Prophets and Markets

Social Dimensions of Economics

City College of the City University of New York

Prophets and Markets

The Political Economy of Ancient Israel

Morris Silver
City College of the City University of New York

Kluwer-Nijhoff Publishing
Boston   The Hague   London

2/1983
Econ.

Distributors for North America:
Kluwer-Nijhoff Publishing
Kluwer Boston, Inc.
190 Old Derby Street
Hingham, Massachusetts 02043, U.S.A.

Distributors outside North America:
Kluwer Academic Publishers Group
Distribution Centre
P.O. Box 322
3300AH Dordrecht, The Netherlands

*Many of the translations in this book are copyrighted
by and used through the courtesy of the Jewish
Publication Society of America.*

Library of Congress Cataloging in Publication Data

Silver, Morris.
    Prophets and markets.

    (Social dimensions of economics)
    Bibliography: p.
    Includes index.
    1. Economics in the Bible. 2. Prophets.
3. Jews—History—953–586 B.C. 4. Sociology,
Biblical. I. Title. II. Series.
BS670.S49   1983   330.933'03   82-7899
ISBN 0-89838-112-6   AACR2

Printed in the United States of America

To my wife Sandy who fills our home
with the warmth of Judaism

Contents

Preface and Acknowledgements

Israel's classical prophets have intrigued not only students of biblical literature and archaeology, but also social scientists, most notably Max Weber. Lewis S. Feuer (1979, pp. 102, 120) has recently demonstrated that modern scholars of the secular left, including Karl Marx and Erich Fromm, found intellectual sustenance in the prophetic writings. The influence of the prophets is evident in Fromm's suggestion that the free market breeds "idolatry" and in Marx's strictures regarding "commodity fetishism" and "alienation." Nevertheless, many modern men and women have encountered the prophets only in their houses of worship. Recently, however, the prophets have evinced a remarkable ability to leap from the pages of the Bible into the center of public controversies. As one columnist noted: "Amos is as current as this morning's news."

I also believe that we moderns can learn from the ancients and I have for long been fascinated by ancient Israel, the Bible, and its prophets. Once I realized that my training as an economist might provide new perspectives, I seized the opportunity. The result is *Prophets and Markets: The Political Economy of Ancient Israel*. In carrying out this study, I have assumed with Martin A. Cohen (1975, pp. 88, 94) that the persons and institutions represented in the Bible are not "qualitatively different from those of any other time and place" and are, therefore, amenable to social scientific analysis without resort to miraculous and supernatural explanations. More generally, I believe that it is high time for ancient economic historians to spend more time looking at modern economic theory and the evidence for market-oriented behavior, and less time looking over their shoulders at

xi

critics. The recent contributions of Frederiksen (1975), Gunderson (1982) and K. Hopkins (1978) are, therefore, deserving of applause.

The term "political economy" is associated with Karl Marx. Like Marx, I recognize that changes in economic variables are capable of causing significant changes in social, spiritual, political and legal variables. Unlike Marx, I stress the fact that changes in the latter "superstructural" variables have significant feedback effects upon the economic variables themselves. Political economy is the study of these interactions or, to use Marx's phrase, of "the anatomy of civil society."

Acknowledgements

This study has benefited from the most willing help of distinguished biblical scholars including Robert T. Anderson, Yehoshua Gitay, J.S. Holladay Jr. and especially, William W. Hallo. I have also profited from the remarks and suggestions of Gordon Tullock, Malcolm Galatin, Arnold Rothstein, and Werner Herzfeld. Needless to say, however, the responsibility for any errors and the views expressed in this work are entirely my own. I owe a special debt of gratitude to the Interlibrary Loan librarians of countless institutions and to Albertha Sears, Jennifer Smith, Donald Petty, and Helga Moody of the City College Library. Without their efforts beyond the call of duty in obtaining the relevant literature this book could not have been completed. Thanks are also due to Helga Johnson, Judith Endlich, and Francoise Dorenlot for their help in translating several articles. My research was greatly facilitated by a grant from a fund created by the will of the late Harry Schwager, a distinguished alumnus of the City College of New York, class of 1911. The most vital contributions of all were made by my wife Sandy and our sons Gerry and Ron.

Prophets and Markets

1 INTRODUCTION: PRIOR TO THE EIGHTH CENTURY

The Israelite settlement of Canaan in the thirteenth century B.C.E. was concentrated in the hill country.[1] (See figures 1–1 and 1–2.) That such areas were so sparsely populated compared to the neighboring plains was due not so much to chance or to a small Canaanite population as to their relative undesirability. The crucial impediment to settlement of the hill areas was the high cost of water. The plains, on the other hand, had cheap water and fertile soil but they also had numerous plainsmen equipped with chariots (Judg. 1: 19)[2]. For the most part, the Israelites were either unable to conquer the plains or (what comes to the same thing) did not think them worth the price in blood. So, we are informed in Joshua 17: 14–18, the Israelites, in their land of milk and honey, bent their backs and lived less than lavishly by the sweat of their brows.

Forests were cleared to provide additional arable land for planting barley, vines, and olive trees. Deep cisterns were cut into impermeable rock and clay. Conduits were dug in order to channel rainwater into the cisterns. To aid them, the cost of water was significantly reduced at this time by the perfection and application of the process of slaking lime to make watertight cement. Several coats of this cement were plastered on the walls of the cistern to prevent the seepage of water. Now herds and flocks could be grazed

1

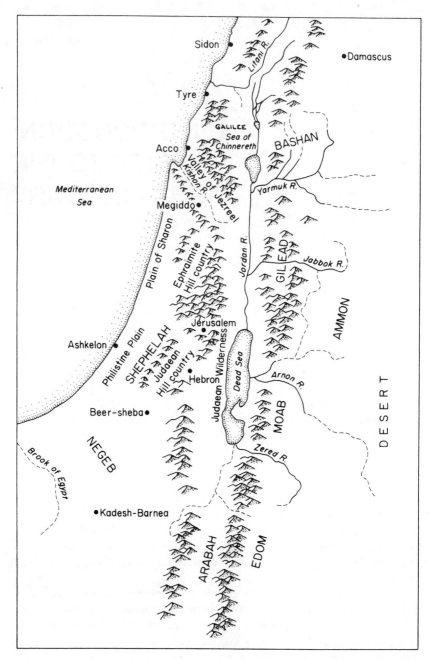

Figure 1-1. General physical features of Palestine. From *Israelite and Judaean History*, edited by John H. Hayes and J. Maxwell Miller. © 1977 John H. Hayes and J. Maxwell Miller. Reproduced by permission of The Westminster Press and S.C.M. Press, Ltd.

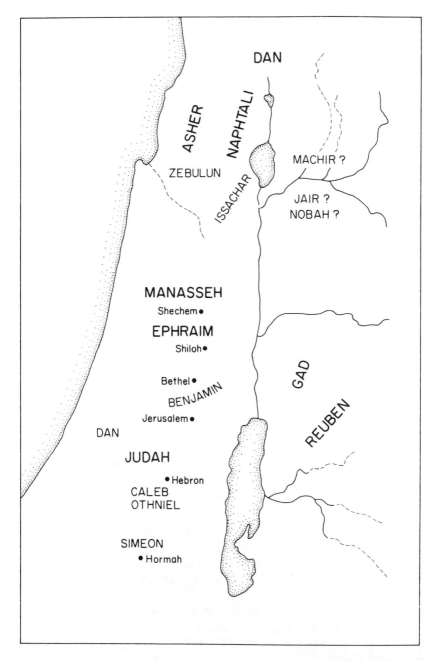

Figure 1-2. Approximate settlement pattern of the Israelite tribes. From *Israelite and Judaean History*, edited by John H. Hayes and J. Maxwell Miller. © 1977 John H. Hayes and J. Maxwell Miller. Reproduced by permission of The Westminster Press and S.C.M. Press, Ltd.

wherever cisterns were available for their daily water (Glueck 1968, p. 10; Wright 1962, pp. 187–88). Perhaps the explanation for this innovation lies in expanded trade opportunities. Indeed, the possibility of mutually beneficial exchange relations between hill and plain may be raised in Genesis 34:21. In this disputed passage Hamor and his son, Shechem, tell the townspeople that Jacob is peaceable, "therefore let them dwell in the land, and trade therein . . . ."[3]

Beginning about 1200, hundreds of new villages sprang up, for example, Geba, Gibeah, Ramah, and Michmash in the vicinity of Jebusite Jerusalem. A town such as Beth-shemesh was to become a "veritable city of cisterns." The remains of large, but crude, two-floored houses dating from this general period have been discovered in towns such as Bethel, Beth-shemesh, and Debir (or Tell Beit Mirsim) (see Albright 1960, pp. 46–7). Perhaps more characteristic of the early Israelite settlements is a four-room house recently excavated at a site that Demsky and Kochavi (1978) identify as biblical Ebenezer. Ebenezer was located on the border of the hill country and the Philistine-occupied Plain of Sharon and served as the Israelite staging area for a decisive defeat by the Philistines in c. 1050 B.C.E. (see 1 Sam. 4:1–2, 10–11). The plan of the house is in the form of a rectangle; one room is possibly an unroofed court for cooking.

By the time of the Ebenezer house the Israelites had, no doubt, made great material progress from the time of settlement[4] but their relative poverty is revealed by a comparison between Ebenezer and Aphek, the nearby Philistine staging area. Philistine Aphek was cosmopolitan and flourishing while Israelite Ebenezer was isolated and barren (see Kochavi and Demsky 1978, p. 21).

The gradual increase in population, wealth, and the Philistine threat all contributed to the demand for and the formation of an Israelite state between 1080 and 1000 B.C.E. The growing strength of the monarchic state facilitated further growth, enrichment, and dispersal of the Israelite population. At this time the carburized-iron plow tip and other steel tools[5] came into wider use; this facilitated terrace construction, increased agricultural yields, and ultimately, lowered irrigation costs (Baly 1974, p. 94; Stech-Wheeler et al. 1981, pp. 246, 254–55). The archaeological evidence suggests a population explosion during and after the tenth century (Cornfeld 1976, p. 99). While marginal sites such as Ebenezer were finally abandoned, it is estimated by Broshi (1978) that Jerusalem (conquered by David) expanded from 12 to 32 acres from 1000 to 930 B.C.E., while its population grew from 2000 to 5000.

Commerce also revived during the period of the United Monarchy. During the late thirteenth and twelfth centuries international commerce was stifled by predations of the sea peoples. However, the weakening of Mycenean seapower, the destruction of the Hittite kingdom, and finally, the limitation on Philistine strength resulting from the alliance between David and the king of Tyre in the eleventh century, combined to open up "for the Phoenicians, in the first quarter of the first millennium B.C.E. vast overseas trading areas" (Oded 1979a, p. 228). By the end of the eleventh century, pottery from Cyprus, after a long absence could once again be found in Israelite-occupied sites (Albright 1960, p. 47). The expansion of the sea trade in the Mediterranean in which, judging by the song of Deborah (Judg. 5), the northern tribes of Asher and Dan (?) (see figure 1–2) would have participated, was accompanied by the inauguration of camel caravans transporting the goods of southern Arabia to and through Israel (see Bulliet 1975, especially p. 36).

Military victories over the Philistines and Syrians, receipts of tribute, and the collection of tolls from the control of trade routes together with the general revival of trade all contributed to Israel's growing wealth. Indeed, the David-Solomon period (most of the tenth century) is often portrayed as the peak of Israelite economic development. In fact there is precious little extra-biblical evidence supporting this portrayal. For example, in spite of the reported activity of David and Solomon's scribes, only one example of "Hebrew" writing from this period, the Gezer Calendar, has been found.[6] Similarly, in spite of the United Monarchy's military power and wealth, not a single contemporary document, including the Phoenician literature, refers to David or Solomon.[7] Indeed, Omri the builder of Samaria who reigned in the northern kingdom (885–874 B.C.E.)[8] is the first Jewish king referred to in the extra-biblical sources. (On the other hand, it is only fair to note that there is no reference to Assyrian kings in the Bible before the ninth century.) From the point of view of this book, however, the most important point is that the archaeological evidence in terms of housing, personal possessions, and the like in no way suggests affluence (Pritchard 1974, pp. 35–6). The greatest days of national wealth were yet to come in the days of the divided kingdoms. The destruction of these kingdoms, the expulsion of the Jewish people from their homeland, and the related tragedies were caused by far more fundamental factors than the decision of the northern tribes to spurn the Davidic dynasty.

After the death of Solomon, the United Monarchy of the Israelites split into a northern kingdom, Israel, and a southern kingdom, Judah, apparently ruled continuously by a single Davidic dynasty. The two kingdoms existed side by side from 928 until 722 when Israel's capital, Samaria, was captured by the Assyrians. Judah was then alone until the Babylonians destroyed it in 587 B.C.E. Several factors played a role in precipitating and maintaining the schism. In the first place the external threat had been greatly reduced as compared to the dark days of Samuel and Saul. Second, the topography of Israel never favored centralized political rule: steep mountain slopes divided various regions, forming natural boundaries difficult for ancient communications technology to cope with (Aharoni 1967, p. 38; Kapelrud 1966, pp. 53–4). Third the construction of cement-lined cisterns and the use of iron tools (de Geus 1975, p. 70) encouraged population dispersal, even further increasing the cost of rule by a single state (see Auster and Silver 1979, chapter 3, on the "Sizes of States"). Under the circumstances it is very possible that Solomon's son Rehoboam was quite rational in his refusal to lower taxes on the northern tribes (1 Kings 12). At a lower tax-price his state would not have been able to cover the costs of protecting the population against external aggression and internal brigands.[9] On the other hand, from the viewpoint of the northern citizen, Rehoboam was overpricing his service, which could be provided more cheaply by a smaller, locally based state. This line of economic analysis of the split finds some confirmation in the failure of Rehoboam to employ his armies to maintain unified rule, and in the historical stability of the division. In any event, Rehoboam was left with Judah and a small part of Benjamin while the remaining tribes were ruled by Jeroboam. The existence of two states whose services must have been viewed by the general Israelite population as rather close substitutes operated to limit the exploitative (that is, monopoly) power of both ruling groups.

Beginning in the early 870s B.C.E. the north under Omri (881-874) and his son Ahab (874-853) and the south under Jehoshaphat (871-849) and his son Joram (849-842) experienced a resurgence in military and commercial importance. Territorial gains were made in the directions of the Mediterranean and Transjordan bordering, on the west, the River Jordan, the Sea of Galilee, the Jordan Valley, and the Arabah between the Dead Sea and the Gulf of Elath; on the east it borders the Syrian-Arabian desert and the Dead Sea (see B. W. Anderson 1967, p. 206; Tadmor 1962, p. 119). This trend is perhaps best symbolized by the complaints recorded on the famous Moabite Mesha Stele celebrating a (later) victory over Israel that is generally dated as 850 or 830 (Price, Sellers, and Carlson 1958, pp. 242–43). According to 2 Kings 3:4, Mesha had paid an annual tribute amounting to the wool of 100,000 lambs and of the same number of rams.

Another indication of wealth and power is provided by the Assyrian monolith inscription of Shalmaneser III (858–824)[10]. It is here stated that Ahab contributed 2000 chariots (this is not a scribal error maintains Elat 1979a, note 61, p. 542) and 10,000 infantry to the Israelite-Syrian allied forces that defeated or stalemated Assyria at a town on the Orontes north of Hamath named Karkar (or Qarkar) in 853 (see, for example, Albright 1960,

p. 64; Hallo and Simpson 1971, pp. 127–28). A chariot cost about 600 silver shekels while the price of the horse was about 150 silver shekels (according to 1 Kings 10:29). To provide perspective, after the siege of Samaria was lifted during the time of Elisha in the second half of the ninth century a "seah" (perhaps about 7.7 liters) of choice flour sold for one silver shekel (2 Kings 7:1). A slave might have cost from about 30 (Exod. 21:32; Hos. 3:2) to about 50 silver shekels (Wiseman 1979, p. 41).

Jehu's (841–813) purge of the Omrid dynasty and his concurrent assassination of the king of Judah, Ahaziah, and other prominent Judeans ushered in a period of serious political weakness in both kingdoms that lasted some fifty years. Jehu himself found it expedient to give gifts to the distant Assyrians and it was no doubt during this period that Mesha made significant military gains against the Israelites (see Astour 1971, pp. 387–88). Toward the close of Jehu's reign, or in the reign of his successor Jehoahaz (813–799), the king of Damascus wrested the whole of Israelite Transjordan from Ramoth Gilead to the south.

To sum up, during the tumultuous ninth century, king strove against king for control over trade-route tolls, aristocrats and generals strove against kings for the throne, and rival priesthoods strove for a larger place at the royal table. Meanwhile, vast cultural, religious, and economic changes were taking place.[11] A national Hebrew script emerged and began to replace the Phoenician script that had been adopted in the twelfth or eleventh century (Cross 1980, pp. 13–14; Naveh 1970, p. 277). Increasing numbers of Israelites began to understand that Yahweh was not only a desert god of war and that his responsibility included agricultural fertility and the like. The recognition that separate, specialized deities were not required moved the popular religion in a monotheistic direction (see Bertholet 1926, p. 353; Worden 1953, pp. 296–97). While kings were preoccupied with weightier matters, ordinary people found themselves in positions, to fulfill a biblical demand that may date from this period: "Be fertile and increase, fill the earth and master it; and rule the fish of the sea, the birds of the sky, and all the living things that creep on earth" (Gen. 1:28).

So the economy grew quietly but steadily. By the beginning of the eighth century it had become evident that, as Bright (1972, p. 252) aptly puts it, Israel and Judah had experienced "a dramatic reversal of fortune" and were now ready to be projected to new "heights of power and prosperity". In this glittering era men and women might well sing Psalm 8:5–7:

> What is man, that Thou art mindful of him? And the son of man, that Thou thinkest of him? Yet Thou hast made him but little lower than the angels, and hast crowned him with glory and honor. Thou hast made him to have dominion over the works of Thy hands; Thou has put all things under his feet.

Notes

1. On the question of settlement versus revolt, dating, and areas of occupation, see Alt (1967); de Geus (1976, pp. 164–81); Kempinski (1976, p. 28).

2. *Bibliographical note*: Reliance has been placed on the Jewish Publication Society's (JPS) English translations of the Masoretic text of the Bible. Specifically: *The Holy Scriptures According to the Masoretic Text* (or JPS, 1917); *The Torah: The Five Books of Moses According to the Masoretic Text* (JPS, 1962, or 1974); *The Prophets: A New Translation According to the Masoretic Text* (JPS, 1978); *The Book of Job: A New Translation According to the Traditional Hebrew Text* (JPS, 1980)

In a limited number of cases the following translations have been cited: Julius A. Bewer, *The Prophets in the King James Version With Introduction and Critical Notes* (Bewer); Charles Thomson (trans.) and C. A. Muses (rev. ed.), *The Septuagint Bible: The Oldest Version of the Old Testament* (Thomson); Arthur Weiser, *The Psalms: A Commentary* (Weiser); Interpreter's Bible, *The Book of Psalms* (Inter.); Jacob M. Myers (trans. and notes), *The Anchor Bible: I and II Chronicles* (Myers).

3. This is the JPS (1917) translation. JPS (1974) renders the Hebrew: "let them settle in the land and move about in it." The underlying issue is the meaning of the verb $s\d{h}r$ in this and several other passages. Elat (1979a, pp. 527–29; for the background of the controversy see Speiser, 1961, and Thompson, 1974, pp. 172–86 versus Albright, 1961) has recently defended the position that this verb refers not to trade, but to travelling and wandering. Perhaps, but to what end? Can we not detect a secular motive in the wandering of the patriarchs?

It will be remembered that, in Genesis 34:25, Simeon and Levi, both sons of Jacob and full brothers of Dinah, took advantage of the after effects of the circumcision ritual to put to the sword and plunder Shechem. Jacob complained that his sons had ruined his name (v. 30). Then, in Genesis 49:5, we find Jacob saying: "Simeon and Levi are brothers, their [uncertain word] became weapons of violence." The uncertain word, *mkrtyhm*, has been rendered in a variety of ways including *circumcision-blades*, *swords*, *counsels*, and *stock in trade* or *wares* (see Young 1981, p. 335). Most recently, Young (1981) has made the ingenious suggestion that, properly understood, the term refers to the *kirru*-vessels that played an essential role in Mesopotamian marriage ceremonies. Nevertheless, the rendition *wares* or *stock in trade*, both of which are supported by a derivation from the verb *mkr*, "to transact business," find further support in 2 Kings 12:5–8, which deals with the *makkārim* who served as business agents for the priests of the Jerusalem Temple (see chapter 6). The interpretation of *mkrtyhm* as "trade-goods" is of course consistent with a reference to trade in Genesis 34:21. It seems possible to defend the following interpretation of Genesis 49:5: "Simeon and Levi are brothers, in the guise of peaceful trade they perpetrated robbery."

Note here that: "The meaning 'trader' for *sōhēr* has never been in doubt, and related values are likewise assured for the three independent noun formations. The only matter at issue is thus the meaning of the finite verb" (Speiser 1961, p. 24). See chapter 6 and chapter 11, footnote 9 and chapter 3, footnote 13 for additional discussion of Hebrew terms for trader.

4. Excavations in the northern Negeb and Tell Masos in strata dating from the late thirteenth century indicate that the four-room house of the late twelfth and eleventh centuries represented a significant improvement over a much more primitive three-room prototype (Kempinski 1976, p. 30).

5. Iron is actually softer than bronze; only carburized iron or steel has hardness exceeding that of coldworked tin-bronze. Carburization involves the absorption of carbon into the metal, thereby creating an alloy. The archaeological evidence clearly suggests that steel was being

produced in tenth-century Israel. However, iron smelting has not been proven at any Late Bronze-Early Iron Age excavated site (Stech-Wheeler 1981, pp. 245, 261).

6. Even this is an oversimplification. Cross (1980, p. 14) points out that: "So similar are Phoenician and Hebrew in the tenth century that it has been impossible for epigraphists to establish whether the Gezer Calendar was written in a Hebrew or in a Phoenician script. I believe that the first rudimentary innovations that will mark the emergent Hebrew script can be perceived in the Gezer Calendar, but they are faint at best." Note that according to 1 Kings 9:16, "Pharaoh king of Egypt had gone up, and taken Gezer, and burnt it with fire, and slain the Canaanites that dwelt in the city, and given it for a portion unto his daughter, Solomon's wife."

7. However, Josephus Flavius, the first-century C.E. Jewish historian says that Solomon was mentioned in the annals of Tyre see Katzenstein's (1973, pp. 77–80) discussion.

8. For the dating of reigns in Israel and Judah, I have relied primarily on Tadmor (1979) and Yeivin (1979).

9. For some evidence relating to royal internal-security forces in the Mesopotamian area during the eighteenth century B.C.E, see Macdonald (1975).

10. For the dating of Babylonian and Assyrian reigns, I have relied primarily on Oates (1979, pp. 199–201).

11. A unique archaeological testimony to the growth of Israelite population, urbanization and engineering prowess is provided by the water tunnels at Megiddo, Hazor, Gibeon and, perhaps, Gezer (fourteenth or ninth century) and Jerusalem's "Warren" or "Jebusite" shaft (Cole 1980).

The Israelite Economy in the Eighth and Seventh Centuries B.C.E.

2 SPECIALIZED PRODUCTION: INDUSTRY AND AGRICULTURE

Archaeology has uncovered the remains of a number of Israelite industrial centers that flourished in the eighth and seventh centuries. (Many of these excavated sites are shown in figure 2–1.) The area around Samaria produced pottery; Debir (or Tell Beit Mirsim) seems to have specialized in woolen textiles; Lachish and Beth-shemesh produced olive oil (Burrows 1941, p. 173); Gibeon made wine, and Elath (or Tell el-Kheleifeh) smelted iron and copper. Tell 'Erani in the eastern part of the coastal plain possessed industrial installations that may have been used in the manufacture of cheese (Yeivin 1975, pp. 93–4; 1 Sam. 17:18[1] seems to refer to cheese). Hazor, Megiddo, Mizpah (or Tell en-Nasbeh), and Arad, among others, were also important but, it would seem, more diversified centers of industry.

It is tempting to slight the importance of industry in the ancient Israelite economy because, by contemporary standards, these sites were very small and unimpressive. Elath, once mistakenly called "the Pittsburgh of Palestine" covered a mere acre and a half, Debir only seven and a half with a population of 2000 to, at most 5000; Gezer, Jericho, and Shechem occupied eight-to-twelve acres; Megiddo included thirteen acres within its walls, Gibeon sixteen, Lachish eighteen, and Beer-sheba twenty five. Even Hezekiah's Jerusalem (ca. 701) included within its walled area some 125

13

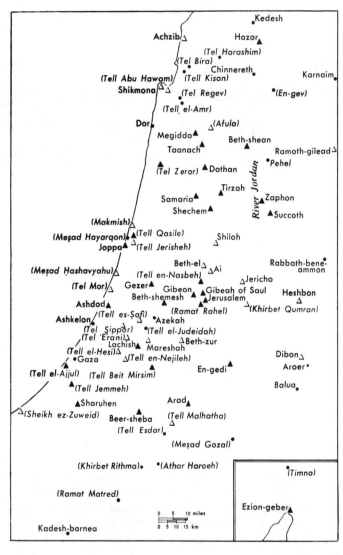

• Trial excavation or minor remains   △ Excavation   ▲ Major excavation

Figure 2-1. The Israelite Period: The Iron Age, 1200 to 587 B.C.E. From *The Macmillan Bible Atlas*, Y. Aharoni and M. Avi-Yonah. © 1977 Macmillan Publishing Co., Inc. Reproduced with permission.

acres and, allowing a generous 200 people per acre, a population of about 25,000. But such measurements do not really come to grips with the issue. The extent of Israelite industrialization should be measured not in absolute terms, but in terms relative to the size of the economy. In this connection it is well to remember the suggestion that in the mid-eighth century B.C.E. the Israelite population numbered about 800,000 in Israel and 200,000 or 300,000 in Judah (see Baron 1972, pp. 61–2; De Vaux 1978, p. 20).[2] Moreover, since the Israelites exported part of their national product, the size of the Israelite population does not fully measure the size of the market, and the consequent potential for scale economies. These points should be kept in mind when examining the evidence on industrial production.

Pottery

The raw-material base for a pottery industry was provided by clay marl of the Jordan and coastal districts. According to Wright (1965, pp. 155–56) the first half of the eighth century saw Israel manufacturing the most beautiful pottery ever produced in Iron Age Palestine. This elegant pottery, called Samaria Ware, because great quantities were found there, seems to have been produced in the surrounding area. More important, Heaton (1968, p. 37) adds that the beginning of the eighth century saw a "minor revolution" in the techniques of pottery production. "In towns like Jericho, Megiddo, Gezer, Lachish, and Hazor, where potters' wheels have been excavated . . . , bowls and jars became standardized in shape and size [the vessels could be nested] for mass-production methods and the employment of unskilled labor." Wright (1962, p. 196) explains that most vessels continued to be made individually on the wheel but special speed-techniques were adopted. Two specialists in modern ceramics, Kelso and Thorley (quoted in Wright 1962, p. 194), concluded in 1943 that Israelite commercial pottery compares favorably in terms of craftsmanship, form, and shape with the corresponding wares of their own time.

Woolen Textiles

The archaeological evidence suggests that Debir functioned as a major center of the woolen-textile (and possibly also olive-oil) industry from ca. 750 to 589 B.C.E. The town was located in southern Palestine some thirteen miles southwest of Hebron at the edge of the southern Shephelah (the low hill country between the mountains of Judah and the Plain of Philistia) on one of the main roads linking Egypt with the Judean hills. The findings there included quantities of iron tools and a great many loom weights. Based on the number of "dye-plants" found in the excavated area there could have been twenty to thirty in the town. If indeed, the objects, each weighing about one ton, were dyeing vats rather than olive presses as has recently been contended by Eitam (1979),[3] the operation seems to have been quite sophisticated as is suggested by the description of McCown (1943, pp. 94–5) who concluded that the dyeing methods of the 1930s "showed some improvements but essentially the same process for simple dyeing." Lachish, in the sheep country of south Judah, and the town of Mizpah (Diringer 1967, p. 320), near the border of Judah some three miles from Bethel, also seem to have been centers for textile production. Excavations in Iron Age strata recovered not only large numbers of cisterns, silos, and presses for wine and oil, but also dye-plants, spinning whorls, and loom weights.

The reference in Lev. 13:48 to "processed skin" (that is, tanning) opens the possibility of an Israelite leather industry (Neufeld 1973, p. 318). Note finally the reference to the manufacture of fine linen in 1 Chronicles 4:21, and the capable wife of Proverbs 31:24 who sold her woven products to the Canaanite (or merchant; see chapter 11, note 9).

Wine

Gibeon in Benjamin was the site of a very significant center for the production of wine (Pritchard 1959, p. 249; 1962, pp. 40, 99; Reed 1967, pp. 234–35). Here were found no less than 63 underground wine vats and cellars (some seven feet deep) capable of storing 25,000 gallons of wine maintained by the underground rock at 65 degrees. In addition, many jar handles with Hebrew inscriptions dating from the seventh (or sixth)[4] century B.C.E. were recovered from the debris of a large rock-cut pool. These inscriptions, the excavator Pritchard suspects, may have been the labels of private firms producing wine for export. Pritchard's conclusion is that the three centuries following the division of the kingdom were a time of "unrivaled prosperity and expansion" for Gibeon "which reached a peak in the seventh century" (Pritchard 1962, pp. 161–63).

Olive Oil

In the ancient Near East, olive oil served a variety of important purposes. It was used for cooking and with many foods (Ezek. 16:13; 1 Kings 17:12-13; Lev. 2:4-7; Num 6:15; 1 Chron. 12:40-41), for anointing the hair, for various cosmetic and medicinal purposes (Isa. 1:6) including cleansing and, perhaps, lubricating the skin to prevent sunburn (Mic. 6:15), and as a base for perfumes (Eccles. 10:1), and for light when burnt in a lamp (Exod. 25:6). Judging by the quantity of olive pits found there, Lachish, beginning in the ninth-eighth centuries, must have hosted a significant olive-oil industry. A Hebrew inscription incised on the base of a bowl from the ninth-eighth centuries seems to indicate that Israelite oil was exported. This ostracon found on the surface at Tell Qasile, a port founded by the Philistines and later destroyed by the Assyrians in ca. 732 B.C.E. is probably a bill or an invoice (no price is mentioned) concerning the shipment of "a thousand oil and a hundred" by one Hiyahu (an Israelite name). Avigad (1979, p. 24) suggests that "since oil was probably not imported into the country this must have been a shipment for export."[5]

Metalworking and Mining

The writings of the eighth- and seventh-century prophets show that the Israelites were familiar with the techniques of metalworking and of the properties of various metals. We read, for example, in Jeremiah 6:28-29: "They are copper and iron, they are stubbornly defiant, they deal basely. All of them act corruptly. The bellows puff; the lead is consumed by fire. Yet the smelter smelts to no purpose—the dross is not separated out. They are called 'rejected silver,' for the Lord has rejected them." ("Rejected silver" probably refers to a method of refining silver by cupulation.) In Ezekiel 22:17-21, we find "The word of the Lord came to me: O mortal, the House of Israel has become dross to Me: they are all copper, tin, iron, and lead. But in a crucible, the dross shall be turned into silver. Assuredly, thus said the Lord God: Because you have all become dross, I will gather you into Jerusalem. As silver, copper, iron, lead, and tin are gathered into a crucible to blow the fire upon them, so will I gather you in My fierce anger and cast you into the fire and melt you." Again, while the traditional translation of Amos 7:7 usually involves a plumb line (anak) Landsberger (1965, pp. 286–87) suggests that is actually refers to tin, "this metal being a symbol of (1) softness, (2) uselessness, unless alloyed to another metal and (3) perishability."[6] Micah's (4:12-13) references to "grain to the threshing floor" and "hoofs of bronze" possibly implies that scrap copper was used to make shoes for the cattle that treaded on the grain. (To date, however, archaeologists have not found any examples.) Note also the reference in Jeremiah 15:12 to the strength of the "northern iron," which may refer to imported steel.

Deuteronomy 8:9 refers to Canaan as "a land whose rocks are iron and from whose hills you can mine copper." High-grade iron ore was available in

Transjordan while the major sources of copper were the Sinai and the Arabah, the depression between the southern end of the Dead Sea and the northern end of the Gulf of Aqaba through which the Jordan flows. One dump in the Sinai contained about 100,000 tons of slag, but the Sinai ores were generally poor, running only 5–15-percent copper. On the other hand, the hills on either side of the Arabah possessed ores running as high as 40-percent (C. F. Pfeiffer 1966, pp. 385–87). Glueck's (1940, pp. 93–4) excavations at Tell el-Kheleifeh (the biblical Ezion-geber/Elath or Eloth?) located halfway between the eastern and western ends of the Gulf of Aqaba, about one third of a mile from its shore, uncovered the ruins of what the archaeologist called the "Pittsburgh of Palestine". Glueck described a system of flues and air channels positioned in such a way that the strong prevailing winds furnished the draft for the furnace rooms, thus enabling the Israelites to dispense with an expensive bellows system. However, Glueck recanted in 1965: the openings in the walls of the buildings were no no longer "flue-holes" but the result of the decay or burning of wooden beams that had served to bond or anchor the walls. Present research suggests that the settlement does not date from the period of Solomon but, on the basis of the total ceramic corpus, to the eighth–fifth centuries B.C.E. (Pratico 1982, p. 6). The buildings served to produce copper ingots from previously "roasted" ores. The main work of smelting was carried out near the mines in small charcoal-fired open-hearth furnaces. The finding (in a Tell el-Kheleifeh stratum probably dating from the time of King Uzziah in the eighth century) of a signet ring bearing the inscription "belonging to Jotham" (Uzziah's son?) and the representation of a bellows, serves to confirm the importance of this site in metallurgical activities (Glueck 1965, pp. 70–5, 85–6). Also, long spikes, heavy cables, and pitch hint at shipbuilding activity.

Industrial installations apparently connected with metalworking and perfume distilling have been excavated at Arad, a town twenty miles south of Hebron (Aharoni and Amiran 1964, p. 51). Another center of the perfume industry in the seventh-sixth centuries was the oasis in the district of ʿEn-Gedi located on western shore of the Dead Sea (Stager 1975, pp. 223–24). Several important sites have been found in the Succoth Valley of Israelite Transjordan, a densely populated area situated on some of the main ancient highways. At Deir ʿAlla (possibly Succoth or Gilgal) a relatively advanced metallurgical center for smelting and casting iron and copper was discovered (Glueck 1968, p. 122). Possibly, use was made here of the iron ore found in the Ajlun district.[7] Also, copper ingots from Elath could have been remelted and cast into instruments.

Residential Housing

What today might be called a housing development was excavated in an eighth-century stratum at Tell es-Sa'idiyeh (near Zarethan in Transjordan). This consists of ten virtually identical houses lying between two straight, paved streets (Pritchard 1965, pp. 10–12). So it would seem that the ancient Israelites applied mass-production methods, and thereby lowered units costs, not only in pottery manufacturing but in the construction of residential housing. Parallels can be found in other parts of the ancient world including (in Egypt) the 73 more-or-less identical houses of the workman's village at Tell el-Amarna dating from about 1350 (B. J. Kemp 1977, p. 127) and the 50 workmen's dwellings at Deir el-Medina (Riefstahl 1964, pp. 69, 73). Additional evidence is provided by the 1980 excavations on the eastern slope of Jerusalem (the City of David), which reveal a terraced complex of buildings whose

> house walls are bonded with each other, with the retaining walls, and with the stone fill of the city wall. Many architectural elements recently uncovered point out that this Iron II quarter, which dates most likely to Hezekiah's time (the 8th century B.C.), was built under one plan; north of the main complex on the slope, a drainage channel was constructed with its walls incorporated into the structures on both sides. The end of the channel and its covering stones are incorporated into the city wall and reach the outer face.[8] (Shiloh 1981, p. 163)

The building of housing developments on slopes must have been difficult and reflects the sophistication of Israelite construction techniques in the eighth century as well as high land values in the Jerusalem area. An impressive engineering project, a 1750-foot water tunnel under the city which, as is explained by the accompanying monumental Hebrew inscription, was cut by two crews starting at either end, also dates from this period (Cole 1980, pp. 10, 19).

Agricultural Practices

Turning now from industry to agriculture one is surprised both by the amount of available data and by the level of technical sophistication it reveals. The use of manure to add humus to the soil, for example, is of special importance in dry lands such as Palestine. That this fact was known to the Israelites can be surmised from the biblical references to the dunghill. (Some of these may refer to the accumulation of dung before being made into fuel, see Stager 1975, p. 73; Ezek. 4:12,15). Hannah's prayer, which is probably much later than the surrounding material, includes the following passage: "He raises the poor from the desert; lifts up the needy from the dunghill" (1 Sam. 2:8). That "the carcass of Jezebel shall be like dung on the ground in the field of Jezreel" is recorded in 2 Kings 9:37. Jeremiah (8:2) says that the bones of the Judeans "shall be for dung upon the face of the earth." Apparently he was aware of the nutritive value of bone meal. Even more to the point is Isaiah's (25:10) prophecy concerning Moab: "And Moab shall be trodden down . . . even as straw is trodden down for the dunghill."[9] The ancient Romans are known to have bedded farm animals on leaves and straw which, when trod down, not only added to the bulk and humus value of the manure, but also conserved the urine. Later, when the material was well rotted, it was spread on the soil and ploughed in (Semple 1931, pp. 410–11). Apparently the Israelites were also familiar with the virtues of the compost heap.[10] Isaiah's (1:11) reference to "fed beasts" and Amos' (6:4) and Jeremiah's (46:21) to "calves from the stalls" suggest that Israelite farmers employed stall feeding to simultaneously fatten livestock prior to slaughter and reduce the cost of manure collection. Archaeological support for these inferences is provided by the finding at Khirbet Abū Tabaq in the Judaean desert in seventh–sixth-century strata, of an area with a series of superimposed layers, each with a burnt-dung fabric over a floor of bricky material. Stager (1975, pp. 54–5, 67–8) sees the area as one where animals were bedded on straw which was periodically fumigated by fire and smoke. Texts dating from the second-millennium B.C.E. demonstrate the existence of the "fattening house" in Babylonia (Page 1970, p. 183).

Leviticus 19:19 contains the puzzling injunction, "thou shalt not sow thy field with mingled seed." Why not? A very interesting theory has been advanced by Semple (1931, pp. 419–20). This prohibition, she suggests, had as its objective "to make the . . . [farmer] scrutinize his seed crop and eliminate adulterations in order to get a clean crop. It was a kind of precautionary weeding. But the sorting process inevitably led to the rejection of imperfect specimens".[11] Semple finds confirmation for her position in the story of the death of Saul's son, Ishbosheth, wherein the assassins were able to creep past "the doorkeeper of his home [who] had been cleaning wheat, and being drowsy, had fallen asleep" (2 Sam. 4:6)[12]. "Thou shalt not sow thy vineyard with two kinds of seed; lest the fulness of the seed which thou hast sown be forfeited together with the increase of the vineyard" commands Deut. 22:9. Does this refer to problems of intercultivation? In relatively arid regions, such as Israel, conservation of soil moisture requires hoe and spade work during the entire growth period (note Isa. 5:6). The planting of other crops between the rows of vines would, perhaps, have interfered with this process and, hence, the biblical injunction against it (Semple 1931, p. 400).[13] Again, Leviticus 19:23–25 forbids the Israelites to eat the fruit of a tree until the fifth year of its growth, "that it may yield unto you more richly the increase thereof." What is the connection? It would seem that the Israelites were aware of pruning techniques that diverted the nutriments of the tree into the fruit. Climatic conditions, however, made it expedient to stress woody growth until the tree was well established. Thus, as Semple (1931, p. 392) explains, the effect of the religious prohibition "was to discourage all pruning for fruitage and to encourage pruning for tree growth." The knowledge of proper pruning techniques is also reflected in Isaiah 18:5: "For before the harvest, yet after the budding, when the blossom has hardened into berries, He will trim away the twigs with pruning hooks, and lop off the shoots." Spring pruning encourages fruit growth while autumn pruning encourages vine growth (Semple 1931, p. 392). Isaiah 17:10 reveals a concern for improving vine quality since, as is suggested in chapter 6 of this book, it probably deals with seed experimentation or the introduction of Syrian vines into Israel.

Isaiah 28:24–26, which dates from the later eighth century, is a gold mine of somewhat obscure information at least demonstrating the systematic nature of Israelite agricultural practices.

> Doth he who plows for sowing plow continually? Doth he continually break the clods of his ground? When he hath leveled its surface, doth he not broadcast black cumin, sow cumin, and plant wheat in rows, barley in a strip, and emmer in a patch? For his God doth instruct him aright and doth teach him.[14]

Verses 27–28 go on to explain the differences in threshing methods appropriate to cumin (a spice) and cereal. First, note with respect to the verses quoted that Isaiah's portrayal of sound agricultural practices as God's instruction is quite consistent with Semple's explanation of the biblical injunctions noted above. The warning against breaking the clods of the soil has to do, I believe, with the fact that a rough soil surface operates like a modern mulch to discourage weeds and to retard evaporation (see Cary and Haarhoff 1940, p. 109; but compare White 1970, pp. 180–81). Isaiah's reference to continuous ploughing has to do with the need for fallow periods or with John Gray's (1962, p. 171; see also Semple 1931, p. 387) observation: "There was no deep ploughing and turning of the soil as in our northern lands. In Palestine the chemicals in the soil are drawn to the surface by the heavy evaporation in the summer heat, and deep ploughing in burying these, does more harm than good. So the top-soil was simply loosened to prepare a seed-bed".

Terracing and Irrigation

Additional information on the cultivation techniques appropriate for hillsides as opposed to valley bottoms is provided in Isaiah 5:1–2,6: "My beloved hath a vineyard in a very fruitful hill; and he fenced it, and gathered out the stones thereof, and planted it with the choicest vine . . . And I shall lay it waste; it shall not be pruned, nor hoed."[15] John Gray (1962, p. 172) explains that, on hills, small narrow plots were cultivated with hoes, and in the absence of protecting turf, the stones removed from the soil were moved to the edges of the plot and built up so as to prevent the soil from being washed away. De Geus (1975, pp. 68–9) presents evidence and arguments that the Israelites constructed irrigation works for their terraces. Using iron tools, they were able to remove the original vegetation from the slopes and then to cut reservoirs, tunnels, and aqueducts that channeled spring water into the terraced fields below. The building of stone tanks represents an alternative to cutting reservoirs out of the rock. Under this system, de Geus (1975, p. 71) explains: "The water of the spring is partly used at the spring and partly transported by aqueducts and/or flow tunnels to one or more such tanks. The tanks, which can contain several cubic meters of water, have a plug near the bottom and from that point water can be distributed once more over the fields below." The archaeologists have not found irrigation water-stowage tanks of this kind but de Geus (1975, pp. 72–3) argues that they correspond to the *gēbim* of 2 Kings 3:16, Isaiah 33:4, Jeremiah 14:3, and, possibly, in Jeremiah 39:10, 52:16, and 2 Kings 25:12 as well.[16] It may be added that spring water was also employed to irrigate the date-palm plantations near the Dead Sea (Stager 1975, pp. 217–21).

Recent excavations indicate that in the environs of Jerusalem during the eighth–seventh centuries soil was actually transported to the terraced slopes (Edelstein and Kislev 1981). This rather expensive practice can no doubt be explained in terms of the special demands of the large Jerusalem market.

Desert Farming

Another example of the adaptation of farming techniques to even more adverse conditions is provided by a farm excavated in the desert of the southern Negeb (today this term covers the area from Beer-sheba to Eilat) that, quite possibly, belongs like the smelting facility at Tell el-Kheleifeh to the eighth century at the time of Uzziah. As described by Schiffer (1960, pp. 34–8; a more technical discussion is provided by Evenari, Shanah, and Tadmor 1971, chapter 7), the farm plot was placed in a small wadi bed (the

Arabic term for a valley gouged out by water) and terraced to slow the momentum of the occasional torrential rains. Much of the rainwater would be absorbed by the desert soil and kept from percolating too deeply by the underlying clay. Then, when the sun came out again, an upper crust would be formed serving to limit evaporation. In addition, grooves leading to cisterns connected to the terraced fields were dug to capture the excess rainwater.[17]

During the seventh century, floodwater farming was carried on with the aid of stone terrace dams and sluice gates in the Buqê'ah wasteland in the northeastern part of the Judaean desert near the Dead Sea.[18] As Stager (1976, p. 157) points out, these desert farmers had no need for fallow periods: "The soils were renewed and enriched each winter by the 'fertilizers' deposited by the floodwaters." That the Buqê'ah settlements were within the kingdom of Judah appears to be confirmed by the finding of a seal of "Badyahū," a Hebrew name that means "in the hand (or under the protection) of Yahweh" (Stager 1975, pp. 79–81, 211).

Agricultural Diversification

The familiar biblical linkage of grain, wine, and oil (see, for example, Hosea 2:24) is actually somewhat surprising since, with the exception of Gilead in Transjordan, they are not normally suited to the same region (Baly 1963, pp. 72–3). Nevertheless, the trio may reflect not only a biblical ideal, but also the actual practice of many Israelite farmers. Sperber (1978, pp. 187–88) reports that in the fourth century C.E. wealthy Palestinian farmers owned numerous scattered plots in which they grew wheat or vines or olive trees. He cites the boast: "I have villages; I have vineyards; I have olive trees." Clearly, as Sperber (1978, p. 192) notes, a system of scattered plots is least disadvantageous "in a country whose topographical characteristics are such that within relatively small distances radical changes of landscape are to be found. Under such circumstances the farmer has ready access to all parts of his scattered estate. This is very true of Palestine, and most especially of the Galilee with its sudden, often startling transitions from hill to valley, from mountain to lowland." But minimal cost is only a permissive factor, not an explanation of scattered holdings. The answer is to be found in Sperber's (1978, pp. 190–91) remarks regarding blight, drought, and reliance on diversification to smooth out the farmer's income stream. No doubt the Israelite farmer took advantage of his opportunity to purchase relatively low-cost insurance by holding a diversified portfolio of crops and plots (see McCloskey 1976, on the medieval English village).

Agricultural Exports

Hosea 12:2 and Ezekiel 27:17 specifically mention that Israel and Judah exported olive oil to Egypt and, to Phoenicia, oil, wheat, wine, and perfume (see also 1 Kings 5:20–25; 2 Chron. 2:9; Ezra 3:7). This pattern of international specialization is quite compatible with modern notions of comparative advantage, based upon Palestine's climate and geography—that is, with the Hecksher-Ohlin theory that countries export the goods that are intensive of their relatively abundant factors of production. Palestine possessed conveniently situated areas capable of producing high-quality wheat. Indeed, the Egyptians actually used the Hebrew-Canaanite word (*qemah*) for top-quality wheat flour (Avi-Yonah and Malamat 1964, p. 264). Cogan (1974, p. 92) points to an Assyrian tablet that employs the Judean measure to record a grain sale. Certainly this is a slender thread, but it is consistent with Judean grain exports to Assyria in the seventh century. The olive oil of Canaan had long been famous; we have already referred to the oil-making facilities at Lachish and Beth-shemesh and the bill of lading for an oil shipment found at the port of Tell Qasile. Reference has also been made to the wine industry of Gibeon and the perfume-making workshops of 'Ên-Gedi.

On a smaller scale but, nevertheless, of great interest is Stager's (1975, pp. 221–22) suggestion that

> The oasis agriculture would have provided a nice complement to the cereal cultivation (impossible along the Dead Sea) that took place in the Buqê'ah. During a series of "good" years in the desert, there might have been a sufficient grain surplus to exchange for oasis crops. . . . The seasonal attention and divergent periods of intensive activity required by these two products—cereals and dates— would not have precluded the same group of cultivators from attending to both in their proximate, but very different, ecological niches.

It should be added that the date palms and spices cultivated along the west coast of the Dead Sea together with the availability of sulfur, bitumen, and salt probably formed the basis of a significant export industry in the eighth–seventh centuries.[19]

The Israelite economy of the eighth–seventh centuries was by no means primitive. It was a living economy whose entrepreneurs, as we shall have further occasion to demonstrate in the next chapter, responded positively and rationally to market opportunities.[20] But is it really appropriate to view markets and entrepreneurs as agents in ancient Near Eastern economic development? The answer, as is shown in appendix A is certainly yes.

To pursue this line of thought briefly, it is sometimes assumed that while the ancient economy was familiar with circulating capital not directly involved in the production process (for example, ships and warehouses) and with the relatively inexpensive tools of the artisan, it did not, in any meaningful way, know fixed capital.[21] However, this kind of rigid formulation clashes with the presence in ancient Israel of industrial installations such as those at Gibeon and, especially, at Debir, with the significant investments in oil-presses, metallurgical facilities, terracing, irrigation, and, no doubt, in tree and vine stock.[22] Obviously there are significant differences between ancient and modern industry, characterized by an increase in the range and variety of the fixed capital goods in which investment is embodied (see Hicks 1969, p. 143). But economic historians should be careful not to exaggerate these differences beyond proper proportions and, consequently, not overlook the possibility, indeed the probability, that the ancient epoch experienced lengthy periods of sharply rising labor productivity and per capita income.[23]

Notes

1. Translations of JPS unless otherwise specified; see the bibliographic note (chapter 1, note 2).

2. But 2 Samuel 24:9 claims 800,000 men of war in Israel and 500,000 in Judah in the time of David.

3. As Eitam (1979, p. 154) notes, however, the olive-press interpretation raises the troubling question of why such installations have been found in the Mediterranean area of Israel but not in the olive-rich Galilee. Note Deuteronomy 33:24: "Most blessed of sons be Asher; may he be the favorite of his brothers, may he dip his foot in oil."

4. The dating is controversial. Many experts prefer the sixth century. Avigad (1972, p. 8) favors the sixth century but, at the same time, he admits "that the Gibeon type of jar is actually missing in all late pre-exilic sites, including the more recently excavated ones at Ramat Rahel, En-Gedi, and Arad."

5. Of course, this line of reasoning is not ironclad. The Egyptians were famous brewers of beer but they also imported "Qode-beer," probably from Babylonia or Hittite country (Lutz 1922, p. 82); equally, "During the Hellenistic period the Land of Israel was famous for its superior wine yet wine from Greece, the Aegean Islands and Cyprus was imported" (Zemer 1977, p. 102).

6. The questions of the sources of Near Eastern tin (Central Europe versus the Caucasus or Zagros areas) and whether the Akkadian word *annaku* refers to tin are debated by Muhly-Wertime (1973) and Dayton (1973).

7. Among the samples so far excavated the frequency of carburized iron (steel) is greater at an Israelite site, late-tenth-century Taanach near the Jezreel Plain, than at Philistine sites even as late as the eighth century (Stech-Wheeler et al. 1981, p. 263). Can this be reconciled with the standard portrayal of the Israelites as technologically stagnant and imitative?

8. Shiloh (1970, p. 186) finds that, at Debir, "some of the buildings . . . were certainly built together with the wall."

9. So translated by JPS(1917) and Bewer. JPS(1978) renders this passage: "And Moab shall be trampled under Him as straw is threshed to bits at Madmenah." Moab is emended to

"Assyria" and Madmenah, a village near Jerusalem, is emended: "As straw gets shredded in the threshing."

10. Semple (1931, p. 410) notes that swine dung is rich in phosphoric acid but poor in nitrogen, the element most needed by Mediterranean soils. See Ginzberg (1931–1932, pp. 363–64) for a negative view of the relationship between divine law and agricultural wisdom.

11. On seed selection and experimentation in classical antiquity, see White (1970, pp. 187–89).

12. So translated by Thomson. JPS(1978) translates 2 Samuel 4:6: "So they went inside the house, as though fetching wheat, and struck him in the belly;" however, it is noted that the meaning of the Hebrew is uncertain and the Septuagint rendering is cited.

13. Is is possible that this injunction was actually meant to encourage farmers to specialize for the market in line with the process of land consolidation described in chapter 6? This intriguing possibility finds support in Coote's (1981, p. 126) remarks concerning the traditional pattern of land use in the hill country; "small holders would devote their . . . plots to mixed farming, interspersing grain rows and garden plots among the vines and fruit trees, thus providing for all the essential needs of the clan . . . .This pattern gave way . . . to the exclusive cultivation of single crops, usually vines or olive trees for commercial gain in the wake of latifundialization."

In classical Rome, the growing of cereals between widely spaced olive trees reduced the fruit yield but helped to offset the biennial yield pattern and, more importantly, the notorious year-to-year variability in olive yields (see White, 1970, p. 48).

14. So rendered by Bewer. JPS(1978) has: "Does he who plows to sow plow all the time, breaking up and furrowing his land?" Bewer's reference to the breaking of the clods seems consistent with the text and makes it more meaningful.

15. So rendered by Bewer. Bewer is merely more compact; both JPS(1917) and JPS(1978) refer in verse 5 to the "wall" of the vineyard.

16. Note the reference to a "tower" in the midst of the terraced vineyard in Isaiah 5:2. Towers (Greek *prygoi*) were a common feature of Near Eastern and Mediterranean agriculture but there is no consensus regarding their function (Pečírka 1973, pp. 123–28).

17. Mayerson (1959, p. 31), consistently with Micah 1:6, connects the numerous stone heaps on the hillsides of the central Negeb with viticulture. We can only wonder whether in Israelite, as in later times, the wine of the Negeb was exported through Gaza. See also Stager (1975, pp. 198–200) on the possibility of grape growing in the neighboring Judaean desert.

18. The terrace dams of the desert farmer "retarded the velocity of the floods, spread the flow of water over a large surface, and allowed the floodwater to be ponded in the fields behind the dams. Because of the permeability of the chalky-marly alluvium, the floodwaters could soak into the soil to insure later crop growth" (Stager 1975, p. 121).

19. Sulfur was used to make medicines and light fires; bitumen for medicines and for calking ships; in Ottoman times the salt of the Dead Sea was made into a government monopoly (Stager 1975, pp. 225–26). Balsam, a wood resin used for making perfumes and medicine was also available. Some archaeologists believe that the inside of wine jars might have been coated with an impermeable substance such as bitumen or resin (see Darby, Ghalioqui, and Grivetti 1977, vol. 2, p. 561).

20. On the role and significance of resident foreign businessmen, see note 9 chapter 11.

20. As Fei and Ranis (1969, p. 396) point out, modern economists have been concerned almost exclusively with fixed capital (for example plant and equipment) "as a permanent and dependable souce of productivity gain, due to changes in the quantity as well as the quality or scientific knowledge embodied." See also Mokyr (1979, pp. 133–34).

22. Note that viticulture involves the continuous application of skilled labor while the olive requires about twenty years before it yields a full harvest, and a great deal of care in the five

years before it is transplanted. (Note the reference to transplanted trees in Psalm 1 (chapter 15). Olive pressing, at least, is a rather complicated technical process.

23. Today we tend to think of rapid growth in terms of rates of 7 to 8 percent a year, which seems unlikely in ancient times. However, I can see no reason why sustained rates between 0.5 to 1.5 percent a year would be outside the realm of possiblity. Such rates are not inconsistent with Starr's (1977, pp. 37–8, 45) estimates of the production of temples and statues (taken as indicators of the growth of physical output) and informed guesses of population growth in Greece from the seventh to the sixth century B.C.E.

While they are focused on the classical economy the comments of the economic historian Gerald Gunderson (1982, p. 255) are well worth quoting:

> The (erroneous) belief that an industrial revolution was the only way out of the problems of the latter classical economy has frequently been accompanied by an assumption that growth could not have occurred in any other environment. It is generally recognized that [increased] output per capita can be achieved by increasing the amount of resources (land and/or capital) at the command of each worker. Ironically the 'increasing labor scarcity' so frequently interpreted as evidence of economic distress in the ancient world was actually a manifestation of such a trend. The other potential source of growth, widely recognized only in recent years, consists of improvements in productivity or efficiency resulting in expanded output from the services of a given stock of resources. In the classical period, one cause of such growth would have been the diffusion of technology. . . . Neither of these potential avenues of growth is precluded by the absence of industrialization.

To take an important example closer to the present, in the eighteenth and nineteenth centuries C.E. French rates of growth in per-capita national product were quite similar to those in Britain despite the absence of an industrial revolution comparable to that which began in Britain during the later eighteenth century.

3 ADAPTATIONS TO SPREADING MARKETS: BRANDS, MANAGEMENT, AND WAREHOUSES

Jar-Handle Stamps, Brands, and Packaging

The numerous, geographically dispersed impressions stamped on the handles of earthenware storage jars for wine and oil symbolize the rich, diversified commerce of the Judean kingdom from the later eighth century B.C.E. Of these, the most widely discussed are those called *lamelek* (*lmlk*), impressions. Each has either a four-winged scarab[1] or a two-winged sun disc and an inscription bearing the word *lmlk* and one of four place-names: Hebron, Socoh, Ziph, and Mmšt (still unidentified). More than 1000 such stamps have been found in sites including Jerusalem, Ramat Raḥel, Mizpah, Gibeon, Gezer, Beth-shemesh, Azekah, Tell el-Judeideh, Lachish, Jericho, and others. The dating of the stamps is controversial, but Stern (1975, pp. 49–50; see also Rosenbaum, 1979, pp. 32–3) after a careful survey of the evidence, cautiously concludes that they probably date from the end of the eighth to the end of the seventh centuries.[2]

It is generally agreed that the word *lmlk* has to do with the throne and it is translated "Belonging to the king (*melek*)" of Judah. Consequently, most interpretations assume royal ownership of the jars and explain the associated place-names accordingly. Avigad (1979, p. 36) provides the following

29

examples: store cities where food was kept in royal storehouses; administrative centers where taxes in kind were collected; key cities of defensive zones where army provisions were stored; royal estates marketing their product in jars stamped with the place of production; the sites of royal pottery factories.[3] On the other hand, some have interpreted *lmlk* as a measure of capacity imposed by the kings of Judah. The symbols are more controversial than the *lmlk* place-name inscription, but they are usually regarded as Judean royal symbols.

There is, however, reason to believe that the jars were not royally owned and that *lmlk* is not a measure of capacity or, if it is, not unique to the kings of Judah. The evidence presented below is consistent with the view that the stamps reflect the existence of numerous more-or-less-concurrent private brands of wine, oil, or pottery. If, indeed, there was a royal brand as well, it faced significant private competition and imitation.

First of all the custom of designating wine by its place of origin pre and post dates the monarchy. In the Bible we find "wine of Lebanon," wine of Izalla," and "wine of Helbon"; "wine of Kerem-hattel" is found in the Samaria ostraca (see below); an early sixth century B.C.E. inscription on a clay vessel at Lachish reads "wine of Ashan;" papyri of Elephantine, the site of a Jewish community in Egypt, refer to "wine of Sidon;" Hesiod praised "Byblian wine;" Talmudic sources refer to the Sharon wine and the Carmel wine. Second, the *lmlk* inscription is found with other symbols, "one the rosette, and another, concentric circles, apparently a schematic version of the rosette. *The rosette is none other than an imitation of an impression of wine cellars from the island of Rhodes and Thasos*" (Stern 1979, p. 258; emphasis added) Stern (1975, pp. 51–2) suggests that on paleographic evidence alone (that is, evidence not substantiated by archaeological findings), the rosette stamps belong to a later period, from the end of the seventh century to the destruction of the Temple. But the possibility remains open that all the so-called royal seals were current at the same time. Moreover, entirely different "royal" symbols with no accompanying *lmlk* inscription, but often with inscriptions such as *y-h-w-d* have been excavated. A six-pointed star (the shield of David) was found near the remains of wine presses in the fill of the pool at Gibeon (Stern, 1975, pp. 51–2). Five-pointed stars (the shield of Solomon) have been found at Gezer and Jerusalem. The prevailing opinion is that the latter date from the end of the Persian period (539–333 B.C.E.) when Judah had no king. It should be noted, however, that Macalister (1912, Vol. II, pp. 209–10) found his five-pointed star in Gezer strata he originally dated from 1000 to 550. Macalister's results are now regarded with suspicion and he may be dead wrong, or perhaps, he was later intimidated by the paleographic argument for the Persian period. Finally, symbols not known to have any royal connection at all, such as birds, have also been found on jar handles.

Again, if the winged scarab and the winged sun-disc[4] were royal symbols, they certainly were not unique to Judean royalty. The winged sun disc is most prominently associated with the Egyptian god-king Horus. In Egyptian mythology it plays an important role in the epic battles between Horus and his arch-rival Seth. The winged sun disc is also known in newly discovered Ebla at the end of the eighteenth century B.C.E., in Kassite Mesopotamia (sixteenth–twelfth centuries), from thirteenth century Ugarit (Ras Shamra) in northern Syria, in royal monuments of Zinjirli dating from the second half of the ninth century, from a fifth-century stele of a king of Gebal, in Neo-Assyrian reliefs, and in Anatolia. The scarab, like the winged sun disc, plays an ancient and important role in Egyptian mythology (Clark 1959, pp. 40, 71, 83; Fairman 1974, pp. 15–16, 27). It is the symbol of Khoprer (or Khepher) "the Becoming One" which is pronounced like the word for a scarabeous beetle. Khoprer is associated with the rising sun and his boat is the seat of ultimate authority from which the world is governed. Khoprer, in his solar barque, plays a role in the great battle for supremacy between Horus and Seth. Usually the scarab is shown with wings folded, but examples with the wings spread have also been found, especially in the twenty-first dynasty—the time of Saul, David and Solomon (Goff 1968, p. 478; Muller 1923, p. 48).

The word *lmlk* appears on Phoenician and Carthaginian wine jars dating from after the destruction of the Judean monarchy (Stern 1975, p. 52). So if the word refers to royal ownership or a royal statutory measure it has this connotation not merely in Judah but internationallly. In this respect *lmlk* resembles the sun disc and the scarab symbols. Direct evidence bearing on the hypothesis that *lmlk* is a statutory measure of capacity is provided by Ussishkin (1978, pp. 77, 80) who was able to reconstruct six of the royal-stamped type-484 jars found at Lachish. The liquid capacities were 43.00, 44.25, 44.75, 45.33, 46.67, and 51.80 liters. The difference between the largest and the smallest jar capacities amounts to 19 percent of the mean capacity. It is difficult to devise a benchmark for such comparison, but I would agree with Ussishkin that a deviation of this magntitude does not seem to support the hypothesis. Further, the excavators of Beer-sheba found the four-winged scarab on an unusually shaped jar with a capacity of 112.5 liters; the accompanying "Ziph" inscription also displayed unique factors (Aharoni 1973, p. 76).

Roughly contemporary preexilic stamps bearing the names of settlements other than the four of the *lmlk* seals have been found, for example, Jerusalem, Gat Carmil (found at Shikmona on the Palestinian coast), Mozah (a town of Benjamin, according to Josh. 18:26)[5], and *khl* (this word might also mean "dark wine") (Avigad 1972, p. 5; Stern 1975, pp. 51–2). Many specimens of eighth-seventh-century stamps bearing a personal name prefixed by the possessive *lamed* ("belonging to") have been found at dispersed locations including Jerusalem, Ramat Raḥel, Samaria, Tell 'Erani, Khirbet el-Qom, Mizpah, Hazor, Lachish, 'Ên-Gedi, Beer-sheba, and Arad. At Arad, in strata he dated to the end of the seventh and early sixth centuries B.C.E., Aharoni (1965, p. 20) found rosettes accompanied by *lmlk* and a personal name. Quite similar finds have been reported at Beth-shemesh and Debir. Macalister (1912, vol. II, pp. 209–10) found at Gezer a single specimen of the two-winged symbol without the word *lmlk*.

Finally, the two-winged and four-winged "royal" symbols themselves are not so standardized as might be imagined. Numerous variants of each seal have been detected. For example, ten variations were found in a sample of 43 four-winged jars, while 19 variations were disclosed when a sample of 86 two-winged type symbols were checked (see Na'aman 1979, p. 80). Similar variations have been noted in the inscriptions including those for a given location such as *lmlk* Hebron (Na'aman 1979, pp. 80–1). Na'aman (1979, p. 81) concludes that "When all the corpora of *lmlk* seal impressions are finally checked, we will probably learn that scores of different seals were employed. It is a matter of pure speculation, of course, why so many seals were required." The picture becomes clearer, however, once we discard the speculation that the *lmlk* jars were royally produced and owned, and follow the evidence where it seems to lead.

By this time one must surely wonder with Stern (1975, p. 52) "why the royal symbols changed so frequently in so short a period"[6] and, with Avigad (1976, p. 299) begin to "allow the existence of organized private enterprise in the country's economy." Indeed, Pritchard (1959, p. 213) recovered 54 jar handles from the pool at Gibeon with inscriptions he dates from the seventh or sixth centuries for which his provisional interpretation was that "the inscriptions were labels on wine jars made for the export of wine from Gibeon. The name of the town is followed by *gdr*, 'the walled enclosure of', and the name of the owner of the vineyard." It is worth noting that the same debris also contained 60 "royal"-jar stamps with examples of all four place names.

Pritchard's interpretation is not so strange when it is recalled that the contemporary potters of Corinth signed their work and, according to Glotz (1967, p. 138), this was "for business rather than the pride of artists."[7] The ancients, after all, were not visitors from another galaxy, but human beings who faced difficulties and opportunities similar to our own. The understanding of this obvious point is deepened by Will (1977, pp. 264, 268):

The Greeks, Romans and other Mediterranean peoples of antiquity were accustomed, as we are, to transporting choice liquids and perishables in disposable bottles of assorted standardized sizes and shapes. Like the buyer of today, the ancient buyer of wine, for example, could tell at a glance what kind and quality of beverage a bottle contained. . . . They restore the names of long forgotten individuals who were active in business and trade. Roman amphoras, like our modern glass and metal containers, were often stamped with the name of the manufacturer.

Interestingly, Rhodian jars of the third century B.C.E. were stamped not only with oblong stamps bearing the name of the manufacturer and the date (represented by the term of an annually appointed official), but also with a circular emblem such as the rayed head of the sun-god Helios. The latter was the very same emblem used on the (presumably) state issued coins of Rhodes. Grace (1961, p. 11) suggests the possibility that the date served to identify "the age or special vintage of the finer kinds of wine and the freshness of the cheaper which were not worth drinking after a year." Egyptian wine jars commonly identified the vineyard, wine maker, and vintage date. Sometimes information was provided on the type of wine (for instance, "sweet") or its quality ("good" or "very good"). (See Yeshiva University Museum 1980, pp. 25–6.)

The ancients with their clay packages also faced the problem of "empties." Usually, as the thick carpeting of pieces suggests, the problem was solved by breakage. But another solution suggested by the stamps is that the containers were returnable, perhaps on a deposit basis. A jar handle found at Ramat Raḥel by Aharoni (1965, p. 11) has two stamps, one the "royal" two-winged disc accompanied by the inscription *lmlk hbrn* and the other "*lmlk* Nera (son of) Shebna." Jars with both "royal" and "private" stamps have also been found at Lachish and, perhaps, at Debir. Possibly the logical explanation is, as Aharoni believes, that the Nera (and the other "private" stamps as well) are merely the marks of royal officials. The explanation for two stamps is not obvious. If it were possible to impress a jar after it had been manufactured, I would be tempted to offer the thought that some of the jars were recycled.[8] Closely related questions are raised by the finding at Tell Defenneh (probably Daphnae), a Greek settlement in Egypt, of numerous jars, amphoras, and amphora handles of Greek make, dating to the seventh-sixth centuries, many of which are sealed with the cartouches of the reigning pharaoh. Austin (1970, p. 37; see also Zemer 1977, p. 113) suggests, as a possible explanation, that the Egyptians were reusing the empty Greek containers. Two less speculative points are that the Rhodian jars described above also have more than one stamp and that the Gibeon inscriptions, which include the place name "and a number of private names (probably of business associates) . . . are regularly written on both handles of the jars" (Avigad 1972, p. 7).[9]

Recent excavations at Lachish have brought to light from the same strata both stamped and unstamped type-484 storage jars (Ussishkin 1978, p. 80). "Generic" pottery? A final piece of evidence consistent with a commercial nature for the "royal" stamps is Tushingham's (1971, pp. 34–5) observation concerning the "crudeness of both devices" relative to the work the lapidaries of the day were able to do on the "private seals cut for officials."

Certainly, Stern (1975, p. 54) is correct in finding the "solution to the problem" of the jar handles in the development of the Judean economy and its integration in the area-wide system of trade and merchandise distribution that flourished in the eighth and seventh centuries B.C.E. However, the seal impressions themselves need not be seen in terms of statutory weights and measures, and still less of royal production and distribution. Evidently the increasingly affluent Judean consumer, like the modern American buyer, was quite interested in the kind of product he or she was purchasing. The Judean entrepreneur responded with product differentiation, labels, and the associated implicit warranties of quality. Again, like the modern entrepreneur, he or she was not above exaggerating the virtues of the wares and creating favorable images. By such means as sun discs, scarabs, five-and six-pointed stars, and, perhaps, certain place names the entrepreneur suggested to the consumer that his wine or oil was fit for kings or even the gods.[10] This is not at all unlikely when it is remembered that Egyptian wines and beers were given names such as "the beautiful," "the heavenly," "the joy-bringer," "for merrymaking," "the addition to the meal," "the plentiful," "the bloodred (of the eye of Horus)," "the divine liquid," and "the unguent of the heart." (R. J. Forbes 1965, vol. III, pp. 88–9) Forbes (p. 73) raises the possibility that these names were actually proprietary brands. Note also an Egyptian bazaar scene of the third millennium B.C.E. in which a woman offers for sale the beverage *nmšt* (beer from a cellar?) while saying, "It is *nmšt* that satisfies thee" (Lutz 1922, p. 73).

Officer Seals and Hierarchic Firms

If ancient Israelite firms produced and marketed, say wine, oil, pottery, cloth, metals, or grain for a national or international market, they, like the throne itself, would have required the services of subordinate functionaries. The recent discovery of two seals has made it possible to distinguish between the *'ebed* seals of royal officers and the *na'ar* seals of nonroyal officers.[11] The *na'ar* seals, which on paleographic grounds are dated to the eighth century by Avigad (1976, p. 297), identify both the employer and his subordinate. A *na'ar*, of course, might have served as a cultic functionary, or as a steward of a king, or as a royal official's private estate officer, or as a civil servant, or as the retainer of a military officer, but not necessarily, nor solely.[12] It is of interest that of the three known pairs of names, one, Eliakim *na'ar* of Jehoiachin (or Joiachin), enjoys a wide spatial distribution: Ramat Raḥel, Beth-shemesh, and Debir. Joiachin was not necessarily the next to the last king of Judah. As Avigad (1976, p. 297) points out, Jehoiachin ruled only briefly in 598, mostly during the seige of Jerusalem, before he was taken prisoner to Babylon. Indeed, Greenfield (1980, p. 84) has recently reported that: "It is now pretty well accepted that these imprints are to be dated to the late eighth, rather than the late sixth century and belonged to the *na'ar* of a private person, rather than the king."

It seems clear that Babylonian firms made use of agents of various degrees of independence (Leemans 1950, chapter 3). Evidently complex firms operated in Ugarit, a north Syrian center for commercial enterprise in the second millennium: one merchant refers to the "merchants under my authority" and another to "my merchants" (Rainey 1964, p. 319). The eighteenth century B.C.E. trade of Assyrian merchants with Anatolia (see chapter 4) was in the hands of "houses" which may be identified as "firms" (Larsen 1976, p. 469). Note also in connection with the existence of hierarchic firms in antiquity, the Roman *institores* who were essentially managers or agents (W. V. Harris 1980, pp. 140–41). Without excluding other functions, there is nothing to prevent the identification of the *na'ar* as a buyer, salesperson, manager, foreman, or agent of a private enterprise. Certainly, this is not inconsistent with Ruth 2:5, which refers to Boaz's "*na'ar* who was in charge of the reapers" and Jud. 19:19 in which a *na'ar* seems to be in charge of servants (*'abadim*). Moreover, this identification of the *na'ar* is quite consistent with the usage of comparable titles in Mesopotamia (*ṣuḥārum*) and Ugarit (*sġr*).[13]

The Samaria Ostraca and Warehouse Facilities

The Harvard Expedition of 1910 excavated numerous ostraca (potsherds written on in ink with a pen) in Samaria, the capital of the kingdom of Israel. These ostraca, which are usually dated to the eighth century, were found in a storehouse and (apparently) record consignments of one kind or another. The storehouse was located within the citadel and, possibly for this reason, the ostraca are usually interpreted as references to taxes in kind. "The fine regular script, the use of almost identical formulae, and the fact that several of the ostraca often form part of the same jar" point to the conclusion that, while the shipments came from various places, the ostraca themselves were "receipts written in the royal storeroom when the delivery arrived" (Avigad 1979, p. 26).

One group of 24 ostraca record the date (in terms of the regnal year), the name of the place from which the consignment was sent, its contents (oil or wine), and the name of the sender. A second group of 28 ostraca is rather mysterious since they appear to mention two place names (or one place name and a regional or clan unit) and make no reference to the goods consigned. In any event, the group of 24 are very clearly receipts or claim-checks for wine and oil deposited in the storehouse.[14] They are particularly interesting documents since they permit a rare glimpse of the linkage between city and suburb.

If not for the location of the storehouse in the citadel (a city within a city), one might reasonably conclude that the texts dealt with transactions between a private storage facility and its private patrons.[15] In fact, the location of the storehouse is not conclusive evidence of either its ownership or its management. Perhaps private warehouses were located within the walled areas of cities for reasons of security. We are fortunate in possessing papyrus documents dating from the third century B.C.E. concerning the affairs of a large Egyptian firm. In one document the owner, Apollonius, tells his manager Zenon: "Take the olive oil which has accumulated with us out of the house to a market place and, having taken it there, put it in a warehouse which is as safe as possible. Then appoint some of the servants to guard it . . . ." (Westermann and Hasenoehrl 1934, p. 55). Another document deals with wine owned by the local government (of Philadelphia) that had been sold to retail merchants or paid out as wages to the guards at the temple. The document bears, apparently in acknowledgment of delivery, the signature of the Nomarch. "This document raises questions as to why an official receipt which belonged in the files of the village secretary should have appeared among the papers of Zenon" (Westermann and Hasenoehrl 1934, p. 145). Perhaps the answer is that the local government kept its valuable property in the numerous storehouses and wine cellars known to have been located on Apollonius's estate.[16]

Interestingly the gem of the 1978 excavation season on the eastern slope of Jerusalem was a large stone plaque fragment with a monumental Hebrew inscription dated to the time of Hezekiah (eighth century B.C.E.). "At this stage of the research it may be agreed that the key word in this inscription is the first, *sbr*, which should be understood as meaning "to heap up," "to accumulate" (Shiloh 1979, p. 170). The inscription, Shiloh believes, "must have come . . . from a public storage building which served the city or the state." For what it is worth, this fragment was found near the top of a terraced Israelite quarter adjacent to but "*outside* the city wall." (emphasis added).

Warehouses have also been located at noncapital cities. At Arad, fragments of business documents were found that include one dealing with "Eliashib (son of) Eshiahu", who may have been connected with the Temple, but who was unquestionably in charge of stores of wine, oil, and flour (Aharoni 1966). Excavations at Megiddo, in strata dating not later than the eighth century, revealed a very large stone-lined granary built against an interior wall. Within the walls of Megiddo several large buildings were excavated in which a central alleyway was divided by rows of stone pillars from stone-paved side galleries.[17] Stone troughs were located between many of the pillars. The buildings were originally called "Solomon's Stables." But as Kenyon (1978, p. 20) points out, the buildings postdate Solomon and probably were not stables. Three very similar buildings with troughs and tethering holes in some of the pillars were uncovered within the walls of Beersheba near the gate. It would seem that they were destroyed during the Assyrian invasion of 705 B.C.E. But these "stables" were stacked with storage jars and uncharred cooking pots. The stables of Megiddo and Beersheba, in short, are storehouses the central aisles of which may have been used to tether and feed the donkeys as they were being unloaded (see Herzog 1973, pp. 25, 29; Pritchard 1970; Ussishkin 1978, pp. 38–41). Warehouses constructed along the same basic lines have also been found at Hazor, Tell 'Abu Hawam, Tell el-Hesi, Tel Malhata, Lachish, Arad, Beth-shemesh, and Tell Qasile.[18]

Phoenician and Ugaritic pottery storehouses have also been found (Grace 1961, p. 11). Further, in northern Syria at Al Mina, Sueidia, on the mouth of the Orontes, excavations revealed storehouses believed to have belonged to a Greek merchant colony dating continuously from the eighth through fourth centuries B.C.E. (Wooley 1938). An additional, most significant point, is that by the sixth–fifth centuries B.C.E. in Babylonia, private firms such as Egibi and Murassu "opened their warehouses for deposits in kind and took a fee for safeguarding these" (Westermann 1930, p. 36).

The presence in ancient Israel of storehouses for consumption goods is suggested in several biblical passages. The eighth century prophet Amos (3:10) condemns Samaria for storing up violence and robbery in its "fortresses" (variously translated as strongly built houses and as palaces). One translation of the Septuagint (Thomson) continues in verse 11: "Therefore, thus saith the Lord God: Tyre is all around." Tyre, let it be noted, is the great symbol for the trader in the Bible (see, for example, Ezek. 27). The verse goes on to prophesy the plunder of the fortresses. Similarly,

Isaiah (1:31) warns that: "Stored wealth shall become as tow" (fiber/inflammable stuff). In his Tyre Pronouncement the prophet adds: "But her profits and 'hire' shall be consecrated to the Lord. They shall not be treasured or stored; rather shall her profits go to those who abide before the Lord, that they may eat their fill and clothe themselves elegantly" (23:18).

Notes

1. Originally the royal symbol of Israel suggests Tushingham (1971, p. 33).

2. On the basis of his recent excavations at Lachish, Ussishkin (1977, p. 56) reports that both the two-winged and the four-winged seals "were used side by side in Level III prior to its destruction." He further suggests that the *lmlk* stamps uncovered in later Lachish contexts may be strays. C. Evans (1980, p. 163) goes too far, however, when he cites these findings as demonstrating that all the *lmlk* stamps "should be dated in the reign of Hezekiah before 701." This conclusion is highly controversial since it places the destruction of Lachish's Level III in 701 instead of 597. Level III may span a century or so. Further, Evans does not refer to the research of Holladay (1976, pp. 266–67) and he repeats (p. 163) a questionable argument against placing any of the stamps in the reign of Josiah.

Na'aman (1979, pp. 72–3) makes use of archaeological data from Ramat Raḥel (see chapter 9 to date the *lmlk* seals: "The finds from Ramat Rahel prove . . . that the *lmlk* seals were used during the reign of Hezekiah; to date them as late as the reign of Josiah is out of the question, since they appear *prior* to the Assyrian 'palace ware,' which is itself prior to Josiah!" Perhaps he is correct but the data for Ramat Raḥel are themselves controversial and it is open to grave doubt whether the finding of Assyrian palace ware necessarily implies "Assyrian hegemony over Judah, i.e. . . . the first half of the seventh century" as Na'aman assumes; the possibilities of domestic imitation (Pratico 1982, p. 9; Aharoni 1965, p. 20) and, especially, peaceful trade should not be ignored. At times these arguments appear to verge on circularity. We are supposed to believe that all the *lmlk* seals date from a single reign and that they are royal seals. We are left to wonder why one king, say Hezekiah, would employ both a two-winged and a four-winged symbol, each in multiple variations (see Na'aman, 1979, pp. 80–1).

3. The reference in 1 Chronicles 4:23 to potters residing at Netaim and Gederah who were "in the service of the king" may, perhaps, point to a royal industry. On the other hand, this pottery may have been produced for use in the king's estates, not for sale. Alternatively, the phrase "in the service of the king" might signify the existence of a guild (or family?, see chapter 13) of potters, as well as of scribes and of linen workers (1 Chron. 2:55; 4:21), that purchased exclusive franchises from the crown as in medieval Europe (see Consitt 1933, pp. 1–28) and probably, in Second Temple Palestine (Mendelsohn 1940, p. 19).

4. Sources on non-Judean sun discs: Bittel (1970, p. 89); Burney (1977, p. 167); Langdon (1931, p. 69); McKay (1973, pp. 35, 115); Matthiae (1979, p. 23); Mendenhall (1973, pp. 33–56); Muller (1923, p. 101); Perres (1966, fig. 7); Yadin (1970).

5. Translations of JPS unless otherwise specified, see the bibliographic note (chapter 1, note 2).

6. This turnover in royal symbols is even more striking if, as some scholars have maintained, all must be dated to either the reign of Josiah or to the reign of Hezekiah. Na'aman (1979, pp. 82–3) suggests that the observed paleographic differences may reflect regional rather than temporal factors.

7. A. W. Johnston (1979, pp. 48, 51) suggests that the names on exported Corinthian and Ionian decorated vases refer not to the potters, but to shippers who may have visited potteries and placed orders.

8. At Khirbet es-Samrah in the Judaean desert, Stager (1975, p. 147) found a *lmlk* handle that had concentric circles incised over the wing after firing. "This," he explains, "is sometimes taken to be a cancellation mark . . . ." On the other hand, he notes the reported finding of a *lmlk* handle with concentric circles applied before firing (fn. 58, p. 169). With respect to this after- or before-firing issue, it is worth noting the remarks of Johnston (1974, p. 140) concerning graffiti on the undersides of Greek earthenware vases: "Most marks are plain graffiti written with a sharp point in the fired clay. Very few marks seem to have been incised before firing, though I concede that it would be difficult to discern between marks made in well-dried unfired, clay and in the finished product." Avigad (1972, pp. 2–3) maintains that the practice of chiselling letters on jars after firing was common in preexilic Judea.

9. Note also that stamps on Roman bricks "usually contain in various combinations a trademark, the name of the brickyard, the name of the owner of the estate on which the brickyard is situated, the names of the different workers on the staff of the brickyard . . . and frequently between 110 and 164 A.D., a consular date is added" (Bloch 1941, p. 3).

10. Signed Roman terracotta lamps of the first century B.C.E. to the third century C.E. sometimes had symbols on their bases. Some of these "consist of a highly stylized and distinctive crown or crown-and-palm branch; and there are also a few uniform leaf decorations. The interesting fact about them is that they appear on lamps of several different 'firms'. Crown-and-palm-branch marks, for instance, are found especially on 'Fortis' and 'Octavi' lamps, but also on Aquileian lamps of ten other 'firms'." (W. V. Harris 1980, p. 138).

11. Note that translating *na'ar* as "young man" is misleading, as in Judg. 8:14 wherein Gideon prevails upon a "*na'ar*" to write down for him the names of Succoth's top seventy-seven personages. Indeed, J. Macdonald (1976, p. 57) finds that the *ne'arim* of the Bible are, by and large, the same kinds of functionaries as are the *n'rm* of the Ugaritic Personnel Lists, the *n'rn* of New Kingdom Egyptian texts and the *suḫārū* of the Mesopotamian area (for example, of the Mari correspondence dating to the eighteenth century B.C.E.).

The word *'ebed* is also an Israelite technical term for a slave. The main difficulty of J. Macdonald's excellent analysis is that he seems to blur the distinction between *'ebed* and *na'ar*. Macdonald (1976, p. 58) equates *wardum* of the Mari correspondence with *'ebed* and suggests that "everyone was a *'ebed* (subject) of the king, whether royal *na'ar* or *'āmāh*. Likewise in the Mari letters everyone is a *wardum*, be he Governor, *suḫāhrum* or slave. All are *wardū*, 'subjects'." But this leaves unexplained the existence of both *na'ar* and *'ebed* seals. Further, it fails to come to grips with a Mari letter cited by Macdonald (1976, p. 58) in which "there is an interesting differentiation of *wardum* and *suḫārum*, when Bahdi-Lim writes to Zimri-Lim his king that 'Napsi-Erah, my lords' servant (*wardum*) and the *suḫārū* of Yasîm-Dagan are well'."

12. For a variety of examples from the Bible, the Ugaritic texts and the Mari correspondence, see J. Macdonald (1975, p. 143; 1976) and Cutler and Macdonald (1976).

13. J. Macdonald (1976, pp. 60, 62, 66) provides examples from Mesopotamia in which *suḫāru* (see note 11) perform such functions as supervising cultivators, participating (as leaders or guards) in a donkey caravan of juniper wood, providing information about grain-carrying boats, receiving money on behalf of the employer and selling copper for silver or gold. Leemans (1950, pp. 34–5) refers to an Old Babylonian text in which it is "expressly stated that a *tamkārum* [merchant] had a *suḫāhrum* . . . The *suḫārum* mainly performed services for the effecting and execution of the liabilities of his master in regard to contracts." Astour (1972, p. 21) cites a Ugaritic text in which businessmen are represented by their *sġr*: "*Sġr* is a North Syrian variant of the common Semitic *sġr* "small, young" . . . which in Ugaritic texts, is used with the meaning of "aide, assistant," and fully corresponds to . . . *suḫāru* . . . ."

On a much more speculative note, the patriarch Abraham whom Gordon (1958, p. 31) believes to have been a merchant prince also had *ne'arim* (Gen. 18:7, 22:3). He offers Genesis 34:10, 21 and 42:34 in support of a merchant role for the patriarchs. For a different interpretation of these passages and some additional evidence, see note 3, chapter 1.

14. Leemans (1954, pp. 52–3) has published wool and barley storage receipts from Larsa (south Babylonia) dating from the eighteenth century B.C.E.

15. In 1955/6 a limited excavation conducted by S. Yeivin (1960, p. 29) east of Tell Hazor uncovered a "series of large commercial (?) buildings outside the city proper, but apparently within a fortified enclosure. Yeivin suggests that this suburb may have been a foreign merchant colony "such as is apparently hinted at in the Bible (1 Kings 20:34) under the term of 'streets'." He explains that the "Hebrew *ḥuṣōt* though used for streets, literally means *outsides*, which may very well refer to suburbs *outside* the city wall, just as well as to open spaces for circulation outside the houses (or streets)."

16. Near Eastern temples may also have provided storage facilities for a price (see R. Harris 1960, p. 129).

17. It might be informative to compare these structures with the Roman *horrea* of the early Empire. The latter buildings were suited for the storage of grain and other goods and, in addition, played a role in the retail trade of the capital (see Rickman 1980, pp. 137–41).

18. According to Shiloh (1970, p. 182), the typical architectural plan of the storehouses (*miskenot*) involves a building of dimensions exceeding those of the average four-room (residential) building with three, probably roofed-over, long parallel halls with well-built walls.

4 TRANSPORT: ROUTES, COSTS, AND MONOPOLY POWER

Highways

Greater Israel is a land of mountains, of long, deep river valleys such as the Jordan, and, to the east of the Jordan Valley, of high desert tablelands. Historically, these geographic features have largely determined and controlled the roads available for commerce.[1] The two major highways follow the main lines of relief from north to south.

The more prominent of the two, the Trunk Road or Via Maris (Isaiah's (8:23) "way of the sea")[2] connects Egypt with Anatolia and Mesopotamia via the northern Levant. From Egypt the Via Maris, the only practical northward route, runs close to the coast through the Plain of Philistia. On the edge of the desert at Gaza, however, there is a division, with one branch cutting east to Petra (in southwestern Transjordan), while the main route continues northward along the coast to the Plain of Sharon. The Via Maris then must turn eastwards to the Megiddo pass leading through the Ephraim and Carmel ranges into the Plain of Esdraelon. From Megiddo, two possible routes lead north to Damascus. The direct route passes through Hazor, strategically located near the Jordan ford; the other strikes through the Plain of Jezreel, Beth-shan (or Beth-shean a fortress town) and the Yarmuk Valley.

From Damascus the Via Maris continues on to Aleppo and Hamath (the Great). A third branch turns westward from Megiddo toward the Plain of Acco, and thence northward along the Phoenician coast through Tyre, Sidon, Gebal (or Byblos), and on to Anatolia. Megiddo, one of the great crossroads of the ancient world, like Hazor lay completely within Israelite territory.

The second-most-important north-south route was the King's Highway (Num. 20:17) which diverged from the Via Maris at Damascus and struck southward past all the important settlements of Transjordan, as Karnaim and Ashtaroth in Bashan, Ramoth-gilead in Gilead, the Ammonite capital Rabbath-ammon, the Moabite towns Dibon and Kirhareseth, Edomite Bozrah and Petra (or Sela), and then through the Wadi Ytem to Ezion-geber on the Gulf of Aqaba and to the Red Sea. From Ezion-geber two branches went out across the desert to Egypt. Along this route the fabled caravans carried their precious cargo of frankincense and myrrh made from trees native to southern Arabia, to Egypt, or to the north, paying transit duties as they went. Ezion-geber, exploiting its links with the gulf ports to collect spices and gold from Arabia, Africa, and Ophir (India?), developed as a transshipment point for caravans travelling west and then north along the Via Maris to Phoenicia. Agricultural and manufactured products, together with metal ingots, moved in the opposite direction.

Several transverse, east to west, roads connected the Via Maris with the King's Highway. The already mentioned Negeb route ran from Gaza through Beer-sheba and Arad. Judah's most important transverse route, the "way of Beth-horon," passed through Gibeon and Jerusalem. Several Judean routes led to the southern Jordan Valley and the Dead Sea the most important of which, the "way of the Arabah," led from Jerusalem through Jericho. Another road led from Lachish to Hebron and 'Ên-gedi on the shore of the Dead Sea and on to Moab.[3] One branch led from Hebron to Beer-sheba and, ultimately, to Egypt. A north-south road through the hills linked Bethlehem, Jerusalem, Mizpah, Bethel, Shechem, Samaria, the Plain of Jezreel, and the Valley of Beth-shan. In the hill country of Ephraim the most important east-west route ran from Socoh in the Plain of Sharon through Samaria and Shechem, and then northeast to Tirzah (Tell el-Far'ah) and then to the fords of the Jordan near the city of Adam.

Economic Importance of Land and Water Transport

The volume of transportation over the highways of ancient Israel cannot be measured and, as a matter of fact, we do not know what these roads were really like. (Perhaps the main roads were paved [see Har-el 1981, pp. 11–

13]; we do know from archaeological excavations that the gateway approach to Dan was paved.[4]) Consequently there is a strong temptation, especially among those economic historians who find economics tedious, to assume that overland trade must have been of negligible importance. Nevertheless, several illustrations and fragmentary cost data drawn from Rome and medieval Europe indicate the potential importance of this traffic.

The archives of the Assyrian merchants operating at Kanesh in Anatolia around the time of Hammurabi in the eighteenth century B.C.E. have richly repaid study. According to Larsen (1976, p. 86) donkey caravans carried "large quantities of tin and textiles . . . from Assur to Anatolia where these goods were exchanged for silver and, occasionally, gold". Utilizing textual references to the shipment of 17,500 textiles as a base, Larsen (p. 89) puts forward, as a conservative estimate, that "about 100,000 textiles [were shipped] from Assur over a period of about fifty years". Some 13,500 kilograms of tin, or 200 donkey loads, are also reported. "Again as a conservative estimate, I suggest an export from Assyria over a period of about fifty years of about eighty tons." Adams (1974, p. 247) notes for the late third-millennium "a single account tablet . . . [that] totals an amount of wool for processing at Ur in excess of 6,400 tons" as well as "indications that almost 9,000 slaves were employed in Ur's textile establishment." Given the relatively narrow markets in the sparsely populated Gulf littoral and mining areas of Oman, production on the indicated scale suggests, "in spite of the high transport costs of overland traffic, a major commitment to caravan traffic—of which the Assyrian outposts in Cappadocia may be only an example . . . ." Two tablets of 551 and 550 B.C.E. from Uruk in southern Babylon record consignments to the merchant Nādin-aḫi of metals (682 pounds for each tablet), dyes, wine, honey, purple-dyed wool, linen, and other merchandise from Egypt, Phoenicia, and various places in Asia Minor. This certainly raises the possibility of a regular and substantial commerce that would have involved a lengthy overland journey even if use was also made of the Euphrates (Oppenheim 1969, pp. 238–39, 253). Birmingham (1961, p. 193) describes a significant overland trade dating from 800–600 B.C.E. in which metalwares produced in Urartu (Azerbaijan) travelled to the Ionian Greeks on the west coast along routes that were "natural highways presenting little difficulty even to wheeled traffic."

The overland movement of grain on a large scale is attested for Sumer in a letter from Ishbi-Erra to King Ibbi-Sin (2028–2004 B.C.E.) at Ur, the capital (Kramer 1963, p. 70). The former reports that he has purchased and transported to Isin 72,000 gur of grain. If we take the gur to be about four bushels (apparently two bushels is also possible, see Contenau 1966, p. 88), this amounts to 288,000 bushels of grain. If the king will now send 600 boats of 120-*gur* each, Ishbi-Erra will deliver the grain, reportedly enough to last fifteen years, to the various cities of Sumer. Another letter (Oppenheim 1967, pp. 98–9) dating from the earlier second millennium illustrates the collection of large quantities of barley at the city of Emar and the shipment by boat down the Euphrates to Mari of 12,000 bushels (assuming 1 *kor* equals 1 *gur* equals 4 bushels).

At Corinth during the reign of Periander (d. 585 B.C.E.) a paved tramway (or *diolkos*) was constructed across the Isthmus "on which ships could be hauled on many-wheeled transporters from sea to sea" (Burn 1968, p. 60). It is also known that some of the grain imported into classical Athens from Euboea and the Black Sea was brought not to the Piraeus (seven miles from Athens) "but to harbors on the northeast coast of Attica, and came to Athens along the Decelea road, a distance of at least 30 miles" (Burford 1960, p. 3).[5] Further, the public works undertaken by Greek cities beginning in the sixth century B.C.E. required the haulage of large quantities of building stone for distances of up to 25 miles. "Blocks weighing 2, 3, or 4 tons are commonplace on many building-sites, and some column drums at Eleusis, by no means exceptionally large weigh from 6½ to 8 tons" (Burford 1960, pp. 3, 6). The Zenon Papyri, mentioned earlier in the discussion of warehouse facilities, once again provide valuable insights. Papyrus No. 2, dated 259 B.C.E., deals with a four-camel caravan moving from Egypt (probably Pelusium) via Gaza and the Via Maris up the coast of Palestine to Sidon, a distance of about 320 miles, and from there inland into Galilee. A load of bricks was carried about 134 miles on the Egypt-to-Gaza leg of the journey. Grain was carried some 115 miles from the lower Galilee, possibly around Beth-shan back to Gaza. The record of the caravan is incomplete, but apparently it more than covered its costs.

Turning to Rome, Varro (d. ca. 27 B.C.E.) mentions how oil, wine, and grain were brought down to the Apulian seaboard on donkey panniers (Brunt 1971, p. 24). Keith Hopkins (1978, p. 44) observes that the fine pottery of the Roman town Arezzo (Arretium) has been found all over the Roman Empire and even in India. Yet this city not only was located deep inland but was far from a sizeable navigable river. Note, even more impressive is the far-flung land and sea trade in "signed" Roman terracotta lamps in the first century C.E. (W. V. Harris 1980a, pp. 127, 136).[6] Keith Hopkins cites several additional facts, for example, that the distribution of lead ingots in Roman Britain shows that Derbyshire's metal was taken long distances to Southampton.[7] He admits that his argument that "there was a significant volume of international trade [in classical antiquity], much of it overland, diverges from the current orthodoxy" (p. 47). An "orthodoxy", I would add, that is sponsored and rigorously enforced by neo-Marxists and linear evolutionists generally.

In medieval England, not insignificant quantities of tin were carried by pack horse from Devon and Cornwall to London (Gregg 1974, p. 76). On the Continent: of the four medieval towns hosting the famous international trade fairs of Champagne, only one was situated on a navigable river and that one was accessible only to small boats. Indeed the participating merchants did not make maximum use of available waterways. In 1296 a contract for transporting cloth to Southern France explicitly called for the use of pack animals as opposed to carts, while the navigable rivers were ignored. Mules and asses laden with silks, cottons, spices, drugs, alum, metal wares, and so forth passed northward through the Alpine passes, and then returned to Italy with cloth, linen, and wool (Boyer 1966, pp. 75–8; East 1967, p. 134). According to Reynolds (1961, p. 34) "the shipments were sent off, winter and summer with clocklike regularity." This happened, it must be remembered, in the twelfth and thirteenth centuries C.E., in spite of stiff gradients, avalanches, winter snows, and the long distances involved. Freighting specialists, the *Vectuarii*, served the fairs on a regular schedule in accordance with an established set of regulations (Face 1959, p. 241). Garnsey (1976, pp. 15–16) presents evidence of a still earlier, regular Transalpine trade in the late Roman Republic and early Empire.

In the eighteenth century B.C.E., Lewy (1958a, p. 93) notes, "Between some towns, . . . copper was shipped in wagons[8] a fact which attests the existence in Anatolia of real highways . . . ."[9] The classical Greeks also used wagons for heavy transport. Archaeological evidence points to the existence of at least partially paved highways long before Roman times[10] in fifteenth century B.C.E. Minoan Crete (*The New York Times*, September 6, 1981) and in thirteenth century Mycenean Greece (W. A. McDonald 1964, p. 236; Michell 1957, pp. 249–50; Vermeule 1964, p. 263). In the eighth–seventh centuries B.C.E. real highways, or at least partially paved roads, linked Etrurian cities such as Caere to mining centers (Grant 1980, pp. 20, 25). Paved road surfaces or cobbles have been discovered in urban areas and their immediate vicinity (Macnamara 1973, p. 144). This period is "remarkable for the number of carts and chariots that appear in graves" (Potter 1979, p. 81). Ultimately, the metals of the western part of central Italy found their way into the holds of Phoenician and Greek merchantmen. The Persian empire of the fifth century B.C.E. was tied together by many roads, one of them, the Susa-Sardis road, 1,677-miles long, divided by 111 post-stations, well-maintained and, perhaps, partially paved (Von Hagen 1967, pp. 20–1).

Some Roman transport-cost data are available for the time of Cato the Elder (234–149 B.C.E.). To take a disassembled mill (an oil-crusher that weighed as much as 3000 pounds) by ox-team wagon from Pompeii to Cato's farm some one hundred miles away nearly doubled the cost of the mill.[11] Information on prices, wages, fodder cost, and so forth provided in

Diocletian's Price Edict (301 C.E.) permit several rough calculations (see Leighton 1972, pp. 159–60). Transporting wheat by ox-wagon, for example, for one hundred miles raised its cost by 75 percent; but transport by pack animal was significantly cheaper. The main pack animals of the first-millennium B.C.E. were the donkey and the camel (Moorey 1980, p. 248) which seems to be confirmed by Isaiah's (30:6) warning to Judah against Egyptian entanglements: "They convey their wealth on the backs of asses, their treasures on camels' humps, to a people of no avail. For the help of Egypt . . . "[12] Provided that the load was evenly balanced, the camel could carry 600 Roman pounds (430 lbs. av.) and the donkey 300. Leighton's data indicate that the carriage of wheat by these animals for one hundred miles increased its costs by some 60 percent of the original purchase price. But this 60 percent probably represents an upper limit since (1) it assumes that each camel or donkey had to have its own individual driver, when, in fact, several animals could be linked together or driven by one man; (2) the calculation assumes the loaded donkey or camel could travel only seven miles per day, the feasible day's journey by ox-team, when, in fact, they could travel faster.[13]

According to Leighton (1972, p. 160) transport charges for unwieldy items, such as wood, rose extremely rapidly with distance: "After scarcely seven miles the freight charge was equal to the original cost. Under such conditions, wood could scarcely be transported far, either by wagon or pack animal." Be this as it may, Leighton's figure 7 shows a Roman wagon specifically designed to accomodate unwieldly loads such as lumber. Of course, Contenau (1966, p. 63) maintains that the transport vehicles of Israelite times were very small and "capable of carrying little more than a few sacks." But Amos 2:13 refers to wagons full of cut grain, and Isaiah (5:18) to "those who drag sin with cords of falsehood and iniquity as with cart ropes." More directly, Lewy's comments on the eighteenth century B.C.E. use of carts in the Anatolian copper trade seem to suggest more than "a few sacks."

In fourteenth century England, wool could be transported one hundred miles by horse-drawn cart for 3 percent of its purchase price. The corresponding percentage for grain was 30 percent. While it must be admitted that these rates reflect the eleventh century's successful adaptation of the horse for heavy transport, data from Diocletian's Edict show that high-grade wool could be carried overland one hundred miles for less than 1 percent of its cost (Jones 1960, p. 186).

Water transport—by river, along the coast, and by sea—and there must have been much of this in the eighth–seventh centuries B.C.E. was very much cheaper.[14] Snodgrass (1980, p. 339) notes that an ancient foundry on the island Pithecusae (Ischia; see chapter 5) worked with hematite imported from Elba, another island located 250 miles to the northwest. Similarly, the ample finds of iron slag at Tell Defenneh and Naucratis in northern Egypt "occur at some distance from known iron ore deposits" (Snodgrass 1980, p. 367), again pointing to import by sea. According to data from Diocletian's Edict, for example, carrying wheat from Alexandria to Rome raised its cost by only 16 percent or about 1.4 percent per-hundred-miles (Yeo 1946, p. 235). Indeed, Yeo (pp. 231–32) points out that: "It was not until the building of the Yankee Clipper . . . that sailing ships of the modern era, even with an improved type of steering-gear, surpassed the speed of ancient ships," some three or four knots. In the third century B.C.E., transporting difficult-to-handle marble by water some 20 miles, from Paros to Naxos, added 25 percent to the cost (Yeo 1946, p. 233). Data on river transport, including boats and barges drawn by teams of animals or men along tow-paths[15] that might have been used in conjunction with the Via Maris, are fragmentary. But Leighton (1972, p. 161) believes that its cost was also relatively low. Some quantitative evidence is provided by an Egyptian papyrus which gives the rate in 42 C.E. of transporting grain by river at 5.9 percent per-hundred-miles (Duncan-Jones 1974, p. 368).

The Philistine Plain in the south and, especially, the Plain of Phoenicia in the north possessed within a few miles of the Via Maris, many harbors capable of handling the ships of the time (see Oded 1979b, p. 223). Underwater archaeology in the Mediterranean reveals that the most common types of anchorages were ports with stone moles for breaking the force of water and wind, roadsteads in the mouths of rivers, and harbors, which were simple anchorages on the seacoast itself. Crown (1971, p. 34) makes the important point that "despite the oft-repeated denial that Israel and the Canaanite coast were not endowed with harbor facilities, it is gradually becoming established that even if there were but few substantial ports on the coast there are a number of roadsteads and anchorages." The sizes of the vessels that could be accomodated should not be underestimated. A twelfth-century-B.C.E. letter in which the Hittite king urgently requests a grain shipment from Ugarit (a north Syrian port) credits the latter with the possession of vessels capable of carrying about 500 tons (J. Sasson 1966, p. 53). For purposes of comparison, note that Roman ocean-going grain transports of the second century C.E. typically ranged from 340 to 400 tons while Columbus's largest ship, the Santa Maria, was only 233 tons.[16] Again, a fourteenth-century-B.C.E. Egyptian tomb depicts humped bulls, large jars of wine and oil, and other merchandise being unloaded at the city of Thebes (?) from Canaanite ships (see deDavies and Faulkner 1947). But Heurgon (1973, p. 62) summarizes research indicating that the turn of the first millennium "witnessed decisive improvements in technique, such as the use of pitch to make the planking watertight, and the invention of the framed hull—from which the longship, intended to face the high seas, derived its classic silhouette and its prospects of success." The sophisticated construction of eighth century seacraft is hinted at in Isaiah 33:21.

The transport picture was also enhanced by the existence of a number of navigable rivers and streams that fed into the sea. Not far to the north of Tyre, the Leontes River comes down from the east. The use to which this river was put is undoubtedly illustrated in a relief of Sargon II (721–705), which shows, however obscurely, Phoenician boats hauling lumber (see, for example, Bailey 1943, p. 107 or Olmstead 1923, p. 273).[17] Also in the north, on the narrow Galilee coast, several wadis from the east ran straight out to sea. The most important of these, the Wadi Qarn, emptied at the port of Achzib. In the central plain of Asher, the little Naaman river emptied at Acco while the Kishon river with its anchorages at Tell'Abu Hawam flowed into the bay not far to the south, providing natural outlets for Megiddo and the rich grain region of the interior. Of course, the usability of the latter three rivers must not be exaggerated. Farther south, a river from the plain of Dothan and a stream from the plain of Shechem entered the sea near the site of Roman Caesarea. In the Plain of Sharon, the Blue river came to the coast south of Israel's Dor (just north of Caesaria) and the streams that fed the port at Tell Qasile included the only lateral river that was navigable upstream to the mountain foothills. The Wadi al-Kabir, which crossed branches of the Via Maris, may, in biblical times, have emptied into a small bay at Joppa (modern Tel Aviv). Although Joppa was, perhaps never in the hands of the Israelites,[18] it was the main port serving Jerusalem some thirty-five miles away. For example, timbers were floated from Tyre to Joppa for both Solomon's (2 Chron. 2:15) and the Second Temple (Ezra 3:7). It is worth noting that a third-century-B.C.E. Sidonian inscription mentions the coastal plain behind Dor and Joppa as a rich grain area (Cooke 1903, Nos. 5, 11, 19). To the south, Gaza, which also had river access, was the port of the Negeb and Sinai.

In conclusion, the transport data summarized above, taken together with archaeological findings, including the growing use of stone in building, specialized industry and agriculture; brand names; warehouse facilities; complex firms; and concentrations of population, such as Samaria and Jerusalem, testify that while costs of moving goods were high by modern standards they were far from prohibitive. Indeed, the natural-resource diversity of the Mediterranean region provides a firm foundation for vigorous trade. The presence of sea coast, plain, scrub uplands, valleys and mountains within relatively compact areas (Semple 1931, p. 376) results in sharp differences in types of production and, consequently, in significant gains from specialization and exchange. This feature was, of course, enhanced by the position of Israel astride the main international trade routes of the ancient epoch, routes that linked regions of widely different productive capacity such as Mesopotamia, Egypt, and Arabia.

We have some interesting quantitative data for the land transport of frankincense and myrrh from southern Arabia to Egypt and up the King's Highway to Mesopotamia:

> The quantities must have been enormous. In the temple of Ammon alone, in the sacred city of Thebes, 2189 jars and 304,093 bushels of incense were burned in the twelfth century B.C. The Chaldeans burned incense to a value of 10,000 talents of silver annually—one talent being 55 lbs—in front of the altar of Baal. (Samhaber 1964, p. 132)

As we have seen, geographic factors determined and sharply limited the number of north-south land routes suitable for commerce. The states controlling the via Maris and, even better, the King's Highway, were in a position to guarantee access to their own citizens and to collect tolls (1 Kings 10:15; see also Num. 20:17) from passing merchants in excess of the costs of providing protection, maintaining bridges, and the like. During an era of Phoenician resurgence and, indeed, of vigorous trade in the entire Near East (see chapter 5), this was precisely the position that Israel and Judah held during the eighth century B.C.E. and that Judah alone seemed to approach in the later seventh century.

Israelite Expansion

The Israelites continuously controlled several key points along the Via Maris, such as Lachish, Hazor, and most important, Megiddo. The Gilead in Transjordan gave them a share of the King's Highway. However, during the eighth century, both Judah and Israel expanded significantly in all directions. In the early part of the century Judah gained a secure foothold on the southern portion of the King's Highway when, according to 2 Kings 14:7, King Amaziah "defeated ten thousand Edomites in the Valley of Salt, and . . . captured Sela and renamed it Joktheel." This victory may have been achieved with the help of Israel (2 Chron. 25:10–13). The report of the Chronicler (2 Chron. 26:2) that Amaziah's son Uzziah "[re]built Eloth and restored it to Judah" suggests control over the southernmost portion of the King's Highway including Ezion-geber on the Gulf of Aqaba. (The latter area may have been lost earlier to the Edomites in the time of Jehoram in the mid-ninth century, see 2 Chronicles 21:8–10). A few years later, Jotham, Uzziah's son and coregent, inflicted defeats on the Ammonites (2 Chron. 27:5) and thereby solidified the Israelite hold over the central portion of the King's Highway. The excavations in the area of several Judean fortresses and settlements whose pottery cannot be dated before the eighth century provide archaeological confirmation of these conquests. An especially interesting finding is a large structure in the northern Sinai dating from the first half of the eighth century which contained inscriptions invoking the blessings of Yahweh, Baal, and the Egyptian god Bes (Meshel, 1979).

While Judah was establishing its hold in the south, Israel won over the rest of the King's Highway. According to 2 Kings 13:17, King Joash, at the beginning of the eighth century, reconquered Israelite Transjordan and made gains in northern Gilead by defeating Aram at Aphek. The excavations at the latter site (En-Gev) confirm that is passed out of Aramean hands in the first half of the eighth century (Mazar et al. 1964). Then Jeroboam II "restored the territory of Israel from Lebo-Hamath to the Sea of the Arabah" (2 Kings 14:25). This claim is supported by Amos 6:13–14: "(Ah) those who are so happy about Lo-debar, who exult, 'By our might we have captured Karnaim'! But I, O House of Israel, will raise up a nation against you—declares the Lord, the God of Hosts—who will harass you from Lebo-Hamath to the Wadi Arabah." Both Lo-debar and Karnaim, the capital of Bashan, are towns in northern Transjordan. The reference to Lebo-Hamath indicates conquests deep within the territory of Aram, as far north as Lebo (Lebweh) bordering the kingdom of Hamath. The account in 2 Kings 14:28 adds that Jeroboam II "fought and recovered Damascus and Hamath for Judah in Israel". Amos (3:12) may have Israelites living in Damascus but the Hebrew is uncertain.[19] It is generally believed that Israel conquered Damascus (see, for example, Tadmor 1962, p. 119) but the reference to "Judah in Israel" is controversial. It may, perhaps, refer to Judean enclaves or merchant colonies.[20] Turning to Israel's southern border, Kings refers to the Sea of Arabah, but Amos speaks of the Wadi Arabah. Aharoni (1967, p. 313) notes that if the latter can be identified with the "Brook of the Willows" (Isa. 15:7), then Jeroboam II "had subjected Moab as well. This would mean that he dominated the entire length of the King's Highway in Transjordan, from the border of Edom to that of Hamath."

As for the west and the Via Maris, we read in 2 Chronicles 26:6–8 of Uzziah that:

> He went out and fought with the Philistines, breaking down the wall of Gath, the wall of Jabneh, and the wall of Ashdod. He also built cities (in the region of) Ashdod and in (the other territory of) the Philistines. God assisted him against the Philistines, the Arabs who lived in Gur-baal, and the Meunites. The Meunites

paid tribute to Uzziah and his fame extended as far as Egypt, for he grew increasingly stronger.

The clear import is that Judah dominated the Philistine Plain. Jabneh and Ashdod are both near the coast while the location of Philistine Gath is uncertain. Perhaps it can be identified with Tell es-Safi (Macalister 1914, p. 72) which, to judge by the absence of destruction layers and by a Judean seal found there, became part of Judah by the end of the eighth century.[21] Moreover, Yeivin (1979, p. 168) understands 2 Chronicles 26:8 to mean that Uzziah ruled "to the entering of Egypt," which means that he probably conquered both Ekron, near the Via Maris, and Gaza, the port at the edge of the desert that served as the place for taking in supplies for the trek to Petra. The defeats of the Arabs on the southwestern borders and in southern Transjordan would have increased the security of the routes from southern Arabia and from Egypt to Gaza, and eastward across the desert. 1 Chronicles 4:24-43 has the Simeonites expanding westward to Gerar and eastward into the Aqaba region during Hezekiah's reign.[22] Further north, an ostracon found at Tell Qasile raises the possibility that this Philistine-founded port fell under the control of Israel during the eighth century B.C.E. The ostracon reading "gold of Ophir for Beth-horon: 30 shekels, "is written in Hebrew characters (Avigad 1979, p. 34; Hallo 1958, p. 326). Whether *Ophir* refers to ancient Suppara near Bombay in India, or to a south-Arabian principality, or is a generic term indicating gold of excellent quality remains a matter of dispute (Barnett 1956, p. 92; Culican 1966, p. 78). It is also unclear whether Beth-horon is the Israelite town or a "house" (temple) of the Canaanite god Horon. (A Philistine temple has in fact been excavated at Tell Qasile.)

On the basis of the above discussion it is not unreasonable to conclude that during the eighth century: (1) Israel controlled Bashan's great granary. (2) Israel controlled the route from Damascus to the sea and several ports including Dor and, perhaps, Tell Qasile, Tell Mor, and Tell 'Abu Hawam (Yeivin 1960b, pp. 208, 212-13). (3) Israel controlled Megiddo and Hazor, key points on the Via Maris. (4) Judah controlled the sea route to southern Arabia and the caravan route across the desert from Ezion-geber in the east to the Via Maris in the west. (5) Israel-Judah controlled the entire King's Highway from the border of Hamath in the north to Ezion-geber in the south. (6) Judah controlled the section of the Via Maris from the "entrance to Egypt" (Gaza). (7) Judah established some degree of control over the fertile Philistine Plain and several of its ports. Perhaps Bright's (1972, p. 255) suggestion that all this must have "poured wealth into both countries" is overly optimistic but, on the other hand, Elat's (1979a, p. 546) belief that "it had only a limited influence on the national economy and on the occupational distribution of the country's inhabitants" is surely too conservative. We return to this question in chapter 10.

Moreover, Israel-Judah's very significant control over the land routes occurred during an era of peak coastal traffic[23] and of sharp competition among ports and shippers. In the north, ports such as Asher's Dor and Phoenicia's Berytus (Beirut), Gebal (or Byblos), and the island Arvad competed for cargo even if they were outshone by Tyre and Sidon. Whether the latter two luminaries were jointly ruled in the eighth century is not clear, but by the time of Esarhaddon (680–669) they certainly were apart (Oded 1979b, p. 227). In the south, the Philistine ports were linked only by a loose sort of league and, according to Oded (1979b, p. 225), they competed "over spheres of influence, markets, and customs duties." In any event, while Ashkelon seems to have remained independent, Uzziah, as we have seen, established some degree of control over Ashdod and Gaza. In the Plain of Sharon, Joppa—though relatively distant from the Via Maris—was still of some significance.

On the seas, Ionian contested with Phoenician. Greeks even began to appear in Phoenician waters (Glotz 1967, p. 118). In the time of Ezekiel, Ionian cities supplied Tyre with metals and slaves. Meanwhile, the Corinthians were breathing down the necks of the Ionians. The Philistines appear to have been active in the coastal trade.

Judah Alone

Of course the picture had changed drastically by about 721 when the Assyrians captured Samaria and put an end to the kingdom of Israel. Then, in 705, they invaded Judah and apparently reduced it to little more than Jerusalem and its immediate environs. The ensuing period, however, was not without redeeming merit from an economic point of view. For one thing, the Assyrians seemed to favor free trade in their huge empire. A text of Sargon II (721–705) boasts: "I opened the closed harbor of Egypt and let the Assyrians and Egyptians engage in trade with each other" (Muffs 1969, p. 191; note also Isaiah 19:23 on the road uniting Egypt with Assyria). He is known to have permitted the establishment of a commercial outpost on the border of Egypt that was populated by both Egyptians and Assyrians. Sargon also claims to have cleared the Mediterranean of pirates (Katzenstein 1973, p. 40). Another favorable factor was the increasingly active role played by Greek traders during the seventh century. The increased economic integration of the Near Eastern area is perhaps best demonstrated by the emergence in the mid-eighth century of Aramaic as the *lingua franca* used by merchants (Bowman 1948, pp. 71–5; Muffs 1969, p. 189; Naveh 1970, p. 279).[24] No doubt the Judeans continued to trade with the Phoenicians. Indications of trade with the Assyrians are provided by pottery findings at many sites, and by a text of 660 B.C.E. describing a sale in Nineveh in which the wheat "was measured 'according to the Judahite *sūtu*' " (Cogan 1974, p. 92). Among the pottery findings are *lmlk* jar-handle stamps (see chapter 3) just across the old Judah-Israel border at Gezer and Jericho. These cities, it is generally believed, were incorporated into the Assyrian empire until the time of Josiah.

Several kinds of evidence at least raise the possibility that, by the time of Josiah (640–609 B.C.E.), the Judean kingdom had recovered not only territorially, but also in terms of affluence. According to Mazar (1978, pp. 57–8; see also Broshi 1974, p. 26). Judah expanded south over Palestine and into the Nebeb. 'Ên-Gedi on the Dead Sea was probably founded at this time. For the north we have the biblical reference to Josiah's religious reform in the area of Samaria (2 Kings 23:4, 15) and to his obscure death, apparently, at the hands of Pharaoh Neco at Megiddo (2 Kings 23:29; 2 Chron. 35:22. For the west we have the findings of four Hebrew inscriptions and a Hebrew ostracon at the coastal fortress, Mesad Hashavyahu. These are dated by Naveh (1960, p. 139) to the latter part of the seventh century. Aharoni (1967, p. 349) concludes: "From this it seems clear that Josiah had annexed the provinces of Samaria and Megiddo to his kingdom and had taken over a certain area in northern Philistia . . . ."[25] On the other hand, it seems that Judah did not recover any of the Israelite possessions in Transjordan.[26]

Notes

1. In this section heavy reliance has been placed upon Aharoni (1967, pp. 46–57, 313–14, 349–50) and Baly (1974, pp. 96–100, 124, 137, 145–46, 150, 203).

2. Translations of JPS unless otherwise specified, see the bibliographic note (chapter 1, note 2).

3. According to Aharoni (1967, p. 55), this road reached Moab via the shallow ford opposite the Lisan (see 2 Chron. 20).

4. At Beer-sheba and Dan the roads were cobbled (Yeshiva University Museum 1980, pp. 60–1).

5. Thucydides notes that before the occupation of Decelea by the Peloponnesians in 413 B.C.E., goods came to Athens overland across Attica from Oropos, instead of by ship around Cape Sunium, which he says was more expensive. Both Oropos and the opposite island of Euboea were steps in the northeastern grain for olive-oil trade with the Black Sea region (see Hopper 1979, pp. 53, 79, 93–4).

6. The existence of this trade is admitted grudgingly by W. V. Harris who, citing allegedly high transport costs and the local availabilities of raw material and qualified potters, wishes to stress the role of branch workshops of Italian firms. However, Harris fails to demonstrate the existence of such firms in the provinces. More basically, Harris ignores the cost to the parent firm of supervising branch firms over long distances and does not explain why the latter would have an advantage over locally based independent firms. In other words, the same kind of argument brought forth against long-distance transport of lamps also applies to branch workshops. The fact remains, however, of "an enormous diffusion of certain lamp types and, even more strikingly, of certain makers' names" (p. 127). Direct evidence of lamp export is available in the form of a "consignment of some one hundred . . . of the maker C. Clodius which was found . . . in a shipwreck in the Balearics, presumably on the way from Italy to Spain . . . " (p. 135).

7. Diodorus of Sicily, writing between 60 and 30 B.C.E., but making use of sources dating as early as the third century, adds that traders loaded British tin on pack horses and carried it across Gaul to the mouth of the Rhone in 30 days (see Chevallier 1976, p. 14).

8. With respect to the innovation of wheeled vehicles, Willetts (1969, p. 101) reports:

> Lower Mesopotamia was perhaps the region from which the use of solid-wheeled vehicles, reasonably efficient for the slow transport of goods gradually spread. Used in Sumer soon after 3500 B.C., in Elam and also probably in Assyria some 500 years later, on the upper Euphrates round about 2250 B.C., [and] . . . in the Orontes valley in Syria about 2000 B.C. Eventually the spoked wheel was invented making vehicles easier to handle and faster moving. The spoked wheel is represented in northern Mesopotamia and in Cappadocia round 2000 B.C., in Egypt soon after 1600 B.C. and on clay tablets from Knossos [Crete] about 100 years later; and it was soon to play a part in Bronze Age warfare when it was used for war-chariots.

See also the recent archaeological survey by Littauer and Crouwel (1979).

9. Somewhat later in the second millennium, the roads of northern Cappadocia were sufficiently good that the annual circuit of the Hittite king was named the "festival of speed" (Goetze 1957).

10. The first Roman paved road dates to the late fourth century B.C.E. and led from Rome to Campania (Via Appia) (see Brunt 1971, p. 23). For a complete discussion of Roman roads, see Chevallier (1976).

11. It is not clear whether this estimate includes the cost of the oxen and the wagons (see Leighton 1972, pp. 157–59).

12. According to 1 Chronicles 12:41, food was brought long distances to Hebron for David's coronation "on asses, on camels, on mules, and on oxen."

13. Yeo (1946, pp. 224–25) who makes somewhat different assumptions (for instance, a load of 250 pounds) argues for a 100-percent increase. One questionable point here is that he includes wages for the return trip in his 100-mile cost figure.

14. The Bible includes sixteen different words for seacraft including "reed ship" (Job 9:26), "merchant ship" (Prov. 31:14), "oared ship/floating ship" (Isa. 33:21), and "Tarshish ship" (1 Kings 22:49). There are references to plying the seas in Psalms 107:23; Proverbs 30:19 and Job 9:26 (see Yeshiva University Museum 1980, p. 54).

A Ugaritic tablet of the fifteenth or fourteenth century B.C.E. appears to be the oldest known shipping gazette: listed are "passenger ships," "war ships," "fishing boats," boats called "land of Mari" or "land of Ur" or "land of Akkad" types, "river boats," and "racing boats," followed by notes on sizes: ships of 60, 50 or 40 *kur*, and so forth (Schaeffer 1939, p. 39). For a recent survey of Near Eastern ships covering the period 2000–500 B.C.E., see De Graeve (1981).

15. Towing

generally occurs . . . when the boat has to be navigated upstream against the current and the wind, or when the water is too shallow. Both cases are represented on the Neo Assyrian reliefs. . . . A relief of Sargon [721–705] depicts a heavy loaded cargo boat being towed by four men who hold a rope upon their left shoulder. The rope is fastened to a vertical pole presumably set in the gunwale behind the stempost. Towing upstream is frequently mentioned in literary documents in connection with cargo ships. There seem to be a special category of men hired for this labor. That towing was a real necessity is illustrated by a Mari text which reports that ships were waiting for one year to be towed upstream! Texts concerning the towing of boats, gid_2-texts . . . ,are of a special type. They mention successively the crew number, the number of days, the kind of ship—occasionally with the load—going from one city to another, sometimes with a return trip . . . .This documentation indicates that a standard cargo boat of 60 gur averaged 9–10 km a day upstream. For faster transport the crew had to be augmented, for lighter goods it could be reduced. Occasionally they were towed downstream in which case they averaged 30–35 km a day. (De Graeve 1981, pp. 151–52)

16. Several Roman grain freighters had capacities of 1200 tons and, in addition, could carry 600 passengers (Rickman 1980, pp. 123–24).

17. Note that for this lumber to reach its ultimate Assyrian destination a not insignificant overland haul was required from the lower reaches of the Orontes. An Old Babylonian tablet reveals the existence of hired ships that carried cargoes such as bricks downstream to Babylon (Saggs 1962, p. 289).

18. According to Yeivin (1960b, p. 205), excavations reveal that Jaffa (or Joppa) was burned and destroyed in the early twelfth century and rebuilt in Israelite times, "but the Israelite stratum (at least within the excavated area) was rather thin and so badly damaged by later settlers . . . that it is impossible to fix exactly the time of the Israelite re-occupation (which ethnically may not have been Israelite at all)."

19. Compare Bewer and JPS(1978).

20. 2 Chron. 8:2,4 has Solomon building or rebuilding cities or store cities in the Hamath-Zobah area. Such enclaves may be referred to in Psalms 48:11 and 97:8 in which "the daughters [banot] of Judah rejoice because of thy judgments" (see I. Hopkins 1980; MacLaurin 1968, p. 89). Also of interest in this connection are names reflecting Israelite influence, including Azriau of Yaudi (Samal) under Tiglath Pileser III (744–727) and of Yaubi'di (or Ibubidi) of Hamath under Sargon II (721–705) (see De Vaux 1980, p. 52; Na'aman, 1974, pp. 36–9).

21. Perhaps it is of significance that Amos 1:6–8 does not mention Gath, the fifth city of the Philistine pentapolis. See, however, Amos 6:2. Note also that Sennacherib's "Letter to God" on his campaign to Judah in 705 describes the capture a a "royal (city) of the Philistines which H(ezek)iah had captured and strengthened . . . ." This city, Na'aman (1974, pp. 26–7, 34–5) suspects was Gath (Tell es-Safi).

22. See chapter 10, note 11.

23. This influence finds some very rough quantitative support in the numbers of large storage jars (used to transport bulk items such as oil and wine) drawn up from the bottom of the sea in the nets of fishing boats along Israel's Mediterranean coast in the period from late 1957 through mid-1959; for the period from the beginning of the second millennium to 1100, ten storage jars were discovered; during the succeeding Iron Age II period (eleventh–sixth centuries B.C.E.) the number leaped to 43 and, reportedly, most of these date from the eighth–sixth centuries. This level was maintained during the Persian period (sixth–fourth centuries) (Barag 1963).

Zemer (1977, p. 114) adds that over this period the shape of the storage jars became better adapted to sea transport.

24. 2 Kings 18:26 established that Aramaic was known to the governing classes in the later eighth century. Note also that when Esarhaddon (680–669) restored Babylon he encouraged merchants and "opened up their ways toward the four winds" for "establishing their tongue in every land" (Ahmed 1968, p. 149).

25. It has been suggested that Josiah's northern expansion must have been rather modest if its limits coincided with the distribution of such trade items as the *lmlk* jars (Stager 1975, pp. 247–48). This is possible, but not at all obvious. The implicit assumption of the argument is that the distribution of *lmlk* jars is determined not by economic factors (for example, competing brands or transport costs from, say, Hebron) but by political (or religious) factors. (Similar arguments have been advanced by Evans [1980, p. 263] and by Na'aman [1979, p. 71] to show that the *lmlk* seals should be dated entirely within the reign of Hezekiah.) However, as we have seen, Assyria apparently favored a free-trade policy within its empire which presumably would have included the former northern kingdom, Israel. Therefore it seems reasonable to assume that economic factors unrelated to the northern limits of Josiah's state are the determining factor in the distribution of *lmlk* jars. On the other hand, Na'aman (1979, p. 82) reports the "lack of a direct correlation between the four towns and the distribution of seal impressions bearing their names . . . ." But geographic concentrations have been observed: "the two-winged seals predominated in the northern part of Judah and the four-winged type in the Shephelah, especially at Lachish" (Na'aman 1979, p. 80). Na'aman (p. 80) attempts to explain this by positing that "the *lmlk* storage jars were produced by two central *royal* potteries, *each having its own seals*" (emphasis added). How much simpler and more in tune with the evidence presented in chapter 3 that private firms were involved. Further, the finding of *lmlk* seals in Gezer, according to Na'aman (p. 76), does not reflect international trade: Hezekiah seized Gath to bolster his defenses "and it would appear that the same fate befell Gezer." Perhaps, but we have no direct evidence that this is what happened. (Na'aman does not refer to the finding of *lmlk* seals at Jericho; perhaps the same explanation would apply.) Evidence that this is at least consistent with an economic explanation is provided by the finding of *lmlk* stamps in the Shephelah that possibly date to the aftermath of the Assyrian invasion of 705—when Sennacherib transferred these areas from Judean soveignty to Philistia (see Na'aman 1979, pp. 71, 83–6 for a different interpretation of this evidence). A final fact of some interest is that *lmlk* jars have not, so far, been recovered from the sea (Zemer 1977, p. 101).

On the question of whether Josiah died at Megiddo or in the vicinity of Shechem, see chapter 17, note 21.

26. However, Hallo and Simpson (1971, p. 143) state that "Josiah annexed the Assyrian provinces of Samaria, Gilead, and Galilee . . . " Jar-handles with the *lmlk* inscription have not been found at East Bank sites.

5 THE ECONOMIES OF ISRAEL'S NEIGHBORS

Naturally one must begin with the Phoenicians whose trade expansion reached its height during the eighth through mid-seventh centuries B.C.E.[1] Phoenicia was famous for its fish[2] but its most famous industry was the production of Tyrian purple, a prestigious substance distilled from two types of sea snails native to its coast, used to produce a color-fast dye for woolen goods. Much of the wool and textiles were probably obtained from Moab and Babylonia while the linen, which was woven, no doubt had its origin in Edom or Egypt or, perhaps, the Jericho area (see Josh. 2:6)[3]. The proximity of the coastal waters to the great cedar forests promoted the production and export of various wood products, ships, and lumber. The Phoenicians also possessed a glass industry[4] and a toiletry industry, that respectively, exported polychrome glass beads and marble scent bottles. Further, making use of imported metals and ivory, they produced bronze and golden bowls and ivory carvings known and coveted throughout the ancient world. Smelters of iron and copper are mentioned on funerary stelae and metalworking tools are depicted. Needless to say, the Phoenicians also played an active role in the export and import of slaves (see, for instance, Amos 1:9). The typical Phoenician red-burnished pottery of the ninth–eighth centuries has been found at coastal sites including er-Retabeh in the Egyptian Delta, Bethpelet and er-Regeish near Gaza, and inland Israelite cities such as Hazor and Samaria.

At Tyre, underwater archaeology has discovered moles constructed of great rectangular hewn stones and, in addition, two great breakwaters south of the island, one 390 meters long,

> the other 500 meters long, and each about 30 meters wide. In building these breakwaters, Tyrian engineers had utilized the reefs along the coast. Researches disclosed that the stones from which the breakwaters were built differed from those found in the sea, and had been brought out from the mainland, where similar rocks are to be found. Undersea divers provided measurements for the cornerstones as 3m. × 3m. × 0.75m. and for the stones in the wall as 3m. × 1m. × 0.75m. We stand amazed at the building technique, which laid these foundations in shallow waters. (Katzenstein 1973, p. 12)

Based upon several admittedly inconclusive pieces of evidence, Katzenstein's belief is that at least one stage of these structures should be dated somewhere between the middle of the ninth century and the time of Sennacherib (705–681 B.C.E.). Similarly, the mole of ashlar blocks discovered at Ṭabbāt al-Ḥammām, a small but international Syrian port, most likely dates to the ninth or eighth century (Riis 1970, p. 152).

Beginning mainly in the eighth century, the Phoenicians established a network of permanent commercial colonies.[5] Certainly there is no strong archaeological evidence of such settlements earlier than this time. In order to gain access to the rich copper deposits of Cyprus they settled the town of Kition on its south coast, probably around 800 B.C.E. The latter had been founded by 1000, but whether by the Myceneans or the Phoenicians is disputed. (Kition is a Semitic name and many Phoenician inscriptions have been found there.) The analysis of pottery and of Phoenician writing on a bronze statuette from southern Spain dates the oldest Phoenician trading establishment to the eighth century and probably to its second half. This was a region rich in gold, silver, copper, and possibly tin. From the famous Nora Stone, found on the southern extremity of Sardinia, we know of a Phoenician army and settlement in the late ninth century. (However, another inscription the Nora Fragment can, on paleographic evidence, be "no later than the eleventh century B.C."; Cross 1974, pp. 492–3). Not very long afterwards a Phoenician port was founded on the west coast of Tharros that possibly had close links with Etruria. Based on the recovery of a bronze figurine of the god Melqart (the chief deity of Tyre) from the sea, a Phoenician colony at Sicily may be dated from the beginning of the first millennium. However, the settlement at Moyta in western Sicily, which was followed by those of Palermo and Solunto, dates from the latter half of the eighth or, perhaps, the seventh century. A settlement may have existed on the island of Pithecusae

(Ischia) beside the bay of Naples prior to the arrival of the Greeks in the earlier eighth century. The settlement on Malta dates from the eighth to the early seventh century, as do those at Gozo, Pantelleria, and Lampedusa. The excavated material in Utica is not older than the seventh century. In view of the finding of an inscribed golden medallion in a graveyard dedicated to the goddess Tanit, the settlement of Carthage probably dates to the eighth century.[6] The paleographic evidence is supported by the fact that pottery found below the Tanit deposits cannot be dated earlier than the third quarter of the eighth century. Archaeological data, especially the pottery, from the Moroccan colonies indicate that they were founded in the seventh or early sixth centuries.

Isaiah (23:3) informs us of the Sidonian carriage trade in Egyptian grain. Perhaps they traded in Egyptian linen as well (see Isa. 19:9). But, with all its obscurities, Ezekiel's (27) prophecy concerning the island Tyre is the most comprehensive account of Phoenicia's rich and varied commercial activity and of the contemporary pattern of the international division of labor.

O Tyre, thou hast said, I am of perfect beauty. Thy borders are in the midst of the seas, thy builders have perfected thy beauty. They have made all thy ship boards of fir trees of Senir (Mount Hermon); they have taken cedars of Lebanon to make masts for thee. Of the oaks of Bashan (northern Transjordan) have they made thine oars; the company of Ashurites (Assyria) have made thy benches of ivory, brought of the isles of Kittim (Cyprus). Fine linen and broidered work from Egypt was that which thou spreadest forth to be thy sail, blue and purple from the isles of Elishash (?) was that which covered thee. The inhabitants of Sidon and Aradus (Arvad) were thy mariners; thy skilled men, O Tyre, that were in thee, were thy pilots. The ancients of Gebal and the crafts thereof were in thee thy calkers; all the ships of the sea with their mariners were in thee to carry thy merchandise. They of Paros (Kush? Persia?) and of Lud (Lydia?) and of Phut (Nubia) were in thine army, thy men of war; they hanged the shield and helmet in thee; they set forth thy comeliness. The men of Arvad and Helech with thine army were upon thy walls round about, and the Gammadims (Kumidians) were in thy towers; they hanged their shields upon thy walls round about; they have made thy beauty perfect. Tarshish (Spain? Carthage?) was thy merchant by reason of the multitude of all kind of riches; with silver, iron, tin, and lead they traded in thy fairs. Javan (Ionia), Tubal (northern Cilicia), and Meshech (Phrygia), were thy merchants; they traded the persons of men and vessels of bronze in thy market. They of the house of Togarmah (southern Armenia) traded in thy fairs with horses and horsemen and mules. The men of Rhodes were thy merchants; many isles were merchandise of thine hand; they brought thee for a present horns of ivory and ebony. Syria (Edom is correct) was thy merchant by reason of the multitude of the wares of thy making; they occupied in thy fairs emeralds, purple and broidered work, and fine linen, and coral, and agate. Judah, and the land of Israel, they were thy merchants; they traded in thy market wheat of Minnith (?) and meal, honey, oil, and balm. Damascus was thy merchant in the multitude of the wares of thy making, for the multitude of all riches; in the wine of Helbon (in Syria?) and wool of Sahar (white wool?) and casks of wine from Izalla (in Anatolia) for your staple wares; wrought iron, cassia (= cinnamon?), and calamus were in thy market. Dedan (Rhodes again?) was thy merchant in precious clothes for chariots. Arabia, and all the princes of Kedar (Arabia), they occupied, with thee, in rams, and goats; in these were they thy merchants. The merchants of Sheba and Raamah (Arabia), they were thy merchants; they occupied in thy fairs with chief of all spices, and with all precious stones and gold. Haran and Canneh and Eden the merchants of Sheba, Asshur, and Chilmad (Mesopotamia) were thy merchants. These were thy merchants in all sorts of things, in blue clothes, and broidered work, and in chests of rich apparel, bound with cords, and made of cedar, among thy merchandise. The ships of Tarshish did sing of thee in thy market; and thou wast replenished, and made very glorious in the midst of the seas. (Translation taken and adapted from Katzenstein 1973, pp. 155–61,Millard, 1962; and Moscati 1968, pp. 84–6.)

That the Phoenicians enjoyed a high standard of living is confirmed by Ezekiel 28:4–5: "By your shrewd understanding you have gained riches, and have amassed gold and silver in your treasuries. By your great shrewdness in trade you have increased your wealth, and you have grown haughty". The Israelites and Phoenicians carried on trade relations but Ezekiel makes no mention of capital and labor market linkages. Nevertheless, between two such complementary, commercially active economies, it is not unreasonable to suppose that they existed and were of some importance.

The Philistines (Dothan 1969; Oded 1979a; Stech-Wheeler et al. 1981, pp. 258–60) undoubtedly specialized in the production of grain, oil, and the coastal carriage trade. Archaeological excavations at Ashdod have uncovered a concentration of pottery kilns dating from the ninth–eighth centuries. Tell Qasile, Tell Mor, and Tell Jemmeh had smelting facilities.[7] With respect to Syria, it seems evident that Damascus was a center of the iron trade, since it once yielded 30,000 pounds to Adadnirari III (810–783) (Oppenheim 1969, p. 241). In addition, archaelogy tells us of a trade in bronze receptacles, sealstones, and elaborately carved spoon-like pipe bowls. The prosperity of this general area is hinted at in inscriptions. One, which belongs to King Azita-wadda of Danuna, is from the late ninth or, more probably, the middle of the eighth century. It reads: "Thus there was in all my days abundance and ease of heart, unto the Danunites and to all the inhabitants of the Plain of Adam" (Marcus and Gelb 1949, p. 116; Obermann 1948, p. 26; Rosenthal 1969, pp. 653–54). Another, which may date from early in the eighth century, has Panammu king of Yaudi suggesting that during his reign the people were well fed and that cities were established (Cooke 1903, pp. 161–65). Somewhat earlier there is the boast: "He who had not (even) seen linen in his youth, in my days he was covered with *bṣ*" (fine quality linen) (Oppenheim 1969, p. 249). The author of this inscription was Kalamu (or Kilamuwa) who also claimed that, unlike his predecessors in whose reigns the Mushkabim (state dependents? fief-holders? the lower classes?) "had gone about like dogs," he was "to one as a father, to one as a mother, and to one as a brother" (Olmstead 1923, p. 184). Turning from northern Syria to Moab, we find that Mesha's stele (see chapter 1) and 2 Kings 3:4 strongly suggest that this nation's wealth was based upon wool export. Micah's (2:12) reference to the sheep of Edomite Bozrah points to a similar specialization. Apparently, Edom also possessed a busy weaving industry (Bartlett 1973, pp. 247–49). Further, the hills on either side of the Arabah, the rift valley between the south end of the Dead Sea and the north end of the Gulf of Aqaba, had rich copper ores running as high as 40 percent copper. Since the eastern side of the valley belonged to Edom they must have smelted and exported copper. When Edom recaptured Elath from Judah in the time of Ahaz (735–716) it must have resumed the export to the Gulf ports of the metal ingots produced there. Indeed, according to Glueck (1971 pp. 238–39): "The settlement that the Edomites created on the ruins of the previous city [at Tell el-Kheleifeh] was one of the largest and most prosperous ever constructed there. Little information is available on Ammonite specializations. Of course, with the expulsion of the Israelites and the deployment of Assyrian military forces against desert brigands, all three Transjordan kingdoms shared in the profits of the booming caravan trade with southern Arabia along the King's Highway:

> The flourishing economy of the Transjordanian kingdoms at this period is emphasized by the plethora of archaeological and epigraphic finds (especially seals) in Ammon, Moab, and Edom. In magnificent tombs excavated in Ammon, many vessels have been discovered which manifest growth in local production, as well as much import, and a wealth which must have originated from the international contacts made with caravans . . . (Oded 1979b, p. 272)

Baly (1974, p. 237) adds that pottery found at Bozrah dating to the seventh–sixth centuries, Edom's period of effloresence, is "the most beautiful ever to be found in Jordan."

Of course, the mainspring of the south Arabian economy was the export of frankincense and myrrh, which are obtained from trees by tapping. Both gum resins were utilized as perfumes in temples and religious rites. In addition, frankincense was known for its ability to stop bleeding, while myrrh was used to relieve inflammation and in wound healing. Perhaps the principal use of myrrh was in the manufacture of cosmetics (Van Beek 1964). The prosperity of the Sabean, Minean, and Qatabanian states during the eighth–seventh centuries is mirrored not only in Ezekiel, but also in the archaeological finds. Widespread literacy is at least hinted at by the literally thousands of inscriptions. The pronounced urbanization of the area is symbolized by the ruins of Marib, the Sabean capital, which covered some 150 acres. An advanced technology is evidenced in irrigated agriculture, metallurgy techniques, including bronze casting by the lost-wax technique, and the first Near Eastern evidence of the drawing of bronze wire (Culican 1966, p. 78; Van Beek 1969, pp. xxii–xxv). Surely, Rostovtzeff (1932, pp. 17–18) is correct in saying that "their gifts" to the Assyrians "were no doubt, a mere trifle in comparison with the profits which the southern Arabs drew from a safely organized trade."

There is evidence that Assyria, perhaps utilizing Phoenician vessels, carried on trade with India since "cotton trees" ("trees that bear fleece" which "people pluck and weave into clothing") were introduced by Sennacherib to Assyria about 700 B.C.E., at which time the Assyrians also began to eat rice (Culican 1966, pp. 78–9; Oppenheim 1969, p. 245). Sennacherib also seems to have introduced coins of small denomination, for in his annals it is recorded: "I caused a mold of clay to be set up and bronze to be poured into it to make [as in making] pieces of half a shekel [1/7 oz]" (Oates 1979, p. 187).[8] Moreover, Assyrian business documents make frequent reference to "Ishtar heads" which are equivalent to a given weight of silver (Olmstead 1923, pp. 321, 537).[9]

As noted earlier, Greek trade with the Near East was rapidly expanding in the eighth and seventh centuries. This is the period when, as Casson (1971, p. 362) puts it, "man-made harbor arrangements stage a sudden and impressive debut" at Delos and other Greek sites. The mainstay of this trade was the export of good household pottery (Roebuck 1972, pp. 116–25) and of cruder undecorated earthernware receptacles probably filled with wine (Starr 1977, p. 68).[10] It is known that, in about 600, the brother of Sappho took a cargo of Lesbian wine to Egypt (Andrewes 1971, p. 133). Judging from the finding of sherds at many sites, including Megiddo and Samaria (Riis 1970, pp. 143–56), the export of pottery from Euboea and the Cyclades probably reached its zenith in the eighth century. In the late ninth or early eighth century, Greek trading posts were founded on the Syrian coast at Al Mina at the mouth of the Orontes and, probably, just to the south at Tell Sūkās (Riis 1970, p. 162; Roebuck 1965, p. 102). Thereafter, Corinthian and Rhodian wares increased in relative importance (Culican 1966, pp. 91–2; Roebuck 1959, pp. 62–5). The Hebrew inscription found at Mesad

Hashavyahu (see chapter 4 and part III) was accompanied by Rhodian vases painted in the wild-goat style of the second half of the seventh century B.C.E. (See Glotz 1967, pp. 118, 135–37, for terracotta paintings that exhibit the various stages in the production and export of Corinthian pottery).

Etruscan metals no doubt made their way to the Near East via the Greek markets at Pithecusae and Cumae (Grant 1980, pp. 39–40). This was also the "first great period" of the Greek "colonies" on the western coast of Anatolia. For the first time, Near Eastern imports such as ivory and bronze objects made their appearance (Akurgal 1962, p. 371). Birmingham (1961, p. 192; see also Burney 1977, p. 185) has brought together evidence of a "thriving commercial activity ... between 730 and 675 B.C." in which merchandise of Urartian and Iranian origin (for example, votive shields, cauldrons with ornamental fittings, and animal-footed tripods) reached the Ionic Greeks by travelling overland across the Anatolian plateau and the river valleys to the west. More generally,

> in the latter part of the eighth and seventh centuries B.C., the material culture of the Mediterranean region (Greece, Italy, the southern parts of France and Spain) is characterized by contact with the Near East. ... We realize how important textiles must have been in conveying Oriental motifs to the West. These new motifs are: interlacing patterns, rays, rosettes, palmettes, lotus and other flowers, volutes, hieroglyphs and figured scenes—human or divine or zoomorphic (which includes both real and fabulous animals). (Rathje 1979, pp. 145–47)

Besides metalwork and ivories, the Oriental influence is marked in terracottas and pottery decoration and seems to be more extensive in Etruria than in Greece.

Looking more closely at the Anatolian plateau, we find that the fragmentary evidence suggests that Urartu, in the eastern highlands around Lake Van, flourished in the late ninth and eighth centuries while the excavations at Gordion the center of the Phrygian kingdom on the river Sakarya

> have revealed a succession of relatively humble occupation levels, yet indicating continuity of settlement, preceding the apogee of the Phrygian kingdom in the eighth century BC, and its subsequent destruction by the Cimmerians (variously dated between 696 and 676, traditionally to 686 BC). ... Not only the skill but also the prosperity of Phrygia in the late eighth century BC is attested to by its arts and craftsmanship. In addition to woodwork and weaving, the products of the bronzesmiths exhibit a facility in mass production, especially in the cast bronze bowls with countersunk (omphalos) base and petal pattern. Such bowls need not have been of Phrygian origin, since they were represented on Assyrian reliefs; but present evidence suggests they probably were. ... Cauldrons with protomes were

imported, using rings for ease of carriage, either from North Syria or, more probably, from Urartu. (Burney 1977, pp. 182–83).

The evidence surveyed in this chapter leaves little doubt that the affluence of Israel-Judah in the eighth–seventh centuries should be seen in the context of a prosperous area-wide system of specialization and trade.

Notes

1. Sources on the Phoenicians: Ap-Thomas (1973, pp. 274–80); Bikai (1978); Cooke (1903, pp. 52–4); F. M. Cross (1971, p. 194); Culican (1966, pp. 78–116); Grant (1980, pp. 34–9); Harden (1962, chapter 4, pp. 147–50, 154–57); Heurgon (1973, pp. 62–75); Katzenstein (1973, pp. 9–25, 155–61); Moscati (1968, pp. 84–6, 98–100).

2. A letter to Sennacherib written about 705 records the receipt of preserved fish: "This might well refer to fish pickled or otherwise prepared as a tasty relish and exported from the shores of the Mediterranean as far inland as Assyria" (Oppenheim 1969, p. 249; see also Neh. 13:16).

3. Translations of JPS unless otherwise specified, see the bibliographic note, (chapter 1, note 2.)

4. Glass fragments have been found at Samaria and other Israelite sites (R. J. Forbes 1966, vol. V, p. 147). Job 28:17 mentions glass.

5. There is, however, evidence of earlier commercial contacts with the West and, possibly, for trading posts and refineries in the forms of the Nora Fragment found at Sardinia and a Phoenician inscription from Crete, both of which are dated prior to 1000 by Cross (1980, pp. 15–17).

6. The founding of Carthage is traditionally dated 814 B.C.E. (Rowton 1950, p. 20) or 825 (Liver 1953, pp. 116–20). Liver is also helpful on the early first-millennium chronology of Tyre.

7. The dating and function of the excavated metallurgical facilities are disputed. According to Stech-Wheeler et al. (1981, pp. 259–60), they should be related to copper and bronze working rather than to iron. Further three iron-smelting furnaces at Jemmeh, which are now dated to the eighth–seventh centuries might be iron forges not iron smelters.

8. In this passage Sennacherib is explaining how he cast great lions and bulls—that is, "the process employed by one already well known; in other words, the casting to half-shekel pieces must have been practiced for many generations before his reign . . . " (S. Smith 1922, p. 178).

9. The introduction of a "guaranteed" money—pieces of metal stampled by merchant or temple or, especially, ruler—testifies to the broadening and intensification of market exchanges (see Hicks 1969, pp. 63–8).

10. Riis (1970, pp. 164–65) suggests that dried mackerel and tuna were also important Greek exports. Bakhuizen (1977, pp. 222–26) emphasizes high quality iron and steel products, including swords and utensils, produced at first by the Euboean Chalcidians.

6 THE MARKET FOR FACTORS OF PRODUCTION: COMMERCIAL LOANS, SLAVERY, AND LAND CONSOLIDATION

Commercial Loans

In contemporary societies interest-bearing commercial loans play a key role in allocating scarce resources to the most valuable of their alternative uses. Did ancient Israel know such loans? Unfortunately, neither the Bible nor archaeology provides definitive answers. The Bible does make numerous references to loans and interest but the motives of the borrower are not explained. When, rarely, we are told something of the debtor's circumstances (for instance, the impoverished widow of 2 Kings 4:1)[1], they seem so dire that we are inclined to assume the loan could only have been for the purpose of consumption.

Four points, however, argue in favor of commercial loans in eighth–seventh century Israel-Judah. First, the existence of such loans in the ancient Near East (for example, Babylon, Eshnunna, Anatolia, Assyria) can be traced back to the Old Babylonian period (ca. 2000–1600 B.C.E.) and even earlier.[2] In many cases we even know the interest-rate differentials paid on different kinds of loans (for instance, silver or grain), to different lenders (for example, private or temple), and by different sorts of borrowers (for example, foreigners and natives, high and low credit risks).[3]

Babylonian documents of the seventh century B.C.E. not only record loans to be used for business purposes, but also often specify the kind of business to be engaged in (Ahmed 1968, pp. 144–45). Olmstead (1948, pp. 82–5) adds that the tablets of seventh–fifth-century Babylonia reveal "a remarkably modern system of doing business. . . . Landed properties, houses, animals, even slaves were bought on credit. . . . Payment of. . . . debt on the installment plan was common and a separate receipt was given each time." Private[4] commercial banking was known in the mid-seventh century.

Next the presumably oldest Elohistic law of Exodus 22:24 did not prohibit the charging of interest on commercial loans (see chapter 18.) Only consumption loans to the poor were prohibited: "If you lend silver to any of My people with you who is poor, you shall not be to him as a creditor, and you shall not exact interest from him."[5]

Third, surely the growing number of Israelite merchants, manufacturers, market-oriented farmers, and wealthy government officials would have included individuals who saw the opportunity to improve their position by entering into loan agreements and then paying or collecting interest.[6] Several biblical references hint that this was in fact the case. Amos 2:7–8 includes the passage: "The man and his father who go to the girl to profane My holy name. And they lay themselves down beside every altar upon clothes taken in pledge." This is usually taken as a reference to some form of prostitution. "But the text doesn't say 'go in to,'" only 'go to'; it doesn't say 'slave'; only 'girl'; and it doesn't say 'the same girl,' only the 'girl' " (Coote 1981, p. 35). Note also that "father" may refer to a priest or prophet (see chapter 13, note 40). Coote (p. 35) connects the "girl" with a Mesopotamian institution: the alewife or innkeeper as pawnbroker (see Finkelstein 1961, p. 99). Thus in the context of the following reference to pledges (and, indeed, to 2:6–8 as a whole) this line may mean that a "man and his father go to the alewife to invest for a usurious return." Another possible Mesopotamian (1800–1000 B.C.E.) identification of the "girl" is with the *naditum* ("one who is left fallow"): this term is "often translated 'priestess;' but these women, although they were attached in some obscure way to the temple, were involved in various kinds of business transactions and played an important role in Babylonian economic life, lending silver and corn, supplying capital for trading expeditions, and so forth. . . . The *naditum*, although she could 'marry', seems to have been under an obligation of celibacy. Despite certain ties and duties to the cloister, the *naditum*, whose background always seems to have been wealthy, lived and functioned as a private individual" (Oates 1979, p. 69). The *naditum* may also have rented out slaves left as pledges for loans (see R. Harris 1975, p. 345). Admittedly, there is no direct evidence of the "alewife" and *naditum* in the Syro-Palestinian area.

It is well known, however, that since the gods offered safe and honest dealing (a sort of implicit surety or guarantee), the temples of the ancient Near East served not only as places of worship, but also as centers of intercity and international commerce.[7] The same was often true in medieval Europe; in Lucca, for example, all money changers or spice dealers wishing to set up shop in the square of the cathedral of San Martino had to swear "to commit no theft, nor trick, nor falsification." This oath was actually inscribed on the front of the cathedral where it is still visible today (Blomquist 1979, p. 55). Moreover, from the earliest times to the sixth century B.C.E., Mesopotamian temples, often using their tithe incomes and "deposits" (?) were involved in making business and consumption loans as well as other types of investments (R. Harris 1960; Milgrom 1976, pp. 58–9; Tyumenev 1969, pp. 86–7).[8]

The role of Israelite temples in economic life is, of course, obscure, but there are several hints. Note the frequent references to the "shekel of the sanctuary" (for example, Exod. 30:13 and Lev. 27:25) and, more importantly, the *makkārim* of 2 Kings 12:5–8 who served the priests of the Jerusalem Temple in the role of merchant, business assessor, or the like (J. Gray, 1970, p. 586).[9] Further, it seems possible that neither the *semel* of the Jerusalem Temple in the vestibule of the gate facing north that so outraged Ezekiel (8:3) nor the one set up by King Manasseh (2 Chron. 33:7) were idolatrous images as is usually believed. The phrase including the term *semel* in Ezekiel 8:3 has been translated variously as "seat of the image of jealousy" (JPS, 1917, and Bewer), "infuriating image that provokes fury" (JPS 1978), and "pillar of the possessor" (Thomson). Myers (1965, Vo. II, p. 197) translates *semel* as "slab-image" in 2 Chronicles 33:7. But Torczyner (1946, pp. 294–95) links *semel* with the Akkadian term *šamala* (or *šamallūm*) meaning a *commercial agent* perhaps representing the *tamkārum*, or "wholesale merchant." Given Ezekiel's hostility to commerce his phrase may refer, not to an idol or even to a stele representing redemption (Torczyner, p. 301), but literally to the "seat of the 'commercial agent' " or lender (banker).[10] Is there a connection between Amos's "girl" and Ezekiel's "*semel*"? It does not seem altogether beyond the realm of possibility that both played a part in the lending process.[11]

The fourth argument involves reference in the biblical literature, to legal documents including a witnessed deed for the sale of land, in duplicate (Jer. 32:9–11) and a written bill of divorce (Deut. 24:1–3; see also Jer. 3:8). Jeremiah's double-document "is of clear cuneiform provenience" and is closely linked with contemporary Assyrian practice in which scribes perpetuated ancient forms by writing the deed a second time on the outer envelope. It is attested later in Egypt and the Talmud (Muffs 1969, pp. 191–

92). Further, as Heaton (1956, p. 174) notes, the scribe of Jeremiah 36:4, Baruch,[12] no doubt represents the existence of a class of professional writers who would have been responsible for drawing up such documents. Scribes of this type are clearly attested to in Mesopotamia (see R. Harris 1975, pp. 284–86). Note also the reference to "families of scribes who lived at Jabez" in 1 Chronicles 2:55. Additional evidence is provided by an ostracon found at the late seventh century Judean fortress Mesad Hashavyahu that records the complaint of a reaper that he had been unfairly deprived of his cloak by an official or contractor (see part III): "The letter is written in simple biblical Hebrew, but in an awkard style. . . . The writing, on the other hand, is that of a practiced hand. These two facts, taken together, may perhaps indicate that the actual writing was the work of a scribe . . . whereas the contents were dictated by the reaper . . . " (Naveh 1960, p. 136; for an opposing point of view, see V. Sasson 1978, p. 61). Archaeological evidence of the use of papyri legal and business documents in ancient Jewish society is provided by several seal impressions dating from our period whose reverse sides bear the marks of the papyrus to which the seal was affixed (for the seal impression of Gedaliah, see Gray 1962, plate 18). Even more relevant are papyri property-transfer and interest-bearing loan contracts in Aramaic found at the Jewish colony on the island Elephantine in Egypt which date to the fifth century B.C.E. (see, for example, Porten 1968). With respect to the loan contracts, the names of debtors, creditors, and witnesses are Jewish, and so, in one of the two contracts, is the name of the scribe who recorded it. Stein (1953, p. 169) adds: "In the Tebtunis Papyri, numbers 817 and 818, we also read of loans at interest between Jews of the Epigone. These documents are written in Greek and belong to the years 182 and 174 B.C. respectively."

To sum up: knowledge, legality, nonprohibitive contracting costs, wealth, and the desire to take advantage of opportunities for material gain are all present. What else is necessary to create a market? Nothing else. It follows that the Israelites must have known commercial loan markets.

Contractual Slavery

In Near Eastern, Greek, and Roman antiquity, contractual slavery or bondage was closely linked to the existence of a credit market. The free individual had the right to pledge himself or a family member as security for a loan (see, for example, Neufeld 1958, pp. 78–81). In the event of default, but only then, the pledged individual was legally obligated to enter the house of the creditor and serve there (see 2 Kings 4:1f).[13] In some times and places this obligation was quite explicit in the lending contract, while in others it was assumed under state law (Driver and Miles 1935, pp. 271–74; Schlaifer 1936, p. 177; Westermann 1938, pp. 10, 16). The debtor served the creditor until the debt was paid or for the period stipulated in the law (apparently, for six years in Exodus 21:2 and for three years in Hammurabi's Code: see R. North 1954, pp. 33, 148–50, 155–56, 206) or in the lending contract (see 2 Kings 4:1; Mendelsohn 1949, pp. 26–33, 88–9). If the contract or the law permitted the control over the pledged individual's services to be transferred to a third party, he became a slave (see Exod. 21:2; Deut. 15:12). If not, his status became that of "bondman" (that is, he is to be treated as a "hired worker" or a "settler," see Lev. 25:35, 39–40 and Driver and Miles 1935, pp. 323–26).[14] Slave-sale contracts are known in Mesopotamia beginning in the middle of the third millennium (Mendelsohn 1949, pp. 34–42) and in Egypt for the sixteenth–sixth centuries B.C.E.[15]

A free individual might also sell himself or a family member into slavery or bondage (see Lev. 25:29–40; Deut. 15:12; Isa. 52:3; Neh. 5). Again, as in the case of debt default, service might be for a limited time, indeterminate, or permanent (Crook 1967, p. 61; Driver and Miles 1935, p. 287; Petrie 1923, p. 24; Schlaifer 1936, p. 177).[16] According to Bakir (1952, pp. 119–20; see also Mendelsohn 1949, pp. 14–19) such contracts were "common in Palestine and amongst the Babylonians. We meet with the passage 'thou hast caused my heart to agree to my money . . . ' " However, the failure of the text to mention the exact amount of money leads Bakir to suspect "that the vendor was discharging his debts through self-sale, and that hence, the formula is simply conventional or fictitious."[17] In any event, it is clear that both self-sale and debt-servitude were known to the ancient Israelites.

"When you purchase a Hebrew slave he shall serve six years; in the seventh year he shall go free, without payment" (Exod. 21:2).[18] The use of the word *Hebrew* has occasioned a great deal of comment (see Lemche 1975) for, as De Vaux (1961, p. 82) notes, it is a term that:

> is applied to Israelites only in certain conditions. It has been suggested that the word means those Israelites who forfeited their freedom by a semi-voluntary slavery. The theory can be supported from 1 Sam. 14:21, where the Israelites who entered the service of the Philistines were called 'Hebrews,' and by analogy to the documents from Nuzu, in which the *hapiru* sell themselves as slaves. The biblical texts would preserve traces of an archaic usage, but they certainly refer to Israelites.

With respect to the Nuzi (or Nuzu) documents referred to by De Vaux, they are witnessed contracts dating from the middle of the second millennium from a site in northeastern Iraq near modern Kirkuk in which, for example, "Mar-Idiglat, a Hebrew from the land of Assyria, on his own initiative has entered (the house of) Tehiptilla . . . as a slave" (Meek 1969, p. 220).

Perhaps De Vaux has here put his finger on the origin of the word *Hebrew*.[19]

One may certainly be dismayed by the fact that individuals found it necessary to pledge or sell themselves or their loved ones into slavery or bondage. One may even doubt whether individuals should have the freedom to make such decisions. One may join Aristotle's applause for the Athenian, Solon, who, at the close of the seventh century B.C.E., "liberated the commons then and there, and for all time, by prohibiting loans on personal security" (Woodhouse 1938, pp. 174, 192). The following considerations, however, should not be totally ignored.

1. The institution of contractual bondage provides the lender (or buyer) with fuller control over the debtor's (seller's) services and consumption level (which includes a debilitating life style) than would otherwise be possible. Contractual slavery, by permitting the lender to transfer (permanently or temporarily) the services to third parties, further increases his flexibility to take advantage of unexpected opportunities and provides a hedge against uncertainty—that is, it increases the lender's liquidity. In the ancient Near East, for example, slaves were often left as pledges for loans (see Driver and Miles 1935, p. 74; Eichler 1973; R. Harris 1975, p. 345). More important, the service-transfer possibility provides division of labor benefits by allowing the lender to concentrate his attention on lending instead of having to take time to control the services of a defaulting debtor. Consequently, the right to submit to contractual slavery or bondage, which severely limits the debtor's permitted range of actions, enhances the expected productivity of his labor services, thereby making him eligible for a larger production or consumption loan than he could otherwise expect (see Barzel 1977).

2. Self-sale or self-security contracts permit a borrower or seller to acquire control over the capital necessary to enhance the productivity of his resources, for instance, by means of irrigating his land or by growing or purchasing tree or vine stock or livestock or by geographic movement. Indeed, an increase in the number of debt-slaves may reflect not economic depression but an expanding economy in which an increased number of people are borrowing in order to invest. Naturally, some of these investors ultimately fail due to inability to run a business or bad luck. Even if these losers constituted a small minority of all borrowers, the total number of people falling into slavery might rise.[20]

It is easily demonstrated that the concept of self-sale or self-security transactions in order to acquire funds for capital investment was not alien to the ancient mind. In the first palce, the Draconian code's recognition of the legality of debt-slavery is probably linked with the new agricultural-investment opportunities offered by the growth in the seventh century of overseas trade at Attic ports (French 1964, pp. 14–15; see also chapter 7). Later, in the middle of the sixth century B.C.E., the Athenian tyrant Peisistratus provided loans to the poor for productive purposes. That is, for developing a plot of marginal land which consisted (in ancient and modern Greek idiom) 'all of stones' " (Hammond 1961, p. 86). Such marginal or hill lands were in fact suited to viticulture and to arboriculture. I can see no reason why small Judean farmers would have gone to the credit market, offering what security they could, to build or irrigate their terraced fields (see chapter 2) and thereby take advantage of the booming Jerusalem market for food. Turning next to Rome, we find in the *Satyricon* of Petronius (d. ca. 66 C.E.) one of Trimalchio's guests asserting: "Actually, my father was a king. Why am I only a freedman now? Because I handed myself into slavery of my own free will. I wanted to end up a Roman citizen, not a tribute-paying peregrine." Dio Chrysostum (d. ca. 112 C.E.) reports that tens of thousands of men sold themselves into slavery "under contract" (Barrow 1928, p. 12).[21] The key lies in the Roman institution of *peculium* ("private purse") under which the slave was able to borrow working capital from his master. As K. Hopkins (1978a, p. 125) notes: "The use by slaves and ex-slaves of their master's capital gave them a decisive advantage over the free poor, and must have been an important factor underlying the prominence of slave and ex-slave enterprises in Roman commerce and manufacture . . . "[22] Hopkins (p. 126) adds that many slaves "worked in positions in which they were able to make a profit for themselves. Indeed, there is evidence that masters paid some of their slaves a regular monthly wage. . . . And eventually they could use their savings to buy their freedom. . . . " Note also in this connection the Greek *apophora*, savings by which the slave might purchase his freedom (Burford 1972, p. 45).

Is it beyond the realm of possibility that ancient Israel also knew institutions whereby the poor but ambitious individual could gain access to capital by self-sale? Apparently not. Note first that Leviticus 25:49 provides that if a slave self-sold to a resident alien "be waxen rich, he may redeem himself." More fundamentally, B. Cohen (1951, pp. 141–43) maintains that the Hebrew term *segullah* corresponds to *peculium* in the Roman literary and juridicial sources. *Segullah* appears to have an ancient pedigree, for it is apparently cognate with the Akkadian *sugullu* found in the cuneiform sources from the earlier second to the first half of the first millennium B.C.E.[23] Indeed, Struve (1969, fn. 52 pp. 52–3,) reports that in Ur III (2112–2004) privately owned slaves "could own a *peculium*." Olmstead (1923, pp. 539–40) asserts that, during this period, Assyrian slaves by purchase or debt (as opposed to war captives) "regularly bought and sold property" while "nearly all the industry and a considerable part of the business carried on in the empire was in their hands." "Their only disqualification," Olmstead continues, "seems to have been their inability to choose their own master and the necessity of remaining more or less closely under their master's oversight. . . . " As in the case of Rome, "we have a fair amount of evidence for manumission". Jacobson (1965, p. 293; see also Dandamayev 1972) adds that, in the early seventh century, Babylonian slaves owned various types of property including orchards "and their right to it was respected, as well as the right of their descendants to inherit it". Dandamayev (1972, pp. 38–9) provides some data indicating that when a slave was sold he carried his *peculium* with him.

In the Bible, *segullah* twice refers literally to royal possessions (1 Chron. 29:3; Eccles. 2:6–8). However, on six occasions the term refers to Israel as the Lord's possession (Exod. 19:5; Mal. 3:17; Ps. 135:4; Deut. 7:6, 14:2, 26:18). The latter usage certainly conveys the idea of dependent property ownership and, indeed, *segullah* is rendered by *peculium* in 19:5 of the Vulgate. Cohen (p. 147) suggests that "*segullah* which was originally a juridicial term in private law meaning property, became charged with theological significance at an early period. The conversion of juridicial expressions into theological terms is a common phenomenon". All this, of course, is not conclusive with respect to the presence of *peculium* (or *segullah*) as a capital-market institution in ancient Israel, but it is more than a little suggestive.

3. Contractual slavery or bondage transfers the ownership of the supply of labor services in the future, the duration being specified in the contract or the law, from the worker to the employer. This heightening of control has the effect of increasing the employer's expected return and, hence, his incentive not only to provide material capital (as shown above), but also to invest in training the worker in a skilled trade. Upon the expiration of the contract, the worker takes title to this "human capital," but until then its fruits are the property of the investor (slaveowner). It is well known that in Near Eastern and Graeco-Roman antiquity slaves learned a variety of skills and trades and became, for instance, arboriculturers, policemen, potters, perfumers, weavers, bleachers, tanners, cobblers, ironmongers, bakers, carpenters, gem cutters, goldsmiths, bookkeepers, doctors, stenographers, architects, merchants, and bankers. There are contracts available that deal with the training of slaves as apprentices or under a formal teaching arrangement.[24]

4. Self-sale or self-security contracts become even more important to the seller-borrower if legal or other obstacles are placed in the way of alternative pledges or sales, for example, mortgage or land sale (see chapter 18).[25]

Land Market

There can be no doubt that the sale and lease of privately owned landed property was familiar in the most ancient Near East. Private contracts involving the bequest, sale, and subdivision of fields are common in seventh-century-B.C.E. Babylonia; they are especially abundant in Mesopotamia during the Old Babylonian period (ca. 2000–1600 B.C.E.). But leases of land are also found in Ur III (2112–2004) and in the records of the second half of the Dynasty of Akkad (2334–2154), which reveal the sale for silver of comparatively small parcels by individual vendors. Indeed, private ownership is confirmed by pre-Akkadian deeds of sale.[26] Private land ownership, sales, and leasing are found in all periods of Egyptian history, including the earliest. To cite one example from the mid-third millennium, the Fourth Dynasty official Metjen states in his biography that he bought "6000 *arouras* from numerous *nswtjw*." The latter vendors, Baer (1963, p. 13) believes, "must have been some kind of small freeholders" and the area they sold was "at least 1/1000 of the arable area of Egypt at the time." Sales of privately owned agricultural land are also recorded at late second-millennium Ugarit in north Syria (Muffs 1969, p. 20). A noteworthy biblical example is Abraham's purchase for 400 shekels of Ephron's field in Hebron in the land of Canaan (Gen. 23:12–18; see also Gen. 33:18–19 and Mendelsohn 1949, p. 107). In the Greek world, the poet Hesiod, who wrote in late eighth or early seventh century Boeotia urged his brother to respect the gods, "so that you may buy another's lot, not another buy yours." (Hesiod's immigrant father had earlier purchased an upland farm.) This, as Andrewes (1971, p. 98) points out, "makes it clear that the sale of land, however unwelcome the necessity might be, was a possibility to be reckoned with . . . ." The often-repeated assertions that the ancient world did not know land markets and lived by a law that land was inalienable collective property worked by a peasantry are romantic or Marxist myths that are unsupported by the evidence.[27]

The existence of private landed property and of an Israelite land market is attested to in several biblical passages. David purchases a threshing floor for 50 shekels (2 Sam, 24:24), 1 Kings 16:24 reports that King Omri "bought the hill of Samaria from Shemer for two talents of silver; he built (a town) on the hill and named the town which he built Samaria, after Shemer, the owner of the hill." The most famous, not to say infamous, example is that of Naboth's vineyard which testifies not only to the existence of a land market, but also of opposition to it.[28] In 1 Kings 21:1–2 we are told that: "Naboth the Jezreelite owned a vineyard in Jezreel, adjoining the palace of King Ahab of Samaria. Ahab said to Naboth, 'Give me your vineyard, so that I may have it as a vegetable garden, since it is right next to my palace. I will give you a better vineyard in exchange; or, if you prefer, I will pay you the price in silver!"[29] Of course, Naboth refused to allow the king to consolidate his holdings, saying (v. 3): "The Lord forbid that I should give up to you what I have inherited from my fathers!" Then, so we are told, Jezebel somehow had Naboth falsely convicted and stoned to death. Isaiah (7:23) refers to "every spot where there could stand a thousand vines worth a thousand shekels of silver." Jeremiah 32:6–9, in which the prophet purchases or repurchases his cousin's land in Anathoth, shows a Judean land market in which the right to permanently alienate land is somewhat attenuated.[30]

Archaeological evidence is provided by a tablet excavated at Gezer, which dates, however, to the period of Assyrian rule in either 674 or 648 B.C.E. The obverse side of the tablet records the sale by Natan-Iahu (Nethaniah or "Yahweh has given") of a piece of land bordering on the property of another individual. The reverse side contains a list of four witnesses, the day and month, and the date-eponymy of the Assyrian governor. (Macalister 1912, vol. I, p. 27).

Of course, land ownership was one of the questions that most concerned the eighth-and seventh-century prophets. First of all, there are critical references to the practice of moving ancient land-boundary stones (Hos. 5:10; see also Deut. 19:14, Provs. 22:28, 23:10). Moreover the northern prophet, Amos, and the later Judean prophet, Isaiah, are quite explicit on this matter. Amos (8:4–5) says: "Listen to this, you who devour the needy, annihilating the poor of the land [Thomson: by your tyranny drive the poor from the land], saying 'If only the new moon were over, so that we could sell grain; the sabbath so that we could offer wheat for sale . . . ' " Isaiah (5:8; see also Mic. 2:1) condemns Israelites "who add house to house and join field to field, till there is room for none but you to dwell in the land."[31] Note also Proverbs 30:14 on the oppressors who "devour" the poor from off "the earth" or the "arable land" (see chapter 15, note 15). Evidently, the Israelites of this period had access to an active land market which they employed not simply to transfer land holdings, but also to consolidate them. It is not unreasonable to accept the evidence of the prophets with respect to the fact of land consolidation, they were, as we saw in chapter 2, in many ways keen observers of the contemporary scene. Moreover, it is known that this was a period of land consolidation in both Egypt (Pirenne 1962, pp. 129–30) and Greece (Lewis 1941, pp. 144–50). But such facts only provide the questions that economic theory must answer. Unfortunately, most modern writers on this period, in this as in other cases, have uncritically taken over the prophets' huge biases but even their primitive, inchoate economic analysis as well. This is unacceptable. Without wishing to single out any particular individual, the kind of approach I have in mind is illustrated by S. Yeivin (1979a, p. 163): "Prosperity brought in its wake a much more acute differentiation between the agricultural population, which became more and more landless, and the *nouveaux-riches* absentee land-lords, living in cities as large dealers and high-grade bureaucrats, exploiting their privileged economic position to the detriment of the population as a whole . . . ." Such explanations raise more questions than they answer. Why, in a period of "prosperity," did the agricultural population sell their land? Where did they go once they had sold out? Why were "large-city dealers" and "bureaucrats" more interested in acquiring land than farmers were in keeping it? In what respect did the buyers enjoy a "privileged" economic position? Did the "absentee landlords" take the land by force? If not, why was land consolidation a "detriment to the population as a whole"? At least since Adam Smith it has been recognized that an uncoerced exchange benefits both parties, the seller as well as the buyer. Unless each of the traders views his postexchange position to be superior to his preexchange position, trade will not take place. In short, trade is a positive-sum game.

The following analysis probes the theoretical connection between economic growth and land consolidation. For the interested economic historian a brief review of the relevant world-and temporal-wide evidence is presented in appendix B.

Now to the underlying theory, the innovating entrepreneur is usually a merchant, larger producer, or traveled individual who has acquired some familiarity with production for markets. He is always, to adopt Leibenstein's (1968) terminology, a "gap-filler." The innovator sees that wheat, or wool, or wine produced in a given region can be sold, in this or another region, for more than its production cost. In order to exploit this discrepancy the innovator offers to purchase, say wheat, from the local farmers. However, these farmers either have not been growing wheat or they have grown it only in small quantities on a subsistence basis. The price is attractive but how can they be sure that after they have made the necessary investments and specialized in wheat (or sheep or vines) that the buyer will be able to fulfill his commitments to them? His request is, after all, rather eccentric. The farmers refuse; the risk is too great.

Now does the entrepreneur bear the cost of explaining the new economic situation to each farmer to gain his cooperation? Here he is faced with the significant problem of information "impactedness, which "is partly an information asymmetry condition: one of the agents to a contract has deeper knowledge than does the other . . . But more than asymmetry is implied . . . It is also costly for the party with less information to achieve information parity." (Williamson 1973, p. 318) Does the innovator, instead of bearing these information-transmission costs, raise the price he offers, in order to compensate the farmers for their excessive (in their own eyes) uncertainty? Or does he sooth the anxieties of the local farmers by placing funds in escrow, putting up a forfeitable bond, and writing detailed conditional contracts (see Arrow 1974, pp. 34–6) specifying how he will react in various contingencies?

The historical evidence presented in appendix B suggests that the entrepreneur often finds his least costly option is to set up his own firm. (The following analysis is based on Silver 1981). This involves purchasing or renting the land and labor services of the local farmers and employing them to produce the desired product. Thus the exploitation of the newly perceived economic opportunity is accompanied by land consolidation. If the new product is relatively labor intensive, say vines, or flax, or grain, additional labor will have to be attracted into the region; if, on the other hand, it is relatively land intensive, say for sheep raising, some local farmers will sell their land and migrate.

Obviously the entrepreneur will have to devote resources to enforcing his labor contracts—hired labor is tempted to shirk. But the additional enforcement costs may be far less than those of transmitting information regarding the existence of new markets. In the employer-employee relationship the employer sets up procedures that the employee is told to follow. Communication regarding procedures, since it is retransmission of a reduced volume of information, is cheaper than communication relating to a desired end result (substantive content). The successful performance of a terminal act—here the production of wheat, as Arrow (1974, pp. 53–4) notes, does not "require for assessment the entire probability distribution of states of the world but only some marginal distributions derived from it." Also, contract enforcement may cost less than higher offer-prices to local producers or conditional contracts.

By way of summation, both economic growth and land consolidation are rational responses to the opening up of new economic opportunities. The entrepreneur who perceives the existence of a new agricultural market and seeks to exploit his insight must gain access to the land of his neighbors. In view of the surrounding uncertainties this usually involves his purchasing or renting the land (that is, land consolidation). But to divert the land from its current uses the entrepreneur must bid up the price. As a result of this bidding process the net gain from the transfer of the land from less-valued, current uses to new, higher-valued uses is shared between the land owner and the entrepreneur. To say the least, it is not at all obvious why the process of land consolidation must be accompanied by the impoverishment of the former free landowners as Neufeld (1960, p. 50) and the prophets assert. It is interesting to note, in conclusion, that we seem to have the word of a prophet that new agricultural products were in fact being introduced. Isaiah 17:10 is somewhat obscure but it surely involves seed experimentation and/or the planting of cuttings from Syrian vines on Israelite soil: "Therefore, though thou plant pleasant plants [or plants of a foreign god] and shalt set it with strange slips; . . ."[32] According to Bewer (1949, p. 49) the Hebrew word for pleasant (na'aman) was a surname for the Syrian god Adonis.[33] Semple (1931, p. 420) casts light on this passage by pointing out that in the first and second centuries C.E.:

> The Jews carried on a trade in seed-corn . . . They tested seed by planting a few in an earthen pot or a manure bed, and judged the vitality by the rapidity of germination. This method recalls the miniature 'gardens of Adonis,' offered to the youthful god of spring throughout Syria . . . They consisted of seedling grains or vegetables raised in earthen pots by some forcing process, and may possibly have been either cause or effect of early experiments in seed testing.

In addition, it is not unreasonable to assume that land consolidation facilitated a transition from grain to stock farming to take advantage of the emergence of an affluent, meat-consuming Israelite public.

Notes

1. Translations of JPS unless otherwise specified; see the bibliographic note (Chapter 1, note 2).
2. In some cases the interest was deducted in advance but additional interest had to be paid if the loan was not repaid on time (Saggs 1962, pp. 290–91).
3. Sources on interest: Ahmed (1968, pp. 143–45); R. Harris (1960, pp. 131–32); Homer (1963, p. 30); Balkan (1974, pp. 30–1); Olmstead (1948, p. 84); Powell (1977, p. 28).
4. "Private" in the sense of not being associated with a temple (see note 8).
5. Within Jewish tradition the Mekhilta, a tannaitic Midrash on Exodus dating from the first–second centuries C.E. stresses the ban on interest-bearing loans to the poor: "To the poor with thee you should not be like a professional creditor, but you may be like a professional creditor to the rich." (Stein 1953, p. 162)
It will not do to say that the Israelites did not need commercial interest because they did not engage in trade. In the first place this is false (see chapters 2 and 3). In the second place, as Leemans (1950a, p. 32, fn. 87) points out, "as is clearly demonstrated by Babylonia, it is not only trade but agriculture which can give rise to lending-transactions."
6. Lang (in press) perceptively suggests that: "Investing income to open up new sources of gain is known from the capable wife of Proverbs 31:16."
7. The nadîtus of Sippar were obligated to bring offerings of flour, meat, and bread to the temple for the festivals. Is it possible that these offerings constituted a kind of payment to the temple for the privilege of carrying out their loan and other business transactions under the auspices of the gods?

8. The importance of temple loans varied from one place and time to another (R. Harris 1960, pp. 127, 130). Falkenstein's (1974) view that temples dominated the Sumerian economy is a mistake resulting from a biased sampling of archival materials (see Yoffee 1979, pp. 18–20) and questionable interpretations of Urukagina's reforms (see chapter 10) and of administrative records regarding the allocation of land (Foster 1981).

Based on their extensive lending role it is reasonable to view the temples of the ancient Near East as relatively efficient financial intermediaries or bankers. Given the degree of trust they enjoyed, the temples were quite probably in a position to charge relatively high fees for holding gold (or silver or grain) for safekeeping and to borrow at relatively low rates of interest in order to relend. Also, since temple bankers had to bear a lesser default risk than most private lenders, they could afford to charge less for a loan. In most of the temple loans the god appears as the creditor, but in many cases "a human agent appears along with the god as a creditor. . . . Several of these human agents are definitely *tamkāru* 'merchants'. . . . It would . . . appear that the human agent appearing alongside the god as a creditor might belong to one of several professions and might occupy a position of great or insignificant importance varying with the temple and city. . . . It was also possible for the agent to appear as sole creditor even when he acted on behalf of the temple." (R. Harris 1960, pp. 128–29).

R. Harris (1960, p. 130), speaking of the Old Babylonian period, notes that the exact relationship between these private individuals and the temple "cannot be determined at the present time. Nor is it known which played the more significant part in the enterprise, for, compared with documents belonging to private persons there are very few temple texts." The declining relative importance of temples as lending institutions may be attributed to the various forces that may conveniently be grouped under the heading of "secularization" and to the conversion of temples from business to charitable institutions.

9. Based on Mesopotamian usage, the term may refer to a commission merchant (see Powell 1977, p. 25–7). On the *mkrm* of Ugarit, see Rainey (1964, p. 314) and Astour (1972, pp. 11–12). See R. Harris (1960, p. 129) on the manifold connections between *tamkāru* "merchants" and Old Babylonian temples. Note that the latter noun is formed from *mkr*. On *mkrtyhm*, see chapter 1, note 3.

10. Article 32 of Hammurabi's Code and a letter written by Hammurabi refer to the role of the temple in redeeming captives of war. In both cases the *tamkārum* or merchant is the agent of redemption (R. Harris 1960, pp. 129, 131). But R. Harris (p. 131) notes that: "Among the temple loans there is one text from Sippar . . . where one Qišušu borrows 24 shekels from Šamaš [the temple] and gives this money to another person for his redemption (*ana ipṭerišu*) . . . However, this may not be an example of a captive being redeemed but rather a case in which a pledge, namely Qišušu, redeems himself with the help of a temple loan. If so . . . the temple aided in alleviating the difficulties of people." The temple aided people, it should be noted, by providing them with loans they desired and were willing to pay for. The same kind of aid is provided by private lenders. Indeed, R. Harris (1960, p. 131) also cites an example from Tutub "of a son borrowing silver in the Sin temple in order to redeem his father who appears to have been a pledge with the temple. However, since he cannot repay his debt he has to sell himself to the *enum*-priest." R. Harris (p. 131) suspects that the *tamkārum*'s mobility suited him for the role of liason between temple and debtor just as he served as the liason between temple and captive. This evidence, I submit, strengthens the case for regarding the *semel* in terms of a lending institution associated with the Israelite temple. For a Ugaritic redemption contract, see Yaron (1960).

11. Can it be that several other biblical passages that seem to refer to cult prostitutes or idolatry are also polemical attacks on the commercial life associated with the temple? 2 Kings

23:7, for example, refers to the "houses of the sodomites that were in the house of the Lord, where the women wove coverings for the Asherah." However, Hawkes (1977, p. 114) reports that in Ur III (2112–2004) textile manufacture was not carried out only by private businessmen but was also in the temples: "In the temple shops both men and women were employed, with the women probably outnumbering the men. Though a large proportion were slaves, there were also free citizens, and it seems they may sometimes have taken spun wool home to weave, bringing it back to the temple as finished cloth." R. J. Forbes (1964, vol. IV, p. 8) notes that at Ur the weaver's house was a separate establishment in the temple complex.

To take another example, in Genesis 38:16 Tamar (Palm) who had disguised herself as a prostitute ("devoted one") by putting on a veil and sitting in the entrance of Enaim, asked Judah for a pledge or a pawn. But a veil is hardly an appropriate disguise for a prostitute and, in any event, the veil may well have been a symbol of respectability in the ancient Near East (see Driver and Miles 1935, pp. 133–34) and within Israelite tradition (Gen. 24:65). What does this tale really signify?

To take an example of another kind, does Ezekiel's (8:17) phrase "they put the branch [or cutting] to their nose" refer to sun worship at the Temple or is it a sarcastic reference to agricultural experimentation? See the discussion of Isa. 17:10 in this chapter.

12. For additional information on Baruch, see chapter 13, note 5.

13. As Neufeld (1958, p. 73) notes, the practice of self-enslavement in lieu of debt repayment is implicit in Genesis 43:9 (see also Gen. 44:32–33). It is possible that Amos had this practice in mind when he spoke of those who "buy" the needy "for a pair of sandals" (8:6). Lang (in press) explains: "The symbolic action of giving a sandal is a feature of concluding an agreement or a transaction; this is understood from Ruth 4:7 which says, 'It was the custom for a man to pull off his sandal and give it to the other party. This was the form of attestation in Israel.' The sandal given to one's partner is the pledge for the transferred property. Hence, the Hebrew word na'alayim 'a pair of sandals' acquired the meaning of 'bond'. Applied to our passage of Amos: the poor man is being 'bought' because of a bond or obligation." In short, in the event of default on the debt obligation signified by the passing of the sandals, the debtor must enter the household of the creditor as a slave. Hammershaimb (1970, pp. 46–7), however, interprets "a pair of sandals" as "a trivial sum." Perhaps there is an element of truth in both lines of interpretation. The "pledge" sometimes "entered the household" of the lender at the time of the loan and his or services constituted the interest payments. (R. North 1954, pp. 179–84).

14. This is also E. Kalt's interpretation of Leviticus 25:39 (cited in R. North 1954, p. 137).

15. Eighth–seventh-century Assyrian slave-sale contracts contain the clause: "The buyer is guaranteed against loss of the slave from . . . disease for 100 days . . . , and against crime for all time." (Postgate 1976, p. 26).

16. In some texts it may be difficult to distinguish between self-sale and an antichretic (to use the classical term) transaction in which the services of the pledge constitute the interest payments on a loan (see note 13 and Eichler 1973, pp. 40–6, 82–3).

Note also in this connection the "mysterious" Roman contract of the fifth–fourth centuries B.C.E. called *nexum* ("binding") "whereby the poor in return for loans had to work in bondage to the rich" (Brunt 1971, p. 51; but compare Finley 1982, pp. 150–66).

In Genesis 49:14–15, Issachar (or "man for hire"? see Herrmann 1975, p. 93) who saw a good resting place and a pleasant land, chose to become a "servant under task-work" or a "day-laborer." But it is difficult to tell whether this refers to wage labor or self-sale or antichresis. Similar ambiguities beset the Greek term "*latris*" (see Finley 1982, p. 150).

17. Terms of satisfaction are common in Aramaic, Demotic, and cuneiform sale documents. "My heart is satisfied with the money" indicates the receipt of the full payment by the seller and,

consequently, that the conveyance was legally incontestable (see Muffs 1969, pp. 27, 47, 56–8). For additional evidence bearing on the nature of Bakir's contract, see Driver and Miles (1935, pp. 271–72, 287–88).

18. The meaning of "without payment" is considered in chapter 18, note 10.

19. The Nuzi documents reveal that in some cases the Hebrew slave "enjoyed the right of refusing to be sold to another owner as long as he did not break his part of the agreement" (Saarisalo 1934, pp. 62–3).

20. According to von Fritz (1943, p. 31) "ancient tradition leaves no doubt that the practice of selling hektemors [Athenian small farmers] into slavery became more and more frequent in the second half of the seventh and sixth century, that is, just at the time when the time when the export of olive oil from Athens experienced its greatest expansion." I would surmise that the explanation is that at this time many farmers pledged their bodies in order to acquire loans to buy or raise olive or vine stock. Correspondingly, self-sale contracts appear to have been prominent in Egypt during the relatively prosperous, international-trade-oriented twenty-sixth (or Saite) Dynasty dating 663–525 B.C.E. (Petrie 1923, p. 24).

21. Without citing a shread of evidence, W. V. Harris (1980, p. 124) dismisses self-sale and debt-enslavement as important sources of Roman slaves and seeks to explain away Dio Chrysostum 15:23 as "presumably metaphorical, the speaker's purpose being to show that anyone may (in some sense) become a slave; i.e. the reference to wage-slaves." Columella (1.3.12) refers to citizens in bondage (*nexu*; see note 16) who worked large estates during the early Empire (Garnsey 1980, p. 36).

22. Of course, we have no way of knowing the fraction of contractual slaves among all the slaves transported from one ancient Near Eastern area to another. The indentured-servitude system of colonial America allowed English emigrants to obtain passage to the colonies by selling claims on their future labor. Galenson (1981, pp. 447–48) summarizes the main features of the system as follows:

> In England . . . a prospective servant signed a contract, or 'indenture' with a merchant . . . The servant was then transported to the specified colonial destination, where the mer-chant . . . sold his contract to a colonial planter or farmer. . . . In return for the commitment of his labor, the servant received passage to the designated colony, maintenance during the term of the contract, and certain freedom dues at its conclusion. Once signed, the indenture was negotiable property, and at any time before its conclusion the servant could be sold to a new master . . . When the contract expired, the servant became a free man."

Diakonoff (1974, p. 70) asserts that the "slave trade . . . is found only *within the community*." But, in Italy under the Empire "Greek-named slaves predominated . . . despite the comparative rarity of Eastern wars." Does the explanation lie, as Duff (1928, p. 3) suggests, in a high birth-rate among the slaves of the Republican age? See also M. V. Harris (1980, pp. 122, 125–28).

23. Greenberg (1951) provides examples of the Rabbinic literature in which *segullah* denotes the savings of legally dependent persons. He rejects (p. 174), however, "the usual connection of *segullah* with Akkaddian *sugullu* 'herd', with the consequent loss of another semantic parallel to *pecu-pecunia, cattle-chattel*" in favor of Akkadian *sikiltu*. The latter term refers to the savings of wives (dependent persons) in the Hammurabi Code (Art. 141) and a Nuzi tablet.

24. Sources on occupations and training of slaves: C. A. Forbes (1955); Diakonoff (1974, fn. 71, p. 76); Mendelsohn (1949, pp. 106, 113–15); Struve (1969, p. 54); Westermann (1955, pp. 102–03).

25. In the first half of the thirteenth century B.C.E. the Hittite king addressed an edict to the king of Ugarit concerning the merchants of Ura, presumably Hittite subjects. Apparently the

latter were to be permitted to seize the persons of defaulting debtors but not their land (see Yaron 1969, pp. 71–4).

26. Sources on Mesopotamian land transactions: Ahmed (1968, pp. 145–47); Bottéro (1967, p. 114); R. Clay (1938); Gelb (1979, vol. I, pp. 68–71); R. Harris (1975, pp. 213–45); Leemans (1975, pp. 137–38); Struve (1969, p. 41).

27. Even the gifted Soviet scholar I. M. Diakonoff (1974, p. 49) seems to twist himself into a circle to conform to the Marx-Engels dogma of collective land ownership while presenting ancient Mesopotamian documents pointing to a private individualistic land market in small farms, date plantations, and gardens. However, another Soviet scholar V. V. Struve (1969, p. 41) wrote in 1933: "Evidently the gentilic order, or rather the patriarchal order, was already on the decline towards the end of the Akkadian dynasty" (2334–2154).

The concept of "peasantry" is quite obscure but apparently one central feature is the absence of individual ownership of land.

28. See chapter 17, note 26.

29. Note Sargon's intriguing cylinder inscription commemorating the founding of his new capital at Dûr Sharrukîn (or Khorsabad) in 706: "In accordance with the name which the great gods have given me,—to maintain justice and right, to give guidance to those who are not strong, not to injure the weak,—the price (*lit.*, silver) of the fields of that town I paid back to the owners according to the record of the purchase documents, in silver and copper, and to avoid wrong (*or*, ill feeling), I gave to those who did not want to (take) silver for their fields, field for field in locations over against (facing) the old." (Luckenbill 1927, vol. II, pp. 63–4).

30. The episode ends as follows: "For thus said the Lord of Hosts, the God of Israel: 'Houses, fields, and vineyards shall again be purchased in this land'." (JPS, 1978). But Thomson and Bewer have "possessed" not "purchased."Torczyner (1946, p. 300) prefers "redeemed." I understand that the Hebrew *qnh* can mean "acquire" in any basic sense; it may or may not mean acquisition by purchase, and can also mean "possess."

31. The student of the ancient Near East may well be struck by the resemblance between these "abuses" and those which Urukagina, perhaps the earliest social reformer recorded in history, sought to remedy in the Sumerian city-state Lagash.

32. So translated by Bewer and JPS(1917). JPS(1978) renders this passage: "That is why, though you plant a delightful sapling, what you sow proves a disappointing slip." "Delightful" is emended to read "true."

33. Note also Amos 5:11 in which those who "trample upon the poor" have "planted pleasant vineyards."

7 LIVING STANDARDS: CONSUMER DURABLES

During the eighth century B.C.E. Israel-Judah's growing economy was embedded in a vigorous international economy. This, together with control over the major trade routes "poured wealth into both countries." There is reason to believe that by the later seventh century Judah had once again become a wealthy nation. But in what forms was this wealth consumed? Both the Bible and archaeology testify strongly to part of the answer: a significant extension in the possession of housing and other consumer durables. The archaeological evidence indicates that this was the case not only in the larger or royal cities, but also in smaller towns and settlements. Kathleen Kenyon (1960, p. 177) concluded that while "Samaria and Megiddo allow us to get some glimpse of royal and official luxury" the finds at other sites "suggest fairly general prosperity but little luxury." On the basis of the review of the evidence that follows I believe that this represents an understatement.

Private Homes

In ancient Israel, as elsewhere in the ancient Near East, bricks made of soft clay were the basic material for house construction (Contenau 1966, p. 27). The clay, which was especially plentiful in the low-lying plains, was mixed with finely chopped straw in order to improve the durability of the product, and then packed into wooden molds and left in the sun to dry (Bertholet 1926, p. 23). At additional cost in terms of fuel and labor the durability of the bricks might be further increased by kiln baking (see Gen. 11:3[1]; Kennett 1931, p. 23). The use of stone in construction was more common in the central highlands where loose stones were abundant. In the earlier Israelite period, stone foundations were usually crude affairs involving roughly trimmed stones and unhewn joints filled with smaller stones or held together with mortar. In the eighth and seventh centuries, however, much greater use was made of the services of the stonecutter. Thus Amos 5:11 warns the Israelites: "You have built houses of hewn stone, but you shall not live in them," while, somewhat later in the eighth century, Isaiah 9:8–9 castigates Ephraim and the inhabitants of Samaria that the Lord "will tumble her stones into the valley and lay her foundations bare." Isaiah 9:9 may also testify to the increasing substitution of high quality cedar for the cheap and common wood of the sycamore (mulberry fig tree): "The sycamores have been cut down, but we will change them into cedars."[2] Several other prophetic passages suggest in more general terms that a dramatic improvement in housing had taken place. Isaiah 5:9, for example, tells Judah that: "Surely, great houses shall lie forlorn, spacious and splendid ones without occupants." In the later seventh century the prophet Jeremiah (9:20) tells the Judeans that death will enter the "windows" of their "palaces" or "strongly-built houses." Note first that "palaces" refers to luxury not royalty: in the mid-second–millennium Nuzi tablets "palaces" are deeded in testaments by people who are not kings (Lacheman 1939, pp. 528–29). Second, while the reference to death coming into the windows recalls the Ugaritic Epic of Baal,[3] it may well be that the windows of the luxurious Judean homes represent some sort of innovation.[4] Such portrayals of an improvement in housing quality are supported by the archaeological evidence.

The town of Tirzah located in the northern kingdom between Samaria and the Jordan River clearly illustrates the change in housing quality. De Vaux describes a group of "very lovely" eighth-century private dwelliings, each with two rooms on either side of a courtyard and one or more rooms at the end, that are not only larger, but also of superior construction to the earlier Israelite homes.[5] "The plan was more regular, the walls built with two lines of stones, the stones better trimmed, and the corners well bonded" (1967, p. 377). Northward, in Hazor, the findings are even more impressive. The excavator Yadin (1975, pp. 151–52, 171) tells us that the eighth-century private houses ranked among the finest buildings of the entire Israelite period at Hazor and "far surpassed [their] predecessors in architectural design." The general plan of the cornered court, pillared house seems to have called for entrance into a large courtyard that led to two large rooms at the opposite end of the house and three smaller rooms along its side. In one specimen the roof above a section of the court was supported "by six well-dressed, square, stone-pillars." Another specimen had an upper story to which access was gained by means of a stone-built staircase with well-dressed steps. Since only foundations were found for the other houses the possibility is raised that many of them possessed upper stories. Shops and workshops were interspersed in the residential quarter.

In Mizpah, a smaller town just south of the Israel-Judah border, the typical house of the later ninth or eighth century was an enclosure with stone walls, but even here the remains of stairways and second floors were found. There were also more carefully constructed buildings of greater architectural distinction. "There are three tripartite four-room buildings, rectangular in shape and of almost the same size, 10 × 12 or 13 meters. They consist of three long rooms, lying side by side and forming an almost perfect square, and a fourth room approximately the same size which ran across their ends. The central room, about 3 meters wide, was always the largest." (Diringer 1967, p. 334) That these were private dwellings rather than storehouses is supported by the similarity in terms of plan and dimensions with houses excavated in Tirzah (see above) and Shechem (see Wright 1965, pp. 158–59; 1978, pp. 153–54). The excavations at Shechem, the first capital of the northern kingdom, revealed private homes dating to ca. 724. One interesting specimen, House 1727, contained seven rooms plus an additional three rooms apparently devoted to some industrial purpose. The residential quarters included cobblestone paved floors[6] and a roof supported by wooden posts standing on two stone pillars. The outline of ceiling beams suggested the existence of an upper floor.

South of Hebron, in Debir, the excavations revealed "pleasant" private homes of a "new type" dating, according to Albright (1932, pp. 116, 126), from the late-eighth or early-seventh centuries. The walls of the second floor, which was reached by a well-built outside stone staircase were constructed of clay brick or, in some cases, wood. The lower walls, however, were of stone. The plan, which in this respect seems to resemble those at Hazor and Gezer, involved a large rectangular room on the lower floor with ceiling supported by a row of four massive stone pillars. The lower floor also included two to four additional rooms. Gezer, located on the boundary of the Plain of Philistia and the foothills of the Judean mountains in Ephraimite territory, contained well-paved rooms and, again, a complex house plan utilizing stone-pillars (Macalister 1912, vol. I, p. 166). Lachish's buildings dating from the eighth or seventh centuries are well constructed (Aharoni 1975, p. 41), as are those recently excavated on the eastern slope of Jerusalem. Indeed, one of the latter possessed an installation tentatively identified by the excavator as a stone toilet (Shiloh 1981, pp. 162–65).

Possessions

The artifacts found within the excavated dwellings further reflect the prosperity of the era. Mizpah reports "numerous beads of semi-precious stones, eyelet pins, fibulae, bangles, and other metal jewellry" together with "metal utensils and implements" (Diringer 1967, p. 320). The most prosperous levels of Tell Abu Selimeh in southern Judah may date from the time of Uzziah (McCown 1943, p. 131). Ample supplies of quality pottery have been excavated in Lachish, Arad, Tell Halif (north of Beer-sheba), Tirzah, Shechem, Samaria, Hazor, and Megiddo, among others. A note-worthy example is provided by an elegant "Cypro-Phoenician" juglet found in House 1727 in Shechem (Wright 1965, fig. 85). An even more interesting find comes from Tell Halif, which overlooked the Via Maris and the route leading toward Hebron and Jerusalem. Excavations in several Judean tombs in the adjacent area led to the discovery of a unique eighth-century bowl with a molded pomegranate in its center (Seger 1979, p. 51).

Ivories were scattered over the entire destruction layer of Samaria. At both Debir and Hazor, numerous decorated-stone cosmetic palettes possibly used for grinding mascara have been recovered (McCown 1943, p. 95; Yadin 1975, pp. 179–80). Most palettes were adorned with simple patterns, but they also came colored dark blue, or inlaid with a gem, and in matched sets of palette and jar. One Hazor house which, to judge by the preserved ruins, consisted of only two rooms built one behind the other plus an open court; nevertheless it contained a wealth of utensils and storage jars. Moreover, this obviously nonroyal domicile also contained an unusual, presumably ex-pensive, ivory cosmetic spoon. The ruins of the neighboring home revealed a beautifully carved mirror handle of bone (Yadin 1975, pp. 154–57). The latter findings bring to mind the diatribe directed at Jewish women by Isaiah 3:16–20.

> Moreover the Lord saith, "Because the daughters of Zion are haughty, and walk with stretched forth necks and wanton eyes, walking and mincing as they go, and making a tinkling with their feet; therefore the Lord will smite with a scab the crown of the head of the daughters of Zion, and the Lord will discover [uncover] their secret parts." In that day the Lord will take away the bravery of their tinkling ornaments, about their feet, and their head-bands and their crescents, the pendants, and the bracelets, and the veils, the head-dresses and armlets and sashes and perfume boxes and amulets, . . .

The sixth-century prophet Ezekiel (23:39–40) charges that "On the very day that they slaughtered their children to fetishes, they entered My sanctuary to desecrate it. . . . Moreover, they sent for men to come from afar . . . For them, you bathed, painted your eyes and donned your finery". (See also Jer. 4:30.) Speaking of children, McCown (1943, p. 95) reports the finding in Debir of many toys[7] including animal and human figurines, rattles, and whistles. Wright (1962, p. 200) adds that during the later eighth and seventh centuries Israelite sites abounded in mass-produced figurines of horseback riders. If, indeed, such objects are toys as they seem to be, this provides a strange contrast with Ezekiel's allegations of child slaughter.

The wooden furniture of Israelite homes has long since become dust. Nevertheless, excavations of eighth-or seventh-century Judean tombs at Lachish have brought to light pottery models of a couch and low wide chair curiously suggestive of the art-deco style of the 1930s (see Heaton 1956, figs. 24, 27; see also Holland 1977, p. 154). Was it on couches such as this that Israelites reclined while they feasted on "lambs from the flock and calves from the stall" (Amos 6:4) and on assorted "dainties" (Lam. 4:5)? Representations on Greek vases and reliefs show us that, in the days before upholstery, both comfort and beauty were served by placing loose covers, hangings, and pillows on wooden furniture (Richter 1965, p. 27). A similar practice is indicated in Ezekiel 23:41, wherein Samaria and Jerusalem sit before the table on "covered sofas" or better on "couches covered with tapestries".[8] (Ezekiel 16:16 seems to refer to the decoration of the "high places" or "platforms" of sacrifices with gaily colored tapestries.) Proverbs 7:16 indicates that the tapestries were imported from Egypt.

Dress

An increased standard of luxury in dress is reflected in several biblical passages. Jeremiah 13:1–2 has the prophet purchasing a "loin-cloth of linen." Ezekiel 7:20 refers to choice apparel that was "laid by for ostentation" or "beautiful adornments in which they took pride" and 16:10 adds: "I clothed you in embroidered garments and gave you sandals of *tahash* leather to wear, and fine linen about your head, and dressed you in silks." Isaiah 3:20–21 lists "armlets, sashes, festive robes, mantles, shawls, purses, lace gowns, linen vests, kerchiefs, and capes." Zephaniah 1:8 refers to those who wear "strange" (imported?) apparel. Then there are the repeated references to clothing in shades of purple. "Be your sins like crimson, they can turn snow-white; be they as red as dyed wool, they can become like fleece" (Isa. 1:18). "They who had been raised in scarlet [purple] were covered with dung" (Lam. 4:5). Jeremiah refers to those whose "clothing is blue and purple" (10:19) and asks "What do you gain by wearing crimson...?" (4:30). The good wife of Proverbs 31:22 wears clothing of "fine linen and purple." As Reinhold (1970, p. 11) observes, "Besides its high cost which afforded a means of conspicuous consumption, sea purple... was the only color-fast dye known to the ancient world, and thus provided upper social strata not only with a fashionable distinction but also the means for assuring the cleanliness of their status garb." For the prophets, as Carmichael (1974, pp. 164–65) notes, the increased use of highly colored material whether of linen or wool was taken as a symbol of wanton luxury.[9] That the fine linen was imported (probably from Edom or Egypt) is indicated by Hosea's (2:7) upbraiding of Israel "because she thought, 'I will go after my lovers, who supply my wool and linen...'." In this connection it is of interest to mention the recent find in a ninth-eighth century building at Kuntillet Ajrud in northern Sinai, some forty miles south of Kadesh-Barnea, of pieces of finely woven linen and a wool-linen mixture (Meshel 1979, pp. 33–4). The building, which apparently served as a waystation for travelers was located at the intersection of three desert trade routes.[10] The Hebrew word for mixtures, *sha'atnez*, being an Egyptian loan word [see Lambdin 1953, p. 155] one would expect that the usage of mixed wool and linen came from Egypt" (Yeshiva University Museum 1980, p. 31).[11]

Notes

1. Translations of JPS unless otherwise specified; see the bibliographic note 2, chapter 1.

2. Perhaps this passage should not be taken literally. The prophet may be making the point that his contemporaries are as extravagant as was King Solomon (1 Kings 10:27).

3. In the Epic of Baal it is narrated that when Baal built his beautiful palace, he gave instructions at the beginning that no window should be opened therein, so that his enemy Mot (corresponding to the Hebrew... 'death') should not be able to enter by way of the windows and kill his wives..." (Cassuto 1971, p. 22).

4. The exact nature of the presumed innovation is, however, unclear. While glass was known to the Israelites (see Forbes 1966) it is quite unlikely that the reference is to windowpanes.

5. According to Shiloh (1970) the Israelite "four-room house" and its subtypes is characterized by a back room the width of the building, with three long rooms stemming forward from it.

6. According to Stern (1979a, p. 269) the floors of Israelite houses "were of stone and packed clay, often with a layer of well-beaten *hawwār* chalk."

7. For a discussion of the question of "toys" versus "cult-objects," see Holland (1977, pp. 134 ff.). The horse on wheels was a popular toy in Athens in the fourth century C.E. and,

according to Brumbaugh (1966, p. 90), "its ancestors, less plump but equally mobile, go back 1800 years." Baby rattles were also known.

8. So rendered by Thomson (23:42) and Bewer; JPS(1978) has "grand couch."

9. Alternatively, Morgenstern (1966, p. 284) has suggested that in the ancient Near East "the color red seems to have been associated with evil spirits or their removal."

10. The building contains benedictory graffiti invoking not only Yahweh but El and Baal; on a storage jar a couple is depicted apparently in the act of sexual intercourse with an accompanying inscription "to Yhwh of Samaria/our keeper and to his Ašrt." "The term *ašrt* with the possessive suffix cannot be a proper name and it seems likely," to Pope (1980, p. 211) "that the meaning here is 'consort.' " Pope (1980, pp. 210–11) concludes that the structure is cultic, possibly a *marzēah*-house (see chapter 16) where various orgiastic funerary rites took place. From the presence of a central bench-room containing "paraphernalia for feasting [as distinguished from mere eating?] and drinking, a large stone mixing bowl and large jars for wine, surrounded by pantries, storage rooms and ovens" Pope deduces that "eating and drinking was an important part of the rites carried on here." Pope does not explain the orgiastic-ritual role of the cloth, but perhaps he will find a clue in note 11 following.

11. Oppenheim (1969, p. 247) suggests that the biblical prohibition (Lev. 19:19 and Deut. 22:11) against mixing wool and linen threads "might conceivably go back to a taboo connected with a technology reserved for textiles destined for contact with the sacred, and therefore inadmissable for profane use." Could such considerations also have a bearing on the attacks on purple-dyed clothing? See Exodus 25:34–35; 26:1, 31, 36; 27:16; 28:4–8; 35:23; 36:8, 35, 37; 39:1–9, 29; Numbers 4:7–8, 14; 2 Chronicles 3:14.

8 LIVING STANDARDS: DIET

A diet that was more nutritious, varied, and tasty was the second form by which eighth and seventh century Israelites consumed their new wealth. Before examining the underlying biblical and archaeological evidence, it is advisable to consider the main facts regarding nutrition and dietary regimens.[1]

Historically, the carbohydrates contained in the endosperm of cereal seeds have been the primary source of glucose in the human diet. Since, however, man's digestive system is ill-adapted to raw starch, the cereals must be cooked in order to predigest them. Gruel or porridge may be prepared by adding water and heating. Two drawbacks are that this food is highly perishable and always more-or-less fluid. The latter difficulties can be overcome by making a paste and spreading it on hot stones until it is baked into a hard sheet (see for example, 1 Kings 19:6).[2] Unfortunately, this process not only removes most of the taste, but produces a thin, and therefore insubstantial, product. A more sophisticated process can produce a thicker product that is difficult to chew once it has cooled.

Bread is by far the most desirable basic cereal food. True bread is raised or leavened bread. Leavening aerates the loaf, thereby lightening it and loosening its texture, but more is required than yeast or some similar fermenting agent. The baking of true bread requires a properly constructed oven and an appropriate cereal. The carbon dioxide gas given off by the fermenting agent must be trapped in the pores of the dough which are then hardened and made permanent by the heat. A well-risen loaf will result only if the flour contains enough gluten-forming protein to form an elastic substance that prevents the gas from escaping. Wheat and rye can sustain the necessary enzymatic action, but barley cannot.

Numerous silos for storing grain have been excavated in Palestine, ranging from one at Beth-shemesh (ca. 900 B.C.E.), which measured 25 feet in diameter and 19 feet in depth, to small plastered silos cut through the floors of private homes (C. F. Pfeiffer 1966, p. 22). Both barley and emmer wheat are native to Syria and northern Palestine. Indeed, Macalister (1912, vol. II, p. 44) actually found a true loaf of bread that had been preserved by having been burnt in debris at Gezer dating from 1800–1400 B.C.E. But the relative yields of barley and wheat vary greatly with soil and rainfall conditions. According to Jasny (1942, pp. 752–53) the excess yield of barley over wheat ranges from 10–15 percent to 50 percent or more in terms of weight. Even after taking account of its greater nutritive value, at most 10 percent in terms of weight, the opportunity cost of growing a pound of wheat was hardly likely to be very much less than a pound and a quarter of barley. The most relevant relative-price data seem to be found in 2 Kings 7:1 in which Elisha prophesies that the Syrian siege (probably in the last quarter of the ninth century) will be lifted and, "Tomorrow about this time a measure of *soleth* [fine flour, very probably wheat] shall be sold for one shekel and two measures of barley for a shekel at the gates of Samaria."[3] In passing, note the prophecy's implication that, contrary to Polanyi (1977, p. 134), an increase in supply would lower price—that is, prices in the gate were determined by market forces.

Further, finely sifted, whiter flour is a luxury compared to the coarser varieties. Basing his information on purity tests conducted by bakers in early modern Rome,[4] Revel (1979, pp. 40–1) reports that

> grain yielded between 68 and 70 percent of its weight when transformed into white bread, and 90 to 95 percent when baked as brown bread. . . . The amount of wheat lost is shown to be even greater if one deducts from the weight of the bread the amount of water added to the dough—about 20 percent of the bread's weight after baking. Then the amount lost would climb to 50 percent for white bread and 30 percent for brown bread.

In short, *soleth* is more a luxury than coarser flour, wheat is more a luxury than barley, and bread is more a luxury than porridge.

Historians of nutrition have placed the preceding considerations in a more general context by, in effect, abstracting from local differences in relative prices and tastes and noting that modern Western societies passed through several identifiable stages or dietary regimens as they developed economically and became progressively more affluent.

Stage 1: The substitution of wheat or rye for secondary cereals such as barley. This, as we have shown, is primarily a matter of increased interest in taste quality as opposed to nutritional quality.

Stage 2: The substitution of whiter for browner bread. Again this is a matter of improvement along the taste dimension, because the bolting process, in which the outer shell of the grain is removed, results in a loss of nutrients, especially under traditional milling techniques.

Stage 3: The substitution of meat (or more generally animal protein), for cereal protein. In this case there is improvement in both taste and nutritional quality. The taste side is obvious; with respect to nutrition, the protein of cereals is short of lysine, an essential amino acid. The critical level for lysine is attained when meat products (or legumes, "the meat of the poor") supply from 22–25 percent of total caloric intake.[5]

Stage 4: The "new dietary model" (the daily meat) that tended to be followed by the entire population. Again there is no question about the taste dimension but questions are now being raised about health. Figure 8–1, which makes use of 1969 data for 84 countries reveals, among other things, how increases in per capita income increase the percentage of calories supplied by animal proteins, and reduce the percentages for vegetable proteins and carbohydrates.

My plan for the remainder of this chapter is, first, to consider the evidence of Israelite progress in Stages 1–2 involving the consumption of wheat and whiter bread, and then to move to Stages 3–4 and trends in meat consumption. In assessing the evidence that consumption of true bread and meat became general among the Israelites during the eighth–seventh centuries it is well to take note first of some archaeological data from Egypt relating to the affluent second half of the second millennium B.C.E. The homes of the (admittedly skilled) necropolis workers at Deir el-Medina contained as many as 15 shapes of bread found upon analysis to be leavened (Saffirio 1973, p. 30; see also Janssen 1975, pp. 166, 169). Also, a detail on a stele commemorating an expedition to the stone quarries in the extreme south indicates that the workers received a daily portion of roast meat. Based on this and other evidence, Saffirio (1973, p. 304) concludes that: "Within the limits of the information at hand, . . . we can say that the Egyptians of the New Kingdom were well-nourished. . . . This fits in well with the prosperity which the country enjoyed during the greater part of the New Kingdom until the first signs of decadence . . . "

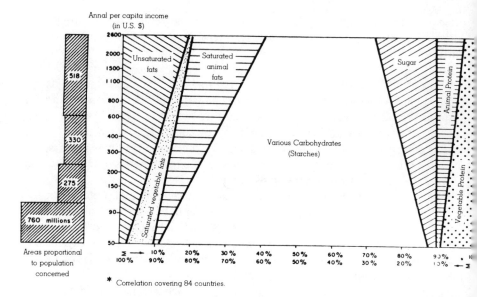

Figure 8-1. Calories Supplied by Fats, Carbohydrates, and Proteins as Percentage of the Total Caloric Intake, by Per-Capita Income of Country. From *Food and Drink in History*, edited by Robert Forster and Orest Ranun. © 1979 The John Hopkins University Press. Reproduced with permission.

Bread Consumption

That barley bread predominated in the diet of the Israelites in the time of the Judges is strongly suggested by an episode during Gideon's battle with the Midianites (Judg. 7:13–14).[6] It will be remembered that Gideon looked down on the Midianite camp in the plain below "just as one man was narrating a dream to another, 'Listen,' he was saying, 'I had this dream: There was a commotion—a loaf of barley bread was whirling through the Midianite camp. It came to a tent and struck it, and it fell; it turned upside down, and the tent collapsed.' To this the other man responded, 'That can only mean the sword of the Israelite Gideon son of Joash. God is delivering Midian and the entire camp into his hands.' " The tough hill-dwelling Israelites, represented by the barley cakes which served as their dietary staple, emerge triumphant over the relatively well-off Midianite plainsmen. The tale also gives us some notion of what it must have been like to eat these cakes.

Another piece of evidence pointing to the predominance of unleavened bread is that Gideon, in Judges 6:19–20, offered it to the angel of the Lord. Of course, it might be objected that Jewish law forbids leavened bread to be offered to the deity. Specifically, Leviticus 2:11 (see also Lev. 6:7–10; Exod. 23:18) forbids the burning of leavened bread upon the altar. But how old is that law? It is difficult to settle the question by appeal to the biblical text since, as G. B. Gray (1925, p. 399) notes: "*lechem* is a term that covers both leavened (*chametz lechem*, Lev. 7:13) and unleavened bread (*lechem matzot*, Exod. 29:2), it is impossible to determine whether the bread that was being taken to God at Bethel (1 Sam. 10:3), or the bread placed before God in Nob (1 Sam. 21:4 ff) was leavened or unleavened . . . " [my transliteration]. But we do know that the eighth century prophet Amos who opposed sacrifices, at least by those who did not "hate the evil, and love the good" (5:15), refers to the burning of leavened bread on the altars of Bethel and Gilgal: "And burn a thank offering of leavened bread; and proclaim freewill offerings loudly. For you love that sort of thing, O Israelites" (4:5). I would agree with G. B. Gray (1925, p. 399) that it is not at all clear that Amos' sarcasm "falls on this feature in particular of the ritual."[7] Moreover, with respect to bread consumed by the priests, Leviticus 2:12 permits the offering of leavened bread as gifts of first fruits while Leviticus 23:17, which deals with the Feast of Weeks (Shavuos), requires for first fruits, two loaves of fine flour (*soleth*) baked with leaven. It seems inconceivable that such a requirement can be very ancient; indeed, it may date from the time of Ezekiel.[8] I suspect that the laws prohibiting the burning of leavened bread on the altar are no earlier than the eighth century and, possibly, were part of a general reform (see part III) aimed at restoring the purer cultic practices of an older and much poorer Israel.

Further consideration of sacrificial practices provides an additional indication of rising consumption standards. Yerkes (1952, p. 166) explains that, while in the earlier traditions *minchah* (also found among the Phoenicians) was a general term for animal or vegetable offerings, it later came to be confined to only vegetable offerings: "Its especial use was for an offering composed of fine wheat flour called *soleth*, to which olive oil, salt, and frankincense were added." In this connection it is also worth taking note of the implication of 2 Kings 7:1 that by the latter part of the ninth century the relatively high price of choice wheat flour (about twice that of barley) did not preclude its being offered for general sale at the gate of Samaria.

Four additional references, one from the eighth-century northern prophet Hosea and the others from the Judeans Ezekiel and Jeremiah in the late-seventh and early-sixth century, strenghten the presumption that during our period Israel-Judah penetrated dietary-regimen Stages 1–2. Hosea (7:4) seems to associate the search after material wealth with the baking of leavened bread: "They all burn with adultery, like an oven fired by a baker, who desists from stoking only from the kneading of the dough to its leavening." Ezekiel (16:13) tells the "people of Jerusaleum": "Your food was choice flour, honey, and oil." Indeed by Ezekiel's time the consumptin of wheat flour must have become so commonplace that the effort to make barley cakes tastier by adding various ingredients could be employed as a symbol of hardship during a seige. "Further, take wheat, barley, beans, lentils, millet, and spelt, put them into one vessel and bake them into bread . . . Eat it as barley cake . . . " (4:9, 12). Finally, "King Zedekiah gave instructions to lodge Jeremiah in the prison compound and supply him daily with a loaf [*kikar lechem*] of bread from the Baker's Street . . . " (Jer. 37:21). The use of a term that may mean "loaf" as opposed to those terms that are usually translated to mean a flat cake or wafer points in the direction of leavened bread.[9] Given that this "loaf" was fed to a prisoner it may, perhaps, be inferred that an inexpensive variety of bread was regularly available on the retail market.[10] Of course, none of this is conclusive.

The archaeological evidence is brief but pointed. First, the preparation of real bread, as noted earlier, requires an oven.[11] Apparently, such ovens have been found in numerous locations; in a rather ordinary two-room house belonging to an eighth-century stratum at Hazor; in seventh-century Gibeon; in an eighth–seventh-century stratum at Tell Halif, a small settlement in Judah; in a mid-ninth to early-eighth century [Aramean?] stratum at En-Gev on the eastern shore of the Sea of Galilee; in Transjordan in ninth–eighth-century strata at Tell es-Sa'idyeh and Tell Deir 'Alla; in an eighth-century level at Dothan; and at Tell en-Nasbeh (Mizpah).[12] Second, we have visual evidence suggesting that by the second half of the ninth century leavened bread may have become common throughout the area. In an Assyrian bronze relief dating from the reign of Shalmaneser III (858–824 B.C.E.) which portrays the preparation of bread in an army camp, the heaped-up loaves appear to be leavened (see Storch and Teague 1952, p. 62). Ninth–eighth century figurines of a female wearing a lamp as a crown and holding an object that is either a loaf of leavened (raisin?) bread, or a baking pan, or a tambourine have been excavated at various sites including Megiddo, Kir Haroseth (Kerah) and Mount Nebo in Moab, and Edomite Bozrah (Glueck 1940, pp. 151–53; Dorneman 1970, pp. 334–35, McKay 1973, p. 116). Most important of all, a terracotta figurine found in an eighth-century grave at Achzib, a port in Asher, has a woman leaning over a kneading trough containing two thick oval lumps of dough suitable for baking true bread (see Pritchard 1958, fig. 22).

Meat Consumption

The more general consumption of meat is surely demonstrated by the sarcastic comments of the eighth-and seventh-century prophets regarding the sacrificial practices of their day: "Though you offer me burnt offerings and your meat offerings of your fat beasts . . . " (Amos 5:22); "I am full of the burnt offerings of rams, and the fat of fed beasts" (Isa. 1:11); "Will the Lord be pleased with thousands of rams, or with ten thousand rivers of oil?" (Mic. 6:7). Isaiah's and Amos's references to fat or fed beasts no doubt refer to the fatted calf. This interpretation is consistent with Leviticus 1:2, in which the Lord tells Moses that the sacrificial offerings shall be chosen from the flock or the herd. That sacrifices from the herd represent a cultic departure is indicated by a comparison of rules regarding the appropriate Pesah victim in Exodus 12:3–5, 21, and Deuteronomy 16:2. The provision in Deuteronomy, which probably dates from the eighth or seventh century (see chapter 16), seems to permit the choice of an animal from the flock or the herd, which would include cattle while the, no doubt older, provision in Exodus calls for a victim from among the sheep and goats. For further discussion of this question, see Segal (1963, pp. 14–5, 23–5, 204).

Another indication of cultic accomodation to the more widespread public consumption of meat is presented in Deuteronomy 12:5–21 which permits nonsacrificial slaughtering (that is, not at an authorized altar). Grintz (1972, p. 93) has argued that this practice goes back at least to the days of Saul, but I find Yerkes's (1952, pp. 123–5, 146–7) arguments more persuasive. It probes the origin of the sacrificial term *zevach*, the best-known rite in both the Israelite and Phoenician literature, in which the animal is partly burned on the altar and partly eaten by the worshippers. The root of this word which, as Yerkes explains, is found in most semitic languages does not merely convey the act of slaying ("to kill" was *shachat*), but it also conveys the idea of preparing an animal for eating. *Zevach* probably harks back to the days when meat diet was rare; if one killed an animal for food, one must have a rite of some kind.[13] Note further that profane slaughter in eighth century Israel may be reflected in Hosea's (8:13) "let them slaughter and eat meat."

Habituation to meat consumption is also suggested by the changes that took place in the manner of determining the priests' sacrificial portions.[14] In 1 Samuel 2:13–14 the ancient tradition of the Shiloh sanctuary is related as follows: the portion belonging to the priests was the meat that happened to be brought up when a fork was thrust into the boiling vessel. But verses 15–16 assert that Eli's sons sinned because they would only accept raw meat from the worshippers. In fact, the arguably later law of Deuteronomy 18:3 and

Leviticus 7:34 specify the priests' portions in advance and may or may not refer to the raw state.[15]

Then, of course, we have Amos's (6:4) warning "to them that are at ease in Zion and confident on the hill of Samaria" who "feast on lambs from the flock and on calves from the stall," and Jeremiah's (46:21) comparison of Egyptian mercenaries with "stall-fed calves." All this not only points to widespread consumption of meat, but also to improvement in its quality via the substitution of beef for mutton and the substitution of fattened for unfattened animals. With respect to dietary-regime, Stage 4 with its daily meat for the entire population we have only Ezekiel's (4:10; Bewer) symbol of the hardships of the coming siege: "And thy meat which thou shalt eat shall be by weight twenty shekels [seven or eight ounces] a day." However, other renderings of this verse have "food" not "meat" which is regarded to be a better rendering of the Hebrew *ma'khat*.

Wine and Oil

Amos (6:6) has Israelites drinking wine (filtered? from bowls?)[16] while they recline on their couches. Isaiah (5:12) refers to the music and wine at the feasts and to "the drunkards of Ephraim . . . who are overcome by wine" (28:1). Amos (6:6) also refers to those who "anoint themselves with the choicest oils" to which Baly (1974, p. 84) adds that "rich olive oil replaced animal fat for cooking and the once longed-for milk and honey . . . became a symbol of poverty." The latter reference is to Isaiah's (7:21–22) warning to king Ahaz that his mistaken Assyrian policy would have as its consequence that "everyone who is left in the land shall feed on curds and honey."

Notes

1. In this chapter reliance has been placed on Aymard (1979), Jacob (1944, pp. 16–17, 26); Jensen (1953, pp. 68–74); Moritz (pp. xviii–xxi); Storch and Teague (1952, pp. 28, 54). Dietary-regimen analysis is consistent with income elasticities estimated by economists.

2. Translations of JPS unless otherwise specified; see the bibliographic note (chapter 1, note).

3. *Soleth* is usually translated "fine flour" and sometimes "groats." The latter is a general term applied to preparations made from cracked wheat, but barley groats are also possible (see Darby et al. 1977, vol. 2, p. 488; Hoffner, 1974, p. 70). The "fine flour" translation finds support in the Mishna which states that *soleth* was sifted 11 to 13 times (see R. J. Forbes 1965,

vol. III, p. 97). Also Hoffner (1974, p. 80) notes that *soleth* is cognate to Akkadian *saltu* whose Hittite translation is derived from the verb *marra/marriya* "to mill, grind up." If, indeed, "fine flour" is correct, wheat is the indicated grain since it seems doubtful that barley, a nonbread grain, would be subjected to repeated sifting. More importantly, Leviticus 23:17 requires *soleth* to be baked with leaven, which would be futile for barley (see also Lev. 6:7–10).

Hoffner (1974, p. 80) points out that Akkadian *saltu* has been identified with "semolina." Today, the latter term refers to a granular, milled product of *Tr. durum* wheat used to make pasta and paste. *Tr. durum* is a naked form of emmer whose kernel hardness makes it difficult to mill. Note, however, that while the modern bread wheats are spelts, the evidence suggests that the ancient bread wheats were primarily (or commonly) emmers (*Tr. durum* or the hulled *Tr. dicoccum*). Indeed, the Mediterranean climate was not well adapted to modern bread wheat. Jensen (1952, p. 70) maintains that the Israelites grew only *Tr. durum* (see also Darby 1977, vol. 2, p. 489–90; Jasny 1942, p. 762; Storch and Teague 1952, pp. 87–8; Hoffner 1974, p. 58).

The available price data also seem to be consistent with the identification of *soleth* with wheat. The account of Lukalla, a merchant in Umma during the reign of Shu-Sin (2037–2029), has the price of barley as 0.43 grains of silver per quart while the corresponding price for wheat is one grain (Curtis and Hallo 1959, p. 126; see also Ashtor 1975, fn. 16, p. 127). An Egyptian papyrus dating to 256 B.C.E. quotes the price of barley at three-fifth that of wheat (Darby et al. 1977, vol. 2, p. 484). The three-fifths ratio also is found in Assyrian texts of the second millennium while calculations from a Hittite text indicate that barley is half the price of wheat (Hoffner 1974, p. 67). These relative prices are of the same rough order of magnitude as Elisha's relative price of *soleth*. All in all, then, it seems reasonable to identify *soleth* with fine wheaten flour.

4. For roughly comparable data for classical Rome, see Storch and Teague (1952, p. 88).

5. During the past several years a number of less-developed countries have experienced rising incomes and responded by sharply increasing their consumption of meat (*The New York Times*, 25 August 1981).

6. According to Ashtor (1975, fn. 16, p. 127; see also Maekawa 1974, p. 41) barley predominated in the Mesopotamian diet as well. For some fragmentary Anatolian data, see Hoffner (1974, pp. 58–9). Dixon (1969) and Saffirio (1973) are valuable sources for Egypt.

7. For a discussion of Exodus 29:23–25, see note 9 following.

8. The "Holiness Code" (Lev. 17–26) is dated below to the period of Ezekiel (probably) in the later seventh or early sixth centuries, (see chapter 18).

9. On the linguistic affiliations of *kikar lechem* (loaf), see Hoffner (1974, p. 167).

The identification of "loaf" (*kikar lechem*) with leavened bread is contradicted by the priestly consecration ceremony in Exodus 29:23 where "one loaf of bread, and one cake of oiled bread, and one wafer" are together in the "basket of unleavened bread that is before the Lord." (The latter are in verse 25 burned upon the altar.) It is always easy to explain away evidence by claiming it to be secondary, but given the discussion noted this may in fact be the case with respect to the equation of *kikar lechem* with unleavened bread.

10. Hittite texts refer to the (solely cultic?) "daily *k.*-bread" (Hoffner 1974, pp. 167, 216–17). In fourth–sixth-century-C.E. Constantinople bakers used to prepare popular or "duty" wheaten bread, as distinguished from the finer loaves consumed by the more affluent (Teall 1959, pp. 41–2).

11. Leviticus 7:9 refers to meal offerings baked in an oven; in Leviticus 26:26 bread is baked in an oven. R. J. Forbes (1966, vol. VI, p. 64) notes that the *tannûr*, the only form of baking furnace named in the Bible, is capable of being operated for real baking of bread. Trays employed in the baking of bread (leavened or unleavened) are mentioned in Leviticus 2:5 (*machvat* or griddle) and Leviticus 2:7 and 7:9 (*marcheshet* or pan). Round, shallow trays

punctured on the convex surface have been found at several Israelite sites. This information is found in Yeshiva University Museum (1980, pp. 20–1).

12. Sources on ovens: Franken (1965, p. 27); Free (1969, p. 8); J. Gray (1962, p. 173); Mazar et al. (1964); Pritchard (1965, p. 12); Reed (1967, pp. 236–37); Seger (1979, p. 52); Yadin (1975, p. 154).

13. Perhaps some sort of ritual was still required. Milgrom (1976a, pp. 3, 15) suggests that the clause "as I commanded you" in Deuteronomy 15:21 does not refer to verse 15 but, instead, "signifies that profane slaughter must follow the same [unknown] method practiced in sacrificial slaughter."

The whole problem is rather complicated. Leviticus 17:3–4 ordains that the sacrificial blood must be brought to the altar to expiate for the murder of the animal (see Milgrom 1971, pp. 154–56). But Leviticus 17:3–4 may be later than Deuteronomy 12:5–21. On the other hand, the former passage may reflect older *P* material entwined with later *H* material. On the dating of *H*, see chapter 18; on *P* as a source for *D*, see Milgrom (1973, p. 160; 1976a, pp. 9–14).

14. Evidence concerning the priest's portion is provided by the animal bones found in a twelfth–eleventh-century-B.C.E. house at Tell Qiri in Jezreel: "After careful examination of these finds, we realized that the bones were almost exclusively the right forelegs of goats. We immediately thought of two biblical passages enjoining the Israelites to sacrifice 'the right leg . . . of a ram of consecration' (Exodus 29:22) and to give 'the right hind-leg of the animal . . . to the priest . . . ' (Leviticus 7:32). This type of sacrifice is also known among non-Israelites . . . " (Ben-Tor 1980, p. 35).

15. In sixth-century-B.C.E. Babylonia the sacrificial shares of high temple officials were "bought and sold on the open market, not only for a given day, but for small fraction of a day" (Olmstead 1948, p.85). For examples of sale contracts see texts (6) and (20) in Finkelstein (1969, pp. 543, 547).

16. See Wolff (1973, fn. 50, p. 18). Note that in warm weather the ancient Greeks served wine from coolers or *psykters*: the long stemmed *psykter* was placed in a deep bowl which was filled with cold water (Brumbaugh 1966, p. 84). A text dating from the second millennium at Tell el-Rimah "shows that ice was used to make drink offerings to deities as well as providing high court officials with iced drinks;" the ice (*šurīpum*) of Mesopotamia was stored in an "ice house" (*bīt šurīpum*) (see Page 1970, p. 181).

9 LIVING STANDARDS: LUXURY CONSUMPTION

Even today's poor American has easy access to amenities (personal transportation, personal entertainment, temperature control, plumbing, health and beauty aids, synthetic fabrics, and so forth.) outside the reach of the wealthiest individuals of past centuries.[1] After studying sixteenth–seventeenth-century-C.E. family-budget data, the economic historian Cipolla (1976, p. 38) concludes that "even when it had overtones of extravagance" the consumption of the rich "never showed much variety. The . . . state of the arts did not offer the consumer the great variety of products and services which characterize industrial societies." But early modern consumption outlets were certainly more varied than those available for the surplus wealth of the genuinely affluent citizen of ancient society. The rich Egyptian or Babylonian or Roman or Israelite finding that climate reduced his basic needs for clothing and shelter, and being necessarily "poor" in terms of modern amenities, chose his bundle of luxuries accordingly. He enjoyed his many children and participated in great feasts; he built winter and summer homes; he made lavish provisions for his afterlife and gave lavish public donations; he maintained a large personal retinue; he enjoyed song, art, and drama; he concerned himself with wisdom, with questions of human character and duty; and he sought to improve the position of those less fortunate than himself.

Cultic Luxury Consumption

How better begin our discussion of luxury consumption than by quoting Amos 4:4: "Come to Bethel and transgress; to Gilgal, and transgress even more; Present your sacrifices in the morning and your tithes on the third day.[2] Here Amos refers to the votive or free-will offerings of eighth-century Israelite worshippers at a feast that lasted three days (see Kaufmann 1960, p. 190). In one of the most important Israelite rites, the 'olah or "burnt offering," the animal was wholly burned on the altar (see, for instance, Deut. 12:11–14). Only the hide was retained as the priest's portion. Yerkes (1952, p. 144) suggests that this type of sacrifice "was chronologically the last to appear," that the 'olah postdated the zevach in which the animal was partly burned and partly consumed by the worshippers. This speculation is not unreasonable since the 'olah is more expensive than the zevach. In any event, 2 Chronicles 29:31–36, which deals with the cleansing and rededication of the Temple by King Hezekiah near the end of the eighth century B.C.E. states that those members of the congregation "with generous spirits [brought] burnt offerings. The number of burnt offerings which the congregation brought was as follows: seventy bulls, a hundred rams, and two hundred lambs . . . " Isaiah (1:11) claimed to know that the Lord was "sated with burnt offerings of rams."

Hosea 10:1 clearly specifies the relationship between affluence and the demand for cultic luxury (or conspicuous) consumption: "When his fruit was plentiful, he made altars aplenty; when his land was bountiful, cult pillars abounded." Indeed there is some evidence that the size of the altar in the Temple was increased during the reign of Ahaz (ca. 735–716). G. B. Gray (1925, pp. 138–39) maintains that the allusions to it in 1 Kings 8:64 and 2 Kings 16:14ff. imply that Solomon's altar of bronze in front of the Temple was relatively small. He believes that Ahaz's replacement altar (2 Kings 16:14) was made of stone (perhaps unhewn, see Exod. 20:22) because this material would more easily have accomodated the increase in size necessary to cope with "the increasing numbers of sacrificial victims commonly, and not as in Solomon's time, as a single special occasion, offered on the altar in Jerusalem . . . " To all this must be added the costs of south Arabian frankincense and south Arabian incense burners such as the one found at Samaria. Note, in this connection that a clay lamp lettered with a south Arabian text has been found at Bethel.[3]

Social Status: Genealogies and Mortuary Wealth

Evidence of an intensified striving for social status in the eighth century is reflected by increased activity in the compilation of genealogies. As Redford (1970, p. 9) notes, "the post exilic writer of the Book of Chronicles had evidence of flurries of activity during the reign of Jeroboam II of Israel . . . " (785–748; see Myers 1965, vol. I, pp. 37–8; 1 Chron. 5:17). He adds Jotham (749–743) and Hezekiah (715–687) of Judah (1 Chron. 5:17; 4:41; 2 Chron. 31:17ff). Perhaps the most concrete example of conspicuous consumption (see Lang in press) and the increased worth of the individual is the construction of elaborate tombs.[4] The earlier Israelites, as their Canaanite predecessors, memorialized their ancestors by making use of sometimes englarged natural caves.

> During the eighth and seventh centuries of the Israelite period, however, much more care was taken by the stone-mason than had hitherto been customary. The typical tomb was made somewhat like a house. A horizontal entrance was cut, sometimes with steps leading down into it. The front was carved from the rock like a doorway, through the opening through this facade was a small square into which a stone, cut away at the edge, was inserted to fit like a stopper. Two or three steps led down from the opening into a rectangular room, on three sides of which stone benches, like beds, had been left. An elaborate family mausoleum has been found at Beth-shemesh. This consisted of a small open court cut into the rock, reached by a descending staircase. From this court four of the bench tombs opened. One of them connected with still a fifth which was provided with its own separate entry. (Wright 1962, p. 199; see also Rahmani 1981, pp. 233–34)

A related practice of the affluent eighth–seventh centuries noted in Samaria and Amman is interment in pottery coffins (Stern 1979a, p. 277). Note should also be taken of the artifacts found in Israelite tombs of this time (see chapter 8). A final point is that Isaiah 1:29–30 may refer to sepulchral gardens (see also note 10 to this chapter).

Plastic Arts

The eighth and seventh centuries also provide evidence of an upsurge in artistic consumption. Yeivin (1979, pp. 170–71) notes finds in mid-eighth century sites including the Shephelah and western Judah, Debir, Lachish, and Tell 'Erani, of unique terra-cotta female figurines. The separately cast heads and bodies contrasted sharply: the bodies were crude and no doubt produced at great speed, but the molds for the heads reflected painstaking attention to details of facial features, coiffure, and even covering veils. Yeivin sees the imprint of the artists also in ornamental graffiti, *dipinti* pottery, ostraca, and seals of the period. All reflect, he believes, a Mesopotamian style, possibly spread through commerce, "which would slowly become almost all pervasive, subsuming the Egyptian patterns that had previously prevailed but that all but disappeared in the second half of the eighth century."[5] To this can be added the finding in the seventh century ruins of Ramat Rahel, possibly the palace of the Judean king Jehoiachim the son of Josiah, of several beakers of elegant Assyrian palace ware, a jar fragment with the drawing of a king, and a seal of the goddess Astarte (Aharoni 1965, p. 22).

Chester McCown (1943, p. 98) provides a balanced, scholarly interpretation of the increased prevalence of Astarte figurines in the eighth century:

> this does not by any means prove that the earlier nomadic period, or "Mosaism," was therefore essentially higher or purer than the religion of the eighth century . . . The increase in luxury of the population would result in new fashions and in more numerous objects in the deposits. Bedouin religion is now much simpler than that of the towns and villages, but it can hardly be said to be more monotheistic or more ethical.

Surely the possibility that the affluent Israelites became lovers and collectors of fine art, archaeological objects, and interesting reproductions must be admitted. Perhaps not only the Astarte figurines but the moon pendants and soul houses Isaiah (3:19–20) includes among the amulets worn by the fashionable women of Jerusalem belong in this category (James 1966, p. 220). It is known that later on, in the second half of the seventh century B.C.E., quantities of apparently genuine Egyptian amulets and other ornaments found their way to Carthage at a time when there was a "renaissance of the old Egyptian culture" and a surge of Phoenician adaptations and imitations of Egyptian art (Katzenstein 1973, p. 300). Fascination with the ancient and obscure is not confined to the twentieth century. In affluent Sung China, for example, "collecting archaeological objects became fashionable in the eleventh century [C.E.] when many tombs were opened" (Goodrich 1969, p. 157). Moreover, two Kings in our period, Assurbanipal (668–627) and Shamash-shuma-ukin (667–648), both displayed a keen interest in ancient arts and culture: "This interest . . . may have been a reflection of what people in general had begun to realize—that the world was old. [Their] interests . . . may, consequently, reflect the spirit of their age." (Ahmed 1968, p. 157)

However, according to one scholar, animal figurines must have been used in exorcisms and female figurines, often with pronounced sexual organs, must reflect "the purpose of stimulating pregnancy—an obsession among Semitic peasants."[6] Along the same line *The New York Times* (23 August

1980) reports that the recent excavations of Jerusalem provide "evidence that . . . the Israelites worshipped idols, at least in the privacy of their homes." The story goes on to remark upon a "unique ceramic cultic figure of a naked uncircumcised man with two pairs of arms . . . uncovered in one of the Israelite homes, where it was probably used as a fertility idol." *The Times* quotes (correctly?) the excavation director about the exotic figure: "The prophets preached against it; but there they are in Israeli homes."[7] On the other hand, I am inclined to think of the prominently displayed fertility figurines in the homes of Semitic peasants like Sigmund Freud, Moshe Dayan, and Sondra and Morris Silver. Those in our home, of course, are only reproductions, which was probably also the case with most ancient Israelites (see Stern 1975, p. 47). It might be added that a good percentage of fashionable Manhattan apartments have at least one idol of some kind.

Interestingly, the excavations at Shechem provide evidence bearing on the question of artistic-archaeological interest versus secretive idol worship. The stamp seals recovered at Shechem include: No. 1, a scarab of white steatite with the design of a human hand from a stratum dated 900–860; No. 2, an ivory seal with a winged beetle from strata ranging from 900–724; No. 3, a white steatite scarab "found in the context of the Israelite period;" No. 4, a scarab of white steatite picked up on the surface of the mound; No. 5, a scaraboid of dark stone with a winged disc and lunar crescent over a sacred tree found on the surface; No. 6, a marble scaraboid with two figures, an altar, and a star found in a stratum dated 748–724. Notice that while Wright (1965, pp. 145, 162–63) states the locations of five seals more or less precisely, in the case of No. 3 he refers to its being "found in the context of the Israelite period." His caution is understandable since No. 3 "bears in hieroglyphs the name 'Rameses' derived from the nineteenth Egyptian Dynasty (late fourteenth to early twelfth century")! Another puzzle is provided by a Middle Assyrian cylinder seal of serpentine dating ca. 1200 B.C.E. found in debris dating between 748 and 250 B.C.E. Of course, it is possible that both objects were forced upward by earthquakes which are relatively frequent in Israel. On the other hand, the possibility remains that these two objects, as well as some of the other finds, were collectors' items.[8]

Performing Arts

The spread of music appreciation to the general Israelite public is suggested by Amos 6:5: "They hum snatches of song and sing to the tune of the lute— they account themselves musicians like David" (Hebrew uncertain). And they may also have enjoyed dramatic performances of the Song of Songs.

The grounds for the dramatic view consist of the fact that the book presents speakers and dialogue without introducing statements or transitional directions and that where action or account of speech are given in the third person, . . . the narrator appears to be one of the actors. The poet-author nowhere appears. Thus if the book is a unity, and if there is a plot, we have the basic features of drama. (Pope 1977, p. 35).

To the objection that it is often difficult to ascertain who is saying what, Pope (1977, p. 36) responds that "If an act of one of Shakespeare's plays were stripped of outward indications of the speakers, attempts to restore them would differ." The argument that the Song of Songs dates to the period of the Second Temple has been significantly weakened by recent research. The late dating is based on the presence of certain Aramaic expressions, but it is now recognized that this can be explained by a northern Israelite provenance (see Bowman 1948, p. 70; Pope 1977, pp. 33–4; Weinfeld 1977, pp. 69–70). Archaeological support for an early date is provided by a store jar found in the destruction layer at Hazor (ca. 732) on which is inscribed the word *smdr*, which occurs only three times in the Bible—always in the Song of Songs.[9] The tenability of a preexilic, even eighth-century, origin for the Song is suggested by the resemblance of its vineyard (8:12) to Isaiah's (5:1): "Now will I sing to my well-beloved a song to my beloved, touching his vineyard: My well-beloved hath a vineyard in a very fruitful hill . . . " Of course Isaiah's Song of the Vineyard has a much different message than the, presumably older, Song of Songs: "And I will lay it [the vineyard] waste; . . . For the vineyard of the Lord of hosts is the house of Israel, and the men of Judah his pleasant plant; and he looked for judgment, but behold oppression; for righteousness, but behold a cry." (5:6–7)

Gardens

The idol issue comes up again in Isaiah 1:29–30: "For they shall be exposed to shame for the idols on which they doted; as they have for the gardens which they coveted" (Thomson). But according to "Isaiah" in the *Encyclopedia Judaica* (Ginsberg 1971, vol. 9, p. 50; see also Kennett 1931, pp. 8–12), the prophet is not speaking about idols in cult gardens, but about luxury or pleasure gardens.[10] (Note the reference to the king's garden in 2 Kings 25:4.) It is worth adding that Assyrian kings such as Tiglath Pileser I (1115–1077) created botanical gardens while Pharaohs instructed expeditions to collect and bring back rare specimens (Contenau 1966, p. 109). It is important to note, however, that in our period beginning with Sargon II (709–705):

the royal interest in gardens definitely shifts from utilitarian to display purposes, from an interest in assembling the largest number of specimens to incorporating a garden into the palace precinct for the personal pleasure of the king. This change is expressed in the replacement of the ancient term for garden, *kirû* by *kirimāhu*. . . . The gardens of the Assyrian kings seem to have been so arranged as to imitate a wooded and hilly terrain of paths and watercourses. . . . In the framework of this development, the inclusion of a *bîtānu*, "little house," in the architecture of an Assyrian palace complex fits perfectly when we assume that it denotes a "kiosk" or "summerhouse." (Oppenheim 1965, pp. 331–32)

Indeed, it has been suggested that gardens were associated even with smaller residential buildings in ancient Egypt (Gallery 1978, p. 48). Further, pleasure gardens were widely distributed throughout the Mediterranean lands (Semple 1931, p. 474). Again, in affluent Sung China, "gardens, once enjoyed only by princes became the fashion for the well-to-do" (Goodrich 1969, p. 150). If the Israelites of Isaiah's time were willing to utilize land and water for primarily ornamental purposes this would provide additional confirmation of their economic affluence. Note, finally, that the Assyrians may have taken over gardens and summerhouses from the West (Oppenheim 1965, p. 331).

Large Families

Chouraqui (1975, p. 126) suggests that "the rich and powerful imitated the kings and established their social positions by increasing the number of their wives and children, who could number several dozen." But the desire for status is not the full explanation for large families. Friedlander and Silver (1967, p. 44) observed in a multiple-regression analysis that the relationship between national incomes and birth rates varies with the level of economic development. "Specifically, in developed countries . . . the relationship is positive, and in underdeveloped countries . . . it is negative." They offer the following explanation:

The progress of economic development probably increases productivity in the market relative to productivity in the home, and the resulting rise in the opportunity costs of children reduces desired family size. Finally, affluence in terms of market-produced goods and services leads couples, in spite of rising opportunity costs, to devote an increasing portion of their time to leisure activities, including the raising of larger families. (p. 52)

The temptation to substitute the enjoyment of children for the enjoyment of material goods would, of course, have been much stronger in ancient Israel than in modern industrialized economies with their myriad market-produced consumption goods.

Education and Wisdom

Several biblical statements seem to imply that literacy and, more generally, education became more widespread during our period. Isaiah (10:19) comments that, "What trees remain of its scrub shall be so few that a boy may record [write?] them." Heaton (1968, p. 174) may be correct in taking this as a passing reference to children learning their ABCs. Better yet note the reference to a spelling lesson in Isaiah 28:10 (Hallo 1958, pp. 337–38). Deuteronomy 6:9 instructs the Israelites to "write them [the laws and the rules] on the doorposts of your houses and gates." Again there seems to be the implication of literacy. The paleographic evidence also points in this direction. According to Naveh (1970, pp. 279–80) Hebrew script developed from early lapidary forms toward later cursive ones. By the eighth century the formal cursive style "was so strong that even stone inscriptions, and seals were engraved in cursive letters which emphasized the shading, a natural by-product of pen and ink writing." Note in this connection that Isaiah (30:8), a prophet of the later eighth century, writes down a prophecy on a "great roll" with a "man's pen"—that is, in the easily read common script. Naveh goes on to add that by the late seventh century two other substyles of cursive, free, and vulgar, "seem to bear witness to the existence of a literate society."

There are no clear references to regular schools in the Bible but we do have some archaeological evidence that seems relevant. Wright (1964, p. 306) reports that at least three skulls in a mass grave at Lachish show evidence of trepanning operations. It would seem, from the growth of the bone of the skull, that in one case at least, the patient lived for some time after the operation. Wright's conclusion is that: "The evidence of these skulls is a surprising testimony to the advanced state of Judean medicine during the time of the prophet Isaiah." Now it is obvious that skills such as trepanning were not taught by itinerants in the open air.[11]

Whybray (1974, pp. 33–41) finds evidence of professional itinerant open-air "wisdom teachers" within the corpus of the wisdom literature itself. Thus Proverbs 1:20 "Wisdom uttereth her song at the gates, and in the streets speaketh boldly . . . " or Proverbs 8:2 in which wisdom "is on the lofty summits, and hath taken her stand in the middle of the highways." Professionalism is suggested by sarcastic comparisons of the wisdom teacher with the woman who sells sex (see Prov. 7:6–12, 9:13–16) and, especially, by Whybray's translation of Proverbs 17:16: "Why should a fool have a price in his hand to buy wisdom, though he has no sense." Here we may have as well indications of resentment among the elite at the spread of higher modes of consumption among the general public. Chouraqui (1975, p. 120) imagines that leisure activities such as "public readings of the prophets and other writers" played an important role.

Indeed there is evidence of a generally increased demand for leisure activities amongst the ancient Israelites. For example, Exodus 12:16 forbids "servile work" on the first and seventh days of Passover (Segal 1963, p. 206; Thomson has "sacrificial service") while Deuteronomy 16:8, which probably dates to the eighth or seventh centuries (see chapter 16), forbids "work." At some point as much as a third of the year might be holiday. It is of interest to note that a similar trend culminating during the affluent reign of Ramses III (late twelfth century B.C.E.) is evident in ancient Egypt: "It is clear ... that the religious festivals became ... more and more numerous. The temple at Medinet Habu provides definite evidence for this phenomenon. During the reign of Rameses III celebrations were held on 162 days, in other words on a number of days which together covered nearly six months of the year." (Bleeker 1967, p. 32).

The increase of individualism within Israelite society is, of course, reflected not only in its dynamic economy, but also in the existence and message of the classical prophets. It is also evident in laws such as Deuteronomy 24:16: "Parents shall not be put to death for children, nor children be put to death for parents; a person shall be put to death only for his own crime." Further, the improved social status of women is reflected in Deuteronomy 5:18 which, unlike the presumably earlier Exodus 20:14, separates the wife from the material possessions of the husband (see chapter 18). But these are not the only manifestations. The Book of Job, for example, is usually dated to the postexilic period. Weinfeld (1977a, pp. 65–9) explains, however, that the issues are not so simple. The Book consists of two seemingly contradictory sections: a framework (1–2, 42:7–17) in which Job graciously accepts his afflictions and a main poetic section (3:1–42:6) in which he seeks to prove that God is unjust. Perhaps the former does date from the postexilic period: it is marked by a heavy concentration of Persianisms and other late linguistic elements (Hurvitz 1974). On the other hand, it is not improbable that the poetic section dates from our period.

Notes

1. The subject matter of the first paragraph is treated in greater detail in Silver (1980, pp. 22–5).

2. Translations of JPS unless otherwise specified; see the bibliographic note (chapter 1, note 2).

3. For information of the authenticity of the stamp see Kelso (1970, p. 65) and van Beek and Jamme (1970, p. 9). These authors are replying to Yadin (1969) who doubted the authenticity of the Bethel stamp.

4. For statistical treatments of the demand for mortuary goods, see Kanawati (1977; see also O'Connor 1974, p. 27) on Old Kingdom Egypt and Randsborg (1974, pp. 58–60) on Bronze Age Denmark. See also Starr's (1977, pp. 37–8) data on the production of statues and temples in seventh–sixth-century-B.C.E. Greece.

5. The nude female holding her breasts is usually termed a "mother goddess." But Ahmed (1968, pp. 152–53) suggests that in seventh-century-B.C.E. Babylonia this type of figurine had become a sort of good luck symbol rather than an object of worship. Particularly interesting: "they were more specifically characterized than had been the case in the immediate past. The great variety of facial types, many of them painstakingly worked, would seem to occasionally suggest crude attempts at actual portraiture."

6. During our period the Astarte or "mother goddess" nude figurine of the solid pillar-base type with a molded head is, in terms of the findings, at least one-and-a-half times as popular as the type whose hands support breasts or point to or touch the genital area (Holland 1977, pp. 124–25). Note further that the latter type is also found in the Early Iron Age (1200–1100) and still earlier in the Bronze Age.

7. This assumption is based less on archaeology than upon the "vision" of the prophet Ezekiel (8:12): "Again He spoke to me, 'O mortal have you seen what the elders of Israel do in the darkness everyone in his image-covered chamber?'" In his report on the 1980 excavations at Jerusalem, Shiloh (1981, p. 167) tells us that the fascinating object noted in the text was found "below the late Israelite houses" in a narrow layer dated by the pottery to the early tenth century.

8. Indeed Horn (1962, p. 2) asserts that "even if a scarab bears a royal name and thus is "below the late Israelite houses" in a narrow layer dated by the pottery to the early tenth century.

clearly datable, its presence in a certain stratum or locus is in itself not enough proof to date the archaeological material which is found with it, for scarabas were sometimes kept as heirlooms for more than one generation."

9. Song of Songs 2:13, 15; 7:13. The word is pronounced *semadar* and is related to the blossoming of the vines or to tender grapes (Yadin 1975, pp. 182–83).

10. Another possibility is that Isaiah 1:29–30 refers to *funerary* gardens such as those known in ancient Rome. J. M. C. Toynbee (1971, p. 95) explains that

> numerous sepulchral inscriptions bear witness to a widespread interest in the Roman world in the endowing of funerary gardens consecrated to the dead as holy and inviolable domains. The texts make it clear that these gardens were enclosed by walls, planted with a great variety of trees and flowers, equipped with wells, pools, and so forth for watering the plants and refreshing visitors, and furnished with buildings such as dining rooms and *species of summer-houses* in which meals of commemoration of the departed could be eaten by the survivors. Arrangements of this kind . . . reflected both the general passion of the Romans for gardens, a passion that the dead when dwelling in the tomb did not, so it was believed, cease to experience, and also the notion that Elysium, with its idyllic landscape, natural amenities, and heavenly banquets, could have its symbolic counterparts on earth (emphasis added; see also chapter 16 on the *marzēah*-house).

Note also the trees bordering the tomb of Sara in Genesis 23:17–19.

11. The existence of doctors in ancient Israel is attested for the reign of Asa (911–871) in 2 Chronicles 16:12 and also by Jeremiah 8:22.

10 LIVING STANDARDS: INCOME DISTRIBUTION

In spite of the very significant accomplishments thus far reviewed, modern assessments of the eighth–seventh centuries B.C.E. are almost uniformly unflattering, so much so indeed that in the social scientist they must strike a note of unreality, that is, of being out of social character. This negativism can be partially traced to religious presuppositions. Israel-Judah was ultimately destroyed. In some Jewish circles where ideas related to theodicy prevail, the fact of destruction is sufficient proof that "the Israelites did evil in the eyes of the Lord," while in some intellectual Christian circles, the destruction symbolizes the coming replacement of "ethnic-nationalist religions by the true and only universal faith" (see Kaufmann 1960, p. 135).

But presumptions of a Marxist-Leninist character are also important. The market economy is visualized as a zero-or negative-sum game in which every gain to the rich is matched, or more than matched, by a loss to the toiling masses (see, for example, Neufeld 1960, p. 52). In short, Marx's concept of the absolute and relative impoverishment of the working class is applied. This approach is clearly reflected in Salo Baron's (1952) writings on ancient Israel:

> General economic decline was accompanied by a steady process of differentiation. Some of the rich grew richer at the expense of their fellows under the prevalent precapitalistic forms of exploitation.

111

Once some families had secured more than their due share, the trend became irresistible for the poorer farmers sooner or later to lose their land, while a group of comparatively few rich landowners accumulated large estates. (p. 68)

Here we have in addition to relative and absolute pauperization, the increasing concentration of wealth, and the operation of mysterious, but irresistible, historical forces, the application of the Marxist-Leninist notion of general economic crisis to an economy that was in fact enjoying significant growth. Notice also that since capitalism according to the dogma, must begin only in Europe after the overthrow of feudalism, the Israelite forms of exploitation are carefully called "precapitalistic." Add next a pinch of imperialism: "Situated in the midst of the most advanced industrial civilizations of the time . . . this small country was flooded with foreign products, and because of political weakness it often had to admit foreign merchants[1] against its will" (Baron 1952, p. 69). So the period of Israel-Judah's greatest political strength, in which it won control over the key trade routes and established trading enclaves in Syria, is pictured as one of political weakness and of economic ruination, as if it were India in the nineteenth century. The next addition must include the element of reserve army of the unemployed:

The poorer peasants were often permanently ruined by their debts, since the income from their agricultural production could not long stand the strain of high interest rates. . . . [T]he number of free landless workers constantly grew. Inevitably they had to accept low wages and often could find no work at all . . . [T]he country seems not to have escaped the evil of permanent unemployment. For this among other reasons, the 'Hebrew' slave sometimes chose to remain with his master even after he had completed his six-year term. (Baron 1952, pp. 69–70)

We are not told why interest rates were high in an economy, whose marginal productivity of capital was assertedly low[2] or why masters would have agreed to lifetime contracts with unproductive slaves.[3] Moreover, even if the data on terracing and irrigation (see chapter 2), as well as other indications that small Israelite farmers produced for the market, are put aside, we are left wondering why assumedly kin-oriented peasants would plunge so deeply and irrationally into debt.[4] As for the emergence of large landed estates worked with hired labor (or labor services of various kinds) the reader is urged to compare Baron's catastrophism with the explanation offered in chapter 6.

Modern liberal-minded attitudes, more or less closely linked to the prophecies of Amos, Hosea, Isaiah, Micah, Jeremiah, Zephaniah, and Ezekiel are, however, the main source of negativism regarding the eighth and seventh centuries. The alleged social features of the time are stated clearly by Irwin (1959, pp. 203–04):

> At one extreme was a selfish and indolent group of courtiers and idle rich living their parasite life of drunken revelry: at the other the peasantry and poorer workers whose slavery was not merely that of an income below a living standard, but sank even to the unqualified legal sort. And between these upper and lower levels a numerous class of greedy business folk cheated and swindled one another and whoever else might fall within their power.

Since little or no information regarding the details of social relations is provided in the historical books, reliance must be placed on the prophetic books alone. This is rather like writing a history of the U.S. economy relying solely on the opinions of Ralph Nader. Nevertheless, let us examine what the prophets had to say about income distribution.[5]

Hosea (12:8–9) compares Ephraim to a "trader who uses false balances" and thinks "Ah, I have become rich, I have gained wealth for myself." Here the prophet displays his bias against the market while recognizing its productivity. More importantly, the entire nation is characterized as wealthy. Similarly, Isaiah (2:7) refers to the house of Jacob in the following terms: "Their land is full of silver and gold, there is no limit to their treasures; their land is full of horses, there is no limit to their chariots." Again there is no reference to poverty or pronounced distributional inequalities. Micah (1:7) adds that the "harlot's wealth" of Samaria will be burned. Writing in the later seventh or early sixth century, Zephaniah (1:17–18) warns that the Lord will bring distress upon the "people" or "men" and that "their silver and gold shall not avail to save them." Ezekiel 7:19 more or less repeats Zephaniah (or is it the other way around?): "They shall throw their silver into the streets, and their gold shall be treated as something unclean. Their silver and gold shall not avail to save them in the day of the Lord's wrath—to satisfy their hunger or to fill their stomach."[6]

Micah (3:10), writing in the later eighth century charges that Jerusalem has been built up with "iniquity" while Ezekiel (16:48–49) accuses Jerusalem of sharing the "iniquity of thy sister Sodom" including "pride, fullness of bread, and abundance of idleness." Ezekiel goes on to condemn the failure to help the poor, but he does not assert that Jerusalem had become rich at their expense. It is quite clear, especially in Ezekiel, that "iniquity" and "Sodom" are not symbols of violence or sexual aberration but of the market and of the material prosperity it produced. Indeed, Plaut (1981, p. 61) remarks that the Midrash linked affluence with depravity: "hand in hand with material prosperity went an overbearing attitude toward God, whom people judged incapable of hearing prayer and of enforcing moral standards."

References to force, and violence, and oppression must also be interpreted carefully.

> Hear this word, you cows of Bashan, on the hill of Samaria, who defraud the poor, who rob the needy, who say to your husbands, "Bring and let's carouse!" (Amos 4:1)

> Therefore because they have beaten the poor with their fists, though you had received from them choice gifts; you have built houses of hewn stone; but in them you shall not dwell. (Amos 5:11)[7]

> The Lord will bring this charge against the elders and officers of His people: "It is you who have ravaged the vineyard; that which was robbed from the poor is in your houses. How dare you crush my people and grind the faces of the poor? (Isaiah 3:14–15)

> Ah, those who plan iniquity and design evil on their beds; when morning dawns, they do it, for they have the power. They covet fields, and seize them; houses, and take them away. They defraud men of their homes, and people of their land. (Micah 2:1–2)

> For among My people are found wicked men, who lurk like fowlers lying in wait; they set a trap to catch men. As a cage is full of birds, so their houses are full of guile; that is why they have grown so wealthy. (Jeremiah 5:26–27)

> O House of David, thus said the Lord: render just verdicts morning by morning; rescue him who is robbed from him who defrauded him. (Jeremiah 21:12)

> Thus, if a man is righteous and does what is just and right: . . . If he has not wronged anyone: if he has returned the debtor's pledge to him and has taken nothing by robbery; if he has given bread to the hungry and clothed the naked; if he has not lent at interest; if he has abstained from wrong doing and executed true justice between man and man . . . (Ezekiel 18:5, 7–8)

But as Jackson (1972, pp. 4–5) points out the prophetic use of terms such as "seizure" and "robbery" (the verb *gazal*) is polemical. Of course, the creditor or the state might employ force against a defaulting debtor.[8] "But though the verb [*gazal*] in this context could still refer to forcible execution of debt, it would be entirely wrong to think it was confined to forcible acts. The prophets certainly intended no such distinction. Exploitation of the poor, whether forcible or not, was alike condemned." From the perspective of the prophets (and many modern social critics) any economic transaction between a rich and a poor person had to be robbery, whether it was legal and uncoerced or not. Indeed terms such as "seizure" (as well as "widow" and "orphan") are probably standard literary elements of a tradition of social reform or amelioration (see Edzard 1974, pp. 154–55) dating back at least to Urukagina (2351–2342; see pp. 230f.). In any event, it is precisely these polemical verses that come closest to asserting that the rich grew richer while the poor grew poorer.

A more concrete notion of income distribution in the northern kingdom, Israel, during the politically unstable period following the death of Jeroboam II can be based upon 2 Kings 15:19–20. Here it is stated that Menahem (in ca. 738 B.C.E.) gave the Assyrian ruler Tiglath Pileser III "a thousand talents of silver that he might support and strengthen his hold on the kingdom. Menahem exacted the money from Israel: every man of means [or man of "valor" in the sense of worth not "courage"] had to pay fifty shekels of silver[9] for the king of Assyria." Assuming with Baron (1972, p. 61) and Parrot (1935, p. 39) that 100,000 talents equals 3 million shekels, it follows that there were 60,000 "men of means."[10]

> Since these men were undoubtedly the owners of large estates, whose income enabled them to purchase their own arms and to pay taxes, some idea can be formed of the size of the population. . . . It is certain that many of the farmers were hired workers and not "men of valor." Likewise, few of the craftsmen and traders in the urban population were among the "men of valor." If we add these free residents and slaves to the "men of valor," the adult male population would be at least three or four times greater than 60,000. If the "men of valor" together with their families numbered approximately 240,000, it would not be an overstatement to say that in Menahem's time the northern kingdom possessed a population of 800,000 to 1,000,000. (Baron 1972, p. 61)

Let us accept Baron's somewhat ideological demography as a working hypothesis and assume a total population of 800,000. Then, converting this total into 200,000 household units of four persons each, and taking each of the 60,000 men of means to represent a household unit of four persons, we find that 30 percent of the population belonged to Israel's upper-income class. Does this figure reflect glaring income inequality? In the United States in 1972, 23 percent of household units earned between $15,000 and 24,999 while 7.3 percent earned $25,000 and over, for a total of about 30 percent.

The excavations at Tirzah in the northern kingdom are often cited as evidence of increasing inequality of income. According to De Vaux (1967 p. 376–77; see also De Vaux 1956, p. 134) in the early Israelite period (mid-tenth-early-ninth century) "the very uniformity of the dwellings shows that there was no pronounced social inequality among the inhabitants." But by the eighth century a long, straight wall separated a rich quarter from a poor quarter "where the techniques of an earlier age perpetuated themselves *in a steady decline*" (emphasis added.) But I am troubled by the fact that neither of De Vaux's articles on Tirzah provides a direct description of the poor quarter or the specifics of its alleged steady decline. My misgivings are further heightened by the fact that in both the 1956 and the 1967 articles we are, on the same page, reminded that Amos and Hosea condemned social inequality and told that the excavation is "a concrete illustration of [their] invectives . . . " In my mind it is an open question whether biblical preconceptions have affected De Vaux's interpretation of the excavations. It is of interest, however, that De Vaux found in both quarters a "wealth of pottery" very similar to that recovered at Samaria and Megiddo.

On the other hand, we are told that the excavations of eighth-seventh-century Debir in Judah, a thriving textile town (see chapter 2), reflect a widely diffused prosperity, and the private homes indicate "a surprisingly narrow range of variation of social scale" (Albright 1960, p. 75; Kapelrud 1966, p. 79). Does this demonstrate that income differentials narrowed or were not very pronounced during the great period of economic affluence? Not really. On the next page Albright tells us that the absence of concentration of wealth in Judah explains "why there is no such bitter denunciation of the dominant social order in Isaiah or Micah as we find in Hosea." Again one must wonder whether biblical preconceptions are affecting the interpretation of archaeological evidence. On the other hand, Isaiah 3:14–15 is bitter and directed against Judah and Jerusalem, both of which are compared to Sodom in verse 9. So perhaps Albright is reinterpreting the prophets to suit the archaeological evidence.

In conclusion, the archaeological evidence does not at this point convincingly demonstrate the existence of trends in income distribution. With respect to the increased control over trade routes noted previously, it is difficult in the absence of information concerning government policies to disagree with Elat's (1979a, p. 546) suspicion that it merely "produced profits for the royal court that enabled it to strengthen the military force of the kingdom and to raise the standard of living of the royal family and of those close to it." Obviously increased control over the trade routes increased toll revenues. Did the kings of Israel and Judah use their increased revenues from tolls and tributes to reduce domestic taxation or construct public works capable of raising national output or consumption? Did control by Israel and Judah result in reduced charges or freer and more assured access for Israelites? As Neufeld (1962, pp. 41–2) points out, "a caravan . . . not only serves to convey goods great distances, it is also a moving market or fair which is opened at successive stages." Thus increased access would lead to lower prices paid for foreign goods and higher prices received for domestic goods, plus the opportunity to provide various ancillary services—that is, brokerage, storage, and the like—to the caravaneers. Answers to these questions are difficult to come by. We do know that, during the eighth–seventh centuries, good arable land and pastures fell under Israelite control, not just highways. Surely some of this new land found its way into the hands of ordinary Israelites. The description of the expansion of the Simeonites into the pasture lands of the Meunites[11] during the reign of Hezekiah found in 1 Chronicles 4:24–43 is certainly relevant in this connection.

Archaeologists are agreed that Jerusalem experienced explosive growth in acreage and population during the eighth and seventh centuries. According to Broshi (1978, p. 12) Jerusalem reached its zenith in ca. 701 when "the walled area was about 125 acres which, at 200 persons per acre, comes to about 25,000 within the city walls." This compares to 32 acres and 5000 people in ca. 930. Broshi maintains further that "the ancient city did not change much during the seventh century even in the reigns of Manasseh (698–642 B.C.) and Josiah (640–609 B.C.)." On the other hand, some archaeologists place greater emphasis on the reign of Uzziah. Mazar (1978, pp. 57–8) seems to emphasize the reign of Josiah. Broshi (1974, p. 23), in defending his position, minimizes the importance of demographic and economic factors in causing the observed growth and suggests that "this growth was probably the result of the arrival in Jerusalem of Israelite refugees who fled south after the fall of the northern kingdom to the Assyrians in 721 B.C., as well as refugees from the eastward migration of the Judahite population which occurred when Sennacherib in 701 B.C. punished rebellious Hezekiah by ceding part of western Judah to the Philistine city states." This is not unreasonable, but neither is it ironclad.[12] 1 Chronicles 5:6, 26 states that Tiglath Pileser III (ca. 733–732) deported many people from Reuben, Gad, and the half tribe of Manasseh in Transjordan. In 2 Kings 15:29 there are the deportations from upper Galilee, which numbered 13,520 according to Assyrian annals. The annals of Sargon II state that some 27,000 were deported after the fall of Samaria. Sennacherib's annals report that 200,150 men, women and children were deported from Judah in 705. (Note that this is about equal to the estimated population of Judah, see Heaton 1968, pp. 21, 131).[13] Hezekiah named his son after the northern tribe, Manasseh, probably to attract support in that region. Aharoni (1967, p. 350) cites the fact that one of Manasseh's wives was from Jotbah in Galilee (2 Kings 21:19) which, again, "shows us that the dense Israelite population was not removed completely by Tiglath Pileser." I would add that in the aftermath of Hezekiah's reforms, which probably triggered defections to the Assyrians (see part III), many Judahites may not have seen Jerusalem as a haven or place of sanctuary.

Nevertheless, for the sake of argument, we can assume that Broshi is correct and explore the consequences for income distribution. Clearly, an increase in the supply of labor within the borders of Judah with no change in the stock of capital goods would operate to reduce income-per-worker while income per-capitalist (that is, employer or landlord) would rise.[14] On the other hand, the expansion of Judah's boundaries under Josiah (and Manasseh?) would tend to have the opposite effect.

Whether or not the income distribution became more unequal there is no reason to believe that the poor became poorer and abundant reason to conclude with Heaton (1968, p. 35) that "an appreciable number of Israelite citizens became men of means" during the eighth and seventh centuries. Therefore, it is not surprising that this period also reverberated with the call for social justice, which can also be viewed as a form of luxury consumption. This "prophetic revolution" is the subject of part II.

Notes

1. See chapter 11, note 9 on the role and significance of resident foreign traders.

2. Is this to be explained by a high risk of default (due, in large part, to the unwillingness of the courts to enforce loan contracts?), or possibly by a paucity of surplus grain or of other forms of loanable material wealth?

3. Did the slave have a legally enforceable right to remain in slavery? See van der Ploeg (1972, p. 80).

4. Perhaps the explanation is to be found in unexpectedly (and therefore unprepared for) frequent or severe crop failures in both Israel and Judah. Did weather patterns change in the eighth–seventh centuries so that the typical alternation of above-and below-average harvests was drastically altered? Did it, consequently, become impossible for the peasants to follow their age-old practice of evening out their consumption streams by storing grain from above-average harvests and consuming the stored grain after inadequate harvests? I can find no reason to believe this. Lang (in press) suggests that the story of the famine in Genesis 47:13–26 "does not fit in with the Egyptian economic system; rather, it reflects how the poor Israelite peasant becomes dependent on a rich lord." Alternatively does it reflect how the author wished the economic process to be visualized? In fact, sharp increases in the volume of debt not only are symptomatic of a market orientation but also are quite consistent with an expanding economy (see chapter 6, especially note 20). For another line of interpretation, see chapter 13, note 47.

5. Translations of JPS(1978) unless otherwise specified; see the bibliographic note (chapter 1, note 2).

6. Comments of this kind do not, of course, mean that there were no poor but rather that affluence had been widely diffused, as in our own society.

7. So translated by Thomson; JPS(1917) renders Amos 5:11: "Therefore, because ye trample upon the poor, and take from him exactions of wheat" while JPS(1978) has: "assuredly, because you impose a tax (Hebrew uncertain) on the poor and exact from him a levy of grain." Lang (in press) suggests that "a more accurate translation may be, 'Because you make tenants out of the weak, and take tribute of corn from him'."

8. See chapter 11.

9. The price of a slave according to contemporary Assyrian slave-sale contracts (Wiseman 1979, p. 41).

10. Brinker (1946, p. 214) has a total of 72,000.

11. See Tadmor (1971) for details on the Meunites. Apparently families of the Meunites were absorbed into Israel, for $b^e n\grave{e}$ $m^e \bar{u}n\hat{i}m$ are listed among those who returned from the Exile with Zerubbabel (see Elat 1979a, p. 536).

12. As Gunderson (1976, p. 52) well notes, urbanization can be an indicator of increasing affluence for "as average incomes rise, the percentage spent on food decreases. An extension of this process would be that for a closed economy (that is, abstracting from imports and exports) the percentage of the economy's resources employed in agriculture would most likely also fall."

13. Na'aman (1979, p. 85) notes that Ungnad (1942–43) has "explained the error of the Assyrian scribe in recording these figures, the actual number of prisoners . . . being smaller by far. The hypothesis that large areas of Judah were deserted following Sennacherib's conquest should therefore be rejected."

14. What happens to the total income of labor and its relative income share is uncertain (see Layard and Walters 1978, pp. 66–7, 265–67).

II THE CALL FOR SOCIAL JUSTICE: PRIESTS, PROPHETS, PROVERBS, AND PSALMS

11 THE PROPHETS AS SOCIAL REFORMERS

In the earliest Israelite literature, Yahweh is a national god concerned primarily with the military security and material prosperity of his people. Threats of punishment and doom directed at this people arise only for the worship of foreign gods whose exemplars are the Baalim. All this changes in the eighth–seventh centuries B.C.E. with the classical prophets.

For Amos and then Hosea, Isaiah, Micah, Jeremiah, Zephaniah, and even for Ezekiel, Yahweh is a god of social justice. The magnitude of this prophetic revolution is clearly brought out by Kaufmann (1960, pp. 355–56):

> The idea that God dooms a whole society for moral corruption is not altogether absent [in the earlier literature], but . . . whenever God's judgment falls upon the nations specific gross sins are the cause: murder, sexual immorality, oppression of strangers, inhuman cruelty . . . Violations of everyday social morality—perversion of justice, bribe-taking, exploitation of the poor, and the like—are never mentioned. These are regarded as "venial sins," subject to the regular process of God's judgment and his individual providence. Classical prophecy radically alters this view; it threatens national doom and exile for everyday sins.

Neither worship of Baal nor of any other specific foreign deity plays a part in the prophecies of Amos, Micah, Isaiah, and Ezekiel. Hosea 1–3, on the other hand, strongly condemns Baal worship, but it is dated to the period prior to

Jehu's purge (ca. 841).[1] As Kaufmann (1960, p. 143) notes, the references to Baal in Hosea 9:10 and 13:1 are reminiscences of past misbehavior. According to the *Encyclopedia Judaica*, (Ginsberg 1971, pp. 1015–16) the first phrase in Hosea 4:17 is corrupt and should be emended to read "Ephraim is a band of lechers" rather than "Ephraim is addicted to idols." Zephaniah mentions Baal once. Thus it would appear that by the time of the classical prophets, Baalism in the sense of the worship of a foreign deity was of little, if any, consequence. On the other hand, the indispensible agri-cultural-fertility aspect of Baalism (see Engnell 1967, p. 172) had long ago become a traditional part of the Yahweh worship, taken for granted even by Amos and Hosea.[2] It is a naive misconception to suppose that the latter had achieved its final form even at the time of Moses and the Exodus. As Morgenstern (1966, p. 64) well notes, the Jewish religion is the product of historical evolution to meet the needs of the Jewish people "from the remote desert period to the present day." The only "pure Yahwism" is a dead Yahwism.

Jeremiah's "Queen of Heaven" and, more generally, the references of the prophets to "eating on the mountains," "high places," "asheroth," "fetishes," "soothsayers," certain types of astral worship (for example, Amos 5:26), "calves," worship of the dead, and others are very probably, as we shall see in part III, hostile, distorted references to ancient indigenous Israelite practices. Indeed it is precisely the most sacred Israelite religious observances, those honoring God (for instance, sacrifices) and ancestors (*teraphim*) that the prophets attack most bitterly, because the ordinary Israelite could not be converted to a new religion of social justice and social reform until he had been robbed of the peace of mind and the sense of belonging provided by the ancient religion.

The Israelite society portrayed by Amos and his successors suffers terribly from severe oppression of the poor, injustice, commercial dishonesty, and official corruption, all of which are linked to the life-style of a well-to-do middle class. The central image is one that is familiar to modern Americans, namely the blight of poverty amid affluence. Several examples of this were provided in chapter 10, several more should be sufficient to demonstrate the point.[3] First Amos:

Ah, you who turn justice into wormwood and hurl righteousness to the ground! (5:7)

They hate the arbiter in the gate, and desert him whose plea is just. (5:10)

Seek good and not evil, that you may live, and that the God of Hosts, may truly be with you, as you think. (5:14)

I loathe, I spurn your festivals, I am not appeased by your solemn assemblies. If you offer Me burnt offerings—or your meal offerings—I will not accept them . . . Spare me the sound of your hymns . . . But let justice well up like an unfailing stream. (5:21–24)

Listen to this you who devour the needy, annihilating the poor of the land, saying, "If only the new moon were over, so that we could sell grain; the sabbath, so that we could offer wheat for sale, using an ephah that is too small, and a shekel that is too big, tilting a dishonest scale, and selling grain refuse as grain! We will buy the poor for silver, the needy for a pair of sandals." The Lord swears concerning the Pride of Jacob: "I will never forget any of their doings." (8:4–7)

Next Hosea:

Hear the word of the Lord, O People of Israel! For the Lord has a case against the inhabitants of this land, because there is no honesty and obedience to God in the land. [False] swearing, dishonesty, murder, and theft are rife. Crime follows upon crime! For that, the earth is withered: everything that dwells on it languished— beasts of the field and birds of the sky—even the fish of the sea perish. (4:1–3)

For I desire goodness, not sacrifice; obedience to God, rather than burnt offerings. (6:6)

You must return to your God! Practice goodness and justice and constantly trust in your God. (12:7)

A trader who uses false balances, who loves to overreach, Ephraim thinks, "Ah, I have become rich". (12:8)

Now Micah:

Will I overlook in the wicked man's house, the granaries of wickedness and the accursed short ephah? Shall he be acquitted despite wicked balances and a bag of fraudulent weights? Whose rich men [of the city] are full of lawlessness . . . I, in turn have beaten you sore, have stunned (you) for your sins. (6:10–13)

The pious are vanished from the land, none upright are left among men. All lie in wait to commit crimes. One traps the other in his net. (7:2)

Next Isaiah:

Hear the word of the Lord, you chieftains of Sodom! Give ear to the law of our God, you people of Gomorrah. What need have I of all your sacrifices. . . . Your hands are stained with crime. Wash yourselves clean; and put your evil doings from My sight. Cease to do evil. Learn to do good. Devote yourselves to justice and the wronged. Uphold the rights of the orphan; defend the cause of the widow. . . . If, then you agree to give heed, you will eat the good things of the earth, but if you refuse and disobey you will be devoured [by] the sword. (1:10–11, 15–17, 19)

Who of us can dwell with the devouring fire, he who walks in righteousness, speaks uprightly, and spurns profit from fraudulent dealings . . . Such a one shall dwell in lofty security, with inaccessible cliffs for his stronghold. (33:14–16)

Then Jeremiah:

Circumcise your hearts to the Lord. Remove the thickening about your hearts. (4:4)

For among My people are found wicked men, who lurk, like fowlers lying in wait; they set a trap to catch men. As a cage is full of birds, so their houses are full of guile; that is why they have grown so wealthy. They have become fat and sleek; they pass beyond the bounds of wickedness, and they prosper. They will not judge the case of the orphan, nor give a hearing to the plea of the needy. Shall I not punish such deeds . . . (5:26–28)

Zephaniah:

Seek the Lord all you humble of the land who have fulfilled His law; seek righteousness, seek humility. Perhaps you will find shelter in the day of the Lord's anger. (2:3)

Finally Ezekiel:

Thus, if a man is righteous and does what is just and right. If he has not eaten on the mountains or raised his eyes to the fetishes of the House of Israel; if he has not defiled his neighbor's wife or approached a menstruous woman; if he has not wronged anyone; if he has returned the debtor's pledge to him and has taken nothing by robbery; if he has given bread to the hungry and clothed the naked; if he has not lent at advance interest or exacted accrued interest; if he has abstained from wrongdoing and executed true justice between man and man; if he has followed My laws and kept My rules and acted honestly—he is righteous. Such a man shall live—declares the Lord God. (18:5–9)

Lo, I will strike My hands over the ill-gotten gains that you have amassed and over the bloodshed that has been committed in your midst. Will your courage endure, will your hands remain firm in the days when I deal with you? I the Lord have spoken and I will act. I will scatter you among the nations and disperse you through the lands; I will censure the uncleanness out of you. You shall be dishonored in the sight of nations, and you shall know that I am the Lord. (22:13–16)

There can be no doubt that the prophets were social reformers. But according to Irwin (1959, pp. 205–06) and Ginsberg (1979, pp. 15–18) this was to be accomplished through personal reform or supernaturally inspired catastrophes, not by state action. But Kaufmann (1960, p. 329) quickly gets to the heart of the matter: the "new moral conception, especially as it was expressed by the prophets, was beyond the scope of ancient, sapiential morality that had never heard of a claim upon society as a whole." For the prophets, as for all social voluntarists, social injustice is neither private nor inevitable; it can and must be eliminated by a resolute act of social will. And this will–that is, the necessary force, was to be supplied by the rulers.

Mendenhall (1976, p. 142) sees the prophets as defending peasant producers against the state. But, as was shown in chapter 6, land consolidation, a presumed peasant grievance, was not the result of state action (see Neufeld 1960, pp. 49–50) but of market forces. There is no reason to doubt that farmers, like other members of the society, shared in the benefits of economic growth. Did government officials collect taxes and bribes? Of course, as always. Indeed, the prophets' term "gift" or "bribe" is probably polemical (see chapter 10). From biblical passages such as 1 Kings 21:8, 2 Chronicles 19:5, Exodus 18:13ff, Deuteronomy 16:18–20, 17:8–9, 19:17–18, and Jeremiah 26:10ff, we know that the Israelites had formal law courts. But did they possess wholly state-subsidized commercial courts? This is to be doubted. It is more likely that Israelite litigants, as those of medieval England, had to pay fees for judicial services. More specifically, the creditor probably had to purchase a writ to enforce a judgment against a defaulting debtor.[4] While evidence relating to court procedures in Israel and the ancient Near East generally is difficult to find, what we have is consistent with this position. Moreover, it stands to reason that in a society with a government, a creditor would have had to obtain some sort of judgment before he (or an officer of the court; see Driver and Miles 1935, pp. 274–75) dared to seize the property or person of a defaulting debtor. Note the reference to judicial investigations in Deuteronomy 19:18 and that the judges of Deuteronomy 16:18 have officials (or officers) at their disposal. The duties of the latter, Phillips (1970, pp. 19–20) suggests, "would not have been confined to recording the result of any criminal or civil action, but they would also have been charged with communicating or enforcing it either as police or court bailiffs."[5] For Amos and the other classical prophets, the sale of such writs or judgments would have constituted "bribery" and "robbery" and "selling the righteous for silver." Indeed, Isaiah (10:1–2) comes close to saying this in so many words: "Ha! Those who write out evil writs and compose iniquitous documents to subvert the cause of the poor, to rob of their rights the needy of My people; that widows may be their spoil, and fatherless children their booty!." Isaiah 1:23 attacks the princes who consort with thieves, love gifts, "follow after šalmōnîm" (rewards or fees) and fail to judge the case of the orphan and widow. Micah's (3:1, 11; 7:3) attack is quite similar. More explicitly, Ezekiel (45:9) calls upon the princes of Israel to make an end "to your evictions of My people" while Hosea (5:10) compares the princes of Judah with "shifters of field boundaries"[6] and Isaiah (3:14) in a probable reference to the trial of Naboth (1 Kings 21:8), accuses the elders and the princes of eating up the vineyard and robbing the poor.[7]

Mendenhall (1976, p. 142) sees the "social gospel" of the classical prophets as "quite opposite to the tired 'liberalism' of modern politics that calls for increased oppression of the producers in order to support a non-productive clientele of the incompetent and lazy both at the top and the bottom of social strata upon which the political power of the 'liberals' depends." But, whether or not we choose to define it in exactly this way, modern liberalism, tired or robust, is the closest contemporary analog to the program of the prophets. Let them speak for themselves:

> For I have noted how many are your crimes and how countless your sins—you enemies of the righteous, you takers of bribes, you who subvert in the gate the cause of the needy! . . . Hate evil and love good, and establish justice in the gate; (Amos 5:12, 15)

> Hear this, O priests, and attend you prophets and give ear, O royal house: for right conduct is your responsibility! (Hosea, 5:1)

> Listen you rulers of Jacob, you chiefs of the House of Israel! For you ought to know what is right. But you hate good and love evil. (Micah, 3:1–2)

> But a shoot shall grow out of the stump of Jesse [King David's father] . . . He shall sense the truth by his reverence for the Lord. He shall not judge by what his eyes behold, nor decide by what his ears perceive. Thus he shall judge the poor with equity and decide with justice for the lowly of the land. He shall strike down the ruthless with the rod of his mouth and slay the wicked with the breath of his lips. Justice shall be the girdle of his loins. And faithfulness the girdle of his waist. The wolf shall dwell with the lamb, the leopard lie down with the kid;[8] (Isaiah, 11:1, 3–6)

> To the House of the king of Judah: Hear the word of the Lord! O House of David, thus said the Lord: render just verdicts morning by morning; rescue him who is robbed from him who defrauded him. Else My wrath will break forth like fire and burn with none to quench it because of your wicked acts. (Jeremiah, 21:11–12)

It is quite true, of course, that the prophets are authoritarians not social democrats. For them extremism in defense of social justice (or *mishpāt*) is the supreme virtue, while the passive acceptance of injustice is a vice. At times the prophets seem to play the role of revolutionaries and, as M. A. Cohen (1979, p. 16) has noted, their oracles have the ring of sedition. "The shrines of Isaac shall be laid to waste, and the sanctuaries of Israel reduced to ruins; and I will turn upon the House of [King] Jeroboam with the sword" (Amos 7:9). "I will give thee kings in my ire, and take them away in My wrath" (Hosea 13:11).

Not unexpectedly, the prophets opposed expansionist militarism and patriotism. Amos (5:18–20 and elsewhere) derides the Day of Yahweh, which was probably associated with the expectation of Israelite victories against external foes. Hosea (10:13) is even more blunt: "You have plowed wickedness, you have reaped iniquity—[and] you shall reap the fruits of treachery—because you have relied on your chariots and on the host of your warriors." Micah (5:9–10) adds that the Lord "will destroy the horses in your midst and wreck your chariots" while Isaiah (31:1) complains of "those who go down to Egypt for help and rely on horses! They have put their trust in abundance of chariots, in vast numbers of riders, and they have not turned to the Holy One of Israel . . . " For Albright (1960, p. 71) the prophets "reflect a gentler more refined age in which love had become more potent than hate and a cosmopolitan spirit looked at Israel and Judah almost as impartially as it considered its neighbors." This aspect is, of course, most prominent in Amos (9:7) wherein the prophet maintains that: "To Me, O Israelites, you are just like the Ethiopians. True, I brought Israel up from the land of Egypt, but also the Philistines from Caphtor and the Arameans from Kir." A similar spirit underlies Isaiah 19:23–34:

> In that day shall there be a highway out of Egypt to Assyria, and the Assyrian shall come into Egypt, and the Egyptian into Assyria; and the Egyptians shall worship with the Assyrians. In that day shall Israel be the third with Egypt and with Assyria, a blessing in the midst of the earth; for that the Lord of hosts hath blessed him saying: 'Blessed be Egypt My people and Assyria the work of My hands, and Israel Mine inheritance'.

But, just as love for social justice can be accompanied by hatred of human beings, so universalism can be transformed into corrosive self-hate. Both tendencies are evident in the writings of Israel's classical prophets.

Amos tells the Israelites that they are "just like" their neighbors but he (3:2) nevertheless insists: "You alone have I singled out [entered into a covenant with? see Seilheimer 1974] of all the families of earth—that is why I will call you to account for all your iniquities." He quickly calls the neighboring peoples to "gather on the hill of Samaria and witness the great outrages within her and the oppression in her midst" (3:9). By the beginning of chapter 4 he is referring to human beings, the Jewish women of Samaria, as "you cows of Bashan" and looking forward to the day that they "will be carried off in . . . fish baskets . . . and flung in the refuse heap" (4:1–3; but see

Pope 1977a, p. 166). From the assertion that the "people's leaders have been misleaders" Isaiah (9:15–16) deduces: "That is why my Lord will not spare their youths, nor show compassion to their orphans and widows. For all are ungodly and wicked, and every mouth speaks impiety." Jeremiah (4:22) begins by declaring: "My people are stupid, they give Me no heed; . . . they are clever at doing wrong but unable to do right." Then he asks (5:1): "Roam the streets of Jerusalem, search its quarters, look about and take note: you will not find a man, there is none who acts justly, who seeks integrity—that I should pardon her." By chapter 6 (verses 11, 13) such thoughts fill him with "wrath of the Lord" that he cannot hold in: "Pour it on the infant in the street, and on the company of youths gathered together! Yes, men and women alike shall be captured. Elders and those of advanced years. . . . From the smallest to the greatest, they are all greedy for gain." Zephaniah (1:10) declares that Jewish businessmen[9] have much to fear: "In that day there shall be— declares the Lord—a loud outcry from the Fish Gate, and howling from the Mishneh, and a sound of great anguish from the hills. The dwellers of the Maktesh howl; for all the merchants have perished, all who weigh silver are wiped out."

Ezekiel's (23:24–26) is the most shocking outpouring of self-hate:

> They [assorted external foes] shall attack you [primarily Jewish women] with fleets of wheeled chariots and a host of troops . . . And I will entrust your punishment to them . . . They shall cut off your nose and ears . . . They shall take away your sons and daughters, and your remnant shall be devoured by fire. They shall strip you of your clothing and take away your dazzling jewels.

But Ezekiel's view that Israel's god Yahweh would use foreigners to punish the Israelites for not helping their poor is also found in Isaiah 10:5: "Ha! Assyria, rod of My anger . . . " and in Jeremiah who urges desertion to the Chaldeans (21:9) and proclaims: "Serve the king of Babylon and live" (27:17). In chapters 15 and 27 and elsewhere, Jeremiah goes so far as to proclaim that Nebuchadnezzar is the servant of the Lord and that those who take issue with this are "false prophets" (27:1–10).

Some modern affluent revolutionaries might appreciate Isaiah's (20:1–6) ploy of warning the Israelites against an alliance with Egypt by going about "naked" for three years. His publicly stated intention to be "intimate with the prophetess" (8:3) may have shocked the bourgeois Judeans.[10] Not even a Trotsky could improve upon Isaiah 8:12: "You must not call conspiracy what this people calls conspiracy [holy?], nor revere what it reveres, nor hold it in awe." Ginsberg (1979, p. 22) interprets Isaiah 8:15 as follows: "The masses, says Isaiah to his children [more likely his followers][11], shall trip; you, the elite, shall not."

Was classical prophecy idiosyncratic or, alternatively, should it be seen as a systematic, conscious response to the social and economic forces prevailing in the eighth and seventh centuries? In a recent, strangely heated denunciation of the "social scientizing" of biblical studies, Mendenhall (1981, p. 190) ridicules the suggestion that the classical prophets might have been "important political authority figures, if not 'radical revolutionaries'." He asserts that this "is hardly a historically useful approach simply because of the radical *ideological* contrasts involved that only accidentally corresponded to social contrasts, particularly between the urban and rural populations." If I understand him correctly, Mendenhall is taking the position that any correspondence between the arguments or the prophets and real social issues is illusory—that is, that the message of classical prophecy was idiosyncratic. This, I will seek to demonstrate, is historically untenable. On the other hand, it would be quite pointless in a scholarly discussion to dispute with Mendenhall on "transcendent factors" or the intentions of "transcendent deity."

The fertile mind of Max Weber linked classical prophecy with Israel's external sociopolitical environment. For Weber I (1952, p. 303), the "patrimonial bureaucracy" of the great kingdoms neighboring Israel "had always given rise to the patriarchal and charitable ideal of the 'welfare state'. . . " But Israel had to "borrow, apparently through Phoenician mediation, the argument that the masses "had a claim on the charity of the ruling strata, above all, the royal officials . . . " Basically Weber's argument is that the demand for a welfare state emerges from a "national bureaucratic machine" and its "corresponding cultural stratum." Since Israel possessed neither of these prerequisites its demand had to be idiosyncratic, that is, copied. But what, it may be asked, is there to prevent a bureaucratic machine from being put in place in response to a preexisting demand for a welfare state? Weber does not discuss this perfectly reasonable possibility. This is precisely what happened when, as Yoffee (1979, p. 12) notes, Hammurabi (1792–1750) and his son Samsuiluna (1749–1712)[12] began to vigorously regulate economic affairs: "The evidence gleaned from a close examination of several ranks of offices indicates that these offices were created or greatly expanded after the time of Samsuiluna." Neither does Weber explain how he knows that Israel's bureaucracy was, or remained, inadequate for such a task.[13]

Weber II (1952, p. 268) views classical prophecy as a response to "the rising external danger to the country and to the royal power." He is obviously troubled, however, by the prevalence of prophecies of doom in a time of "political and economic prosperity." A similar argument has recently been advanced by Holladay (1970, pp. 30, 39) who has, however, supported it

with evidence suggesting that national exile is an innovation of the eighth
century B.C.E. He cites a provision of a ca. 750 treaty between Assyria and
Arpad that calls for exile of the latter nation as the penalty for violation. In
ca. 740, Arpad became the first Western state to fall to Assyria and,
presumably, the exile provision of the treaty was implemented by Tiglath
Pileser III. On the other hand, Amos began to utter his threats during the
reign of Jeroboam II (Amos 1:1) who died ca. 747. So Amos was active long
before 740 and, quite probably, long before 750. In support of the latter
point, we have two pieces of evidence. First, the solar eclipse noted in Amos
8:9 and also recorded in Assyrian eponym lists, according to modern
astronomical calculations, took place in 763 (see Haran in *Encyclopedia
Judaica* 1971, vol. 2, p. 881). Second, Amos 1:1 tells us that he prophesied
"two years before the earthquake" which is dated to ca. 760 by the
excavators of Megiddo and, by Yeivin to 749 (see Yeivin 1979, pp. 162,
168). Further, as Gottwald (1964, pp. 101–2) points out, even as late as
750, the Assyrians were still fighting for their lives against Urartu in the
north and the Arameans in the south and west. Gottwald rightly concludes
that "Amos sounded his threats at an utterly improbable time."[14] Neither is it
necessarily the case that Israel's armed forces from an estimated population
of 800,000 were very badly outnumbered by the native Assyrian forces.
Basing his conclusions on fragmentary data such as a seventh-century total-
population census at Harran, a city on the western limit of Assyria proper,
Burney (1977, pp. 165–66) boldly estimates that in ca. 705 "the Assyrian
homeland must have had a population of between 250,000 and 500,000 in
all, not necessarily much less in the early ninth century B.C."

Moreover, little in the prophesies of Amos, or of Hosea for that matter,
requires us to think of an Assyrian threat[15] or that the Israelites were
concerned about an external danger to their national existence. Amos 6:6–7
asserts that those Israelites who enjoy good food and wine at festive meals
but "are not concerned about the ruin of Joseph" (the downtrodden?; but see
also note 18 of this chapter) "shall head the column of exiles." The Lord "will
raise up a nation against you" (Amos 6:14) who will "drive you into exile
beyond Damascus" (Amos 5:27). In the face of such vague threats is it any
wonder that the Israelites were able to "ward off" [the thought of] a day of
woe" (Amos 6:3) and instead, were "at ease in Zion[16] and confident on the
hill of Samaria" (Amos 6:1)? Indeed, Amos (6:8) had to cope with stubborn
"pride of Jacob" (the northern kingdom) and his fortresses. Vriezen (1967, p.
216) notes that the absence of a political reason for Amos' prophecy of woe
"is especially evident in the visions through which he received his call."
Finally, Amos' prophecy concerning a mysterious nation (6:14) appears to
have come on the heels of Israel's military victories at Lo debar and Karnaim

in nothern Transjordan (Amos 6:13). These were probably the most significant since 853, when Israel and its allies defeated or stalemated the Assyrians themselves at Karkar (Qarqar; see Hallo and Simpson 1971, pp. 127–28). Hosea includes only one passage (9:3) that seems to link Assyria and exile: "They shall not be able to remain in the land of the Lord. But Ephraim shall return to Egypt and shall eat unclean food in Assyria." Even this statement is undermined in Hosea 11:5, which asserts only that: "They return to the land of Egypt [for aid?], and Assyria is their king [patron?]." Examination of the context of Hosea chapters 4–14 shows that the prophet was aware of the assassinations of Zechariah (the son of Jeroboam II) and of the usurper Shallum in 747. Analysis of the material surrounding the prophecy that the Israelites will eat "unclean food in Assyria" shows that exile is contemplated, not as the result of military defeat, but as the result of famine (see 9:2–6). Such a perspective the *Encyclopedia Judaica* (Ginsberg 1971, vol. 8, p. 1017) reasonably points out, would be inconceivable after the Assyrian invasion of 734–732:[17] "In other words, the prophet has not witnessed the events of 734–732 but he vividly recalls the ghastly civil wars of 747"[18] (see Hosea 10:14; 14:1). Even the (presumably) pre-705 Isaiah shows little awareness of an imminent Assyrian threat. Isaiah 9:11 has the northern kingdom being devoured by Aram and Philistia. Since this verse is immediately preceded by Israel's rebuilding with "dressed stone" and "cedar" (v. 9) it was probably written shortly after the civil war of 747. Isaiah 28:1–4, which has Israel being "trampled underfoot," is taken to reflect King Hoshea's defection from the Assyrians in ca. 725. However, 28:2 provides not the slightest indication of which (if any) nation may be represented by the Lord's "something strong and mighty." Similarly, the Assyrians are supposedly referred to in Isaiah 5:26–29 as the "nation from afar," from "the end of the earth." But as the *Encyclopedia Judaica* (Ginsberg 1971, vol. 9, p. 51) points out, the enemy comes equipped with "fangs" and is nothing more than a legendary nation of barbarians.

According to Neufeld (1960, p. 22), "the masses . . . had to cope with an extremely low standard of living and great unemployment." Baron (1952, pp. 68, 77, 87) does not for a moment doubt that "lofty and intense prophetic utterances" were a direct response to the general economic decline of the eighth and seventh centuries. Economic depression triggered "mass dissatisfaction" and the prophets served as the vanguard of a precapitalist proletariat in their struggle against the precapitalist capitalists. Nevermind that the classical prophets never call upon the oppressed to resist their oppressors: "The direct relation of prophet and people helps to explain how, with no real financial or military backing these messengers of God wielded such influence." The most obvious difficulty here is that Baron's great depression is a figment of Marxist dogma. It never happened. The eighth and later-seventh centuries, the periods of classical prophecy, were the most prosperous periods in Israelite history. Marxists are well known for their tendency to see depressions around every corner; they cannot cope with the "paradox" that political and social ferment typically increases after a marked improvement in economic conditions.[19]

By now the reader has, I trust, become somewhat more receptive to the idea that ancient Israel was a real society, capable of being analyzed in systematic social-science terms. I will now put forward a general framework for understanding the events of the eighth and later-seventh centuries. This is done, I might add, with some trepidation, for it is predictable that some of you will angrily slam this book closed and accuse me of sins such as "importing the twentieth century into ancient Israel" or engaging "not in historical scholarship, but in a conservative polemic against liberal social reformers." Please be assured that the evidence presented in the remainder of this study is as carefully considered and researched as that in Part I. Why not wait until it is presented? Then, if you wish to dismiss the argument as a mere "conservative interpretation of history" you can do this in complete fairness.

The central theme of my 1980 study on *Affluence, Altruism, and Atrophy* is that altruism or the "taste" for helping others is one of the higher needs described by the psychologist Abraham H. Maslow. An examination of the implications of modern consumer-choice theory together with a review of a substantial body of behavioral evidence—anthropological field research, voting studies, public-opinion survey data, econometric studies of charitable giving—suggests that affluence markedly increases the demand for altruistic consumption. Consideration of affluent societies, including not only contemporary Sweden and the United States, but also classical Athens and Rome and Sung China and Victorian England, suggests that this often takes the form of state actions to improve the lot of the poor.

Before going on, it is well to note, for example, that in the earlier stages of Roman affluence, in the late first century B.C.E. and first century C.E., one's chances of pleasing the gods depended primarily on the proper performance of traditional rituals. But it was only during the second century C.E. (Silver 1980, pp. 65–7) when affluence had peaked

> that Persius could assert that the only acceptable offering to the gods was "holiness of mind and purity of heart" (Satires II, pp. 73–4) or the younger Pliny could write: "The gods rejoice more in the innocence of worshippers than in elaborate prayers; the man who enters their temples with a pure heart is more agreeable to them than one who recites a carefully prepared litany" (*Panegyric* 3). (Ogilvie 1969, p. 18.)

It is interesting to note that exactly the same tendency toward "works" seems to be manifested in the "Admission Torah" (Ps. 15: "Lord who shall sojourn in Thy tabernacle? . . . He that walketh uprightly, worketh righteousness, and speaketh truth in his heart") and in Psalm 24 ("Who shall ascend into the mountain of the Lord? . . . He that hath clear hands and a pure heart.") As will be seen in chapter 15 where both psalms are quoted more fully, there is reason to believe that they date to the eighth–seventh centuries. Meanwhile, note the resemblance of both psalms to Isaiah 33:14–16.

I would modify Baron's conclusion as follows: The direct relation of prophets and affluents explains how these messengers of God were able to acquire the financial and military backing to exert influence.[20] Although this element is not entirely absent, the ensuing struggle for social justice (described in part III) should not be seen as a confrontation between the wealthy and the royalty. Rather, the wealthy, royal and nonroyal (for instance, the House of Shaphan), sought with the guidance of the prophets to employ the state power to nullify the laws of economy and society. The elite, as Coote (1981, p. 100) neatly puts it, was "talking to itself." As we shall see, these well-meaning but uncomprehending efforts backfired disastrously.

Notes

1. See chapter 16.

2. Note Amos 4:6–9, in which Yahweh determines the rainfall, and 5:8, in which he creates the Hyades and Orion: "In Hebrew cosmology the stars are one source of rain . . . The Hyades (Greek 'water stars') and Orion are constellations that rise high in the sky at sunrise near the autumnal equinox. They are thus the cosmic harbingers, if not the cause and source, of the rainy season. . . . [God] controls the equinoxes, making nights shorter in the spring when the rains stop, and days shorter in the fall when they return." (Coote 1981, p. 79) Also note Yahweh's blessing on the crops in Hosea 2:21–23, at least in the renderings of Bewer and Thomson.

Bernhard Anderson (1975, p. 251) credits Elijah with having challenged Baal in the sphere of his power, namely fertility: "The central concern of the stories is to portray Yahweh's authority over the fertility of the land, and, to affirm that people's lives are wholly in his hand."

3. Translations of JPS(1978) unless otherwise specified; see the bibliographic note (chapter 1, note 2).

4. On the sale of writs in medieval England, see Hogue (1966, esp. pp. 12–15, 157–59). On "bribes" as a component of the incomes of medieval-English law-enforcement officials (for instance, sheriffs), see chapter 18, note 5.

5. Some extra-biblical evidence is available for Rome and the Near East. Driver and Miles (1935, pp. 288–89) cite a custom of Rome described by Gellius (second century C.E.) in which "after debtors in default had been seized, an interval of time was allowed in order to discover

whether the parties could come to terms and then, if no settlement was reached, the debtors were kept in chains for 60 days; during this period they were brought before the praetor [an official] on three successive market-days and the amount of the debt for which they had become judgment-debtors was publicly announced. The object of this procedure was presumably to discover if any friend or relation of the debtor would pay the debt for him."

Note that article 114 of Hammurabi's Code (see Meek 1969, p. 170) implicitly provides a debtor with the right to sue in the event of false distraint. Also in the second millennium, Larsen (1974a, pp. 289–90) takes note of tablets from Kanesh, the Assyrian commercial colony in Anatolia, in which witnesses swear "by the life of the city (Assur)" or "by the life of (divine) Assur." (This practice reminds me of Amos 8:14 and Hosea 4:15 which condemn those that swear oaths involving Samaria or Dan or Beer-sheba.) Larsen informs us that the Anatolian texts "frequently refer to documents which could be issued by the City and/or the *rubāum* . . . with the help of which one could pressure debtors or opponents in lawsuits." The *rābisu* (Sumarian *maškim*), he adds, seems to be "a kind of attorney who could be hired by private individuals to represent their interests in lawsuits that took place in Anatolia." In the local court documents (*ditilla*) of the Ur III period (2112–2004) the *maškim* holds pretrial investigatory hearings in cases of slavery and breach of contract (Edzard 1967, pp. 151–52). Most interesting, during the Sargonic period (2334–2154), Foster (1977, fn. 52, p. 35) notes: "It was . . . customary to give silver to the judge and the *maškim* of court proceedings, perhaps as 'court costs'." Related practices are found in later times in the Middle Assyrian legal documents called *šulmānu*-texts. *Šulmāmu*, like *ṭātu* in the Nuzi texts, is well known in the meaning "gift" or "bribe." In both cases, Finkelstein (1952, pp. 79–80) concludes, we are dealing with a common, legally sanctioned gratuity (witnessed in the Middle Assyrian texts) the aim of which "might be to induce an official to hear a lawsuit."

Perhaps the traditional translation "bailiff" is too narrow (see Kang 1972, pp. 248–56) but it is quite suggestive in view of the later transformation of the *rābisu* into a demon apparently visualized as crouching in wait to ambush human beings. This transformation is noted by Oppenheim (1968, p. 179) who also calls attention to "a parallel in the well-known passage 'sin lieth at the door' from Genesis 4:7 which uses the Hebrew *rōbeṣ* in exactly the same way." Note also Von Rad (1972, pp. 375–76): "In the statement 'I remember my faults' (*mazkîr hᵃtā'ay*) the butler of Gen. 41:9 probably refers to an actually existing office for bringing suit." It is suggested below that the Joseph story may date from the time if not the pen of Amos.

6. For the concrete circumstances of Hosea 5:10, see chapter 17.

7. For a hypothesis concerning the legal role of "princes" or "nobles" or "gods" (?), see chapter 18, note 5.

8. The picture of a paradise in which all creatures live in nonviolent harmony is a recurrent one in Egyptian and Mesopotamian mythology.

9. The most common biblical term for trader or merchant is "Canaanite". Elat (1979a, pp. 529–30) raises the question "whether they were called Canaanites because of their ethnic affiliation or origin, or whether this was a term for merchants of every nationality created as early as the premonarchic period, when those traders whom the Israelites met were, invariably, Canaanites." (Elat ignores the possibility that the term "Canaanite" is pejorative.) The answer seems evident from references in the prophetic literature cited by Elat (p. 529) himself. "Isaiah prophesied about Tyre, 'whose merchants (*sōḥarêhā*) were princes, her Canaanites were men honored on earth' (Isa. 23:8). 'Her Canaanites' has no ethnic meaning, but is a parallel expression for 'her merchants'." Similarly, Ezekiel (17:4) terms Babylonia *'Eres Kᵉna'an* (or "land of trade"). Perhaps the most important point, however, is that it is simply absurd to suggest that as late as the eighth–seventh centuries there were still no native Israelite merchants. Note the shipment of oil by Hiyahu (see chapter 2).

Neither can it be deduced from the presence of resident foreign merchants (for instance, the "metics" or resident aliens of ancient Athens) that the natives are uninterested or hostile to the occupation of trader. This is, of course, the position usually encountered in discussions of classical economic history; here Starr (1977, pp. 87–9) is a notable and welcome exception. Indeed the opposite may be the case; the acceptance of foreigners may reflect the fact that trade has grown to a point where the opportunities for traders exceed the domestic supply of traders. This is beautifully explained by Hicks (1969, p. 48):

> If the newcomers were to do exactly the same business as was being done by established merchants, their competition would probably, at best, be harmless; as soon as there was even a temporary check to expansion it would be a nuisance. But in fact they do not need to do just the same business; their best opportunities will be to fill gaps in the already existing structure. The former merchants (we may suppose) will not all of them be doing just the same business; there will be things which they have not been able to avoid doing for themselves and which they will prefer to let the newcomers do for them. By the expansion in the number of merchants operating, the trading center as a whole will benefit from specialization and division of labor; so that a larger center will be able to trade, up to a point, more effectively than a smaller one. . . . The expansion which the newcomers make possible is . . . at that stage to the general advantage. . . . The benefits in question are not only in direct reductions in cost; even more important, perhaps, are reductions in risk. Every trader is operating in an environment of which he has fair knowledge only as concerns those parts that are 'nearest' to him; he has a much weaker knowledge of parts that may concern him intimately, though they are 'farther away'.

The knowledge of these "farther away" parts can be increased and risk reduced, precisely by importing merchants from these parts.

10. It is often assumed that "the prophetess" was his wife. But as Crenshaw (1971, p. 58) points out: "Such an interpretation is in no way demanded by the text, however, this being an unusual way of addressing one's wife. Furthermore, why would the prophet need reliable witnesses if he merely went in to his wife? If the prophetess were not his wife, the desire for witnesses becomes understandable, since this is a dramatic symbolic action."

11. The prophetic "father" is the leader of his group (1 Sam. 10:12; 2 Kings 2:12).

12. On Samsuiluna see also chapter 18, note 11.

13. The Bible provides formal lists of state officials only for the reigns of David and Solomon (see 2 Sam. 8:15–18; 1 Kings 4:1–6).

14. Coote (1981, pp. 20–4) wishes to place Amos closer to 722, but his case hinges on a hypothesis I find difficult to accept. Specifically, that Jeroboam II was inserted into the book of Amos by a seventh-century Judean editor so that the great prophet would clash with the namesake of the founder of the despised Bethel cult and the northern kingdom of Israel. One small problem here is that Jeroboam II receives relatively favorable treatment in Kings (see chapter 13).

15. Assyria is not mentioned by Amos. The Masoretic text of Amos 3:9 reads as follows: "Proclaim it upon the palaces at Ashdod, and upon the palaces in the land of Egypt . . . " The Septuagint has Assyria not Ashdod, but this is usually regarded to be secondary. "The names Ashdod and Egypt represent wordplays on 'plunder' and 'foe' respectively" (Coote 1981, p. 21). A similar wordplay is found in 6:13. It must be admitted, however, that Amos 6:2 may refer to an Assyrian threat. In this rather obscure passage the prophet cites Calneh, Hamath the Great and Gath of the Philistines as lessons for Israel. Na'aman (1974, p. 37) is of the opinion that "Amos was alluding to Tiglath Pileser's campaign to Syria in 738 B.C., during which the Assyrians conquered Kullania and Hatarikka (the northern part of the land of Hamath)." But

what then is the significance of the reference to "Gath of the Philistines"? According to 2 Chronicles 26:6, Judah conquered Gath during Uzziah's reign. Would the Israelites have taken this as an "example and warning . . . not to rely upon her strength against Assyria"? Note further the difference of opinion among scholars concerning whether Kunalia and Kullania are two different places (see Na'aman 1974, fn. 51, p. 37).

16. This reference need not refer to Jerusalem. J. Gray (1965, p. 287; see also Roberts, 1973) notes that: "With the discovery of the Ras Shamra [Ugarit] texts . . . came the discovery of a Canaanite 'Olympus' *ṣpn*, specifically the seat of Baal, the god who triumphed over the powers of Chaos and ruled as King in an ordered world." Thus, Fohrer (in Lang, in press) may be quite correct in suggesting that Amos is here using the term "Zion" as a (sarcastic) metaphor for the "hill of Samaria."

17. I do not wish to suggest that the Israelites became aware of Assyrian power only after 734. Tiglath Pileser I (1115–1077) may be alluded to in Psalms 83:9 while an Assyrian inscription mentioning an Israelite payment in ca. 797 is consistent with the suggestion that the unnamed deliverer of 2 Kings 13:5 may be Adad-nirari III of Assyria (810–783) (see Hallo 1981, p. 11 and fn. 14; Page 1969).

On the other hand, the Bible ignores (obfuscates?) the defeat or stalemate of the Assyrians in 853. My point is that the evidence does not demonstrate that the Assyrians were viewed as an imminent, mortal threat in the times of Amos and Hosea.

Hosea 5:13 and 10:6 seem to refer to certain Israelite attempts to purchase the military help of the Assyrians. Hosea 10:14: "And all your fortresses shall be ravaged as Beth-arbel [Arbêla in northern Transjordan?] was ravaged by Shalman," may refer to Israel's civil war and the Shallum of 2 Kings 15:10ff or, as Astour (1971, pp. 386–87) cogently argues, not to Shalmaneser V (727–722), but to an earlier invasion of Israel by Shalmaneser III in 841.

18. Andersen and Freedman (1980, pp. 35–7) suggest that the central events of the book of Hosea best fit 750–740 or 755–740. Hallo and Simpson (1971, p. 137) counter as follows: After the Assyrian invasion of 734–32 Israel was shorn of Gilead and much of the Galilee— "the proud kingdom of Israel was reduced to little more than a vassal state, which Isaiah and Hosea now properly called simply Ephraim, where Amos had still called it Joseph." But see chapter 13 on the Amos-Joseph connection.

19. See Auster and Silver (1979, chapter 7 and appendix II). The reader's attention is also called to Genesis 41 in which Joseph convinced Pharaoh to make drastic changes in agricultural policy during a period of abundance.

20. The socioeconomic origin and function of classical prophecy cannot be gainsaid. The perspective of the social reformers is well stated by Coote (1981, p. 102): "There may be no alternative way to institutionalize justice. There may be no alternative way to bring prophecy effectively to bear on power but to institutionalize it, in writing as in other ways, and call it prophecy grown up, or justice in the process of being achieved in the midst of the ambiguities of human affairs."

12 THE POLITICAL POTENCY
OF THE PROPHETS

Amos, Micah and the other classical prophets must not be seen as poor peasants, hermits, or eccentrics outside the mainstream of Israelite life, but as intellectuals competing for the support of the affluents in the sphere of public policy.

Heaton (1968, pp. 12–13) has pointed out that "the influence of educated men in Israel is only just beginning to gain recognition from students of the Old Testament." But Weber (1952, p. 267), in a work first published in 1917, was able to view the prophets as "above all, political demagogues and, on occasion, pamphleteers." He went on to add that "In all these motivations for Yahweh's wrath," that is, buying and selling, usury, and the like, and "even in the deliberate paradoxes of Amos, may be discerned the impact of an intensive culture of intellectuals." All this contrasts sharply with traditional Jewish and Christian interpretations. For Robert H. Pfeiffer (1961, pp. 124, 158, 163): "In the Northern Kingdom, the bulk of the nation, the prophets failed to have any influence on its policies; The Prophetic Movement, was apparently a total failure in the days of the great prophets . . . the prophets played no role even in connection with the Deuteronomic reforms" (see part III). Irwin (1959, p. 207) adds that "The weakness of the prophetic program of reform was that, in modern phrase, it lacked teeth . . . the prophets met with little success: the majority of their compatriots thought them misguided nuisances. Their reforms did not come about, some only after centuries and then imperfectly." But let us like modern dentists look inside the patient's mouth before diagnosing the vigor of his teeth.

When the (nonliterary) prophet Micaiah saw "all Israel scattered over the hills like sheep without a shepherd" (1 Kings 22:17)[1], King Ahab (874–853) reacted to a death threat: he had Micaiah locked up and wore a disguise. When Jeremiah proclaimed, "Serve the king of Babylon and live!" (27:17) he was opposed by the "false prophet" Hananiah[2] to whom Jeremiah said: "Listen Hananiah! The Lord did not send you, and you have given this people lying assurances. Assuredly, thus said the Lord: I am going to banish you from off the earth. You shall die this year, for you have urged disloyalty to the Lord. And the prophet Hananiah died that year, in the seventh month" (28:15–17). Does this story represent myth, hypnotic suggestion, coincidence, or political assassination? Jeremiah 29:20–21 also has the prophet addressing the Jewish exile community in Babylon as follows: "Thus said the Lord of Hosts, of Maaseiah, who prophesy falsely to you in My name. I am going to deliver them into the hands of King Nebuchadnezzar of Babylon, and he shall put them to death before your eyes."[3] Mere bombast? Jeremiah 38:19–22 finds this "toothless" prophet offering to protect King Zedekiah from "the Judeans who have defected to the Chaldeans" in return for his surrender of Jerusalem. The sad fate of Pelatiah the "prince of the people" in Ezekiel 11:13 should also be noted.

Isaiah has disciples (8:16) and is consulted by Kings Ahaz (7:1–9) and Hezekiah (chapters 37, 38). He also authors royal records (2 Chron. 26:22; 32:32) and, apparently, is capable of driving a high government minister, Shebna, from his office (Isa. 22). Beebe (1970, p. 262) suggests that Isaiah 9:2–6 was the accession hymn composed by the prophet for Hezekiah's coronation.[4] Yeivin (1979, p. 174) thinks it possible that Isaiah was a high royal official (a scribe) under Uzziah and, possibly, Ahaz. (This question will be dealt with in chapter 13). Hoschander (1938, p. 260) calls attention to the rabbinical tradition (Babylonian Talmud) that Isaiah was a member of the royal family—that his father Amoz is a brother of King Amaziah. This possibility, Hoschander notes, cannot be dismissed on linguistic grounds alone. Jeremiah, the "priest" from little Anathoth has supporters among the elders and the priests (19:1–2); is consulted by representatives of King Zedekiah (21:1–2); is protected by officials and principal men of the elders (26:4, 16–17); has his messages to the Babylonian exile community delivered by the king's own messengers (29:3), and officials (51:59); has a person of substance, Baruch son of Neriah son of Mahseiah, as his personal secretary (32:12–14; 36:2–10);[5] has access to chambers at the Temple (35, 36:10); colludes with the highest officials to bring his writings to the attention of the king (36:10–25); receives protection and reverential treatment from two houses, Shaphan and Achbor, which participated actively in King Josiah's reform (36:12, 25; 2 Kings 22); is hidden by the Lord (in the Temple probably) when the king orders his arrest (36:26); has family connections in the highest circles in the land (Jeremiah's father Hilkiah may even have been Josiah's chief priest); and, finally, is treated with the utmost respect by King Nebuchadnezzar of Babylon, who "had given orders to Nebuzaradan, the chief of the guards . . . 'Take him and look after him; do him no harm, but grant whatever he asks of you.' " (39:11–12). Zephaniah 1 traces this prophet's ancestry back to Hezekiah, most probably King Hezekiah; this would also make him a distant relative of King Josiah.

Even Baron (1952, pp. 86–7) admits that "Isaiah and Zephaniah were members of the highest aristocracy" while Jeremiah "belonged to a financially independent family of provincial priests." His explanation is that they were "more thoughtful members of the privileged classes." Baron insists, however, that some of the prophets "belonged to the oppressed classes," but he does not specifically name even one, not even Micah or Amos. Another scholar suggests that Micah "rose from the ranks of the peasants" but adds "if his denunciation of the landlords and the principal officials can be taken as an indication of his status." But by this reasoning Marx and Lenin would end up as proletarians. In the end, Baron (1952, p. 86) contents himself with the conclusion that "whether wealthy or poor, all these preachers safeguarded their independence by refusing to benefit financially from the performance of their duties." So we are left with the question of how they made a living. Even if one believed that Amos was literally a "shepherd" and a "sycamore dresser," he would still have to explain how Micah and Hosea earned their bread. As far as I am aware, the only scholars that have specifically raised this question are Greenberg (1979, p. 101) and, especially, Coote (1981, p. 100).

The outstanding Jewish scholar Kaufmann (1960, pp. 157–58) takes a position similar to those of Pfeiffer and Irwin, but his main concern is quite understandably to combat the Wellhausenist school, which sought to belittle Judaism by suggesting that the Torah is only a later popular formulation of the prophetic teaching. Kaufmann (pp. 158, 162) seeks to demonstrate the "small influence" of the literary prophets in their own age by pointing to the facts that, with the exception of Isaiah, they are not mentioned in the historical books and that they were not advocates of the cultic centralization called for in Deuteronomy. A possible answer to his first point is given in chapter 13. He is probably wrong with respect to the second: Jeremiah actively campaigned for centralization in Anathoth and, as he informs us, it nearly cost him his life (18:18–23).[6] More will be said about the roles of the prophets in part III.

What is a prophet and what is a priest? Who was Amos and what was he trying to accomplish? These questions are taken up in the next two chapters. I would like in advance to acknowledge my intellectual debt to the research of the Uppsala School and Mowinckel.

Notes

1. Translations of JPS(1978) unless otherwise specified; see the bibliographical note chapter 1, note 2.

2. According to Albright (1960, pp. 83–4) Hananiah was a self-styled patriot" who whipped "Judahite chauvanism" into a "frenzy."

3. In verse 23, Jeremiah adds that both patriots "did vile things in Israel, committing adultery with the wives of their fellows". One is immediately reminded of the similar attack directed at the Mosaic priests of Shiloh. According to 1 Samuel the priest Eli's sons, Hophni and Phinehas, were "scoundrels" (2:12) who "lay with the women who ministered at the entrance of the Tent of Meeting" (2:22). And, of course, both men died in battle against the Philistines at Aphek (4:11). It is interesting to note that Jeremiah (7:12) actually refers to the ruins of the Shiloh temple as a warning to his contemporaries.

4. The connection between the prophets and the psalms is explored in chapter 15.

5. The recent finding of a seal impression bearing the inscription "Belonging to Berechiah [or Baruch?] son of Neriah the Scribe" in an "archive amidst bullae of royal scribes . . . seems to indicate that at some time Baruch belonged to the category of royal scribes . . . (Avigad 1979a, p. 118). An additional seal "Belonging to Seraiah son of Neriah" can, perhaps, be identified with the royal minister who carried Jeremiah's oracle of doom to Babylon (51:59; 59:64). According to Avigad (1978, p. 56) Seraiah and Baruch were brothers "and both were close friends of Jeremiah." Note should also be taken here of a seal bearing the inscription "Belonging to Amos the scribe" which may date to the eighth century (Yeivin 1979, fn. 187, p. 339).

6. Why was Huldah rather than the great Jeremiah consulted about the book of the Law found during the repairs of the Temple? (2 Kings 22:13–14) Huldah, it should be noted, advised King Josiah that he would be gathered to his grave "in peace" (2 Kings 22:20; see also chapter 17, note 21). Actually he died in battle, or more likely, he was assassinated. One scholar, A. van den Born (in Vos 1968, p. 185) has commented on several striking similarities between Huldah's language and that of Jeremiah. One can only speculate on the significance of this point.

13 PROPHETIC SYMBOLS AND AMBITIONS

The classical prophets created a new literature of social reform, but it is evident that they were deeply versed not only in the older Israelite literature, but also in the literature, including international treaties, of the entire ancient Near East (McCarthy 1978, pp. 289–90). If we are to gain a deeper understanding of these men, who they were and what their ambitions were, it is necessary to penetrate some of their apparently obscure allusions to ancient traditions. As Hosea (14:9) warned: "Whoever is wise will understand these things; whoever is discerning will know them."[1]

Amos with his notable rhetoric and even more notable paradoxes is the key to positioning the prophets within Israelite society (see Craghan 1972). In the first place, the fact that neither Amos nor Micah is provided with a genealogy does not prove that they were scions of obscure families. Indeed, such an omission might point to their social prominence. "It was the custom of Neo-Babylonian scribes to write the names of very high officials without statement as to ancestry" (Dougherty 1929, pp. 29–30). More important, genealogical concreteness would have clashed with the literary image they were seeking to create. Amos after all was a shepherd or herdsman and a tender of sycamore figs (1:1; 7:14)[2] from a small town, Tekoa (1:1). Micah the Morashite (1:1) apparently came from Moresheth, another small town.[3]

But Amos in addition to his knowledge of ancient literature and world history was, as Beebe (1970, pp. 222–23) points out, a man with a "rich vocabulary" whose "use of the ancient and honored poetic form of balanced lines indicates his facility with Hebrew literary art." "Balance," Beebe adds, "is also registered in the repeated phrases which serve as introductions for new stanzas." Wolff (1973, pp. 10–12) suggests that Amos' "*interrogative form* must be regarded as a style of wisdom rhetoric." Terrien (1976, p. 109) points to the many words and expressions indicating Amos's familiarity with the Israelite wisdom literature as well as his knowledge of astronomy and geography. Watts (1956) detects command over hymnic forms and Würthwin (1950, especially pp. 40ff) is struck by the intimate contact between Amos's accusations and divine law. Strangely, two very sophisticated scholars, H. W. Wolff (1973, p. 56) and Cyrus Gordon (1965a, p. 223), seem to believe that Amos was a simple shepherd who gained his knowledge of international affairs from "caravan personnel" who stopped at the "watering holes frequented by shepherds." Prophets, however, were also referred to as "watchmen." The Lord said to Ezekiel (3:17): "O mortal, I appoint you watchman of the House of Israel." Isaiah (21:6) was told, "Go, set up a watchman [sentry]; let him announce what he sees."[4] Does this mean that Ezekiel and Isaiah learned about politics, literature, and the foreign commerce of Tyre and Egypt by reading scrolls during the long and lonely hours of vigil atop the town walls? Kapelrud (1956, p. 6) puts a halt to this sort of nonsense by observing that to say that Amos was a humble herdsman "would be as if one could say that the poems of T. S. Eliot were written by an uneducated person . . . T. S. Eliot is unthinkable without a long literary and religious tradition behind him. So also is Amos."

As a matter of fact it has been noted in the literature that such occupations as sheep or cattle breeder, wool farmer, shepherd, and herdsman need not be humble, or even wholly secular. During the Ur III period (2112–2004) some individuals describing themselves as "shepherds" (*sipa*) had personal seals (Sollberger 1972, p. 185). The scribe who wrote out the Hittite laws was the grandson of the chief shepherd (Neufeld 1951, p. 69). In the Near East generally, and specifically in eighth-century Assyria it was common business practice for sheep owners to sign written commercial contracts entrusting their flocks to shepherds (Postgate 1974, p. 109). An Assyrian letter (722–625) addressed to the king reports that "Abni, the chief herdsman of the country (around) Arpad, is coming into the presence of my lord. . . . In the matter of sheep my lord may trust him (implicitly)" (R. H. Pfeiffer 1935, p. 106). Further, Near Eastern temples kept large herds of sheep for sacrificial purposes. Ezekiel (36:38) refers to the "sacred flocks . . . the flocks of Jerusalem on its festivals." A Ugaritic text (northern Canaan, ca. fourteenth century B.C.E.) includes the colophon: "The scribe is Il-mahki, the šbn-ite; the student is Atn-prin, chief of the priests and chief of the shepherds (rb. khnm, rb. nqdm), the T'-ite;[5] Nqmd is the king of Ugarit . . . " (Kapelrud 1956, p. 6; see also Ringgren 1973, p. 166). Assyrian archives dating from 808–710 that were found at the governor's palace at Calah (Nimrud) list shepherds and herdsman among the extramural staff of the temple (J. V. K. Wilson 1972, p. 29). According to Kapelrud (1956, p. 6; see also R. Harris 1975, pp. 253–56), Mesopotamian temple herds were under the supervision of a few rabi-buli who had under them several naqidu (shepherds). The latter lived in special towns (like Levites?) and were in charge of the actual herders, the rē'ú.[6] A Neo-Babylonian text dating from the sixth century B.C.E. has King (or coregegent) Belshazzar issuing an order to the chief temple officer at Erech calling for the latter to hand over 2000 sheep to a specified individual for shepherding (Dougherty 1929, p. 131). Shepherds were included among the officials of Hittite temples (Goetze 1969a, p. 210).

Weisberg (1967, pp. 81–8) has even suggested that in seventh-and sixth-century-B.C.E., Babylonia the terms māru and aplu, which are usually translated as "sons" of a particular trade or "member" of a specific guild or, perhaps, I would add "among" the practitioners of an occupation, do not indicate a vocation at all. Instead they refer to an individual's family name, for example, "the family of shepherds" or simply, "Mr. Shepherd." So Amos who was "among" the shepherds (noqedim) of Tekoa (1:1; JPS, 1917) could mean "Mr. Amos Shepherd from Tekoa."

In the Near East, kings and other government officials were sometimes referred to as "shepherds" or "herdsman" (Ringgren 1973, pp. 42, 103). Hammurabi of Babylon (1792–1750 B.C.E.), for example, was the "shepherd named by (the god) Enlil" while Sin-kashid of Uruk (ca. 1850 B.C.E.) was "established a faithful shepherd" by the goddess Nanaya, and Assurbanipal II of Assyria (668–627 B.C.E.) was appointed by the goddess Ishtar to be "Shepherd of Men," and so on. A letter to the same Assurbanipal concerns "the ceremony of the shepherdship" (R. H. Pfeiffer 1935, p. 168) and may refer either to his own (perhaps annual) enthronement or to that of his vassal rulers. The term "herdsman" is applied to Israelite rulers on numerous occasions (see, for example, Jer. 10:21, 23:1, 25:34; Ezek. 34:1–10)[7]. A particularly interesting, if paradoxical, example is provided by 2 Kings 3:4 in which King Mesha of Moab who "used to pay in tribute to the king of Israel the wool of 100,000 lambs and of 100,000 rams" is called a noqed (shepherd). In the Masoretic text of the Jewish Bible the word noqed is used only twice, once in reference to Mesha and the other in reference to Amos (1:1). Elsewhere, for example in Amos 7:14[8] the word boqer is used.[9]

The role of shepherd and herdsman also have definite cultic overtones (Haldar 1945, p. 76). The Lord is a shepherd (for example, Ps. 23:1; Gen. 48:15; Ezek. 34:12–16).[10] Rachel, who is called a shepherdess (Gen. 29:9), later takes the household idols from her father's home (Gen. 31:34). The testament of the patriarch Jacob, who had served as Laban's shepherd (Gen. 31:4–6), includes the passage: "By the hands of the Mighty One of Jacob— There, the Shepherd, the Rock of Israel" (Gen. 49:24). Moses, the great lawgiver, tended the flock of his father-in-law Jethro, the priest of Midian (Exod. 3:1). Moses's wife, the priest Jethro's daughter, Zipporah, performed a circumcison ritual (Exod. 4:25–26). Evidently, the prophet Jeremiah (1:1) "son of Hilkiah, one of the priests of Anathoth" was also a shepherd.[11] He vows (17:16): "But I have not evaded being a shepherd in your service." Moreover, Jeremiah (3:15), while preaching in northern Israel, promises "shepherds after My own heart, who will pasture you with knowledge and skill." Here the word "shepherd" or "herdsman" seems to refer to extra-mural cultic functions—that is, to priestly duties performed not in the Temple of Jerusalem but in the surrounding country. Note in this connection that archaeological excavations at the temples of Arad and Lachish in Judah reveal that they may have remained in use even after their sacrificial altars had been removed, presumably during the reign of Hezekiah. Note further the priests whom King Josiah "brought out of the cities of Judah" when he "defiled the shrines where these priests had been making offerings—from Geba to Beer-sheba" (2 Kings 23:8). A final point is that the word nāweh, which Haran (1978, p. 14) translates as a habitation or abode of shepherds and flocks, is applied to temples (houses of God). He cites in this connection 2 Samuel 15:25, which refers to the abode of the Ark and to Isaiah 33:20.

Now Amos who in fact prophesied at Bethel, (7:13) told "Amaziah the priest of Bethel": "I am [was?] no prophet, neither am [was?] I a prophet's son; but I am [was?] a herdsman . . . "(7:14). Does this mean that Amos was not a priest, that he did not earn his living within the cult?[12] Even if the possible use of the past tense (the statement has no verbs in the Hebrew) is put aside, this is not at all self-evident. Amaziah carefully informs Amos that Bethel "is a king's sanctuary and a royal palace" (7:13) and tells him (7:12) to "eat bread" in Judah. Interestingly, the expression "eat bread" was in use among twentieth century Sinai Arabs for whom akl eysh evidently meant to live at the expense of the government (see Jarvis 1936, p. 170). Although they may date from the Greek period in the fourth century B.C.E., the remarks of Zechariah (13:4–6) seem quite relevant in understanding the true meaning of Amos's denial.

> In that day, every "prophet" will be ashamed of the "visions" (he had) when he "prophesied." In order to deceive, he will not wear a hairy mantle, and he will

[not?] declare, "I am not a 'prophet'; I am a tiller of the soil; you see, I was plied with the red stuff (Hebrew uncertain) from my youth on." And if he is asked, "What are those sores between your arms?" he will reply, "From being beaten in the homes of my friends [for making drunken scenes?]."

Obscure? Very. But it looks very much like an attack on the older ecstatic "prophets" of the Elijah-Elisha type.[13]

It is known that in high Neo-Assyrian circles (eighth–seventh centuries B.C.E.) the behavior of the trancer and ecstatic were viewed as forms of insanity (R. R. Wilson 1980, pp. 103–06). The first trace of this negative attitude in the Israelite literature is found in 1 Kings 22:19–23 where the northern prophet Micaiah ben Imlah claims that the Lord sent a "lying spirit" to deceive all the other prophets and through them King Ahab. This attitude was shared by the classical prophets. Mowinckel (1934, p. 204) translates Hosea 9:7 as follows: "The prophet is a fool (without morality), the man of spirit wild with folly; on account of his great wickedness ... " Note also Micah (2:11): "If a man were to go about uttering windy [related to spirit] and baseless falsehoods; 'I'll preach [prophesy?] to you in favor of wine and liquor' he would be a preacher [acceptable] to that people." Isaiah 28:10 is probably a caricature of the ecstatic prophets, the Hebrew represents a sarcastic reference to a spelling lesson (Hallo 1958, pp. 37–8) or meaningless baby-talk. Finally, Jeremiah 5:13: "The prophets shall prove mere wind [related to spirit] for the word is not in them." Of course, Amos in spite of his denials of ecstasy did, in fact, claim to have experienced visions (see 7:1–9, 8:1–11, 9:1). Indeed, it is difficult to see how he could have hoped to transform the "God of the Fathers," Israel's only protector in a hostile, tribalized (that is, ethnically unified) world, into a God of Universalism and Social Justice without some sort of direct contact with God Himself (see Gitay 1980, p. 299). However, the same visions that may have increased his credibility among the less-educated Israelites made him vulnerable to the ridicule of his educated competitors. Amos's outstanding rhetorical skills[14] helped to persuade the doubters that he was one of their own. Still, the sophisticated priest Amaziah ("Yahweh is strong") did not miss the opportunity to link Amos with the "madmen of wind." In 7:12, Amaziah calls Amos a "seer" (hozeh), a term that has ecstatic overtones and that, according to Zevit (1975, pp. 788–89), refers to "an institution which first appeared in Israel after the establishment of the monarchy in the tenth century [and] may have been borrowed from a cognate language spoken in a neighboring country where the institution already existed." At the same time, Amaziah told Amos not to "drip" (or drool?) against the house of Isaac (7:16) and advised him to take his foreign method of prophesying to (backward?) Judah (7:12). It appears to me that Amos defended himself against the charge of being an ecstatic prophet (visionary) by asserting that he was not a prophet, it was just that he had experienced a vision in which the Lord told him: "Go prophesy to My people Israel",[15] that is, he claimed he had been told to tell the people the meaning of what he had seen in his visions.[16] Amaziah's retort is not recorded.[17]

We must not overlook Amos's other occupation, that of "tender" or "dresser" of the sycamore fig tree (7:14). It is a large tree also known as the mulberry fig. Its rounded masses of foliage, I understand, provide dense shade and are so widespreading that from a distance one tree may give the impression of several. Again multiple meanings present themselves. Shepherds or herdsman can refer to a civilian occupation or to a royal official, and so also can sycamore tender. In 1 Chronicles 27:28 is the report that under King David an official was specifically charged with oversight of the royal olive and sycamore plantations.[18] On the other hand, pinching or puncturing each sycamore fig while it was still green shortened the ripening process, increased the number and size of the fruits, and enhanced edibility by permitting the escape of astringent juices (Bertholet 1926, p. 202). Again just as shepherd and herdsman can be a cultic functionary so can a sycamore tender. In Greece, around the turn of the first millennium B.C.E., the god Apollo spoke to his prophets at Pytho (Delphi) from a laurel tree, while at Dodona, Zeus utilized an oak. The gods provided oracles to their servants, the tenders of the trees, presumably, by rustling the leaves (Parke and Wormell 1956, pp. 3, 25). The oracles were, in turn, expounded by the sanctuary personnel. At Claros the latter included a *thespiodos* or religious poet who cast the utterances of the prophet into poetic form (Mireaux 1960, pp. 84–5). The Greek word *prophētēs* can be literally translated "he who stands (or speaks) in front of". Östborn (1945, p. 25) and other scholars have suggested that in early Israel "*tōrā* consisted in part of 'signs,' *omina* from holy trees, or was based on such."

Strong support for this hypothesis is provided by analysis of Genesis 12, Judges 4, 6, and 9, and Deuteronomy 11. In Genesis 12:6–7, Abram arrives at the site of Shechem and there, "at the terebinth of Moreh,"[19] the Lord appears to him and says, "I will give this land to your offspring." Abram builds an altar at Shechem and then departs. In Deuteronomy 11:29–30, the Lord instructs the Israelites that when they enter Israel they "shall pronounce the blessing at Mount Gerizim and the curse at Mount Ebal.—Both are on the west side of the Jordan, toward the setting sun, in the land of the Canaanites who dwell in the Arabah, near Gilgal, by the terebinths of Moreh". Judges 9:6 has Abimelech made king at Shechem "by the oak of the pillar,"[20] while 9:37 refers to the "tree of the soothsayers." Judges 4:4–5 tells that the "prophetess" Deborah "sat under the palm-tree of Deborah between Ramah and Bethel in the hill country of Ephraim; and the children of Israel came to her for judgment."[21] In verses 6–7 she commissions Barak the son of Abinoam to rescue Israel from the hand of the Canaanite King Jabin. (Palm trees are also prominent in Ezekiel's vision of the Temple [40:26, 34; 41:20].) In the Gideon narrative the Lord's messenger (angel) sat under a terebinth (Judges 6:11) and gave Gideon, a king (Jud. 8:18), the commission to deliver Israel from the hand of Midian (Jud. 6:14). Saul also sat under trees and in one case, at least, he was accompanied by a priest wearing an ephod (1 Sam. 14:2–3; 22:6). Note also Hosea 4:12 "My people ask counsel at their stock [literally "wood" or "tree"], and their staff declareth unto them."[22] Östborn (1945) points out that while *allon* is usually translated "terebinth" or "oak" it probably means no more than "large trees." For Hammershaimb (1970, p. 5) such words "mean originally 'a large tree in which a divinity dwells'." Thus the "large tree" itself "or else a person owning or tending the tree[23] (the latter opinion seems to be more common), would thus be '*tōrā*-yieldings' . . . One is here justified in speaking of *tōrā* communicated by a god . . . " (Östborn 1945, pp. 25–6).[24] This is not all.

In 2 Samuel 5:22–25, the oracles of the sycamore fig[25] are explicitly stated to have been instrumental in King David's great victory over the Philistines in the Valley of Rephaim:

> And when David inquired of the Lord, He said: "Thou shalt not go up; make a circuit behind them, and come upon them over against the mulberry trees. And it shall be, when thou hearest the sound of marching in the tops of the mulberry trees, then thou shalt bestir thyself; for then is the Lord gone out before thee to smite the host of the Philistines.[26]

Of course, David did as he was told and he "smote the Philistines from Geba unto Gezer." The Septuagint (Thomson) makes no mention of mulberry trees:

> And when David inquired of the Lord, the Lord said, Thou shalt not go up to meet them in front, wheel about from them, and come upon them near Wailing. And when thou hearest the sound of rustling in the grove of Wailing, then thou shalt go down against them.

But where is "Wailing"? The Masoretic text is silent but the Septuagint rendering of Judges 2:1 identifies it as Bethel. Further, Genesis 35:8 informs us that "Deborah, Rebecca's nurse died, and she was buried below Bethel under the oak; and the name of it was called the oak of wailing" (*allon-bacuth*). By calling himself a sycamore tender, Amos identifies himself as a savior of Israel. If his oracles are heeded the Israelites will be permitted to abide in the Promised Land. He also seems to link himself with the cult and, more specifically, with the Bethel cult or, possibly, that of Shechem.

The switch from shepherd (*noqed*) in Amos 1:1 to herdsman (*boqer*) in Amos 7:14 is sometimes taken as an error. This indeed may be the case. On the other hand, it may provide additional evidence linking Amos with the cult. Sigmund Mowinckel (cited in Rowley 1967, pp. 158–59) sees the word as a reference to sacrificing for omens. Before examining his reasoning let us review the procedure of the Mesopotamian *bārûs*. R. R. Wilson (1980, pp. 95–6; see also Hallo and Simpson 1971, pp. 158–63) who studied texts of the Assyrian kings Esarhaddon and Assurbanipal (680–627 B.C.E.) dealing with extispicy, lists the following steps:

1. A question is posed to the gods through the diviner.
2. A prayer is offered asking that a favorable omen be placed in the midst of the sacrificial sheep.
3. A sheep is sacrificed.
4. With the aid of standardized rules the exta (sheep entrails) are studied for omens.[27]

Returning to Mowinckel's views, he sees *bōḵēr* in the word *bōḵer* (morning) in Psalm 5: "In the morning will I order my prayer unto Thee, and I will look forward." (verse 4, JPS 1917); "In the morning thou shalt hear my voice: in the morning I will wait on Thee and look up." (verse 3, Thomson); "O Lord, in the morning thou dost hear my voice; in the morning I prepare a sacrifice for thee and watch." (verse 3, Inter. IV). Mowinckel also takes the word "seek" (*bikkēr*) in Psalm 27:4, ("One thing I have asked of the Lord, that I will seek after", to mean "find out the token" or "take omens." All this is, of course, rather speculative but it is not inconsistent with the concept of prophet as "watchman":

> Ephraim watches for my God. As for the prophet, fowlers' snares are on all his paths, harassment in the House of his Lord. (Hosea 9:8; JPS, 1978)

> Ephraim was a watchman with God, [but that] prophet was a cunning snare in all his ways; they made madness in a house of God; . . . " (Hosea 9:8; Thomson)

> "O mortal, I appoint you watchman for the House of Israel." (Ezekiel 3:17)

A final point of some interest is that Bic (1951), basing his conclusion primarily on a piece of Akkadian evidence, suggests that the title *noqed* is also related to divination. Murtonen (1952, pp. 170–71), however, disagrees and offers an alternative line of explanation:

The meaning of the Akkadian sentence upon which his theory is based is quite uncertain, as Bic himself says. The puncturing of the liver is, in my opinion, best explained by supposing that it means its preparation for the examination, e.g. by means of dividing it into various areas. In any case the shifting of the meaning from "puncturing" to "divination" is too great to be supposed without any intermediate phase between them. . . . The meaning of "sheep-raiser" is very easy to derive from the original meaning of the root *nqd* "to puncture". We know from the OT that the ancient Israelites marked their slaves with an aul (Ex. 21:6). What is more natural than to suppose that they marked also their sheep and other animals in an analogous way to distinguish them from those of other cattle raisers? The meaning of the root *nqd* fits very well the sense of such a marking. . . . [Further], in Arabic *naqqad* means without doubt "shepherd", the word being the denominative from *naqad* "a kind of sheep".

Perhaps Murtonen is correct in insisting that Bic's "puncturing" is unrelated to divination but he downplays the relevance of the Ugaritic Personnel Lists that seem to link *khnm* with *nqdm* and he seems unaware of the evidence indicating that a "sycamore tender" may not be a "gardener."

Shepherd-herdsman, sycamore tender-dresser, the Bethel cult, salvation, and the king are linked on another level. In the Bible "shepherd" has the deeper sense of help and protection. The sycamore fig (*nht*) is a symbol of welfare in Egyptian mythology. Indeed, when it is written with the house terminative instead of the tree it means "refuge" (Buhl 1947, p. 80). The deep roots of the sycamore fig allow it to flourish, as if by a miracle, at the edge of the desert. (Note Hosea 9:10: "Your fathers seemed to Me like a ripe fig in a waterless waste.") Not surprisingly it is associated with ideas of salvation and of the hereafter. "The soul (ba) of the deceased . . . was allowed like the gods to sit on the branches of the sacred [sycamore] tree" (Buhl 1947, p. 89). The latter were pictured as being "like shepherds sitting at the edge of the [heavenly] pastures." (Kees 1961, p. 79). The goddess Nut was depicted rising from a sycamore tree extending her arms toward the deceased with a tray of food in one hand and, in the other, a jar pouring streams of water into the hands of the deceased or his wife. Another goddess, Hathor, was portrayed in a sycamore tree holding a basket of figs in one hand and with the other pouring several streams of water from a vase for a ba-bird (soul bird) with a human head on the ground below (Buhl 1947, pp. 91–5). The tomb of Osiris was also associated with a sycamore tree (De Vaux 1971, p. 216).[28]

Note that Amos 5:16 may associate the herdsman with mortuary rituals: "Assuredly, thus said the Lord . . . In every square there shall be lamenting, in every street cries of 'Ah, woe!' and the farmhand shall be called to mourn, and those skilled in wailing to lament." Here the "farmhand" or "husbandmen" or, perhaps, "herdsman" clearly plays a cultic role in mourning the deceased (see Worden 1953, p. 290 cn lamentation rites).

The goddess of the sycamore guided the deceased into a world in which he not only continued his earthly life but enjoyed a higher standard of living. The sycamore, however, also protected the living: "shepherds . . . [placed] a loaf and a jar of water under [the] tree [in order] to escape the wrath of the goddess who dwelt in it, and who might afflict the household with sickness in her wrath" (Breasted 1912, p. 341). While the Israelites apparently rejected immortality they did recognize a "tree of life." In Genesis 3:22, the Lord said: "Now that man has become like one of us, knowing good and bad, what if he should stretch out his hand and take from the tree of life, and live forever."[29] Moreover, both the Egyptian and Israelite religions stressed purity and the purifying properties of water. The Egyptian ideogram of the priest who cleanses is a vase from which water flowed. Aaron and his sons were consecrated as priests by being washed with water (Exod. 29:4). Water cleaned away what was unacceptable to God and revitalized the individual being purified. The Egyptian king could not act as high priest until he had been purified by two priests representing the gods Horus and Seth. The water that they poured down on the king consisted of a stream of hieroglyphs of life (Bleeker 1966, pp. 86–7; Witt 1971, p. 88).

Genesis 41:45 has Joseph married to the daughter of the priest of On (Heliopolis). On was the capital of Egypt's thirteenth nome, called the "Shepherd of Prosperity" or the "Prosperous Shepherd." The walls of the temple at Gurneh at the site of On portray three gods writing (or dressing?) the name of King Ramses on the fruits and leaves of On's sacred sycamore (Barton 1934, pp. 127, 191).[30] The intention was to provide the ruler with a long life. In Jewish tradition "the king carries a branch from the Tree of Life as a sign of his possession of Life and his distribution of Life"[31] (Widengren 1963, pp. 205–6).

A great deal more can be learned about Amos's intentions and techniques from a consideration of the popular Egyptian tale of the "Eloquent Peasant." First of all, as Erman (1927, p. 116) points out, calling the hero of the tale the "peasant" is only a custom and terms such as "dweller in the wilderness" (or herdsman?) are more accurate. The story which probably dates from the Twelfth Dynasty (ca. 2000 B.C.E.), begins with a peasant leading some donkeys with the produce of his village (called the Salt-Field) and traveling to Heracleopolis to trade for grain. On the way he must pass the estate of Thutenakht, a subordinate official of Rensi the grand steward of the Pharaoh. Thutenakht sees the approach of the peasant and devises a plan for seizing the donkeys. He has pieces of linen spread out across the public highway from the water of the canal on the lower side to the edge of his grain field on the upper side. Finding his way blocked and fearing the water below, the peasant turns upward and skirts the edge of the grain field. Just as Thutenakht planned, one of the donkeys bites off a mouthful of grain. When he emerges from his hiding place leveling accusations "the peasant pathetically maintains the attitude and the speech of deprecatory but not servile courtesy, until with loud complaint Thutenakht seizes the asses" (Breasted 1912, pp. 217–18).

Before continuing with the story let us note its evident connection with Amos 2:7: "Ah, you who trample the heads of the poor into the dust of the ground, and make the humble walk a twisted course!" Emendation yields: "Who crush on the ground the heads of the poor, and push off the road the humble of the land."[32]

Returning to the story we find in Simpson (1972, pp. 31–49) that the peasant appeals to the grand steward Rensi, whom he refers to as "father of the orphan, a brother to her who is divorced, a garment to the motherless; let me make your name in this land [in accord with] every good law . . . a magnate who destroys falsehood and fosters truth, and comes at the voice of the caller." Upon hearing this Rensi tells the Pharaoh, "My lord, I have found one of those peasants who is really eloquent." Pharaoh orders that "his speech be brought to us in writing that we may hear it." The peasant makes some eight appeals, which are written down and brought to Pharaoh. Note how this story provides a rationalization for a major innovation of the eighth–seventh century-Israelite prophets, that of written prophecy or books. Prophecy is written so that the king may "hear it."[33] As Jeremiah was well aware written prophecy was also considerably safer for the prophet than appearances in the flesh. In the midst of a terrible drought (Jer. 14:1–6) when the entire Judean community was fasting and the leaders were gathered in the Temple to pray, Jeremiah "commanded Baruch, saying, "I am detained [in hiding?]; I cannot go into the house of the Lord. Therefore go thou, and read the roll which thou hast written from my mouth the words of the Lord in the ears of the people in the Lord's house upon the fasting day, and also thou shalt read them in the ears of all Judah that come out of their cities'." (Jer. 36:5–6). We learn what he wrote in Jeremiah 14:11–12: "Then said the Lord unto me, pray not for this people for their good. When they fast, I will not hear their cry; and when they offer burnt offering as an oblation, I will not accept them. But I will consume them by the sword, and by the famine, and by the pestilence" (see Hoschander 1938, pp. 91–4). Is is any wonder the prophet was indisposed? Again in Jeremiah 36:19, Baruch reads Jeremiah's prophesies to the nobles and elders who instruct him to take Jeremiah and hide before they read the scroll to the king.

Let us again return to the story and to the content of several of the peasant's appeals. "Restrain the robber, take counsel for the poor man, do not become an innudation against the petitioner. Beware of the approach of eternity; will to live long according to the saying: 'The doing of justice is the breath of the nose" (third appeal). (Note in this connection King Shabaka's inscription in the later eighth century B.C.E.: "Justice means life" [Morenz 1973, pp. 57, 116]) "O grand Steward my Lord! [Destroy] falsehood, bring about justice" (sixth appeal). "Seek justice and do justice, for it is mighty . . . and it leads to the blessed state . . . " (eighth appeal).

Note in connection with the Egyptian material the following passages in Amos:

Seek the Lord, and you will live . . . (5:6)

Seek good and not evil, that you may live, and the Lord, the God of Hosts, may truly be with you as you think. (5:14)

But let justice well up like water. Righteousness like an everflowing stream. (5:24)[34]

This is what my Lord God showed me: There was a basket of figs. He said, "What do you see, Amos?" A basket of figs, I replied. And the Lord said to me: "The hour of doom has come for My people of Israel; I will not pardon them again. (8:1–2; see also Jeremiah 24)

Add to this Hosea 10:12: "Sow for yourselves for righteousness; gather in the fruit of life. Light up for yourselves the light of knowledge. Seek the Lord until the fruits of righteousness come to you."[35] Were these lessons addressed primarily to Israelite kings? I believe so. A hint of support is provided by Genesis 20:7 which is usually taken to be late and is attributed to the Elohistic-source (see Plaut 1974, p. 36; Orlinsky 174, p. 59). King Ahimelech of Gerar who had taken Sarah without knowing she was Abraham's wife is told by God in a dream: "But you must restore the man's wife—since he is a prophet [navi'], he will intercede for you to save your life."

We have provided a great deal of data linking Amos's occupational identifications with cultic functions. Now, at last, we begin to concentrate on his objectives by combining the Sethite genealogy in Genesis 5, Micah 5:4, and a Sumerian-king list. According to Mesopotamian mythology, seven apkallus[36] (angels, sages, or seers) taught the eight primeval kings that reigned before the flood the seven attributes of kingship. King number five is Dumuzi "the shepherd" while king number six is Ensipazianna. The latter name A. T. Clay (1923, p. 143) translates to mean "the shepherd who was taken to heaven" or "who was taken by the god El." Now Micah 5:4 states that should Assyria invade Israel's soil "then shall we raise against him seven shepherds and eight principal men [princes? first-born?]". Now with respect to the eight principal men we can refer to Genesis 5, which lists the line of Adam up to the flood in the time of Noah as Seth, Enosh, Kenan, Mehalalel, Jared, Enoch, Methuselah, and Lamech, for a total of eight. Of Enoch, number six on the list corresponding to Ensipazianna,[37] Genesis 5:24 tells us: "Enoch ealked with God; then he was no more, for God took him." Note first that H. H. Cohen (1974, pp. 124–25) citing the "walking" of Samuel and Israelite kings (1 Sam. 12:1–3; 2 Kings 20:3) plausibly infers that the term "should be understood as meaning the execution of the responsibilities of one's office." Thus Enoch, and Noah after him (Gen. 6:9), "played the special role of God's agent". Second, in the extrabiblical Jewish tradition, Enoch had visions, gained much knowledge of heaven and earth, and was able to fortell the future. In the *Testaments of the Twelve Patriarchs*, especially *Testament Levi*, reference is made to the enthronment ritual of Jewish Hasmonaean priest-kings during the Hellenistic-Roman period (see Widengren 1963, pp. 202–4). One passage reads, "And I saw seven men in white saying unto me: "Arise put on the robe of priesthood, and the crown of righteousness, and the breast plate of understanding, and the garment of truth, and the plate of faith, and the turban of justice, and the ephod of prophecy."

Here we have seven attributes of kingship. Are the seven "men in white" Micah's "seven shepherds"? I believe so. This would mean that a "shepherd" (the counterpart of the Mesopotamian *apkallu*) has knowledge of earth and heaven and is an advisor to kings.

Even so, is a Hasmonaean ritual relevant for preexilic kingship? Surely such rituals may have been preserved just as various biblical writings were. More concretely, two pieces of evidence may be cited. First, the list of seven sacred garments matches those of the high priest in Exodus 28 of the Septuagint. Second, Ezekiel (8:3) tells of how "a spirit lifted me up between heaven and earth and brought me in visions of God to Jerusalem."

We come still closer to Amos and to the other prophets of social reform by considering a tablet ("Advice to a Prince") found in the library of the Assyrian king Assurbanipal (668–627) which certainly dates between 1000 and 700 and, most likely, to the last quarter of the eighth century (see Diakonoff 1965): "If the king does not give heed to justice, his people will come into anarchy and his land will go to ruin. If he does not give heed to justice in his land, Ea, the lord of fates, will alter his fate and bring another [fate] for him. If he does not give heed to his *apkallu*, his days will be cut off." (Langdon 1907, p. 150; see also Lambert 1960, pp. 110–15) Note first of all that in Isaiah 3:1–12 anarchy is also the result of social injustice. Now, *apkallu* (or *abgallu*) means, as shown above, "great teacher" or "advisor."[38] The tablet goes on to name the god Marduk "*apkallu* of the gods." In Mesopotamia the governments of men and gods had to be congruent (Speiser 1967, pp. 278–79). Marduk advised the gods and his priest advised the king.[39] Moreover, the title *apkallu* is known to have been "applied to certain types of priests and diviners" (R. R. Wilson 1977, p. 149). In epics of most ancient Egypt, the "chief lector priest and scribe" was the consultant of kings and a great magician (Simpson 1972, p. 18). Note also the "viziers" who authored moralistic "instructions" and "admonitions" for the pharaohs (see for instance Breasted 1912, pp. 204–16). More specifically, Genesis 45:8 explicitly states that the Lord made Joseph the *'abh* ("father") to Pharaoh.[40] This ties in nicely with the tale of Ahiqar recorded in a fifth-century-B.C.E. Aramaic text found at Elephantine, the site of a Jewish colony in Upper Egypt. In the story Ahiqar is described as a "wise scribe" and called "the father of all Assyria, by whose counsel King Sennacherib [688–681] and all the host of Assyria were guided." Ginsberg (1969, p. 427) suggests that Ahiqar "may be a reflex of Adadšumuṣer, a priest who officiated in the reigns of Sennacherib and Esarhaddon and exerted a certain amount of influence over them."[41] Ahiqar is attested to as *ummânu* (apparently an alternative term to *apkallu*), of Esarhaddon by a cuneiform text from Urak dated 165 B.C.E., published and discussed by Van Dijk (1962, especially p. 45). The *apkallu* tradition was also known in Phoenicia (R. R. Wilson 1977, pp. 152–54).

While the Bible certainly includes references to a divine council (see, for instance, Deut. 32:8; 1 Kings 22:19–22; Isa. 6; Ps. 82, 89, and 95) there is no reasonably clear reference to an office of "divine counsellor" (or the like) whether filled by a subordinate god or by Yahweh himself (see Whybray 1971, especially pp. 44–5, 66–77). Nevertheless, even if its theological or mythological rationale is absent (censored?), the reflections at the Israelite royal court of an *apkallu*-like office (hereafter *apkallu*) are unmistakable. First of all, the qualifications of Israelite priests to play a scribal role in the royal government are attested to by Ben Sira (Ecclesiasticus 38–39 in the Apocrypha) who wrote in ca. 190 B.C.E. that:

> He who devotes himself to the study of the law of the Most High will seek out the wisdom of all the ancients, and will be concerned with prophecies; he will preserve the discourse of notable men and penetrate the subtelties of parables; he will seek out the hidden meanings of proverbs and be at home with the obscurities of parables. He will serve among great men and appear before rulers; he will travel through the lands of foreign nations, for he tests the good and the evil among men. He will set his heart to rise early to seek the Lord who made him, and he will make supplication before the Most High: he will open his mouth in prayer and make supplication for his sins. (in Heaton 1968, p. 171).

In considering whether Israelite kings had an *apkallu* several names come immediately to mind: Samuel, Nathan, Gad, Elisha, Jehoiada, Jonah the son of Amittai ("the true one"), and, for that matter, what of Jonathan the Levite who served Micah, a personage of some importance (see Judg. 18:22), as "a father and a priest" (Judg. 17:10)? Further, 2 Chronicles 25:15 tells how after King Amaziah of Judah had defeated the Edomites, he brought their gods home: "The anger of Yahweh blazed against Amaziah and he sent a prophet to him who said to him, 'Why do you inquire of the gods of the people who could not even deliver their own people from your hand?' While he was still speaking to him, he said, 'Have we made you a royal adviser? Stop, or you will be struck down!' " Evidently, as R. T. Anderson (1960, p. 57) notes, prophetic utterances were expected of royal counselors. Amaziah's son, Uzziah, was guided by Zechariah "who had understanding in the vision of God" (2 Chron. 26:5). The Chronicler provides ample evidence of prophets and seers who wrote histories of various kings (see chapter 14). Even King Manasseh reportedly had several seers whose oracles are "in the records of the kings of Israel" (2 Chron. 33:18). Shemaiah the "prophet" who was an author of King Rehoboam's history (2 Chron. 12:15) was also the "man of God" ('*ish ha-'Elohim*; 1 Kings 12:22–24) who, after the northern tribes had rejected Rehoboam's kingship, told him: "Thus said the Lord: You shall not set out to make war on your kinsmen the Israelites. Let every man return to his home for this thing has been brought about by Me." The narrative in 1 Kings 12:24 continues, "They heeded the word of the Lord and turned back . . . " Evidently Shemaiah was Rehoboam's *apkallu* (man of God?) while the "prophet Ahijah of Shiloh" played the same role for his northern rival Jeroboam son of Nebat (1 Kings 11:29–39; but see also 14:1–20). Elisha, "the man of God," is called "father" by the kings of Israel whom he advises (2 Kings 5:8; 6:21; 13:14). It seems quite possible that "Gemariah son of Shaphan the scribe" was *apkallu* during the reign of Josiah's son, Jehoiakim. In Jeremiah 36:10 we are told that this individual has a chamber in the Temple, while in 36:11–12, the list of all the officials who were in session in the "chamber of the scribe" in the king's palace includes the same Gemariah son of Shaphan. He is not given a specific title, but Elishama is called "the scribe."

Isaiah himself is reported to have composed royal records of Uzziah and Hezekiah (2 Chron. 26:22; 32:32). Further, in 2 Kings 20:11, Isaiah moves a shadow, and in 20:7 he cures King Hezekiah who was dangerously ill by applying a "cake of figs" to his rash.[42] These are the kinds of miracles associated with Egyptian "chief lector priests and scribes." Moreover, Mesopotamian medical texts attribute various remedies to the *apkallus* (R. R. Wilson 1977, p. 149). It is not unreasonable to assume that Isaiah spent parts of his career as an *apkallu*, while Amos, at least, sought to become one.

(Perhaps the reason that Isaiah is the only classical prophet mentioned by name in Kings is that he was the only one who actually held this office for a Judean king.)[43] The reality of Amos's ambition is supported by the biblical story of Joseph which at the same time confirms that Amos's political objective involved socioeconomic reform. In support of this hypothesis note first of all that the cycle of Joseph stories that concludes Genesis may actually be dated, at least roughly, to the Amos era. Hallo (1980, p. 17) points out that:

> The cycle has long proved troublesome to all interpretations of Israelite historiography because (with the exception of some intrusive elements such as the story of Judah and Tamar in Gen. 38[44] it resists facile literary analysis into separate strands which would link it to those identified by one means or another elsewhere in Genesis or the tetrateuch. On the contrary, it contains late technical terms—neo-Assyrian or Saite—and late literary motifs which call into question its ostensible early Egyptian coloring and literary models. It seems then, to constitute a discrete literary unit best described as a novella which was only slightly modified in order to be ingeniously inserted into the seam between the (primeval and patriarchal) traditions of Genesis and the more vivid memories of the oppression.

With respect to the question of literary motifs alluded to by Hallo, note should be taken next of Redford's (1970, pp. 96–100) outline of the standard story line in ancient Egypt and the Near East: (1) a savior appears who is the only hope for the kingdom; (2) the savior is disgraced and rehabilitated; (3) the savior is slain by wild animals (or said to be). The savior, it should be noted, is often a high government official: "The wise vizier, whose wisdom his king has not heeded, . . . when a need arises for him he will be reinstated" (Reiner 1961, pp. 7–8).

In the Joseph story, it will be remembered, "at seventeen years of age, Joseph tended the flocks with his brothers" (Gen. 37:2). However, Joseph seems to have been a shepherd who had little to do with sheep. While his brothers are pasturing the flock at Shechem, his father, Israel, tells Joseph, "Go and see how your brothers are and how the flocks are faring, and bring me back word" (Gen. 37:12–14). Indeed, earlier in Genesis 37:2, we are informed that Joseph "brought bad reports of them [his brothers] to their father." Joseph's "dreams" (or visions) in Genesis 37:5–10 reveal that he will rule over his parents and brothers. Redford (1970, pp. 15–16) adds that verse 2, which has Joseph tending the flocks, is semantically a double entendre and means "to shepherd the human flock, to rule." So Joseph's credentials as a savior have been established. In Genesis 37:28, Joseph's brothers sell him into slavery.[45]

Once in Egypt, Joseph is disgraced, that is, placed in Pharaoh's dungeon (Gen. 39:19–23). His God-given ability to interpret dreams once again establishes Joseph's credentials as a savior (see Niditch and Doran 1977, p. 187). Ultimately he is released from prison, that is, rehabilitated, and appears before Pharaoh (Gen. 41) to interpret his dreams. Interestingly, Joseph, like the Mesopotamian *bārū* priests both interpreted dreams and received revelations by their means. Pharaoh then recognizes that Joseph is a savior and installs him as the highest official in the nation (Gen. 41:40).[46] Significantly, Joseph's seven-year plan for national salvation calls for the Egyptian state to institute a drastic economic reorganization during a period of prosperity.

> God has revealed to Pharaoh what He is about to do. Immediately ahead are seven years of great abundance in all the land of Egypt. After them will come seven years of famine, and all the abundance of the land of Egypt will be forgotten. . . . Accordingly, let Pharaoh find a man of discernment and wisdom, and set him over the land of Egypt. And let Pharaoh take steps to appoint overseers over the land, and organize (or take a fifth part of) the land of Egypt in the seven years of plenty. Let all the food of these good years that are coming be gathered, and let the grain be collected under Pharaoh's authority as food to be stored in the cities. Let that food be a reserve for the seven years of famine which will come upon the land of Egypt, so that the land may not perish in the famine. (Gen. 41:28–36)

Of course, as in the dreams of economic advisers, the reform not only worked, but also enriched the ruler. In Genesis 47:20–26 Joseph trades the stored grain for land, excluding temple estates, and Pharaoh emerges as the landlord of Egypt.[47,48]

While the parallel is far from complete, it appears that Amos is also a national savior who interprets visions. He is disgraced by being dismissed from cultic participation at Bethel. But did he win rehabilitation and become King Jeroboam's *apkallu*? In order to answer this question it is necessary first of all to note with Staples (1966, p. 112) that the "writing prophets" show striking parallels with the epic literature of Mesopotamia. Therefore we must not be misled by "the rejection of the 'writing prophets' by their age, and [by] the prophetic view of inevitable calamity, these are literary motifs derived from the epic rather than historical facts." Second, we have some biblical evidence that bears directly on the question of what happened to Amos. The narrative in 1 Kings 12 has the northern tribes rejecting the kingship of Solomon's son, Rehoboam, and proclaiming Jeroboam I as their king. The chapter ends with Jeroboam setting up calves and non-Levitic priests at the Dan and Bethel sanctuaries. In the next chapter a "man of God arrived at Bethel from Judah" (1 Kings 13:1). This "man of God" tells Jeroboam who is standing on or by the altar: "O altar, altar! Thus said the Lord: a son shall be born to the House of David, Josiah by name; and he shall slaughter upon you the priests of the shrines who bring offerings upon you. And human bones shall be burned upon you" (verses 1–2). The "man of God" offers as a portent that "this altar shall break apart, and the ashes in it shall be spilled" (v. 3). Note that in Amos 9:1 the prophet sees the Lord, who, "standing by the altar" threatens the destruction of the Bethel sanctuary and its personnel.[49] After the altar breaks apart, Jeroboam invites the "man of God" to "come with me to my home and I will give you a gift." But he refuses and departs Bethel (verses 5–10). However, he is pursued by "an old prophet living in Bethel" who finding the "man of God" sitting under a *terebinth* invites him to "Come home with me and eat bread," assures him that "I am also a prophet [*navi'*] just as you are" and, ultimately, convinces him to return. (verses 11–19). This return violated the Lord's command and he was therefore told: "Your corpse shall not come to the grave of your fathers" (v. 22). So on the road out of Bethel the "man of God" was killed by a lion[50] (v. 24) and his corpse was placed in the tomb of the "old prophet living in Bethel" (v. 30). The latter told his sons, "when I die bury me in the grave where the man of God lies buried; lay my bones beside his" (v. 31). In 2 Kings 23:15–16, King Josiah defiles the graves and altar of Bethel. An exception is made, however, for the grave of the "man of God who came from Judah" whose bones were "together with the bones of the prophet who came from Samaria" (verses 17–18).

As I understand all this, the "man of God from Judah" and the "old prophet living in Bethel" had their bones mixed together because they were one and the same person, namely Amos. Eissfeldt (cited in Lemke 1976, fn. 94, p. 325), it should be noted, believes that 1 Kings 13 preserves information not found in the Book of Amos and that the tomb of the unknown prophet was the tomb of Amos. I would conjecture that Amos stayed in Bethel and "ate bread"—that is, he served Jeroboam II as his *apkallu*. By the time he died and was buried at Bethel he was indeed the old prophet. This hypothesis is at least consistent with the fact that the book of Amos ends not with the prophet's confrontation with the priest Amaziah, but with some rather optimistic verses.[51] It is also consistent with the relatively favorable portrayal of Jeroboam II in 2 Kings 14:27: "And the Lord said not that he would blot out the name of Israel from under heaven, but He saved them by the hand of Jeroboam the son of Joash." The story of his death at the hands of a lion helps to explain why Amos the first and greatest social reformer was buried in the idolatrous cemetery at Bethel. It may also help to explain away the failure of Amos's reforms (he somehow disobeyed the Lord) and the consequent turmoil and ultimate destruction of the northern kingdom. Note, finally, that Joseph was not really killed by a wild beast (Gen. 37:33).

If indeed Amos is the "man of God" he may very well have come from

Judah, but certainly not from Tekoa. The prophet Samuel who was a "man of god" (1 Sam. 9:6–10) had a vision (or dream) at the Shiloh sanctuary (1 Sam 3:15) during an era in which "there was no frequent vision." We are told that Samuel "judged Israel as long as he lived. Each year he made the rounds of Bethel, Gilgal, and Mizpah, and acted as judge over Israel at all these places" (1 Sam. 7:15–16).[52] And Samuel's "sons" Joel and Abijah "sat as judges in Beer-sheba" (1 Sam. 8:2). This raises the possibility that members of Samuel's house continued to serve as "men of God" or "messengers of God" making the rounds from Beer-sheba in Judah to Bethel in Israel, and other places. What I am suggesting is that, just as Ramah served as Samuel's home base (1 Sam. 7:17), so Beer-sheba could have been Amos's. Amos (5:5 and 8:14) in fact twice refers to such pilgrimages (*haggim* or processional circuits): "Do not seek Bethel, nor go to Gilgal, nor cross over to Beer-sheba;" and "Those who swear by the guilt of Samaria, saying, 'As your god lives, Dan', and 'As the way to Beer-sheba lives' they shall fall to rise no more." Terrien (1976, p. 113) points out that Amos was the only prophet to refer to Beer-sheba.[53] Further, while Amos threatens Bethel and Gilgal, no explicit threat is directed at Beer-sheba. Also Joseph, whose career may well mirror Amos's ambitions, is from Beer-sheba. Joseph's father Israel (Jacob) worships and experiences a vision at Beer-sheba before journeying to Egypt (Gen. 46). This, taken together with various details of Genesis 37, suggests that the author of the Joseph story placed the patriarch's homestead in Beer-sheba (see Redford 1970, p. 21).[54] To the extent that the biblical attack on Samuel's sons ("they were bent on gain, they accepted bribes, and they subverted justice," (1 Samuel 8:3) reflects the rejection of Samuel's house by the Davidic monarchy, Amos would not have had much chance to "eat bread" at the Judean court.[55] Finally, a sacred tree is mentioned at Beer-sheba (Gen. 21:33).

Amos was certainly not a simple "herdsman" or "sycamore dresser" and the evidence does not require us to believe that he came from Tekoa.[56] "Tekoa" can be viewed as another of Amos's symbols having to do with how a king, in Amos's view, could and should conduct himself. In 2 Samuel 13, one of David's sons, Absalom, murders his half brother, Amnon, so that the responsibility for blood vengeance falls upon David. In chapter 14, Joab recruits a "wise woman[57] of Tekoa" who tells David that one of her two sons has killed the other so that if her family fulfills its duty of blood vengeance she, a widow, would be left with no one. "Your maidservant thought, 'Let the word of my lord the king provide comfort; for my lord the king is like an angel of God, understanding everything, good and bad" (v. 17). David pardoned Absalom, thus demonstrating as Gordon (1965a, p. 173) puts it, that "the king was the highest court of appeals and could even reverse the basic laws of society." Calling it basic is putting it mildly, for the Lord had told Noah: "Whoever sheds the blood of man, by man shall his blood be shed; for in the image of God was man created" (Gen. 9:6). By recalling Tekoa, Amos was, in effect, telling Jeroboam: "If David in exercising the king's special *mishpāt* could ignore the Noahide laws, surely you can set aside traditional cultic practices and property rights" ("the statutes of Omri" in Micah 6:16?). Given however, Absalom's later revolt against David (2 Sam. 15–18) an alternative interpretation is possible. "Tekoa" may symbolize the unpleasant consequences for the nation of the king giving heed to social reformers and violating basic laws and traditions. This message would be consistent with Jeroboam having implemented his *apkallu* Amos's policies with disastrous consequences including the revolt of Pekah (see chapter 17).

Neither must we believe that Jeremiah's patriotic opponent Hananiah, the son of "Azur" come from "Gibeon" (Jer. 28:1). Gibeon was a symbol for liar. The Gibeonites by making themselves look poor, had fooled Joshua about their origin in order to achieve peaceful assimilation into Israelite society (Josh. 9:3–15). And Micah the "peasant" probably did not come from little Moresheth. Instead, this town was probably a symbolic warning to Judah's rulers not to rely of foreign alliances (probably with Israel against Assyria or with Egypt), but on God. In 2 Chronicles 20:37, Eliezer ben Dodavahu of "Mareshah" prophesied against King Jehoshaphat as follows: "Because you became a partner with Ahaziah [the king of Israel] Yahweh has wrecked your work." The Chronicler adds: "So the ships were broken and could no longer go to Tarshish." Indeed, there is reason to suspect that even the name "Micah" is symbolic. According to 1 Kings 22:1–38, King Ahab of Israel was mortally wounded in a battle against the Arameans in northern Transjordan. But Astour (1971, p. 387) recalls that "in the last year of his rule (853), far from being an enemy of Aram, he was its ally against Assyria and commanded the Israelite army in the battle of Qarqar." Astour concludes that: "The story of Ahab's death is clearly a piece of moralizing fiction . . . As we have it now, the story reflects the conflict between the defeatist 'true' prophets and the patriotic 'false' prophets, first expressed in sharp terms in Micah 3:5–12. The author of 1 Kings 22:1–38, inspired by Micah's invectives, even gave his 'true' prophet the same name— Micaiah."[58]

To conclude: Amos and the other classical prophets were intellectuals, social activists, important public figures, and quite probably, cultic "priests." With all due respect, I must reject Mendenhall's (1981, p. 190) "fact" that "except for Isaiah, all of the prophets of whom we know the relevant facts stem from the villages." Motivated by idealism or personal ambition, the classical prophets sought, with the support of Israel-Judah's affluents, to commit the rulers to programs of social amelioration and regeneration. The next chapter deals more specifically with the possible role of the prophet in the Israelite cult. The suggestion that Amos and the other classical prophets had positions in the cult is not an indispensable building block of the overall thesis presented in this study. However, the plausibility of this thesis is increased by evidence that tends to place the prophets within the Israelite Establishment.

Notes

1. Some scholars (see for instance Blenkinsopp 1977, p. 100) believe that this passage is secondary.

2. Translations of JPS unless otherwise specified; see the bibliographic note (chapter 1, note 2).

3. Genealogical data may also be misleading. Hosea is the "son of Beeri" (1:1) who is otherwise unknown. But does this refer to Hosea I, whom some scholars place in the ninth century prior to King Jehu or the eighth century prophet Hosea II? Is there a connection between "Hosea son of Beeri" and "Balaam son of Beor" (Num. 22–24)? In Numbers 31:8, 16 Balaam is slain by the Israelites because of his guilt in connection with a "trespass against the Lord in the matter of Peor" (see also Num. 25:1–5). Interestingly, Hosea II (9:10) refers to the incident of "Baal-peor." That there is much more to the Balaam story than we are told is indicated because (1) the name Balaam is related to the name of a Levite town in Asher, Bileam (Ibleam; Josh. 17:11; see Daiches 1975, p. 202); (2) according to old Jewish folklore, Hosea was from Bileam (Torrey 1946, p. 40); (3) an Aramaic inscription found at Tell Deir 'Alla in Transjordan dated on paleographic grounds to ca. 700, tells of a vision experienced by Balaam son of Beor who is here called "Seer of the Gods" (see chapter 17 for additional discussion and references).

4. See also Hosea 9:8.

5. It is fascinating to speculate whether the Ugaritic term T'-ite has any connection with the obscure "Tishbite" in 1 Kings 17:1 and 2 Kings 1:8. The prophet Elijah who was "from" or "among" the settlers of Gilead is called the "Tishbite." He is also described in a manner evoking the image of a nomadic shepherd: "a hairy man with a leather belt tied around his waist."

6. In Ugarit the nqdm-shepherds had 'ubdy-fields (fields held in consideration of services rendered to the king) which were attached to the gt or royal estate (?) and are listed among those receiving weapons from the royal stores (Heltzer 1979, vol. I, pp. 463, 472). A Mesopotamian letter transmits a royal order to "levy one hundred bowman from among the shepherds" (Oppenheim 1967, p. 191).

7. See also 2 Samuel 5:2; 2 Kings 10:12; 22:17; Hosea 13:4–6. King David had been a shepherd (1 Sam. 17:34–37) and so had Joseph (Gen. 37:2) who ultimately became a high Egyptian official.

8. The Septuagint has noqed in Amos 7:14.

9. The term boqer raises additional questions considered below.

10. Hosea 13:5–6 has the Lord looking after Israel in the wilderness and grazing it; The Septuagint (Syr.) uses the word "shepherd."

11. So translated by JPS(1978) and Bewer; Thomson does not have "shepherd".

12. Here two points are in order: (1) Amaziah calls Amos "seer" (*hozeh*) in 7:12, a title which may well have derogatory overtones, but elsewhere in the Bible is specifically applied to prophets composing royal records (1 Chron. 29:29; 2 Chron. 9:29; 12:15; 19:2 and 20:34) or otherwise enjoying royal patronage (2 Sam. 24:11; 1 Chron. 25:5; 2 Chron. 29:25; 33:18; 35:15). See Paul (1971, col. 1154–1155) and Zevit (1975, p. 785). (2) Basing his conclusion on a comparison of Amos' oracle against the nations (1:2–2:16) with Egyptian "execration texts," Bentzen (1950, p. 94) believes that "curses against sinners inside the people, together with curses against foreign and demoniac powers, belonged to the [New Year] ritual of judgment."

13. Both the niphal and hithpael forms of the (assumed) root *nb'* are usually translated "to prophesy." Some scholars link the hithpael form with ecstatic behavior. See R. R. Wilson's (1980, pp. 137–38) critical analysis.

14. Gitay (1980) has perceptively applied the tools and framework of classical rhetoric to Amos 3:1–15. The prophet's usage of such devices as rhetorical questions, *anaphora*, and mixed genres, Gitay concludes, was designed not only to persuade his listeners but to prod them into action.

15. Another technique may have been to claim that Samuel, a venerated Israelite prophet of the past, had experienced visions. Thus Samuel explicitly experiences a vision (dream) at a time when "The word of the Lord was rare . . . ; there was no frequent vision" (1 Sam. 3:1, 15). Note also that at Gibeon, Solomon the wise king had a dream concerning social justice (1 Kings 3:9–11).

16. Alternatively: "A lion has roared, who can but fear? My Lord God has spoken, who can but prophesy?" (Amos 3:8).

17. The superscription over Amos' book characterizes him as one who "had visions (*hāzāh*) over Israel."

18. A similar position seems to have existed in Mycenean Greece (ca. 1200 B.C.E.). According to Chadwick (1976, p. 122): "An official at Pylos (in Messenia) appears to have a title (*opisukos*) which must mean something like overseer of the figs; but the context in which this title appears does not suggest his duties were restricted to figs."

19. So translated by JPS(1974); Thomson has "lofty oak." In fact the two trees are close relatives.

20. An Assyrian relief in the throne room at Nimrud depicts Assurnasirpal II (883–859) "twice on either side of the sacred tree [a fig tree?], one of the recurring themes of Assyrian Art. He is receiving the authority of kingship from the national god Assur, represented as usual in a winged sun-disc . . . From its position this relief obviously had a special importance." (Burney 1977, p. 167)

21. The Roman poet Juvenal (d. 140 C.E.) called a trembling Jewish fortune-teller "great priestess of the tree" (see Wiesen 1980).

22. So translated by JPS(1917); JPS(1978) reads (as emended): "My people it consults its stick, its rod (its phallus meaning 'its lust') directs it!" The Septuagint (Thomson) rendering is "They consulted by symbols . . . and gave answers by their staves."

23. The Talmud notes sacred trees under which the priests sat but did not eat the fruit (Cook 1908, pp. 25–6).

24. This is quite consistent with Jastrow's (1915, p. 243) argument that the Hebrew word for law *tôrāh* has its equivalent in the Babylonian *têrtu* which means "oracle," that is, a divine decision. However, I am informed by William W. Hallo that *têrtu* is from the root *W'R* while *tôrāh* is from the root *WR'*.

25. Interestingly, sycamore (Greek, *sȳkómoros*; Hebrew, *shiqmāh*) bring to mind "Moreh." This raises the possibility that the lofty trees at Shechem near Gilgal were sycamore (mulberry)

fig trees. Also, "Mareh" or "Morah" is the place of the bitter waters (Exod. 15:22–25). Here the Lord, after showing Moses a tree that made the waters sweet, revealed his law to the Israelites. Note also that the verb *mārah*, "to annoint a wound," which is found only in Isaiah 38:21 in connection with the treatment of Hezekiah's illness with a cake of figs (see also 2 Kings 20:7) appears to be an Egyptian loan word. Lambdin (1953, p. 152) suggests that the widespread occurence of the root *mrḥ* in Semitic points to a comparatively early borrowing but warns against confusing the root *mrḥ* with a different in meaning Semitic *mrḥ*. Mayes (1979, p. 219) suggests that the epithet Moreh is derived from the same root *yārāh* as that from which *tôrāh* is derived. Wiliam H. Hallo, however, informs me that there is no connection between *shiqmāh* and *moreh*.

A final point is that it is not at all clear that Dodona's "oak" was literally an oak (see Parke 1967, pp. 29–30; see also the discussions of Albright 1968, pp. 189–90 and Farbridge 1923, pp. 27–49).

26. So translated by JPS(1917); JPS(1978) has "baca trees." The passages in 1 Chron. 14:10–11 omit any reference to the role of tree oracles in David's victory. See also Worden (1953, p. 290).

27. In 2 Kings 16:15, "to inquire" refers to something that is done on the altar in connection with sacrifices (see Ringgren 1963, p. 3). In the Mari literature we find that after his "prophetic utterances" the *āpilum* of Adad is "watching" at the *maškānum* (or "tabernacle"?) (Weinfeld 1977b, p. 187).

28. Fig trees were also sacred in Crete, Greece, and Rome (Evans 1901, pp. 101–04, 128–29).

29. Note the special position of the seven-branched-tabernacle menorah with its tree motif (see Myers 1976).

30. Note the obscure passage in Hosea (5:7–9) in which Beth-aven is a pun on Beth-on. In a vignette in the Saite recension of the Book of the Dead: "The sun-god . . . is represented with a falcon head and a sun disc with uraeus . . . standing in a boat with a calf with a shining star over its head . . . placed before him and the deceased behind him" (Buhl 1947, p. 88). Danelius (1967/68) presents arguments suggesting that the "calves" at Bethel and Dan represented the goddess Hathor.

31. In the days of the Hasmonean priest-kings of the Hellenistic-Roman period the branch came from an olive tree. "Now tradition differs as to the botanical species of the Tree of Life in the Israelite Paradise. Some of the rabbis held it to be a date palm, others the olive, and even the fig tree had its advocates." (Widengren 1951, p. 38)

32. See JPS(1978); Job 24:4 refers to those who "chase the needy off the roads." Indeed this Book contains many speeches strongly reminiscent of Amos.

33. Note Coote (1981, p. 101): "Without the writing down of prophecy . . . the claim for justice . . . would arise, but not among the ruling elite in such a way as to have a lasting effect on policy." The "divine letters" to Assyrian kings probably "represent admonitions from the clergy revealed through the medium of god-sent letters rather than by the voice of a prophet" (Oppenheim 1977, p. 280).

34. A hymn to the sun-god Shamash, the Mesopotamian god of justice, contains several passages that resemble Amos: "He who receives no bribe but takes the part of the weak, it is pleasing to Shamash, and he will prolong his life. . . . The honest merchant who holds the balances (and gives) good weight, everything is presented to him in good measure. . . . He will enlarge his family, gain wealth, and *like the water of a never failing spring (his) descendants will never fail.*" (emphasis added). According to Thomas (1958, p. 108) the tablets are Assyrian and date from the seventh century B.C.E., but some of the material incorporated may date from the first half of the second millennium.

35. So translated by Thomson, JPS (1978) renders the verse: "Sow righteousness for yourselves; reap the fruits of goodness; break for yourselves betimes fresh ground of seeking the Lord, so that you may obtain a teacher of righteousness."

36. The seven *apkallus* were represented as carrying *ēru*-branches (cedar) or those of the date palm (Widengren 1951, pp. 20–1, 48). The *Babyloniaca of Berossus* (the latter name meaning "Bel is his shepherd"), composed about 281 B.C.E., as well as two first-millennium cuneiform texts list not only the pre-Flood kings but their *apkallu* (Burstein 1978, pp. 8–9; see further Reiner 1961, p. 7 and Van Dijk 1962). Tradition connects the reestablishment of civilization with a second series of *apkallu* (Burstein 1978, p. 21).

37. For this correlation of chronologies of antediluvians I have relied on the Sumerian king list in Kramer (1963, p. 328 or Walton 1981). There are, however, inconsistencies and contradictions in the cuneiform literature concerning "the number, the names, the order and the lengths of reign of the antediluvian kings" (Hallo 1970, p. 62; see also Hallo 1963, pp. 174–75). Hallo and Simpson (1971, p. 32) present a parallel Mesopotamian tradition in which the fifth-antediluvian king Dumuzi (the shepherd) corresponds to Enoch while Ensipazianna is number seven, corresponding to Lamech. Note also that the Kenite genealogy of Genesis 4 runs parallel to Genesis 5.

38. Reiner (1961, pp. 8–9) lists the alternative *ummânu* which is usually translated as "master craftsman" and refers to a learned man.

39. "An interesting feature in the 'Advice to a Prince' is its striking formal resemblance to the omen texts. The omen style is used effectively to give the cautions a general wording, avoiding any direct references to a particular king: 'If a king does not heed justice . . . ' This way of beginning the sentence with a conditional clause is typical of omens (though curiously enough the introductory *šumma* 'if' is not expressed in this text, contrary to the characteristic omen formula). The author is dependent on the omen style in other respects as well, especially in the loose syntax and in some of the phraseology." (Albrekston 1967, p. 61). Can the same perhaps be said of the prophetic literature generally?

40. See De Boer (1960, pp. 57–8) and Hallo (1981, p. 10) on *abrek/abarakku* in Genesis 41:43. "As the father is provider, so he is also protector and intercessor with higher powers. In fact the Akkadian term for 'fatherhood' (*abbûtu*) tends to become specified because of this typical role of the father to meaning 'intercession'." (Jacobsen 1976, p. 159).

Egyptian tradition knows a "Sacred Scribe" who, every morning, recited to the reigning king the accomplishments of his predecessors from the sacred books. Joseph and Moses were reputed to belong to this category (Witt 1971, pp. 93–4). The "vizier" Ptahotep (ca. 2350) was called "Father of God" (Von Rad 1972, p. 399).

41. It is interesting to note that the graduated numerical sequence ("for three . . . and for four") found in Amos' oracle against the nations which, possibly, played a cultic role occurs in a "two-three" version in the Aḥiqar tale (see Ginsberg 1969, p. 428; Wolff 1973, pp. 34–44).

42. See the discussion of Hezekiah's illness in chapter 17. See Hallo (1976) for a Sumerian analogue to the so-called Psalm of Hezekiah in Isaiah 38.

43. See the discussion of Kaufmann's argument in chapter 2. On the other hand, Jonah the son of Amittai, the prophet who guided Jeroboam II during the period of his great military victories is mentioned (2 Kings 14:25). So perhaps the criterion for inclusion is success.

44. On the Judah-Tamar story, see chapter 6, note 11.

45. Amos 6:6–7 refers to Israelites who enjoy the pleasures of good food but "are not concerned about the ruin of Joseph" while 5:15 refers to the "remnant of Joseph."

The good-evil contrast in Amos 5:14, "Seek good and not evil that you may live" and 5:15, "Hate the evil, and love the good" is also present in Genesis 50:20, "you meant evil against me, but God meant it for good" (see further Wolff 1973, pp. 67–70).

46. Note that Jeremiah, who was beaten and placed in the stocks by Pashur (an Egyptian name) the priest in Jeremiah 20, is asked for an oracle by the king's officials in 21. Further, in chapter 37 Jeremiah is placed in a cistern. Compare this with Joseph's pit (Gen. 37:22–24) and his dungeon (Gen. 41:14). Jeremiah's plight was brought to the attention of King Zedekiah by "Ebed-melech the Ethiopian, a eunuch who was in the king's palace" (38:7–9). Compare this with the "chief cupbearer" who brought the imprisoned Joseph to the attention of Pharaoh (Gen. 41:9–13). King Zedekiah not only rescues the prophet but consults with him (38:14–28). Finally, the Babylonians destroy the Temple, release Jeremiah from prison, and install him as *apkallu* in the quisling government headed by Gedaliah the grandson of Jeremiah's protector Shaphan (40). Compare this with Joseph's Egyptians.

47. Genesis 47 may of course, be aetiological or, alternatively, it may reflect a call for some sort of land reform or nationalization or, perhaps, for regulation of the land market.

48. Recalling the tale of the "Eloquent Peasant," Israel sends his sons to trade for grain with items such as balm, honey, gum, ladanum, pistachio nuts, and almonds (Gen. 43:11). Gordon (1965b, p. 113) notes: "The device of the Pharaoh and Rensi is essentially the same as that of Joseph, who humanely keeps his brothers and their family supplied while enjoying the act that he obliges them to put on, including speeches that he draws out of them."

49. Note that in Jeremiah 35:3–5 the prophet makes use of a Temple chamber belonging to a "man of God." The projection of Amos backward in time to Bethel is not unprecedented. In Judges 2:1–5 (Thomson):

> There went up a messenger of the Lord from Gilgal to Wailing, namely to Bethel, to the house of Israel, and said unto them, thus saith the Lord: I caused you to come out of Egypt, and brought you into this land which I solemnly promised your fathers, and I said I will never break My covenant with you; therefore you shall not make a covenant with the inhabitants of this land, nor worship their gods; but you shall break to pieces their graven images, and demolish their altars. But you have not harkened to My voice. Because you have not done these things, therefore I have said, I will not drive them out from before you; but they shall be as curbs for you; and their gods shall be to you a stumbling block; And when the messenger of the Lord had spoken these words to all the children of Israel, the people wept aloud, so that they called the name of that place Wailing, and there they sacrificed to the Lord.

If a nationalist "messenger of God" of the Elijah-type can be projected back to early times to curse idolatrous altars, why not an Amos-type "man of God" who curses social injustice?

50. "A lion has roared, who can but fear? My Lord God has spoken, who can but prophesy?" (Amos 3:8; see also Amos 3:12).

51. Amos 9:13: "Behold, the days come, saith the Lord, that the plowman shall overtake the reaper, and the treader of grapes him that soweth seed."

At this point, however, a large caveat is in order. Undoubtedly the book of Amos was reworked more than once. It is hard to believe, for example, that Amos really said that "Yahweh roars from Zion and bellows from Jerusalem" (1:2) or that he was greatly concerned with what Coote (1981, p. 48) terms the "religiopolitical opposition between Bethel and Jerusalem as cult sanctuaries" (Bethel versus Shechem is perhaps another situation). But the term "Zion" which is apparently related to the Canaanite "Olympus," *spn* may be a mythological reference or, perhaps, a reference to a sanctuary other than Jerusalem's. Note the references to the north in Isaiah 14:13 and Ezekiel 1:4. Most importantly, note the reference to "Mt. Zion in the far north" in Psalms 48:3, a northern psalm ("of the sons of Korah") possibly belonging to Shechem. Doubts can also be expressed concerning the reference to Jerusalem; perhaps the original text had "Salem" (or "Shalem") a town of the Shechemites according to the Septuagint

(Thomson) rendering of Genesis 33:18 and according to the Samaritans (Purvis 1968, p. 13–14). Note the references to "Zion" and "Salem" in the northern "of Asaph" (see Chapter 15) Psalm 76:3. (There is also the question of whether King Josiah died "in peace" or "in Shalem" see chapter 17, note 21.) I would agree with Coote (1981, pp. 7–8, 47) that slanting of this type is best dated to the period between Hezekiah and Josiah. Perhaps Amos 7:12 in which Bethel's priest advises Amos to flee to Judah and prophesy there is also polemical and secondary.

To return to Amos's optimistic closing verses, 9:11–15 may well date as some commentators believe to the late exilic or postexilic period. But why should we deny that "the earlier prophets were concerned with the new society as well as with the old?" (Coote 1981, pp. 122–23). Perhaps the reference to David's "falling tabernacle" in 9:11 is secondary or, perhaps, as Coote (1981, pp. 123–24) suggests, the "reference is to the early David, the folk hero, the protector of the disenfranchised [note 1 Sam. 22:2] . . . the ruler who knew his subordination to Yahweh . . . The image of the hut controls the figure of David rather than the other way around. That is, the monarchist glory of David is overshadowed by the humbleness of the hut." Perhaps. I would add that David represents Israel's "golden age" and that Amos may well be contrasting his simplicity with the extravagance of later kings of whom Solomon is the prototype. Deuteronomy 17:15–16 which may, like Amos, have its origin in the north, also seems to be aimed against Solomonic extravagance.

Gordis (1980, pp. 253–54, 259–62) places Amos 8–9 in the prophet's post-Bethel period, pointing out that "he continues to use the same techniques, terms and phrases in the second period that he had used in the first." However, Gordis believes the optimistic verses refer to Judah.

52. In 2 Chronicles 17:7–9, King Jehoshaphat sends out officials, Levites, and priests: "And they taught in Judah having the book of the Law of the Lord with them: and they went about throughout all the cities of Judah and taught among the people."

53. The linkage between Amos and Samuel's house is strengthened by the inclusion in the book of Samuel of an attack on sacrifice that is forced into the surrounding material. Samuel tells King Saul, "Does the Lord delight in burnt offerings and sacrifices as much as obedience to the Lord's command?" (1 Sam. 15:22). Also compare 1 Samuel 17:34 and Amos 3:12 on shepherds and lions.

54. Wolff (1973, pp. 76–80) notes Amos's "unique linguistic usage" regarding Israel's father, Isaac, who is tied to Beer-sheba in Genesis 26:23–25, 33; 46:1–4: "This curious double observation is above all noteworthy because, on the one hand, Amos always speaks of Isaac only in clear parallel to the Northern Kingdom of Israel and also mentions Beer-sheba in the same breath with northern sanctuaries; however, on the other hand Beer-sheba, as an oasis in the Negeb, itself lies deep in the south of Judah."

55. According to Redford (1970, p. 21) a later glossator wished to locate Israel's residence in the vicinity of Hebron (see Gen. 37:14).

56. Note that Tekoa lies too high for the sycamore fig to flourish. Indeed, King Solomon "made silver as plentiful in Jerusalem as stones and cedars as plentiful as sycamores in the Shephelah (Lowland)." (1 Kings 10:27).

57. See Petrie (1924, p. 450 on ancient Egypt's "wise woman."

58. Note that both Micah (2:11) and Micaiah (1 Kings 22:19–23) launch attacks on ecstatic (nationalist?) prophecy. Also suggestive is the striking similarity of 1 Kings 22 and Isaiah's "Throne Vision" (Isa. 6; see Tsevat 1980, pp. 161–64).

14 THE JOINT MINISTRY OF PRIESTS AND PROPHETS

There is good reason to believe that the higher Israelite clergy, the "priests," consisted of two orders, *kohēn* and *navi'* who exercised a joint ministry before Yahweh (see B.W. Anderson 1975, p. 230). *Kohēn* is usually translated as "priest" while *navi'* is rendered "prophet" but literally means "mouth" or "spokesman" (Orlinsky 1974, p. 59). The Levites were (or became) a minor priestly order, subordinate to the higher clergy or to the king.[1]

The biblical evidence supporting the existence of two priestly orders, the priests and the prophets, ranges from Exodus to Zephaniah:[2]

> The Lord replied to Moses, "See, I make you an oracle to Pharaoh, and your brother Aaron shall be your spokesman (*navi'*)." Exod. 7:1

> And let Zadok the priest and Nathan the prophet anoint him there king over Israel. 1 Kings 1:34

> The king [Josiah] went up to the House of the Lord, together with all the men of Judah and all the inhabitants of Jerusalem, and the priests and the prophets. 2 Kings 23:2

> Shall the priest and the prophet be slain in the sanctuary of the Lord. Lam. 2:20

Let no man rebuke, let no man protest! For this your people has a grievance against [you], O priest! So you shall stumble by day, and by night the prophet shall stumble as well. Hos. 4:4–5

Her rulers judge for gifts. Her priests give rulings for a fee, and her prophets divine for pay. Mic. 3:11

Priest and prophet are muddled by liquor, they are muddled in their visions, they stumble in judgement. Isa. 28:7

The priests shall be appalled and the prophets stand aghast. Jer. 4:9

The prophets prophesy falsely, and the priests rule[3] accordingly. Jer. 5:31

They are all greedy for gain; priest and prophet alike. Jer. 8:10 (see also Jer. 6:13)

Both priest and prophet roam the land they know not where. Jer. 14:18

Come let us devise a plot against Jeremiah—for instruction (or law; Thomson) shall not fail from the priest, nor counsel from the wise, nor the word [oracle] from the prophet. Jer. 18:18

For both prophet and priest are godless; even in My House I find their wickedness. Jer. 23:11

The priests and prophets and all the people heard Jeremiah speaking these words in the House of the Lord. And when Jeremiah finished speaking all that the Lord had commanded him to speak to all the people, the priests and the prophets and all the people seized him. Jer. 26:7–8

They, their kinds, their princes, their priests, and their prophets. Jer. 32:32

Then they shall seek a vision from the prophet in vain; instruction [or law] shall perish from the priest. Ezek. 7:26

Her priests have violated My teaching: they have profaned what is sacred to Me, they have not distinguished between the sacred and the profane, they have not taught the difference between the unclean and the clean, and they have closed their eyes to My sabbaths . . . Her prophets, too, daub the wall for them with plaster: they prophesy falsely and divine deceitfully. Ezek. 22:26–28

Her prophets are wanton and treacherous persons; her priests have profaned that which is holy, they have done violence to the law. Zeph. 3:4

Other biblical passages point to the existence of two priestly orders without specifically distinguishing between priests and prophets:

O house of Israel, bless ye the Lord; O house of Aaron, bless ye the Lord; O house of Levi, bless ye the Lord. Ps. 135:20

Zakok son of Ahitub and Abiathar son of Ahimelech were [David's] priests. 2 Sam. 8:17.[4]

And the king [Josiah] ordered Hilkiah *kohēn hārō's* (head priest?, head of the first order?), the *kohēn misne* (second priest?, head of the second order?), and the guards of the threshold to bring out of the Temple of the Lord all the objects made for Baal and Asherah, and all the Host of Heaven. 2 Kings 23:4 (see Sabourin 1973, p. 143)

But in 2 Kings 25:18, Seraiah is identified as the "head priest" and Zephaniah, who is probably the classical prophet of that name, as the "second priest" (JPS 1917; JPS 1978 has "deputy priest") or "head priest of the second order" (Thomson). Taking 2 Kings 23:4 and 25:18 together, we have strong evidence for the existence of two priestly orders, priests and prophets, each with its own head or chief priest. Finally, it appears reasonable to assume with Johnstone (1965/66, p. 47) that the "sons of Hanan" who in Jeremiah 35:4, possess a chamber in the Temple represent a "guild" of prophets.

What were the distinctive priestly functions of the two orders? The passages quoted above link the priests with questions of instruction (law) and ritual purity and the prophets with oracles or divination. Based upon this finding and the evidence linking Amos with oracle-giving and, perhaps, divination,[5] I am now prepared to refine my earlier suggestion that Amos was a cultic priest and identify him as a member of the second or prophetic order of priests.

If, however, we are to appreciate the complementary roles played by *kohēn* and *navi'* in the crucial rituals of Israelite worship, we must first adopt a more general perspective and survey the evidence for other ancient Near Eastern societies. Yerkes (1952, p. 124) has pointed out that: "All religious rites are primarily doing something with something. A later addition was the saying of something, either to a deity or to the worshippers or to both; by way of accompaniment or explanation of what was done." The word focuses and actuates the power of the act. In the religious rites of ancient Egypt, for example, things done were represented by the Celebrant (*sem* or *setem*) priest[6] and things said by the Reader (*kherheb* or "Holder of the Roll" or lector priest).[7] Both actions and utterances of the rites in the god's shrine are enumerated in service books dating from the New Kingdom (sixteenth–twelfth centuries B.C.E.). In each case the words provide a mythological interpretation of the actions undertaken. The funerary service set forth in the Book of the Dead includes not only the things to be said by the lector or psalmist priest (here also called "Opener of Heaven's Gates"), but also marginal rubrical directions addressed to the *sem* priest: "Here water should be sprinkled;" "here [pour] the fresh water and [burn] two portions of incense;" "here offer a cake;" and so on.[8] Moving north to Ugarit in Canaan we find texts (for example, the Gaster Nikal text) in which one priest would perform the prescribed acts of sacrifice and prayer, while another would explain the actions to the assembled multitude. Engnell (1967, p. 104) concludes that: "We are dealing with cult dramas accomplished in cues, narrative passages, gestures, and ritual actions; words and actions supplementing each other." (Some Assyrian evidence for the combination of agenda and dicenda is presented in note 10 of this chapter.)

A number of scholars have found a basically similar procedure in Israelite rituals. Gunkel (cited in Welch 1936, p. 130), and Mowinckel (cited in Rowley, 1967, pp. 136–37) for example, see the actions being carried out by the priest while the prophet speaks the rubric in the form of an oracle. Welch (1936, p. 130) concludes that a "combination of priestly practice and prophetic teaching is unmistakable" in Israelite services. Several key biblical passages support this interpretation:

> The Lord became angry with Moses, and He said, "There is your brother Aaron the Levite . . . . You shall speak to him and put the words in his mouth . . . . Thus he shall be your spokesman, and you shall be an oracle to him. And take with you this rod, with which you shall perform the signs. Exod. 4:14–17

> Then Moses and Aaron went and assembled all the elders of the Israelites. Aaron repeated all the words which the Lord had spoken to Moses, and he [Moses?] performed the signs in the sight of the people. Exod. 4:29–30.

> He sent forth Moses His servant—Aaron whom he had chosen: to them He committed the words of His signs—of His wonders in the land of Egypt. Ps. 105:26–27[9]

> The prophets prophesy falsely, and the priests rule accordingly. Jeremiah 5:31. (Rowley (1967, p. 151) maintains that accordingly" should be translated "according to the directions of.")

However much their roles may have been confounded in later years, Moses is the ideal priest (see Ps. 99:6) who performs the "signs" (that is, the actions) while Aaron, the ideal prophet, supplies the "words" (that is, the interpretations). If Rowley's translation of Jeremiah 5:31 is correct we have strong evidence that the ritual distinction between things said and things done persisted to the very end of the Israelite monarchy.

Rowley (1967, p. 161) adds the important point that the utterances accompanying, say, ancient sacrificial rites provided them with a Yahweh intention. In the main the traditional rituals (recorded in Leviticus 1–7; 14:10–32; 22:7–30; 27 and Numbers 18–19) were accompanied by prophetic words that recalled and praised the great deeds that the Lord had performed for his people the Israelites.[10] Indeed in the older literature the "prophet" is closely linked to "historicization" (see, for example, Muilenberg 1961, pp. 110–11).

Then Miriam the prophetess, *Aaron's sister*, took a timbrel in her hand, and all the women went out after her in dance with timbrels. And Miriam chanted for them, "Sing to the Lord for He has triumphed gloriously; Horse and driver He has hurled into the sea." Exod. 15:20; (emphasis added)

Deborah, wife of Lappidoth, was a prophetess . . . On that day [after the victory over King Jabin of Hazor] Deborah and Barak son of Abinoam sang: . . . Hear, O Kings! Give ear, O potentates! I will sing, will sing to the Lord, will hymn the Lord, the God of Israel. O Lord, when You came forth from Seir, advanced from the country of Edom, the earth trembled; the heavens dripped, yea, the clouds dripped water. The mountains quaked before the Lord, Him of Sinai, before the Lord, God of Israel. Judg. 4:4, 5:4–5

When the Israelites cried to the Lord on account of Midian, the Lord sent a prophet to the Israelites who said to them, "Thus said the Lord, the God of Israel: I brought you up out of Egypt and freed you from the house of bondage. I rescued you from the Egyptians and from all your oppressors; I drove them out before you, and gave you their land. Judg. 6:7–9.

If, as suggested in chapter 13, the classical prophets were cultic priests, then to which order did they belong? In order to answer this question let us see whether their books contain passages of praise for Yahweh's historic deeds.

Yet I destroyed the Amorite before them, whose stature was like the cedars and who was as stout as the oak, destroying his boughs above and his trunk below! And I brought you up from the land of Egypt and led you through the land of the Amorite! Amos 2:9–10.[11]

Only I the Lord have been your God ever since the land of Egypt; you have never known a God but Me, you have never had a helper other than Me. I looked after you in the desert, in a thirsty land. When they grazed, they were sated; when they were sated they grew haughty; and so they forgot Me. Hos. 13:4–6

My people! What wrong have I done you? What hardship have I caused you? Testify against Me. In fact, I brought you up from the land of Egypt, I redeemed you from the house of bondage, and I sent before you Moses, Aaron, and Miriam. My people remember what Balak king of Moab plotted against you, and how Balaam son of Beor responded to him. From Shittim to Gilgal [the crossing of the Jordan?] and you will recognize the gracious acts of the Lord. Mic. 6:3–5

Assuredly, thus said my Lord God of Hosts; "O My people that dwells in Zion, have no fear of Assyria, who beats you with a rod and wields his staff over you as did the Egyptians. For very soon My wrath will have spent itself . . . The Lord of Hosts will brandish a scourge over him as when He beat Midian at the Rock of Oreb, and will wield His staff as He did over the Egyptians by the sea. Isa. 10:24–25.[12]

Hear the word of the Lord, O House of Jacob, every clan of the House of Israel! Thus said the Lord: What wrong did your fathers find in Me that they abandoned Me and went after delusions and were deluded? They never asked themselves, "Where is the Lord who brought us up from the land of Egypt, who led us through the wilderness, a land of deserts and pits, a land of drought and darkness, a land no man had traversed, where no human being had dwelt?" I have brought you to this country of farm land to enjoy its fruit and its bounty. Jer. 2:4–7.[13]

On that day that I chose Israel, I gave My oath to the stock of the House of Jacob: when I made Myself known to them in the land of Egypt, I gave my oath to them. When I said, "I the Lord am your God, that same day I swore to them to take them out of the land of Egypt into a land flowing with milk and honey, a land which I had sought out for them, the fairest of all lands . . . . I brought them out of the land of Egypt and I led them into the wilderness. I gave them My laws and taught them My rules, by the pursuit of which a man shall live. . . . But the House of Israel rebelled against Me in the wilderness; they did not follow My laws and they rejected My rules . . . Then I thought to pour out My fury upon them in the wilderness and to make an end of them; but I acted for the sake of My name, that it might not be profaned in the sight of the nations before whose eyes I had led them out. Ezek. 20:4–14

With the possible exception of Isaiah, the prophetic books include passages praising Yahweh's mighty deeds of the past. This finding is at least consistent with the classical prophets having been members of the second priestly order, the prophets. Surely, given the total weight of the evidence, this conclusion cannot be dismissed as a "posthumous ordination of the prophets."

Ancient Egypt's learned priest, the *kherheb*, was also known as the "Scribe of the God's Book." There is some concrete evidence linking even the older, preclassical Israelite prophets with learned endeavor, specifically the writing of royal histories. Before reviewing the evidence it must be noted that according to 1 Samuel 9:9, "the prophet (*navi'*) of today was formerly called a seer (*ro'eh*)."[14] If, in addition, the terms *ro'eh* and *hozeh* (both meaning "one who sees") can be roughly identified (the terms are parallel in Isaiah 30:10), it follows that in every case the writer of a royal history is identified as either a prophet or a "seer."

> David's history was written by Samuel the seer, Nathan the prophet, and Gad the seer. 1 Chron. 29:29. (In 1 Samuel 3:20 Samuel is "established to be a prophet of the Lord" while 1 Sam. 22:5 and 2 Samuel 24:11 identify Gad as a "prophet.")

> Solomon's history was written by Nathan the prophet, Ahijah the Shilonite, and Jedo (Iddo?) the seer. 2 Chron. 9:29. (1 Kings 11:29 identifies Ahijah as a "prophet" while Iddo is called a "prophet" in 2 Chron. 13:22.)

> Rehoboam's history was written by Shemaiah the prophet and Iddo the seer. 2 Chron. 12:15.

> Abijah's history is found in the treatise of Iddo the prophet. 2 Chron. 13:22.

> Jehoshaphat's history was written by Jehu son of Hanani. 2 Chron. 20:34. (In 2 Chron. 19:2, we find "Jehu the son of Hanani the seer."[15]

The prophet is an ancient figure in the Israelite cult but the prophetic books constitute evidence suggesting that with the passage of time he evolved from a relatively junior to an equal, or even senior, partner in the priestly enterprise. Possibly prophetic sermons" became a regular feature of the Israelite cult. Some scholars, for example, see the cultic occasion for Amos in an annual covenant renewal festival. This much is known for sure: in later Egyptian times at Edfu and Thebes a "prophet" lectured the assembled worshipers regarding the contemporary meaning of the ancient texts *after* the ritual had been performed.

Notes

1. Translations of JPS unless otherwise specified; see the bibliographic note chapter 1, note 2.

2. Fortunately, a determination of the exact status of the Levites is not crucial for the present study and it shall not be attempted (see Milgrom 1970).
Noted without comment: In the epic period, the oracles of Zeus' "oak" at Dodona were interpreted by the Selloi or Helloi who have unwashen feet and sleep on the ground. It is uncertain whether the latter were a tribe or a priestly family. In classical times the Selloi fade out and oracles are by means of lots (Parke 1967, pp. 8–9, 75–6).

3. See Rawley (1967) for an alternative translation.

4. The text of 2 Samuel 15:27 may be corrupt but it refers to both Zadok and Abiathar and seems to mention both priest and seer. Note also that 1 Chron. 24 divides the family of Aaron the priest into two branches, one descended from Eleazar and the other from Ithamar.

5. Chapter 13 showed that one of Amos' "occupations," tender or dresser of sycamore figs is almost certainly linked to oracle-giving, while the other, herdsman (*boqer*), may also be related to divination.

6. The image of the *sem* priest or at least the leopard's skin he wore, were excised from monuments during the reign of the monotheist Akhenaton.

7. In much later times the higher clergy appears to have been divided into "Keeper of the Robe" and "Servant of the God" (or "Prophet"). The former held the cubit of justice and the cup for libations and was an expert in the rituals of sacrifice, prayer, and so on. The latter knew the seven "hieratic books," held the water vase, controlled temple revenues and made pronouncements concerning questions of morality (Morenz 1973, pp. 103, 224–25; Witt 1973, pp. 93–4). A similar distinction is observed in ancient Rome in which one group of cultic professionals, that is, priests, superintends the various forms of worship while the other interprets signs and portents (Sabourin 1973, p. 40).

8. Sources on Egyptian religion: Budge (1967, cxxxix–cxli); Champdor 1966, pp. 62, 71); Clark (1960, pp. 27–8); A.R. David (1973); Erman (1927, p. 36); Morenz (1973, pp. 87–8); Petrie (1924, pp. 48–9).

9. So translated by Thomson, JPS (1917) renders the verse: "He sent Moses His servant, and Aaron whom He had chosen. They wrought among them manifold signs, and wonders in the land of Ham."

10. In Deuteronomy 26:3–10, the priest performs the sacrifice while the *offerer* summarizes the great deeds of the Lord in Israel's history. An interesting contrast is provided by an Assyrian "ritual [which] clearly describes with rare explicitness the *dromena* and the *legomena*, that is, what is to be done and what is to be said during the religious act in which the two 'actors' are engaged. One of them is the supplicant who, as the one who has brought the sacrificial animal is referred to as 'owner of the animal,' the other is the priest (called *šangù*) of Ištar . . . . The distribution of roles is the following: the supplicant performs in two parallel scenes acts of adoration directed not toward the goddess herself but toward certain cult objects. The priest does not participate actively in the ceremony; he only speaks, that is, he pronounces declarations in the name of the goddess Ištar after each of the two scenes of the ritual." (Oppenheim 1966, pp. 252–53)

11. Wolff (1973, fn. 123, p. 55) says that "Amos 2:10 is most probably . . . secondary."

12. Some scholars question whether this passage was written by Isaiah I, the prophet of the eighth century. Note, however, that Isaiah mentions the pillar of cloud and pillar of fire (4:5) and the day of Midian (9:3) and is aware of the drawing out of water in the Wilderness.

13. See also Jeremiah 10:6–12.

14. See also Chapter 13, note 13.

15. Note: "seer" is *ro'eh* in the case of Samuel; elsewhere "seer" is *hoseh*. However, in 2 Chronicles 16:7, 10, Hanani is called *ro'eh*.

15 SONGS AND WORDS OF SOCIAL JUSTICE

"Cult or ritual" has been defined by Mowinckel (1962, vol. I pp. 15–17) as the totality of "holy acts and words in which the encounter and communion of the Deity with the congregation is established, developed, and brought to its ultimate goal." What the Israelite congregation sought to achieve "is *life*—in the most comprehensive sense of the word . . . The Israelites experienced the . . . idea by the word 'blessing'." In ancient times both sacrifice and prayer were seen as part of the process of receiving "blessing." As Mowinckel (1962, vol. I, p. 22) has observed, the psalm, is the natural form of cultic prayer. "From Babylonia-Assyria, Egypt, the Hittites in Asia Minor . . . we have a long series of psalms with indications of the definite cultic performance at which they were to be recited. The Ugaritic texts give strong reason to believe that the same was done by the Canaanites." Now as Peters (1922, p. 1) has pointed out the title of the Israelite book of Psalms is *tehillîm* which means "sacrificial praise songs." (The word *tehillîm* is from the same root as *hallel* which is, of course, familiar to us in the form of *halleluiah*.) "Ritual sacrificial use is indicated in headings: 30, 38, 70, 88, 100, 102, and perhaps 8, 9, 22, 32 as by first lines: 105–107, 118, 136, 138, 145" and elsewhere. But at some point in time,

177

Peters (1922, p. 4) notes, psalms with no obvious connection with sacrifice (for example, 9, 10, 34, 37) were introduced into the Psalter.

Literary anthologies such as the books of Psalms and Proverbs bear few signs that would enable them to be precisely dated. Consequently, the objectives of this chapter must be rather modest:

1. To show that the social-justice theme penetrated the literature of prayer and wisdom.
2. To show that special stress came to be placed on the role of the king and his officials in caring for the poor and downtrodden.
3. To distinguish between psalms of northern and southern provenance.
4. To show that the social justice-social reform theme was especially prominent in the 8th-7th centuries B.C.E., the period of affluence and of the classical prophets.

The Psalms are taken up first.[1]

The social justice theme can be illustrated by Psalms 1, 4, 10, 12, 14, 15, 24, 45, 58, 72, 73, 75, 82, 94, and 101.

> Happy is the man that hath not walked in the counsel of the wicked, nor stood in the way of sinners, nor sat in the seat of the scornful. But his delight is in the law of the Lord; and in His law doth he meditate day and night. And he shall be like a tree planted by streams of water, that bringeth forth its fruit in its season, and whose leaf doth not wither; and in whatsoever he doeth he shall prosper. Not so the wicked; but they are like the chaff which the wind driveth away. Therefore the wicked shall not stand in the judgment, nor sinners in the congregation of the righteous. For the Lord regardeth the way of the righteous; but the way of the wicked shall perish. Psalm 1

There are no obvious clues to the dating of this psalm, but in the references to "a tree planted [or transplanted] by streams of water . . . " and "whose leaf doth not wither" we come very close to Ezekiel 47:12, Jeremiah 17:5–8, Hosea 9:10, and Hosea 4:1–3.

> Tremble, and sin not; commune with your heart upon your bed, and be still. Offer the sacrifices of righteousness, and put your trust in the Lord. Psalm 4:5–6

Apparently this psalm played a part in the regular morning and evening sacrifice. The passages quoted above bear a striking resemblance to Hosea 6:6 and 12:7.

> Why standest Thou afar off, O Lord? Why hidest Thou Thyself in times of trouble? Through the pride of the wicked the poor is hotly pursued: they are taken in the devices that they have imagined. For the wicked boasteth of his heart's desire; and the covetous vaunteth himself, though he contemn the Lord . . . . His

ways propser at all times; ... He sitteth in the lurking-places of the villages; in secret places doth he slay the innocent. His eyes are on the watch for the helpless. He lieth in wait in a secret place as a lion in his lair; he lieth to catch the poor; he doth catch the poor, when he draweth him up in his net .... Wherefore doth the wicked contemn God, and say in his heart: 'Thou wilt not require'? Thou hast seen; for Thou beholdest trouble and vexation, to requite them with Thy hand; Unto Thee the helpless committeth himself. Thou hast been the helper of the fatherless. Break Thou the arm of the wicked; and as for the evil man, search out his wickedness, till none be found. The Lord is King for ever and ever; the nations are perished out of His land. Lord, Thou hast heard the desire of the humble: Thou wilt direct their heart, Thou wilt cause Thine ear to attend; To right the fatherless and the oppressed, that man who is of the earth may be terrible no more.[2] Psalm 10:1–3, 5, 8–9, 13–18

The theme of the wicked businessman who sets traps and ambushes for the righteous poor is prominent in Jeremiah 5:26–28 and Micah 7:2 (see chapter 10).

For the oppression of the poor, for the sighing of the needy, now will I arise, saith the Lord; I will set him in safety at whom they puff. The words of the Lord are pure words, as silver tried in a crucible on the earth, refined seven times. Psalm 12:6–7

The references to smelting and the puffing of the bellows bring to mind Jeremiah 6:28–29 or Ezekiel 22:17–21 (see chapter 2).

The fool hath said in his heart: "There is no God"; they have dealt corruptly, they have done abominably. There is none that doeth good. The Lord looked forth from heaven upon the children of men to see if there were any man of understanding, that did seek after God. They are all corrupt, they are together become impure; there is none that doeth good, no not one. "Shall not all workers of iniquity know it, who eat up My people as they eat bread, and call not upon the Lord?" There are they in great fear; for God is with the righteous generation. Ye would put to shame the counsel of the poor, [You would confound the plans of the poor,] but the Lord is his refuge. Oh that the salvation of Israel were come out of Zion. When the Lord turneth the captivity of His people. Let Jacob rejoice, let Israel be glad. Psalm 14

The references to fools and universal corruption bear a close resemblance to Jeremiah 5:1 (see chapter 11). Psalm 14 duplicates Psalm 53 with the exception that the divine name Yahweh, usually associated with Judah, is employed in 14, while the northern name, Elohim, appears in 53 (see Peters 1922, p. 18).[3] Perhaps the Psalm was composed or adapted for the period when Jeremiah preached in the territory of the former northern kingdom (see Jeremiah 3:12–15).

Lord who shall sojourn in Thy tabernacle? Who shall dwell upon Thy Holy mountain? He that walketh uprightly, worketh righteousness, and speaketh truth in his heart; ... In whose eyes a vile person is despised, but he honoureth them that fear the Lord; he that sweareth to his own hurt, and changeth not; he that putteth not out his money on interest, nor taketh a bribe against the innocent. He that doeth these things shall never be moved. Psalm 15:1-2, 4-5

The references to unjustified profits, being truthful, and security bring strongly to mind Isaiah 33:14-16 (see chapter 10).[4]

The earth is the Lord's, and the fulness thereof; the world, and they that dwell therein. . . . Who shall ascend into the mountain of the Lord? And who shall stand in His holy place? He that hath clear hands and a pure heart: who hath not taken My name in vain, and hath not sworn deceitfully. He shall receive a blessing from the Lord, and righteousness from the God of his salvation. Such is the salvation of them that seek after Him, that seek Thy face, even Jacob. Lift up your heads, O ye gates, and be ye lifted up. ye everlasting doors; that the King of glory may come in. . . . Lift up your heads, O ye gates, yea lift them up, ye everlasting doors; that the King of glory may come in, "Who then is the King of glory?" "The Lord of Hosts; He is the King of glory." Psalm 24:1, 3-7, 9-10

According to Peters (1922, p. 3) this Psalm is associated with the return of the Ark. The use of the word "gates" which is characteristic of Deuteronomy links it with the eighth or seventh centuries.[5] The linkage of righteousness and "blessing" or "life" is characteristic of Amos (see chapter 13).

O Lord, Thou God to whom vengeance belongeth, Thou God to whom vengeance belongeth, shine forth. Lift up Thyself, Thou Judge of the earth; render to the proud their recompense. Lord, how long shall the wicked, how long shall the wicked exult? . . . They slay the widow and the stranger, and murder the fatherless. And they say: 'The Lord will not see, neither will the God of Jacob give heed.' Consider, ye brutish among the people; and ye fools, when will ye understand? He that planted the ear, shall He not hear? He that formed the eye, shall He not see? He that instructeth nations, shall not He correct, even He that teacheth man knowledge? . . . Shall the seat of wickedness have fellowship with Thee, which frameth mischief by statute? . . . But the Lord hath been my high tower, and my God the rock of my refuge. And He hath brought upon them their own iniquity, and He will cut them off in their own evil. The Lord our God will cut them off.[2] Psalm 94:1-3, 6-10, 20, 22-23.

Because of the use of the divine name "Yahweh," Psalm 94 may be placed in Judah (see Peters, 1922, p. 5 and note 3 to this chapter). The reference to "framing mischief on the basis of statutes" closely resembles Isaiah 10:1-2 (see chapter 10). The remainder of the psalm strongly resembles Isaiah 6:9-10: And He said, "Go say to that people: 'Hear indeed but do not understand; see indeed, but do not grasp.' Dull that people's mind, stop its ears, and seal its eyes—lest seeing with its eyes and hearing with its ears, it also grasps its mind, and repents and saves itself."

Psalms 73, 75 and 82 may be discussed together.

Surely God is good to Israel, even to such as are pure in heart. But as for me, my feet were almost gone; my steps well nigh stopped. For I was envious at the arrogant, when I saw the prosperity of the wicked. . . . They scoff, and in wickedness utter oppression; they speak as if there were none on high. . . . Behold such are the wicked; and they that are always at ease increase riches. Surely in vain have I cleansed my heart, and washed my hands in innocency; . . . Until I entered into the sanctuary of God, and considered their end. Surely, Thou settest them in slippery places; thou hurlest them down to utter ruin . . . . As a dream when one awaketh, so O Lord, when Thou arousest Thyself, Thou will despise their semblance. . . . Thou wilt guide me with Thy counsel, and afterward receive me with glory. Psalm 73:1–3, 8, 12–13, 17–18, 20, 24

For God is judge; He putteth down one, and lifteth up another. For in the hand of the Lord there is a cup, with foaming wine, full of mixture, and He poureth out of the same; surely the dregs thereof, all the wicked of the earth shall drain them, and drink them. But as for me, I will declare forever, I will sing praises to the God of Jacob. All the horns of the wicked will I cut off; but the horns of the righteous shall be lifted up. Psalm 75:8–11

God standeth in the congregation of God [gods?]; in the midst of the judges [gods?] He judgeth [gods?]: How long will ye judge unjustly, and respect the persons of the wicked? Judge the poor and fatherless; do justice to the afflicted and destitute. Rescue the poor and needy; . . . I said: Ye are godlike beings [gods?], and all of you are sons of the Most High. Nevertheless ye shall die like men, and fall like one of the princes. Arise, O God, judge the earth; for Thou shalt possess all the nations.[6]Psalm 82:1–4, 6–8

Psalms 73, 75, and 82 are all "of Asaph" and use the divine name El rather than Yahweh. This, it would seem, not only places their origin in the northern kingdom Israel, but also distinguishes them from the psalms of the "sons of Korah," which use Elohim but never El (Peters 1922, pp. 296, 305). Peters (p. 64) suspects that the Asaph psalms had their origin in Bethel.[7] The references to ease and purification in Psalm 73 are somewhat reminiscent of Amos 5:14 (see chapter 13) and 6:4 (see chapter 7). Of course, the universalist outlook of psalms 75 and 82 is quite prominent in Amos, especially 9:7. With respect to Psalm 82, Johnson (1967, p. 136) points out that the "helpless, the poor, and the humble not merely in Israel but throughout the world, may look forward to an era of universal righteousness and peace, as the one omnipotent God comes with judicial power to destroy the wicked."

A similar theme is found in Psalm 58:1–3, 11–12:

Do you indeed speak as a righteous company? [Do you indeed decree what is right, you gods.[6] (Weiser, 1962).] Do ye judge with equity the sons of men? Yea, in heart ye work wickedness; . . . The righteous shall rejoice when he seeth the vengeance; He shall wash his feet in the blood of the wicked. And men shall say:

"Verily there is a reward for the righteous; verily there is a God that judgeth in the
earth.

Here, of course, the theme of universalism is permeated by a brutality and
vindictiveness characteristic of later prophets such as Jeremiah, Zephaniah,
and Ezekiel.

The duty of the state and, more specifically, the king to take special care of
the poor and to root out sin and wickedness and avarice from society—all in
the name of God—is strongly stated in several psalms.

> Thou are fairer than the children of men; grace is poured upon thy lips; therefore
> God hath blessed thee forever. Gird thy sword upon thy thigh, O mighty one, thy
> glory and thy majesty. And in thy majesty prosper, ride on in behalf of truth and
> meekness and righteousness; and let thy right hand teach thee tremendous
> things. . . . Thy throne given of God [O God] is forever and ever; a scepter of
> equity is the scepter of thy kingdom. Thou hast loved righteousness, and hated
> wickedness; therefore God, thy God, hath anointed thee with the oil of gladness
> above thy fellows. Myrrh, and cloes, and cassia are all they garmets; out of
> ivory palaces stringed instruments have made thee glad. Psalm 45:3–5, 7–9

This psalm, at least in origin, is a royal wedding hymn and there is little doubt
that the reference is to a king of the northern kingdom, Israel. The
identification of the psalm with the "sons of Korah," Aramaisms. and the
preference for Elohim as opposed to Yahweh place the psalm in the north,
possibly at the Dan sanctuary (Peters 1922, pp. 5, 9–10) or at Shechem. The
latter possibilities are at least raised by verse 5 of Psalm 46 which, is also
identified with the sons of Korah: "There is a river, the streams whereof
make glad the city of God, the holiest dwelling-place of the Most High." Dan
is situated on the river Jordan, while Shechem is located on a watershed with
part of its numerous streams flowing to the Jordan, while others flow to the
Mediterranean. The reference to ivory palaces seems to clinch the matter of
location both biblically ("the ivory palaces shall be demolished," Amos
3:15, "the ivory house which he [King Ahab] built," I Kings 22:39) and
archaeologically (see Parrot 1958).

Just as interesting, note the parallelism of Psalm 45:8a with both Amos
5:15 "hate the evil and love the good, and establish justice in the gate" and
Micah 3:2, which attacks the "rulers of the house of Israel" because they
"hate the good and love the evil". Mulder (1972, p. 123) discusses this rather
close fit and then notes another correlation between Psalm 45:8a and Amos.

> The anointing of the king is typical for Palestine, and there are several parallels in
> the Old Testament, but never the verb *mashach* is connected with shemen except
> in Amos 6,6. where it is used for anointing for festivities: *v'raysheet shmahneem
> yimshechu*, "they anoint themselves with choice oils." [transliteration mine]

Mulder also provides indirect evidence supporting a preexilic origin for Psalm 45. He lists (pp. 148–49) a variety of parallels with the Akkadian literature and notes that while some of these are attested to during the second millennium (p. 150), "none . . . is found in texts of the sixth century B.C. unless they are also found in earlier texts" (p. 153). Mulder (p. 158) concludes that Psalm 45 "originated probably in the seventh century B.C. in the Southern kingdom, with a good chance that Josiah is the king who is celebrated in the psalm." But this runs counter to the previously cited internal evidence, without reference to the Akkadian texts, which favors a northern origin. Mulder's (p. 157) strongest argument "is formed by the list of expressions in Psalm 45 that have parallels occuring in the royal inscriptions of the last Neo-Assyrian kings only, Sargon II [721–705] and his successors, especially Esarhaddon [680–669]." But as Mulder is well aware, correlation does not establish the direction of influence. The nations of the ancient Near East were continually interacting and there is no reason to assume that the culture of the Israelites was always the dependent variable. Israel, as the others, was both a borrower and a lender. Here I would call attention to the discussion of Piankhi's stele in chapter 16 of this book and, much more importantly, to the striking resemblances between Amos 5:24 and a Neo-Assyrian hymn (chapter 13, note 34); the similarity between Amos's curses and Esarhaddon's vassal treaties (chapter 16 of this book); the concern for the poor reflected in the inscriptions of the last Neo-Assyrian kings (chapter 18 of this book.)[8] Possibly the Assyrians were influenced by the writings of Amos. Clearly he was not influenced by theirs.

Next we have Psalm 72, which was probably sung at the king's enthronement, a festival that Mowinckel (1962, vol. I, p. 60) believes was commemorated annually just as in Egypt, Babylon, Assyria and other Near Eastern states. Note that consistently with this position is the kingship-renewal ceremony for Saul in 1 Samuel 11:14.[9] The parallel between "justice" and "righteousness" found in Psalm 72:2 is, of course, prominent in Amos (5:7, 24; 6:12) but it is clearly and specifically focused on the king by Isaiah (9:6) and Jeremiah (22:3, 15; 33:15).

> Give the king Thy judgments, O God, and Thy righteousness unto the king's son [this member of the royal line]; that he may judge the people with righteousness and Thy poor with justice. . . . May he judge the poor of the people, and save the children of the needy, and crush the oppressor. . . . Yea, all kings shall prostrate themselves before him; all nations shall serve him. For he will deliver the needy when he crieth; the poor also, and him that hath no helper. He will have pity on the poor and needy, and the souls of the needy he will save. He will redeem their soul from oppression and violence, and precious will be their blood in his sight; [from usury and injustice he will redeem their lives; and their name will be precious in his

sight; v. 14, Thomson] that they may live, and that he may give them of the gold of Sheba, that they may pray for him continually, [yea bless him all the day, and he shall live, and to him shall be given the gold of Arabia; and prayers shall be made for him continually; and he will be blessed all the day long. v. 15, Thomson] Psalm 72:1–2, 4, 11–15

Psalm 101 which Mowinckel (1959, p. 293; see also Kenik 1976) views as the "charter" of the king as annointed of God is more easily placed and dated. Because of the use of the divine name Yahweh, as opposed to Elohim, the psalm is of Judean origin (see Peters 1922, p. 5). The picture of the ideal king brings to mind Isaiah 11:1, 3–6 while the "morning to morning" reference suggests Jeremiah 21:11–12.

> I will sing of mercy and justice; unto Thee, O Lord, will I sing praises. I will give heed unto the way of integrity. Oh when wilt Thou come unto me? I will walk within my house in the integrity of my heart. . . . Mine eyes are upon the faithful of the land, that they may dwell with me; he that walketh in a way of integrity, he shall minister unto me. He that worketh deceit shall not dwell within my house. He that speaketh falsehood shall not be established before mine eyes. Morning by morning will I destroy all the wicked of the land; to cut off all the workers of iniquity from the city of the Lord. Psalm 101:1–2, 6–8

A final example, Psalm 2, is somewhat controversial. It is often understood as a threat against foreign "nations" and their "kings," but according to Daiches (1930, pp. 37–44) it is actually a warning to Israelite magnates to dispense justice and judge righteously.[10]

In summation, the objectives set forth have been achieved. A strong social-justice–social-reform theme can be detected in psalms originating in both Israel and Judah. Given the striking resemblances to passages in Amos, Hosea, Isaiah, and Jeremiah it is not unreasonable to date most of these psalms in the eighth or seventh centuries. These resemblances provide additional evidence, if it is still required, of both the influence and the probable professional cultic status of the classical prophets.[11]

The special value of the book of Proverbs is that it gives our analysis of the call for social justice a new dimension. Unlike the psalms and the prophets they have no obvious cultic links, they are fairly characterized as secular and "humanistic" in content. As Kaufmann (1960, p. 316) observes: "Wisdom literature makes no allusion to covenants between man and God. It conceives of morality rather as a kind of natural law that God implanted in the hearts of men." The special disadvantage of the proverbs is that we have no way of knowing whether they occupied a particularly important place in Israelite secular life.

Among the proverbs only the Second Collection of Solomon's Proverbs, 25:1–29:27, is even reasonably well dated. This collection is said to have been edited by the men of king Hezekiah (25:1), which is generally accepted as authentic, and places the collection in Judah near the end of the eighth century (see Inter. 1955, pp. 774–75 and Heaton 1968, p. 186). The procedure employed is as follows:

1. Proverbs 1:1–9:18 and chapter 31 are eliminated from consideration because the long essay style, which differs from the short two-line proverbs that predominate elsewhere, makes it more difficult to apply procedure 2 objectively.

2. The remaining proverbs are grouped into two subcategories: those that display a social justice theme (SJT) and those that do not (NSJT). In the interest of reproducibility, the social justice subcategory is strictly limited to those proverbs that display an explicit concern for the welfare of the poor, debtors, and the like. This means that many proverbs that dwell on righteousness or are critical of sacrifice, or are otherwise related to the social message of the prophets must be placed in NSJT.[12]

3. The percentage of SJT in Hezekiah's eighth-century collection is calculated and compared to the corresponding percentage in all remaining proverbs.

The SJT proverbs in Hezekiah's collection of some 122 proverbs are the following:

28:3 A mighty man by wicked acts oppresseth the poor . . . [13]

28:6 Better is the poor that walketh in his integrity, than he that is perverse in his ways, though he be rich.

28:8 He that augmenteth his substance by interest and increase, gathereth it for him that is gracious to the poor.

28:15 As a roaring lion, as a ravening bear; so is a wicked ruler to poor people.

28:27 He that giveth unto the poor shall not lack; but he that hideth his eyes shall have many a curse.

29:7 The righteous taketh knowledge of the poor; the wicked understandeth not knowledge.

29:13 The poor man [debtor] and the oppressor [creditor] meet together; the Lord giveth light to the eyes of them both.

29:14 The king that faithfully judgeth the poor, his throne shall be established forever.

The SJT proverbs in the remainder of the book, some 418 proverbs, are the following:

14:21 He who despitheth the poor, sinneth; but he who compassionateth the poor is blessed.[14]

14:31 He that oppresseth the poor blasphemeth his Maker; but he that is gracious unto the needy honoureth Him.

19:17 He that is gracious unto the poor lendeth unto the Lord, and his good deed will He repay unto him.

21:13 Whoso stoppeth his ears at the cry of the poor, he also shall cry himself, but shall not be answered.

22:2 The rich and the poor meet together—the Lord is the maker of them all.

22.9 He that hath a bountiful eye shall be blessed; for he giveth of his bread to the poor.

22:16 One may oppress the poor, yet will they gain increase; one may give to the rich, yet will want come.

22:22–23 Rob not the weak, because he is weak, neither crush the poor in the gate; for the Lord will plead their cause, and despoil of life those that despoil them.

23:10–11 Remove not the ancient landmark; and enter not into the fields of the fatherless; for their Redeemer is strong; He will plead their cause with thee.

30:14 This is a generation whose teeth are as swords, and their great teeth as knives, to devour the poor from off the earth,[15] and the needy from among men.

For the Hezekiah collection, the percentage of proverbs with a social-justice theme is 6.5 while the corresponding percentage for the remainder of the proverbs is 2.4. Treating the two percentages as if they were samples we can statistically test the hypothesis that they were drawn from the same population, and that the observed difference is due to chance (including errors in classifcation). The null hypothesis, however, must be rejected: the computed t value is 2.29, which exceeds the critical value, 1.64, for a one-tailed test at the 5-percent-level of significance. The difference between the percentage of SJT proverbs in the Hezekiah collection of the later eighth century and the SJT theme in the remainder of the proverbs is too great to be attributable to chance. Note further that if only the last two chapters of the Hezekiah collection (probably the latest) were considered (some 55 proverbs), the SJT percentage would rise from 6.5 to 14.5.

In conclusion a social-justice theme can be detected in both the cultic psalms and the secular wisdom literature. In both cases this theme is closely linked with the eighth–seventh centuries B.C.E.

Notes

1. Translations of the psalms and proverbs from JPS (1917) unless otherwise specified; see the bibliographic note (chapter 1, note 2.).
2. This is the translation of JPS (1917); Weiser's translation differ in several minor respects.
3. Scholars do not automatically take the alternatives "El" and "Yahweh" as indicative of Israel or Judah, but the possibility is widely acknowledged.
4. Psalm 112, which has an acrostic structure, provides a similar picture of the social virtues. Because of the use of the divine name Yahweh it is probably of Judean origin (Peters 1922, p. 5).
5. Carmichael (1974, p. 261) notes that "gates" is used 25 times in Deuteronomy and rarely elsewhere.
6. On the question of whether Psalms 82 and 58 are directed against mythical gods or earthly judges, see Tsevat (1980, pp. 131–47).
7. Compare Amos 1:2 and Asaph Psalm 76:3 on Zion and (Jeru?)salem. Note that Psalm 74:15, which is also "of Asaph," includes the phrase "everflowing rivers" found in Amos 5:24. Wolff (1973, pp. 10–12) notes the similarity of Amos's interrogative style as manifested, for example, in 5:25: "Did you bring to Me sacrifices and offerings in the wilderness, O house of Israel?" with verse 13 of Asaph Psalm 50: "Do I eat the flesh of bulls, or drink the blood of goats?" Peters (1922, p. 65) believes that the Asaph priests of Bethel later joined Josiah's "Levites." The favorable references to Joseph in Asaph psalms 77:16, 80:2, 6 and 81:6 point to a northern origin while Joseph is rejected in favor of Judah in Asaph Psalm 79:67. Peters (1922, pp. 5, 9–10, 18, 65) links the Korah psalms with Dan (42–49) and, later, with Jerusalem (84–89).
8. Langdon (1914, pp. 145–47) cites several priestly oracles communicated to Esarhaddon and his son and successor Assurbanipal and then notes: "In certain of these oracles the reader will have observed minor subsections introduced by the word here translated 'saying.' This word corresponds precisely to the word *lĕmōr*, 'saying,' so characteristic of Hebrew prophecy. Both words imply a preceding verb of saying or thinking or an idea of some sort, and both introduce the oracular utterances of the deity. The similarity of style between these oracles and the Hebrew Prophets is altogether striking. . . . The use of the tenses . . . reminds strongly of the prophetic use of past tenses in Hebrew prophecy."
9. Tsevat (1980, p. 97) counters: "The installation was a one-time series of acts performed in different places. This explanation, which is the preferred one . . . , is supported by the Mesopotamian custom of coronations, multiple and in different cities." But why then the word "renewal?"
10. Daiches' view seems to be supported by Causse (see Kimbrough 1966, p. 147).
11. It is worth noting that there is evidence linking the Mesopotamian *apkallus* with cultic hymns, possibly as authors: the name of an antediluvian *apkallu* appears as the incipit of a hymn to Enki and King Ur-Ninurta (see Hallo 1963, p. 176).
12. Wolff (1973) points out numerous parallels between Amos and the proverbs.
13. So translated by Thomson; JPS (1917): "A poor man that oppresseth the weak . . . " makes little sense.
14. So translated by Thomson: JPS (1917) renders the verse: "He that despiteth his neighbor sinneth; but he that is gracious unto the humble, happy is he."
15. "Arable land" according to Wolff (1973, p. 73).

III THE IMPLEMENTATION OF SOCIAL REFORM

16 THREE CULTURAL REVOLUTIONS

In the view of the prophets and their allies social injustice was both sinful and avoidable. How simple and obvious was the solution. There need be no national doom, there need be no poverty, if only people behaved correctly: "There shall be no needy among you—since the Lord your God will bless you in the land which the Lord your God is giving you as a hereditary portion—if only you heed the Lord your God and take care to keep all this Instruction that I enjoin upon you this day . . . You will dominate many nations, but they will not dominate you" (Deut. 15:4–6). But the people were "dull" and "foolish" and, could not seem to grasp "all this Instruction." Indeed, they were incapable of understanding even the one sentence instruction that covered them all: "Righteousness and only righteousness you shall pursue."! (Deut. 16:20).

The Program of Social Reform

Salvation required concerted action on two fronts to produce "a holy people" (Deut. 26:17–19). First there had to be an immediate improvement in the behavior of Israelites. To this end a program of economic reforms would be implemented. Second, the Israelites had to learn to think more righteously. This would be accomplished by means of a program of indoctrination which, ultimately would raise behavior to a higher, even godlike, level: "Physical man, dominated by his instincts and desires, his hate and violence, [would] be transformed into a new being who . . . repudiated his nature and became similar to the ideal image of the just person created in God's image. He [would] live by the law of love and refrain from evil . . . Social justice, peace, and the metamorphoses of mankind [would] come about because YHWH [had] willed it" (Choraqui 1975, pp. 186, 197). Deuteronomy was designed to fulfill both programmatic objectives: on the one hand it outlined the necessary economic reforms, and, on the other, it was a textbook of righteousness.

Basically Deuteronomy is a revision and expansion of the old divine-law code[1] in favor of the poor and underprivileged (Irwin 1946, p. 340). Carmichael (1974, p. 258) sees this book as a synthesis of the secular-wisdom teaching (see for instance, Deut. 4:6)[2] with the "prophetic revolutionary morality." He goes on to take note of its pronounced "instructional character": "The frequent indication that a teacher is instructing his pupils is a factor of importance. It is tempting to conclude that this background may be close to the actual life setting of D." Weinfeld (1972, pp. 44–5) adds that Deuteronomy is the only book of the Torah requiring the recitation of liturgies (Deut. 21:7–9; 26:1–11, 12–15). But no scholar has more fully grasped the unique construction of Deuteronomy than Kaufmann (1960, pp. 174–75).

> The books of earlier tradition were testimonials and memorials (cf. Ex. 17:14) rather than books of study. . . . The priestly laws were "handled" and known only by the priests. . . . Deuteronomy is the first to conceive of a Torah book, the possession of the people, to be studied, taught by fathers to sons, its precepts to be bound on the hand and written on the doorposts and gates (Deut. 6:7ff; 11:18ff). Israel's king is to write a copy of the Torah and read in it all his life (17:18ff). It is to be inscribed publicly on stones (27:3, 8); the priests are to read it to all Israel every sabbatical year (31:10ff). The very style of Deuteronomy, repetitive and horatory, is inspired for this purpose.

On the ideological side, however, the distinction between the covenant with the fathers and the covenant at Horeb is absolutely basic. Polzin (1980, p. 44; see also Weinfeld 1970, pp. 195–96) perceptively notes that whenever the concept of divine election (the oath that God made to the fathers) is mentioned, it is carefully neutralized by "controlling retributive statements or else by the insinuation that the covenant at Horeb is *somehow* a necessary condition for the fulfillment of the unconditional oath and covenant God swore to the fathers." In this connection, one is struck by the evident correlation between Deuteronomy 4:1: "And now O Israel, hearken unto the statutes and unto the ordinances, which I am teaching you to perform, so that you may live and go in and possess the land which the Lord, the God of your fathers, gives you."[3] and Amos 5:14: "Seek good and not evil, that you may live, and the Lord, the God of Hosts, may truly be with you as you think." The point is clear: no social justice, no land of Israel.

To accomplish their immediate and long-range objectives, the social reformers needed force. This was applied by the state which not only implemented the proposed social reforms but, via cultic centralization, sought to make Deuteronomy the only and required religious textbook for all Israelites. Further, not only does Deuteronomy call for the appointment of legal officers in each town (16:18–20; most probably it seeks to reform or enlist already existing professional legal functionaries for its purposes), but it also appears to project (reintroduce?) priests into local justice administration (19:17, 21:5; see Phillips 1970, p. 22), and requires that hard cases be brought to the place of cultic centralization ("the place which the Lord your God shall choose") to be settled by "the priests the Levites and the judges that shall be in those days" (17:8–9).[4] Those who disobey are to be executed in order to "exterminate evil from Israel" and so that: "All the people shall hear, and fear, and do no more presumptuously" (17:12–13). Köhler (1956, p. 147) notes with some exaggeration, but, nevertheless, perceptively: "Deuteronomy is at one and the same time a source of the proclamation of the unification of places of worship and of the unification of justice. The old local legal assembly *has* had its useful period of life and has served its purpose but now is replaced."[5]

Bertholet (1926, p. 371) provides a concise summary of the course of events:

> If, as the prophets said, it was the sin of the people that was calling down the judgement, then the task before them was to restate as prohibitions and commands those things which the prophets declared to be the cause of the judgement, and to make them part of a regular constitution which the nation would be compelled to keep. The secular arm gave its aid to the spiritual pedagogues, and as a result Deuteronomy was solemnly introduced as the law of the land in the year 621.

My only modification of this would be to add to 621 the years ca. 751 and ca. 716/5. Ancient Israel experienced no less than three cultural revolutions which, like the editions of Deuteronomy that inspired them, differed in detail but not in their basic thrust.

But the history of the social reforms in Israel beginning in ca. 751 under Jeroboam II was suppressed in the interests of Hezekiah's reforms, which probably date from ca. 716/5, and the history of Hezekiah's reforms was suppressed in the interests of Josiah in ca. 621. This point is well illustrated by a comparison of the accounts of Hezekiah's reign in Kings and Chronicles. As Rosenbaum (1979, pp. 41–2) has noted, the omissions in the preexilic Kings "have one thing in common: they are complimentary to Hezekiah. Such material would have detracted from the accomplishments of . . . Josiah." More basically, Rosenbaum continues, Hezekiah presented a "problem" to the editors of Kings because Hezekiah's reforms were extremely similar to those which governed Josiah except that they eventually proved to be Hezekiah's undoing . . . "Of course Josiah's reforms were also disastrous. Consequently, in the hands of later editors they became more obscure and less praiseworthy.

Chapters 17 and 18 seek to reconstruct the salient features of all three episodes. First, however, the foundations must be laid by demonstrating the probable northern origin of Deuteronomy.

The Northern Origin of Deuteronomy

There is little doubt that Deuteronomy is associated with the book found in the Temple during Josiah's reign. However, the presence of a variety of distinctively northern features has led a number of scholars to conclude that Deuteronomy, or its basic core, originated not in Judah, but in Israel.[6] McCurley (1974, p. 311), for example, concludes his careful survey of this literature with the cautious statement that "it is probable that the home of Proto-Deuteronomy or at least the major traditions of that work, lies in northern Israel." The more important evidence pointing in this direction is summarized below.

Several kinds of evidence make it reasonable to credit the authorship of Deuteronomy to the periods in which the two Hoseas prophesied if not to the two northern prophets themselves.[7] Given the emphasis of Hosea I (1–3) on the sins of Baal worship and Jezreel (a reference to the Naboth incident (1 Kings 21)?) it would seem that he should be placed in the reign of Ahab, that is ca. 874–853 (see Haran in *Encyclopedia Judaica*, 1971, vol. 8, p. 1022). As we saw in chapter 11, the prophesies of Hosea II (4–14) show a definite awareness of Israel's civil war of 747, but not of its invasion by the Assyrians in 734–732. H.L. Ginsberg in the *Encyclopedia Judaica* (1971, vol. 8) suggests several striking linguistic affinities between Deuteronomy and the two Hoseas which may be compactly stated as follows:

1. Hosea 1–3 (ninth century)
The juxtaposition of nakedness and thirst as features of destruction in 2:5, the phrase "I lavished silver and gold on her (*hirbeti lah*)" in 2:10 and fourfold use of *ahav* in 3:1 in the sense of "to befriend" are "deuteronomisms," of Deut. 28:48; 8:13; and 10:18–19 respectively. (p. 1022)

2. Hosea 4–14 (eighth century)

With the exception of Hosea 11:8 and Deut. 29:22, biblical allusions to the destruction of the cities of the plain (see Gen. 14, 19) take specific note only of Sodom and Gemorrah or of Sodom alone. Hosea 11:18 names just Admah and Zeboin while Deut. 29:22 lists all four. [pp. 1022–23] The chain *sava'* ("to be sated") . . . *ram levavo* ("to become haughty") . . . *shakhah ('et YHWH)* ("to forget YHWH") occurs only in Hosea 13:6 and Deut. 8:12. (p. 1023).

Deuteronomy repeatedly (11:28; 13:3, 7, 14; 29:25) warns the Israelites against worshiping "other gods whom you have not known." Hosea condemns Baal, molten images, idols, and calves and adds "thou knowest no God but Me" (13:4). Both are making the point that other entities are "not gods." (pp. 1023–24)

Other connections worth noting are the analogy between father-son and Yahweh-Israel relationships (Hos. 11:1 and Deut. 1:31; 8:5), the strong wisdom element in both Deuteronomy and Hosea (see Andersen and Freedman 1980, p. 70), reference to nonsacrificial slaughtering (Hos. 8:13 and Deut. 12:15), and the threat of return to Egypt (Hos. 8:13; 11:5 and Deut. 17:16; 28:28; 68). More generally, Levine (1974, pp. 51–2) concludes: "Not all of the received text is original to Deuteronomy, of course, but what is original shows striking Hoseanic influences, on the one hand, and no influence whatsoever from Isaiah, hardly conceivable if the book were of Judean origin and a product of the late seventh century.[8]

Perhaps the most important northern feature of Deuteronomy is the presence of an earlier, or at any rate rival, tradition in which cultic centralization is visualized not in the south at Jerusalem, but in the north at Shechem. Deuteronomy (11:31–32; 12:4–6) tells the Israelites that when they "cross the Jordan and occupy the land which the Lord is giving you" they are not to worship in the manner of the Canaanites, but instead to "look only to the place that the Lord your God will choose amidst all your tribes of His habitation, to establish His name there. There you are to go, and there you are to bring your burnt offerings and other sacrifices, your tithes and contributions, your votive and freewill offerings, and the firstlings of your herds and flocks." Both the Masoretic and Septuagint texts of Deuteronomy 11:29 have the Israelites crossing the Jordan and pronouncing "the blessing at Mount Gerizim and the curse at Mount Ebal." These are twin mountains on either side of *Shechem*, some forty miles north of Jerusalem. According to the Masoretic texts of Deuteronomy 27:4–5 and Joshua 8:30, the central altar is to be erected on Mount Ebal; the Septuagint and Samaritan Torah have Mount Gerizim. It is known that in the Persian period, a Samaritan temple was built on Gerizim. Scholars such as Beebe (1970, p. 144) and Gordon (1965a, pp. 146, 189) both favor Gerizim over Ebal. In any event, the central altar seems to be clearly linked with Shechem. The text does not mention Jerusalem and does not even hint that it is "the place which the Lord your God will choose."[9] Gordon (p. 146) adds two additional points in support of Shechem over Jerusalem. First, Solomon's altar of bronze (see chapter 9 of this book) is inconsistent with Deuteronomy 27:6 and Joshua 8:31 both of which command that the central altar be built of "unhewn" or "whole" stones. Second, the ancient claim of Shechem is suggested by the fact that, when Solomon's son, Rehoboam, wished to be acclaimed king, he and "all Israel" went not to Jerusalem but to Shechem (1 Kings 12:1). Moreover, Abimelech was made king at Shechem (Judg. 9:6). The stress on the Josephite tradition as in the Blessing of Moses (Deut. 33) and the emphasis on the Egyptian captivity links Deuteronomy with the Josephite shrine of Shechem, suggests Peters (1922, p. 10; on the Joseph-Shechem connections, see chapter 17 of this book.) An additional point made by McCurley (1974, p. 312) is that "both the covenant renewal pattern [Deut. 28:69] and the Holy War [Deut. 7:16–26; 9:1–6; 20:1–10; 31:3–8] point to the north, for the former is known to have been used at Shechem [Josh. 24] and at Gilgal [1 Sam 12], and the latter seems to be a particular concern of the [northern] Rachel tribes." Wright (1962, pp. 59–63) argues that the lawsuit form of Deuteronomy 32 had its origin in the north.

Deuteronomy repeatedly uses the phrase "God of my [thy, and so forth] father" which, as Jenks (1977, p. 124) points out, is also prominent in many Elohist (E) passages (for example, Gen. 31:5, 29, 42, 53; 46:1, 3; 50:17; Exod. 3:13–16). Peters (1922, p. 10), along the same line, points to the emphasis on the divine name Elohim as opposed to Yahweh in Deuteronomy 32 and 33. The Elohist, of course, is linked by scholars with the northern Israelite tradition.[10]

Deuteronomy 17:15 assures the Israelites that, upon entering the Promised Land, "you shall be free to set a king over yourself, one chosen by the Lord your God." Von Rad (1966, p. 26) argues that, even when account is taken of 17:20 which raises the possibility of a dynasty,[11] the degree of flexibility in choice visualized here simply does not fit the circumstances of Judah, where by the time of Josiah in the later seventh century, the Davidic dynasty had long since become inviolate. On the other hand, Deuteronomy 17:15 is consistent not only with the dynastic instability of the northern kingdom but also with the specific complaint of the eighth-century Hosea (8:4): "They have made kings, but not with My sanction."

Segal (1963, pp. 208–9) points out that the passover of Deuteronomy 16 has two unique aspects. First, in 16:8 the seventh day is called *'asereth*— which has no parallel in any other account of Passover. Second, after having recalled the linkage between Passover and the Exodus, Deuteronomy 16:7 tells the Israelites that on the morning after the Pesah they should "go" or "turn" to their "tents."[12] Interestingly, the linkage of Exodus, tents, and, it would seem, passover, is also found in the eighth-century prophet Hosea:

> I the Lord have been your God ever since the land of Egypt. I will let you dwell in your tents again as in the fixed season. (12:10)

> For, lo, they are gone away from destruction, yet Eygpt shall gather them up, Memphis shall bury them; their precious treasures nettles shall possess them. Thorns shall be in their tents. (9:6)[13]

The Egyptians it will be remembered gave the Israelites jewels, gold, and silver either just before (Exod. 11:1–5) or just after (Exod. 12:35–36) the plague of the first born and the Lord's passover (Exod. 12). It would seem that Deuteronomy 16:7 reflects the passover celebration of eighth-century Israel wherein the northerners recalled the Lord's deliverance by living in tents and wearing silver ornaments (see Segal 1963, pp. 213–14).[14] Note, finally, that in the Samaritan passover celebration the sacrifice took place at sunset after which the participants returned to the tents they had pitched on Mount Gerizim (see Welch 1924, 74–7).

There is also the singular fact that "the dog did not bark." *Am-haaretz* is taken by some scholars to refer to a "national council" and by others to the "landowning class" or a "power group." Talmon (1967, pp. 71, 74) tells us that this term is mentioned 74 times (27 independent references) in the biblical literature dealing with events ranging from the mid-ninth to the beginning of the sixth century. In the majority of cases, *am-haaretz* appears in connection with the affairs of Judah, especially Jerusalem, in 2 Kings, 2 Chronicles, Jeremiah, and Ezekiel. Deuteronomy, however, does not mention the word even once. This is rather strange if we are to believe that the book originated in Judah at the time of Josiah or even of Hezekiah. Levine (1980, p. 451) adds that *māqôm*, "which is undoubtedly a term of northern usage" is used for "cult-place" in Deuteronomy, while Kings employs *bāmâ*, which "appears to be a term of southern origin."

Several other pieces of evidence link Deuteronomy with eighth century Israel. The word "gate" (or "assembly" or "synagogue"?) is used 25 times in Deuteronomy and rarely elsewhere (Carmichael 1974, p. 261). The word is, however, used three times in Amos (5:10, 12, 15).[15] The Egyptian ruler Piankhi (ca. 751–730) who besieged the city of Medum had the following words inscribed on a stela: "See two ways are before you; you must choose as you wish: open up, and you shall live; close, and you shall die" (Williams 1971, p. 267). Compare this message with Deuteronomy 30:15, 19–20: "See I have set before you this day life and prosperity, death and adversity . . . I have put before you life and death, blessing and curse. Choose life—if you and your offspring would live, by loving the Lord your God, heeding His commands and holding fast to Him." It seems more reasonable to assume that Piankhi influenced Deuteronomy, or that Deuteronomy influenced Piankhi, than that Piankhi's formulation was recalled and adapted a century later in Josiah's Judah. I would add that the passage in question is reminiscent of Amos 5:6: "Seek the Lord and you shall live." Note also the correlation of the latter and 5:14 with Deuteronomy 4:1.

Even more reminiscent of Amos is the devaluation of Israel's special status with respect to Yahweh's gift of land. Compare Amos 9:7–8

> To Me, O Israelites, you are just like the Ethiopians. True, I brought Israel up from the land of Egypt, but also the Philistines from Capthor and the Aramaeans from Kir. Behold the eyes of the Lord God are upon the sinful kingdom, and I will destroy it from off the face of the earth;

with Deuteronomy 2:4–5, 9–12, 19–23:

> And command thou the people, saying Ye are to pass through the border of your brethren the children of Esau, that dwell in Seir; . . . contend not with them; for I will not give you of their land . . . because I have given Seir unto Esau for a possession . . . . And the Lord said unto me: Be not at enmity with Moab, neither contend with them in battle; for I will not give thee of his land for a possession; because I have given Ar unto the children of Lot for a possession. The Emim dwelt there aforetime . . . these also are accounted Rephaim, as the Anakim; . . . And in Seir dwelt the Horites aforetime, but the children of Esau succeeded them; and they destroyed them from before them, and dwelt in their stead; as Israel did unto the land of his possession, which the Lord gave unto them. . . . And when thou comest nigh over against the children of Ammon, harass them not, nor contend with them; for I will not give thee the land of the children of Ammon for a possession; because I have given it to the children of Lot for a possession. That also is accounted a land of Rephaim . . . but the Lord destroyed them before them; and they dwelt in their stead; as He did for the children of Esau, that dwell in Seir, when He destroyed the Horites from before them; . . . and the Avvim, that dwelt in villages as far as Gaza, the Caphtorim, that came forth out of Capthor, destroyed them, and dwelt in their stead.

and Deuteronomy 9:4–5:

> Speak not thou in thy heart, after that the Lord thy God hath thrust them out from before thee, saying: For my righteousness the Lord hath brought me in to possess this land; whereas for the wickedness of these nations the Lord doth drive them out from before thee. Not for they righteousness, or for the uprightness of thy heart, dost thou go in to possess their land; but for the wickedness of these nations the Lord thy God doth drive them out from before thee, and that He may establish the word which the Lord swore unto they fathers . . .

Here we find the most pronounced linkage between the central ideology of Deuteronomy and the lesson taught by Amos at Bethel in the northern kingdom. Moreover, Coote (1981, p. 53) points out that "the language of Amos 5:5. 'Do not *seek Bethel*, nor *enter in* at Gilgal,' is similar to the language of Deuteronomy 12:5, '*The place* which Yahweh chooses you shall *seek*, and there you shall *enter in*' . . . " He adds that the verb "seek" takes an object of place only in these two passages and in 2 Chronicles 1:5, where it refers to the temple built by Solomon in Jerusalem.[16]

With respect to the question of later editions of Deuteronomy note should be taken not only of the resemblance between Deuteronomy 10:12–13 and Micah 6:8 and between Isaiah 31:1, but of numerous striking linguistic affinities between Deuteronomy 28, an unusually lengthy chapter of blessings and curses, the prose sermons of Jeremiah, the book of Lamentations, and Leviticus 26. The language of Deuteronomy 28 as a whole, however, cannot be claimed to be the same as that of these other sources (see Sturdy 1980, pp. 144–47). In this connection it is well to note the marked resemblances between the "curses" found in Amos (2:15–16; 4:6–11; 5:11; 6:7, 11–12; 7:17), those in Esarhaddon's (680–669) vassal treaties, and those in Deuteronomy 28:15–68.[17] Finally, Frankena (1965, pp. 153–54) notes the striking similarity between Deuteronomy 29:24–28[18] and Jeremiah 22:8–9 (dealing with the penalty for violating the covenant with Yahweh) and a passage of the Annals of Assurbanipal (668–627).

The Assault on Ritual and Tradition

Traditional observances such as rituals have a high survival value, because, by reducing anxiety and raising confidence, they enhance the ability of individuals and peoples to cope with reality (Wallace 1966, pp. 233–36). Nevertheless, if the obstacles in the path of Israel's social reformers could be summarized in two words, those words would be "ritual" and "tradition" ("all kinds of cant" according to Albright 1960, pp. 83–4). The expanation is provided by Gouldner's (1980, p. 118) observation that ritual is "an instrument in principle capable of achieving any goal set by will; it is open to any ambition . . . A religious hostility to ritual, such as Puritanism's requires that there be methodological conformity to ethical principles that . . . limit the will, bending it, disciplining it, not permitting it just any ambition, and requiring at all times a conscientious conformity to these principles in the everyday life." But, as we have seen, long before the Puritans, the Prophets attacked ritual in the name of "ethical principles," specifically in the name of social justice. This, however, was far from enough. The Israelites were "beguiled by the delusions after which their fathers walked" (Amos 2:4). For the teaching process to be effective, for the masses to fully commit themselves to the worship of social justice, the context of worship had to be controlled. Accordingly, the distracting influences of such "vanities" as multiple communal altars and such "fetishes"[19] as household (or ancestral) religion, were to be swept aside into the dustbin of discredited history.

Deuteronomy 16 mandates the removal of the very ancient Passover sacrifice and cermony from the household and local sanctuary to a central sanctuary. As Morgenstern (1966, pp. 170–71) concludes, the Deuteronomic reform

> divested the festival ritual of all its original character and meaning . . . . The blood of the sacrifice was no longer sprinkled upon the doorposts and lintel, the bunch of hyssop was no longer used nor could the sacrifice be eaten any longer within the house and in haste by the worshippers with their loins girded, their staves in their hands, and their sandals upon their feet, nor could the prohibition of leaving the house during the entire night be observed in any manner. . . . Moreover . . . it tended to abrogate a custom of long-established practice, upon which in great part the safety and protection of every home and all its inmates were popularly thought to depend.

Social justice would now protect the Israelite household.

The fountainhead, however, of the attack on multiple communal altars is Deut. 12:2–6:[20]

> You must destroy all the sites at which the nations you are to dispossess worshiped their gods, whether on lofty mountains and hills or under any luxuriant tree. Tear down their altars, smash their pillars, put the sacred posts to the fire, and cut down the images of their gods, obliterating their name from that site. Do not worship the Lord your God in like manner, but look only to the site that the Lord your God will choose amidst all your tribes as His habitation, to establish His name there. There you are to go, and there you are to bring your burnt offerings and other sacrifices, your tithes and contributions, and the firstlings of your herds and flocks.

In short, one altar is legitimate while all the others, regardless of their function or historical connection to the Israelites, are condemned as foreign and idolatrous.

As if to leave no doubt that this is exactly what is meant, 2 Kings 17 explains that the Jews of the northern kingdom were exiled in part because they "had feared other gods" (verse 7) and in part because they "did impute things that were not right unto the Lord their God, and they built them high places in all their cities, from the tower of the watchman to the fortified city; and they set them up pillars and Asherim [sacred posts] upon every high hill and under every lofty tree; and there they offered[21] in all the high places, as did the nations whom the Lord carried away before them." (verse 9). Here the temples built by the Israelites in their cities are like the pillars and sacred posts on the hills, explicitly categorized as "high places" (*bamath*). In fact it is quite possible that the shrines or temples in the cities and those in the surrounding countryside had distinct functions that were not only nonforeign and nonidolatrous, but also highly efficacious.

There is little or nothing to choose among the urban temples dedicated to the worship of Yahweh. If Dan and Bethel in the north had calves, then Jerusalem had cherubs, a brazen serpent (2 Kings 18:4: see Sarna 1975), and horses and chariots of the sun (2 Kings 23:11). All, as Kaufmann (1960, p. 136) points out, belonged to the same ancient Israelite traditions. Were they of foreign origin? Is there anything under the sun that is entirely new and original?[22] At Tepe Gawra in the district northeast of Nineveh in Assyria excavations recovered from a temple dating not later than the end of the fourth millennium a phallic object that is obviously intended to emphasize circumcision (Speiser, 1935, p. 99).

Was there a cultic substitute for the smashed temple altars? Perhaps. It has been suggested that in prophetic times the term "gate" (or perhaps "synagogue") referred to a rendezvous place in which the prophets held their meetings (see Rowley 1967, pp. 216–17 and Silber 1915, pp. 18, 22). Bowker (1969, pp. 9–10), pursuing a somewhat different line, has studied the *ma'amadoth*, that is, the divisions of the people corresponding to the twenty-four courses of priests in the Temple. He presents evidence from the targums and rabbinic literature of later times suggesting that, when the course of a local group met, it assembled under prophets to read passages of scripture corresponding to the sacrifices taking place in Jerusalem. Several scholars have hypothesized that, after the altars of the high places were broken, these shrines continued in use as "gates" or "synagogues" for the reading of scripture and the delivery of sermons. This, of course, would have meant the study of Deuteronomy and social justice. Several pieces of evidence support this theory. In the Diaspora, there were houses of prayer that were distinct from the synagogues. Synagogues were places for the reading and the study of the Torah. Philo, in fact, described the synagogue as a school. Further, the Palestinian synagogues were built on the highest sites in the towns and, in still later times, this placement became the explicit rule (see Rowley 1967, p. 230; Silber 1915, pp. 18–19). Bowker (1969, p. 10) suggests that when the destruction of the Temple made sacrifices impossible, the houses of prayer and of study were fused. At this time the study of the Torah was set in a liturgical context Archaeological evidence is also consistent with the posited conversion of the high places into centers for indoctrination. Aharoni's (1979, pp. 303–5) disputed conclusion is that the sanctuary at Arad, which was built on the site of an ancient high place, continued in use even after the destruction of its altar. Possibly this holds for the sanctuary in Beer-sheba as well.

While the urban high places undoubtedly focused on the worship of Yahweh, the high places of the countryside may well have served as centers of household or clan religion. It is well known that in ancient Greece and Rome it was the duty of a son to make libations and sacrifices in honor of his deceased father and his ancestors. His wife, an outsider, was consecrated to the ancestral worship by means of a sacred ceremony. The bible tells us that the Hebrew patriarchs sacrificed (Gen. 31:51–54; 46:1)[23] to the "God of the Fathers" and, more specifically, it reveals that each patriarchal clan seems to have visualized its relationship with the deity in a special way (Fohrer 1972, pp. 38–9). These include: "Fear of Isaac" (probably "Kinsman of Isaac"), "Mighty One of Jacob," "Rock of Israel," "God of Abraham," or, perhaps, "Shield of Abraham" (Gen. 15:1). Further, until the tenth century, biblical names frequently reflect a kinship relation with God. Abiezer, for example, means "My (divine) father is (my) help." while Eliah means "My God is (my) father," and Ammiel means "(The God) of my clan is (my) God." Exodus 22:19 declares that "He who sacrifices to the *elohim* is to be destroyed" and probably refers to the household gods. Apparently, the sacrifices to the *elohim* or ancestors were offered in the shade of trees at "high places."

The conception of a stone or pillar (*maṣṣēbāh*) or stela as the witness of a covenant before Yahweh is quite frequent in the Bible (see, for example, Gen. 28:18, 22; 31:51–52; 35:14; Exod. 24:4; Josh. 24:27; Isa. 19:19–20; 2 Chron. 29:10; see further McCarthy 1978, p. 195). But the pillar may also have witnessed a covenant before the deceased ancestors. This possibility is supported by several Phoenician inscriptions (Cooke 1903, pp. 64, 70):

The pillar among the living which 'Abd-osir set up to his father Arketha.

This is the pillar which Eshmun-ṣillaḥ and Mar-yehai set up for their father Melexenos.

This pillar (is that) which Arish, chief of the brokers, erected to his father, Parsi, chief of the brokers, son of Arish, chief of the brokers, son of Menaḥem, chief of the brokers, son of Mashal, chief of the brokers, and to his mother, Shem-Labul, daughter of Ba'alram, son of Milk-yathon, son of 'Azar, chief of the prefects (?), over their restingplace for ever.

A Ugaritic text refers to "One who sets up the stela of his ancestral gods in the shrine" (Iwry 1957, p. 227). A corresponding Israelite usage is indicated in 2 Samuel 18:18 which reveals that "Absalom, in his lifetime, had taken the pillar which is in the Valley of the Kings [in the neighborhood of Jerusalem] and set it up for himself; for he said; 'I have no son to keep my name alive'." Earlier, of course, Jacob set up a pillar at Rachel's grave (Gen. 35:19–20). Albright (1968b, pp. 105, 107) argues that, in the Sinai and Arabia, burial cairns evolved into altar platforms with one or more memorial pillars, while some *bamoth* served as places of sacrificial feasts. He compares the latter to the Islamic *welis* or shrines of saints.[24] Excavations in Canaanite "high places," Heaton (1968, p. 133) adds, reveal such large numbers of pillars that it is possible they served as cemeteries. In the Bible we read that in the midst of desecrating the altar and shrine of Bethel, "Josiah turned and saw the graves that were on the hill." (2 Kings 23:16). We are further informed that this cemetery included the graves of two revered figures, the "man of God from Judah" and the "old prophet from Samaria [Bethel]" (2 Kings 23:17). Nevertheless, in Deuteronomy 16:21–22, Yahweh appears to repudiate both groves and pillars. Then, in Deuteronomy 26:14, the bringer of the tithe protests: "I have not eaten thereof in my mourning, neither have I put away thereof, being unclean, nor given thereof for the dead." Note the apparent connection with Hosea 9:4: "Their sacrifices are as the bread of mourning unto them; all that eat thereof shall be polluted."

It is known that ancient Egypt possessed a specialized class of funerary priests (or cemetary chaplains) that had nothing to do with the cult of the gods (Sauneron 1960, p. 108). Did the Israelites also have funerary priests? If so, can they be identified with the *kemārim* (usually translated as "idolatrous priests") whom, according to 2 Kings 23:5, "the kings of Judah had ordained to offer in the cities of Judah, and in the places round about Jerusalem"?[25] We know that the word *kmr* occurs frequently in Phoenician and other Near Eastern inscriptions with the meaning "priest" (see, for example, McKay 1973, pp. 36–7).

The obscurities surrounding the function of the Israelite high places serve to remind us how little we know concerning the preexilic relationship between the living and the dead. The practice in the Bible, for example, of naming the burial places of patriarchs, judges, and kings may reflect institutions similar to the Assyrian *kispum*—that is, temples of food and drink offerings to the dead[26] (Grayson 1972, pp. 24–5). Also, Amos 6:7 calls or compares the festivities of the affluents to a "*marzēah* feast." Is this reference entirely sarcastic? In Ugarit, El's *marzēah*-feast involved the god's drunkenness (Pope 1977a, pp. 164–5). However, nonmythological Ugaritic texts refer to "*marzēah*-men," to the "house of the *marzēah*-men," and to the fields and vineyards of the *marzēah* (Porten 1968, p. 180). Other inscriptions dating from the third century B.C.E. to the third century C.E. refer to the *marzēaḥ* in terms suggesting a religious guild or association which held banquets in honor of the gods, worthy members of the guild, and the dead (Porten 1968, pp. 181–83). A fifth century B.C.E. ostracon found at at Elephantine, the site of a Jewish colony in Egypt, is a communication between two individuals concerning "the money for the *marzēaḥ*." From the materials reviewed above, Porten (1968, p. 184) surmises that it deals with raising funds for a banquet to honor a late member. The connection of the *marzēaḥ* with the dead is quite consistent with Jeremiah 16, in which the Lord tells the prophet not to marry or have children or to mourn or comfort the mourner. Porten (1968, pp. 180–81) explains that the prophet "was to stay away from the 'house of feasting' and the 'house of *marzēaḥ*'." (See Jer. 16:5, 8; Job 30:23; Isa. 14:18) "It is clear from the context that these two terms are parallel. A *marzēah* was a 'revelry' or a 'banquet.' The house of *marzēah* was the house of mourning where one broke bread for the mourner and offered him the cup of consolation (Jer. 16:7)."[27]

Quite reasonably, Greenberg (1979, p. 96) wonders "whether the surviving literature has not in fact censored certain popular notions in which the dead played a part in the religious life of the living." Some of the surviving literature seems to equate the remembrance of the dead with soothsaying and witchcraft, just as it equates the ancient cultic role of women with prostitution.[28] In fact Jews today offer prayers for the dead and erect "pillars" and visit the graves of their loved ones. The practice of commemorating the dead by lighting a lamp can be traced as far back as the third millennium in ancient Egypt (see Leibovitch 1953, p. 110).

Turning again to Roman household worship we encounter a small image, the Lar, which served as the guardian spirit of the family.[29] More ancient, in the legal texts of Nuzu (middle of the second millenium) the word *ilāni* is used for the ancestral images. In Gen. 31 and Judges 18 the word *elohim* the usage of which closely parallels that of *ilāni* alternates with the word "*teraphim*" (Draffkorn 1957, pp. 216–17). Evidently *elohim* and *teraphim* refer to the Israelites' ancestral images. We read in Judges 17:5 that the wealthy Israelite Micah "had a house of God [god?] and he made an ephod [an ark or box?] and teraphim, and consecrated one of his sons who became his priest." Once more we are reminded of Roman practice: usually the Lar was placed in a niche near the hearth, but in wealthier homes it stood on a pedestal in a small shrine.

Deuteronomy does not explicitly single out the teraphim but 4:16 warns the Israelites "not to act wickedly and make for yourselves a sculptured image in any likeness whatever; the form of a man or woman, the form of any beast on earth, the form of any bird that flies in the sky, the form of anything that creeps on the ground." The warning is repeated in 4:23, 25; 5:8–9; and 27:15. Joshua 24, which is usually classified with the deuteronomic literature (see De Vaux 1978, pp. 581–84) explicitly urges the Israelites assembled at Shechem to "put away the gods that your forefathers served beyond the river [Euphrates? The "gods of the fathers"?] and in Egypt, and serve the Lord" (verse 14). Several other biblical passages ridicule or explicitly condemn ancestral worship. In Genesis 31:20–23, Rachel "steals" the teraphim from her father Laban's house and he pursues her to recover them. Obviously, this suggests the importance of the images to both parties. Most probably, Rachel counted on the gods of her father for protection during the journey prior to her formal induction into Jacob's household.[30] But in verses 34–5 we find Rachel displaying contempt toward the teraphim. She places them in a camel cushion and sits on them pretending to be having her period while Laban searches. Similarly, in verse 37, Jacob refers to the teraphim as household "objects" or "stuff." Again, in Judges 17–18 money that had been stolen is used to make teraphim which, in the end, are themselves stolen. Another sly attack on the traditional veneration of ancestors is inserted into 1 Samuel 19:13, wherein David's wife Michal helps him to escape from Saul's officers by placing the teraphim in the bed and pulling a quilt of goat's hair over them. Not only is this usage similar to Rachel's demeaning, but we also have the small items magnified into life-size images. Another, less subtle, passage, 1 Samuel 15:23 asserts: "For rebellion is as the sin of witchcraft, and stubborness is as idolatry and teraphim."[31] Yet Hosea 3:4 which, as we have seen, may well date to the middle of the ninth century reads: "For the children of Israel shall sit solitary for many days without king, and without prince, and without sacrifice, and without pillars, and without ephod or teraphim." Is this passage sarcastic? Or does it, as I suspect, mean that the Israelites will be deprived of cherished traditional values?

Within each cycle of economic-cultic reform the prophets, equipped with the state's scalpel, carefully and successfully cut social injustice from the body politic and thereby saved the Israelite nation. Banished were the bad old days of Judges 17:6, and elsewhere, "when there was no king in Israel and every man did that which was right in his own eyes." But the patient, that always backsliding and stiffnecked Israelite, could not comprehend that he had been cured, and his condition always deteriorated. So the social reformers had to probe for previously undetected economic sins. Cultic forms that had long since been emptied of their original meaning were blamed for the new symptoms and were amputated. As debacle followed debacle it became necessary to invent abominations.[32] Witches were sought and destroyed.

The process begins with thinly veiled attacks.[33] As Ginsberg (1961, p. 345) notes, Jacob "a revered figure of the past [is] secondarily . . . made ridiculous in the interests of religious reform." He is portrayed in Hosea 12:5 as building an altar in Bethel dedicated to the angel he wrestled with and defeated there. But Genesis tells us that the altar was erected at Bethel prior to Jacob's arrival in Aram (35:1–7), while the wrestling match took place after his departure from Aram at Penuel (in Transjordan). The attack on "angels" is at the same time an attack on the living Mosaic traditions. (Note, in this connection, the sins of Moses in Deuteronomy 32:51). So also is the story in Judges 17–18, which suggests that Moses's[34] grandson, a Levite "na'ar" named Jonathan, participated in the theft of Micah's idols and then set them up in the sanctuary he founded at Dan. Hosea refers to the ancient shrine at Bethel as Beth-aven or "Delusionsville" (4:15; 5:8; 10:5). Another giant of the past, Aaron, is portrayed as a maker of idols, a weakling, and a fool: "They said to me, 'Make us a god [angel?] to lead us; for that man Moses, who brought us from the land of Egypt—we cannot tell what has happened to him.' So I said to them, 'Whoever has gold, take it off!' They gave it to me and I hurled it into the fire and out came this calf!' " (Exod. 32:23–24). In Hosea 10:5 this great symbol of the Exodus becomes the "calf of Beth-aven" and the priests are *kemārim* ("idoltrous priests") Both Aaron and the calf are attacked in Deuteronomy 9:15–21.

The process of total social destruction in the name of total social justice achieves its culmination in Jeremiah and Ezekiel. First we have the "vexing problem" of the "cult of Molech." Green's (1975, p. 186) conclusion is that: "We simply do not know precisely what was the nature of this ritual." But we do know, as Cogan (1974, p. 77) points out, that the prophetic denunciations lose track of the distinction between actual child sacrifice and a divinatory fire cult: "The verbs 'transfer/pass through fire' and 'burn' are freely interchanged and new vocables 'sacrifice' and 'slaughter' are introduced" (see Jer. 7:31; 19:5; 32:35; Ezek. 16:20–21). There is in addition the question of the extent to which the adherents of exotic religious practices such as child sacrifice at Topheth (2 Kings 23:10) were resident aliens rather than Israelites. Leviticus 20:2, for example, specifically includes "strangers residing in Israel" in its ban on giving "offspring to Molech." Cogan concludes from his analysis that we are dealing with "prophetic polemics."[35] This conclusion finds support to what we know of the household religions of Greece and Rome. According to Fustel de Coulanges (1896, p. 67), within a short time after the birth of a son, the child was inducted into the ancestral cult by a female, no doubt the mother, carrying him several times around the sacred fire in the domestic hearth.[36]

Is this Baal worship? Kings does not hint at any anti–foreign-god movement during the century or so following the mid-ninth-century purges of Jehu and the priest Jehoiada in Israel and Judah respectively. In 2 Kings 21:3 there is the report that the evil (to the social reformers) King Manasseh had "erected altars for Baal and made a sacred post, as King Ahab [earlier 9th century] of Israel had done" and 2 Kings 23:5 reports that Josiah suppressed "those who made offerings to Baal." Given this vagueness it is not at all surprising that when Jeremiah leveled charges of Baal worship, his puzzled contemporaries replied: "I have not gone after the Baalim" (2:23). With respect to "astral worship" which is condemned by Jeremiah (8:2) and figures in Ezekiel's vision (8:16–18), we are told that Josiah suppressed those who made offerings "to the sun and moon and constellations—all the host of heaven" that he "did away with the horses that the kings of Judah had dedicated to the sun at the entrance of the House of the Lord," that he "burned the chariots of the sun," and also "tore down altars made by the kings of Judah on the roof by the upper chamber of Ahaz, and the altars made by Manasseh in the two courts of the House of the Lord" (23:5, 11–12). What does this all come to? An unspecified number of those who made offerings were suppressed and some mostly venerable masonry was turned into rubble. We do not really know how the ancient Israelites understood the "host of heaven" but we do know that a heavenly court presided over by Yahweh was traditional in their conceptualization of the divine realm (see, for instance, 1 Kings 22:19). With respect to horses and chariots of the sun, we know, for example, that Solomon's temple possessed a golden model of the "chariot of cherubs" (1 Chron. 28:18) and that Elijah was taken to heaven by a chariot and horse of fire (2 Kings 2:11).[37] As McKay (1973, p. 34) observes, Elisha's words, "Oh father, father! Israel's chariots and horsemen!" must have had some relationship to Israelite cultic traditions.[38]

The worship of the "Queen of Heaven" is doubly perplexing because it brings to the forefront the role of women in the ancient cult. According to Jeremiah (7:18; 44:19) Judean women vexed the Lord by making "cakes" for the "Queen of Heaven." But in 2 Samuel 6 the ark is brought into Jerusalem, and at the conclusion of the ceremonies (verse 9), David gives each person "a cake of bread, and a cake made in a pan, and a sweet cake" (raisin cake?).[39] Moreover, can we be sure that the rite for the female deity is really very different from that of the "facial bread" (lehem hepānîm) in Leviticus 24:8? Perhaps we have all the answer we need in Jeremiah 44:17–19 wherein the Jewish-exile community in Egypt belatedly puts the prophet squarely in his place: "We will do everything which we have vowed—to make offerings to the Queen of Heaven and to pour libations to her, as we used to do, we and our fathers, our kings and our officials, in the towns of Judah and the streets of Jerusalem. For then we had plenty to eat, we were well-off, and suffered no misfortune. But ever since we stopped . . . we have lacked everything, and we have been consumed by the sword and by famine." If the ancient Jews worshipped a goddess she certainly could not be classified among the "strange gods" whom the Israelites had not known.

Let us now turn to the cultic and economic reforms and their consequences.

Notes

1. Note that Exodus 20–23 (the Covenant Code) is written in the manner of Near Eastern case law, as are several Deuteronomic laws.
2. Israel's righteous laws of the wise have their Old Babylonian counterpart in the *dīnāt mīšarim* of the wise (see Weinfeld 1972a, p. 151).
3. Translations of JPS unless otherwise specified; see the bibliographic note (Chapter 1, note 2.).
4. Milgrom (1973, p. 159) stresses that "it is the new judicial status that D bestows on the priest that constitutes one of its far-reaching innovations." An explicit judicial role for the priesthood in the (presumably) earlier biblical literature is found, according to Phillips (1970, p. 22), only in cases of disputed property requiring an oath (Exod. 22:7 ff.). Does Moses represent king or priest in Exod. 13:1?
5. It is likely that centrally appointed judges predate the Deuteronomic reform (Chapter 18, note 5). Does the central appeal court represent an innovation? It is unclear whether the Jerusalem court established by Jehoshaphat in the first half of the ninth century (2 Chron. 19:8) had final jurisdiction over all Judah or only over the residents of Jerusalem (compare JPS, (1917) with Myers and Thomson).
6. See, for example, von Rad (1966, pp. 26–7) and Welch (1924). Sellin and Fohrer (1968, p. 175) do not provide supporting evidence or an explanation, but they state that Deuteronomy "came into being in Northern Israel . . . probably not later than the first half of the eighth century" and find the "answer" in the "great prosperity of the kingdom under Jeroboam II."
7. Andersen and Freedman (1980, p. 64) believe that "the strong thematic and verbal association between chapter 2 and the latter part of the book, especially chapters 4–5, militate against the views that the parts of the book belong to different centuries or refer to different prophets." But they admit that chapters 1–3 and chapters 4–14 contrast sharply, not only in literary style and construction, but also in the frequency of prose particles: 11 percent of all words in chapters 1–3 as opposed to 3 percent of all words in chapters 4–14. In the end they suggest that "chapters 1–3 . . . have been put together by someone else, especially the large central section (2:4–25)."
8. However, Deuteronomy 17:16, which forbade the king to "multiply horses" and, therefore, chariots, by dealing with Egypt strongly resembles a passage in Isaiah (see Chapter 11 of this book). Another possibility is that this represents an attack on Solomon (the Davidic dynasty) who bought horses and chariots in Egypt (1 Kings 10:28–29; see note 11 following.).
9. Because of the repeated references to "the mountain of the height of Israel," J. Smith (1931, pp. 66–8) suggests that Ezekiel wished the central temple to be built not at Jerusalem but at Shechem-Gerizim.

10. For additional links between Deuteronomy and E and references on the northern origin of E, see Levine (1976, p. 16); Eissfeldt (1965, pp. 203–04); Jenks (1977, pp. 48, 93).

11. Some scholars consider this verse to be a later Judean insertion. On the other hand, it is not totally inconceivable that the prohibition against making a foreigner the king (Deut. 17:15) is aimed at Judah's Davidic dynasty. Certainly Bathsheba's son Solomon could have been regarded as a foreigner. Indeed, even David himself might not be immune from such a charge. "According to what evidence has survived his [David's] family was closely connected with Kenite and Kenizzite elements in the south, contained a strong Moabitic element [Ruth 4:17–22 and possibly 1 Sam 22:3–4], and may even . . . have had some ethnic relationship with groups settled at an early date in or near Kiriath-jearim" (Blenkinsopp 1972, pp. 85, 24–5, 29). Deuteronomy 17:16, which forbade the king to multiply horses may also be an attack on Solomon and the Davidic dynasty (see note 8 above).

12. So translated by JPS (1917); JPS (1962), JPS (1974) and Thomson do not mention "tents" but only that "in the morning you may start back on your journey home."

13. So translated by JPS (1917); JPS (1978) emends "destruction" to "to Assyria" and replaces "tents" with "(old) homes."

14. The unleavened bread, roasted (as opposed to boiled) meat, and bitter herbs (related to the astringent sycamore figs?) are also ways of going back to origins. Note that in the affluent second century C.E. Graeco-Egyptians consumed barley gruel three times a year, during the three major religious festivals (Darby, Ghaliougui, and Grivetti 1977, vol. I, p. 481).

Daube (1963, p. 57) goes further than Segal even suggesting that the bestowal of valuables on the departing Israelites is "closely *modelled*" on Deuteronomy's (15:13–14) provision for the proper release of a slave: "When you set him free, do not let him go empty handed; furnish him out of the flock, threshing floor, and vat" Morgenstern (1966, pp. 197–98), however, sees the wearing by dancing maidens of borrowed clothes and ornaments as protective devices in an ancient initiation festival.

15. Note that the Egyptian lector or psalmist priest is also called "Opener of Heaven's Gates".

16. Peters (1922, p. 310) adds that the phrase "everflowing streams (or rivers)" in Deuteronomy 21:4 is found elswhere only in Amos 5:24 and Psalms 74:15. The latter is a psalm "of Asaph" with possible links to both Bethel and Amos. Note, with respect to the Masoretic text, the translation "perennial stream" is found in Deuteronomy 21:4 by JPS (1962), but not by JPS (1917) and JPS (1974).

17. See Frankena (1965, especially pp. 144–50); Reiner (1969, pp. 538–41); Weinfeld (1965, pp. 417–19). Frankena argues strongly that several passages in Deuteronomy 28 are dependent on Esarhaddon's vassal treaties. His case seems strongest in the following instances: Esarhaddon 526–33 with Deuteronomy 28:3; Esarhaddon 425–27 with Deuteronomy 28:26; Esarhaddon 422–24 with Deuteronomy 28:28. On the other hand, several Esarhaddon passages cited by Frankena as sources for Deuteronomy 28:21, 25, 30–34 are arguably dependent on (presumably) earlier passages in Amos: Esarhaddon 455f "May Nergal, hero of the gods, extinguish your life with his pityless dagger; may he send slaughter and pestlilence between you" with Amos 4:10 "I sent against you pestilence in the manner of Egypt; I slew your young men with the sword"; Esarhaddon 453f "May Ištar lady of battle and war break your bow in hard-fought battle; may she bind your arms [and] make you seat at your enemy's feet" with Amos 2:15–16 "The bowman shall not hold his ground, and the fleet-footed shall not escape. Nor the horseman save his life. Even the most stouthearted warrior shall run away unarmed [naked] that day-declares the Lord"; Esarhaddon 428–30 "May Dilbat, the bright[est] of stars, make your wives lie in the lap of your enemy before your eyes; may your sons not possess your house; may a foreign enemy divide your goods" with Amos 5:11 "You have built houses of hewn stone, but you shall not live in them; you have planted delightful vineyards, but you shall not drink their

wine" and Amos 7:17 "but this, I swear, is what the Lord said: Your wife shall play the harlot [be ravished] in the town, . . . and your land shall be divided up with a measuring line."

18. Wolff (1973, pp. 17–21) detects a structural similarity between Amos's "woe-cry" (5:18, 6:1 and possibly elsewhere) and the series of "curses" found in Deuteronomy 27:15–26: "Here there are present all the formal characteristics mentioned for the 'woe-cry,' except that the opening word 'woe' is replaced by the term 'cursed'." The "woe-cry" is also found in Isaiah 5:11–13.

19. See, for example, Ezekiel 20:24, 27–31, 39.

20. See also 1 Kings 14:23. It is not necessary to postulate an ancient central sanctuary in order to explain Deuteronomy's call for sacrificial centralization. de Geus (1976, p. 212) has concluded from his extensive analysis that it is "not possible to show the existence of a central shrine or a central cult" or of "any amphictyonic office or institution." Possibly he is underestimating some of the evidence pointing toward a positive conclusion. In any event, I fully agree with de Geus's (1976, p. 197) position that "the foundation of Deuteronomy's motive is clearly theological and not historical. Deuteronomy is concerned to keep Yahwism pure, which can only be done with a single sanctuary and a single cult." Of course, "purity" here must be identified with social justice.

21. So translated by JPS (1917); JPS (1978) has "offered sacrifices" while Thomson has "burned incense."

22. Dietrich (1974, p. 2) well notes that "any religion which hopes to capture popular imagination and endure for any length of time must make use of older and existing beliefs, such as had been acceptable to every worshipper for many generations."

23. They erected altars in Genesis 12:7–8; 13:4; 26:25; 33:20; 35:7.

24. Albright's views have recently been strongly challenged by Vaughan (1974, esp. fn. 61, p. 63) who finds no evidence of a cult of the dead being associated with *bamoth*. Note, however, that in 1 Samuel 28:13 the ghost of the revered Samuel is called *elohim*.

25. See also Zephaniah 1:4.

26. Note also "the house of freedom" (or "house of the dead") in 2 Kings 15:5 and 2 Chronicles 26:21 (see Cassuto 1971, pp. 22–3).

27. Note also Amos's (2:7) reference to revelry "in the house of their god."

28. Compare Exodus 38:8 with 1 Samuel 2:22, Genesis 38, and Hosea 4:13–14. Also compare Exodus 35:25–26 with 2 Kings 23:7. See also Morgenstern (1966, pp. 93–9, 145–49) and Otwell (1974, pp. 160–61). Note that in the Deir 'Alla inscription, Balaam sought the aid of a *khnh* "priestess" in his efforts on behalf of the goddess.

29. Sources on Roman household worship: Bailey (1932, pp. 46, 49); Fustel de Coulanges (1896, pp. 43, 54–5, 63); Laing (1963, pp. 16–17); Ogilvie (1969, pp. 101–02).

30. Since the relationship between Jacob and Laban does not conform to the legal requirements of a Nuzi adoption tablet, Rachel's theft of the teraphim would not have given her a legal right to an inheritance (see Greenberg 1962). For a survey of the recent scholarship see Weeks (1975–76, p. 75). See also Speiser (1965, p. 391) on the bodyguard functions of the *talil* figures.

31. See also Leviticus 19:31; Deuteronomy 18:10–11; 1 Samuel 28:3.

32. According to Willis (1972, p. 56): "Drunkenness and prostitution were a part of the syncretistic religion which emerged from the amalgamation of Israelite and Canaanite cultic practices." His authorities for this informative statement are Amos, Hosea, and Isaiah.

33. If the position presented by Ahlström (1963, p. 56) is correct, the process begins with Amos 5:25–26. In verse 25 Amos goes so far as to assert that the sacrifices during the Exodus were not offered to Yahweh, but to foreign gods mentioned in verse 26. Amos 9:7, of course, undermined the belief that the Exodus from Egypt represented a unique election by God.

34. The Masoretic text of Judges 18:30 says "Manasseh." The difference between "Moses" and "Manasseh" in Hebrew script is only the letter *n*. It is known that the name was deliberately altered since the *n* is written at a higher level than the rest of the letters (see, for instance, JPS (1978), p. 93). The Greek reads "Moses" not "Manasseh".

35. See also Weinfeld (1972b; 1978) versus M. Smith (1975).

36. It was the duty of the woman of the home to keep the sacred fire alive. The other sacred spot was the door through which evil spirits might gain entry. The door played a similar role among the Hebrews (see Exod. 12:7, 23–4 and elsewhere). I am inclined to doubt that the "Molech ritual" had to do with dedication and initiation to a *foreign* god as Weinfeld (1978, p. 411) suggests.

37. Other instances of solar imagery include Isaiah 66:15–16; Habakkuk 3:8; and Psalms 19:2–8.

38. See also Psalms 58 and 82.

39. Hosea 3:1 may refer to "raisin cakes" or "cakes with dried grapes" or "cups of wine." Isaiah 16:7 may refer to "raisen cakes" or "foundations" or "men".

17 CULTIC REFORMS AND CONSEQUENCES

The Bible provides several striking but apparently overlooked or misunderstood indications that the Deuteronomic laws were not only composed but *implemented* in the northern kingdom. Perhaps the most important of these is Hosea 10:1–2: "Israel is a ravaged vine and its fruit is like it. When his fruit was plentiful, he made altars aplenty . . . Now that his boughs are broken up, he feels his guilt; *he himself pulls apart his altars, smashes his pillars*" (emphasis added.).[1] Moreover, Hosea 8:6 promises "the calf of Samaria shall be broken in pieces" and the prophet (10:5) adds: "The inhabitants of Samaria fear for the calf of Beth-aven; indeed its people and priestlings, whose joy it once was [Hebrew uncertain], mourn over it for the glory that is departed from it." (JPS, 1917 and Bewer have "for its glory, because it is departed from it"). It would seem that the calves were removed from Bethel, and, possibly, destroyed, which upset the "people and priestlings." It is worth noting that the account of Josiah's defilement of Bethel in the later seventh century makes no mention of the calves.

How the above passages can refer to anything other than a violent splurge of cultic centralization of the type experienced in Judah under Hezekiah and Josiah is difficult to see. Reasoning from the political disruptions triggered by the latter reforms,[2] I would be inclined to date the beginning of Israel's

213

cultural revolution to ca. 751. It was in this year that, apparently without any warning, Pekah revolted against Jeroboam II (Yeivin 1979, p. 167). Note in this connection, Hosea 10:3: "Truly now they [Israel] say, 'we have no king; for since we do not fear the Lord, what can a king do to us?' " If, as Yeivin (p. 167; see also Hallo and Simpson 1971, p. 136) suggests, Pekah's rival kingdom was in Gilead (in Transjordan) additional linkages can be made. In the Masoretic text of 2 Kings 15:25 Pekah killed King Pekahiah (ca. 734) with the aid of "fifty men of the Gileadites." (But the Septuagint (Thomson) has "fifty men of the guard of four-hundred.") Also, according to Isaiah 7:6 (see also 2 Kings 16:5), Pekah wanted to set the son of Tabeel on the throne of Judah instead of Ahaz: "Presumably, the name Tabeel is related to ^{kur}Ta-ab-i-la-a-a+a, situated east of the Jordan." (Ishida 1977, pp. 167–68).[3]

Joshua 22:9–34 projects cultic centralization backward in time to the distant past. The Reubenites, Gadites, and the half tribe of Manasseh are suspected of "treachery," "turning away from the Lord," and "rebelling against the Lord" by offering sacrifices to Yahweh on "a great conspicuous altar" they built near the Jordan in or just opposite to Gilead (see Snaith 1978). In the end these tribes rebutted the charge by arguing along the following lines: We were concerned that the descendents of the Israelites on the west side of the Jordan "might say to our children, 'What have you to do with the Lord, the God of Israel'. . . . So we decided to provide for ourselves by building an altar—not for burnt offerings or sacrifices, but as a witness between you and us and between the generations to come—that we may perform the service of the Lord before Him [in Israel proper] with our burnt offerings, our sacrifices, and our offerings of well-being" The point is quite clear: the rather important communal altar in Gilead was never intended to be used for sacrifices.

Both 1 Samuel 15 and Micah 6:5–8 lecture the Israelites on the relative value of sacrifice, and both are linked to Gilgal. In the former, Samuel castigates King Saul for his failure to "proscribe" all that belongs to Amalek. In reply to Saul's plea that his pious soldiers had but saved some of the sheep and oxen for a sacrifice to Yahweh in Gilgal, Samuel retorts, "Does the Lord delight in burnt offerings and sacrifices as much as in obedience to the Lord's command? Surely, obedience is better than sacrifice, compliance than the fat of rams" (verse 22). (In chapter 13, note 53 of this book it was suggested that this passage might be linked to Amos.) It is also of interest to note the analogy between the defenses offered by Saul and Aaron. Saul says "I did wrong to transgress the Lord's command and your instructions; but I was afraid of the troops and I yielded to them" (verse 24). In Exodus 32, after the Israelites had sacrificed to a molten calf, Aaron tells the furious Moses, "Let not my Lord be enraged. You know that this people is bent on evil. They said to me, 'Make a god to lead us' " (verses 22–23).

Micah, who we are told (1:1), began to prophesy in the reign of King Jotham of Judah (ca. 750–735) offers a different route to the same destination. The translation of the (possibly corrupt) Masoretic text of 6:5–8 is as follows:

> O My people, remember now what Balak king of Moab devised, and what Balaam the son of Beor answered him. From Shittim unto Gilgal, that ye may know the righteous acts of the Lord, "Wherewith shall I come before the Lord, and bow myself before God on high? Shall I come before Him with burnt-offerings, with calves a year old? Will the Lord be pleased with thousands of rams, with ten thousands of rivers of oil? Shall I give my first-born for my transgression, the fruit of my body for the sin of my soul?' It hath been told thee: only to do justly, and to love mercy, and to walk humbly with thy God.

The Septuagint (Thomson) version of verse 5 is more coherent: "My people call now to remembrance what counsel Balak, king of Moab, took against thee; and what answer was made by Balaam, son of Beor, that from [the example of?] Shittim the righteousness of the Lord may be made known to Gilgal." Shittim, east of the Jordan, is the site of the idolatrous worship of Baal-Peor.

> While Israel was staying at Shittim, the people profaned themselves by whoring with the Moabite women, who invited the people to the sacrifices for their god. The people partook of them and worshiped that god. Thus Israel attached itself to Baal-peor, and the Lord was incensed with Israel. The Lord said to Moses, "Take all the ringleaders and have them publicly impaled before the Lord, so that the Lord's wrath may turn away for Israel. (Num. 25:1–5)

Note also Amos's (4:4; 5:5) bitter attacks on Gilgal. But where is Gilgal?

The location is disputed, or perhaps, there were several Gilgals. Simple inference and archaeological inscription connect Micah's Gilgal with Gilgal I, the site in or just opposite to Gilead near Jericho (Josh. 4:19) where, after the Israelites had arrived from Shittim, Joshua (4:20–23) set up twelve stones to commemorate that "Here the Israelites crossed the Jordan on dry land" (see Snaith 1978). The inference is that Micah would not have quoted Balaam to Gilgal unless that prophet were a revered figure there. The inscription in Aramaic[4] that was found at Deir 'Alla in Gilead refers specifically to Balaam son of Beor who is called "seer of the Gods." On both archaeological and paleographic grounds the inscription is assigned to ca. 700, or possibly earlier in the eighth century (see Hoftijzer 1976; Hoftijzer and Van Der Kooij 1976, pp. 12, 271; R.R. Wilson 1980, pp. 132–33).[5] Interestingly, the excavator of Deir 'Alla identifies it with Gilgal

(Franken 1969, pp. 5–8). The Bible and archaeology combine to provide a piece of circumstantial evidence that is consistent with this hypothesis. Judges 3:19 makes mention of "the quarries that were by Gilgal" while, as mentioned earlier a metallurgical center was discovered at Deir 'Alla which could have made use of the iron ore found in the Ajlun district.

Evidently the east-Jordan tribes accepted neither the "witness" theory, nor the admonitions to be obedient, nor Micah's advice to "make justice not sacrifice."[6] Led by Pekah (?), the people forcibly resisted the efforts of Jeroboam (and Amos?) to trample their sacred traditions.[7] Note in support of this contention that, according to 2 Kings 15:28, Pekah "did that which was evil in the sight of the Lord; he departed not from the sins of Jeroboam the son of Nebat, wherewith he made Israel to sin." On the other hand, of Hoshea, the man who killed and replaced Pekah, we are told that "he did that which was evil in the sight of the Lord, yet not as the kings of Israel that were before him" (2 Kings 17:2). But it would seem that Hoshea's redeeming feature was that he "made a conspiracy against Pekah" (2 Kings 15:30). But who did he conspire with? Verse 29 hints that the nameless coconspirator was Tiglath Pileser, the king of Assyria. Indeed, Wiseman (1979, p. 41) cites a broken text of that king in which he claims to have instigated the murder of Pekah and put Hoshea on the throne. Ishida (1977, p. 167) presents the following translation: "The land of Beth Omri (i.e. Israel) . . . (his troops,) all his people, . . . I carried off to Assyria. Pekah, their king, I smote (?) and I installed Hoshea (king) over them."

Hosea provides additional evidence supporting this general line of explanation. "Gilead is a city of them that work iniquity, it is covered with footprints of blood" (6:8). "Is there iniquity in Gilead, surely they are vanity; they sacrifice bullocks at Gilgal; yea their altars are as [stone] heaps in the furrows of the [plowed] fields" (12:12). Once again Gilead is linked with Gilgal I. Indeed, it becomes more probable that Gilgal was the very site of the altar named "Witness" (Josh. 22:34). Seen in this light Hosea 9:15 takes on a new dimension of interest: "All their wickedness is in Gilgal, for there I hated them; because of the wickedness of their doings I will drive them out of My house; I will love them no more, all their princes [officials] are rebellious." But what did they rebel against? Here we find the frustrated social reformer expelling a group that had already made good its secession.

Was Shechem the designated site of sacrificial centralization? According to Genesis 33:18–19, Jacob purchased land at Shechem and erected an altar there. In Genesis 48:22 Jacob willed Shechem to Joseph. (On "portion" versus Shechem, see Brinker 1946, p. 146). One naturally thinks of the convenant-renewal festival portrayed there in Joshua 24 and of the great tree of Moreh (see chapter 13 of this book). Abimelech was made king at

Shechem "by the oak of the pillar" (Judg. 9:6) while Rehoboam, Solomon's son, went there to be crowned king of "all Israel" (1 Kings 12:1). Indeed, Jeroboam's capital was at Shechem until he "went out" to Penuel in Transjordan (1 Kings 12:25). Next, Jeroboam set up the calves at Dan and Bethel in order, we are told, to counter the cultic attraction of Jerusalem (1 Kings 12:26–29). But Jerusalem, after all, was a relative newcomer. Was it perhaps, *Shechem* that Jeroboam feared? Does the break with Shechem (a city of Levites; Joshua 21:21) underlie the charge that Jeroboam "made priests from among all the people, that were not of the sons of Levi" (1 Kings 12:31)?[8] Is this break also reflected in Hosea's (8:4) later complaint that: "They have set up kings, but not by Me"? A strong hint of centralization at Shechem is provided by Hosea 6:7–9, which is translated by Andersen and Freedman (1980) as follows:

> They as at Adam, broke the covenant; there they practiced deception against me. Gilead is the city of evildoers, a deceitful city, because of bloodshed. Those who lay in wait, bands of men, gangs of priests, committed murder on the Shechem road. They have perpetrated enormities.

Andersen and Freedman (1980, p. 436) identify Adam as the town in Gilead at the Jordan crossing (see Josh. 3:16) on the main road linking Shechem (the principal road junction of central Palestine) with such Transjordanian centers as Succoth and Mahanaim. Possibly the "gang of priests" ambushed those who had come from Shechem to defile the Transjordanian altars (see 2 Chron. 31:1). It is known from 2 Kings 15:16 that the Shechem area was devastated during the civil war in 747 and the archaeological excavations suggest that Shechem itself was destroyed (see Wright, 1965, pp. 157–58).

A final hint of the magnitude of the reforms in the northern kingdom is provided by Jeremiah 3:6–7:

> The Lord said also unto me in the days of Josiah the king, "Hast thou seen that which *backsliding Israel*[9] hath done? She is gone up upon every high mountain and under every green tree and there hath played the harlot. . . . And her treacherous sister Judah saw it." (emphasis added)

It would seem from the reference to "backsliding" that Jeroboam's reforms included an attack on the ancestral funerary practices as well as on the multiple Yahweh altars.

The period following the revolt of Pekah in 751 and the death of Jeroboam in 748/7 was one of unparalleled anarchy in which six kings rose and fell. Several royal inscriptions of Tiglath Pileser III from Nimrud indicate that during this period Damascus not only regained its independence, but also took Bashan and Golan as far as the town of Ramoth-gilead (Tadmor 1962,

p. 119). At the same time, Judah moved in and stripped away some territory on its northern border with Israel while Hosea (5:8–15) protested the injustice. Obviously the Assyrians must have seen that the tough Israelites who helped stalemate or defeat them at Karkar in 853 were now militarily vulnerable. They attacked and Israel suffered a series of defeats beginning in 734–732 and culminating in the destruction of the northern kingdom in ca. 721.

Let us now turn to Hezekiah's reforms in the later eighth century. Upon becoming king, at the age of twenty-five, he cleansed and rededicated the Temple and offered generous sacrifices (2 Chron. 29). Possibly it was at this time that he "broke into pieces the bronze serpent which Moses had made, for until that time the Israelites had been offering sacrifices to it; it was called Nehushtan." (2 Kings 18:4). Then Hezekiah issued "an invitation to all Israel to celebrate a passover at Jerusalem." (2 Chron. 30:1). At that time, "they arose and removed the altars that were in Jerusalem; they also removed the incense altars and cast them into the Kidron Valley." (2 Chron. 30:14). Having "cleansed" Jerusalem, Hezekiah and "all Israel" went out "to the cities of Judah, broke the pillars, broke to pieces the Asherahs, and wrecked completely the high places and the altars from all Judah, Benjamin, Ephraim, and Manasseh." (2 Chron. 31:1). The text of 2 Kings 18:4 is more parsimonius in its account of these events: "He removed the high places, and broke down the pillars, and cut down the Asherah. . . . " These events are confirmed in 2 Kings 21:3 and 2 Chronicles 33:3, both of which report that Manasseh, Hezekiah's son, rebuilt the high places.

The archaeological evidence suggests that Hezekiah's exploits were by no means imaginary. At Beer-sheba, Aharoni (1974, pp. 2–4) located a dismantled horned altar. The stones, including the four altar horns, had been used to repair the wall of a building belonging to an eighth century stratum. A twisted snake (note the reference to Nehushtan above) was engraved on one of the stones. Aharoni is of the opinion that the altar was destroyed during the reign of Hezekiah, while the building, its stones patched, was itself destroyed during the attack by Sennacherib (see below). Aharoni's (1969, p. 38; 1979, pp. 303–5) earlier excavation at Arad convinced him that its temple was "rebuilt through five strata, but the altar only through four." His explanation for this "strange fact" is that Hezekiah centralized sacrifices at Jerusalem but did not, as did Josiah later on, abolish all cultic functions for the nation's temples. On the other hand, basing their judgments on aspects of the architecture and stratigraphy of the late casemate and wall and the use there of the toothed chisel, several scholars maintain that Arad's temple was functional well after the time of Josiah. Nylander (1967, p. 59), for example, dates the Arad masonry to the much later Hellenistic-Roman period.

Aharoni's hypothesis is not inconsistent with the biblical evidence. The Assyrian Rabshakeh, whose speech will be discussed shortly, credits Hezekiah with "telling Judah and Jerusalem, 'You must worship only at this altar in Jerusalem' " (2 Kings 18:22). The narrative in 2 Kings 23:8 adds that King Josiah brought up all the priests out of the cities of Judah where the priests burned incense[10] from Geba to Beer-sheba". The praise of Hezekiah is unstinting in 2 Kings 18:5–7:

> He trusted only in the Lord the God of Israel: there was none like him among all the kings of Judah after him, nor among those before him. He clung to the Lord; he did not turn away from following Him, but kept the commandments which the Lord had given to Moses. And the Lord was always with him; he was successful wherever he turned.

The Chronicler (31:21) is not quite so enthusiastic, but he concludes that "Every work which he undertook, whether in the service of the house of God or in the law or in the commandments, he carried out with utter devotion in the worship of his God, and so succeeded." In fact, to say that Hezekiah was not a success would be a grotesque understatement. Hezekiah's reign ranks among the greatest disasters in the history of the Jewish people.

The Chronicler (2 Chron. 32:1) sadly notes that "*After* these faithful acts, Sennacherib the king of Assyria came and invaded Judah" (emphasis added). According to Tadmor (1979, p. 158), this disastrous invasion which is "reported in detail in Sennacherib's Annals, is fixed beyond any doubt in the year 705 B.C.E." (as opposed to the traditional 701). If 2 Kings 18:13, which places the invasion in the fourteenth year of Hezekiah's reign is correct, it follows that his accession took place in 716/5.[11] It follows also that Hezekiah's cultural revolution took place between 716/5 and 705. After the Assyrians had seized all the fortified towns of Judah:

> King Hezekiah sent this message to the king of Assyria at Lachish: "I have done wrong; withdraw from me; and I shall bear whatever you impose on me." So the king of Assyria imposed upon King Hezekiah of Judah a payment of three hundred talents of silver and thirty talents of gold. Hezekiah gave him all the silver that was on hand in the House of the Lord and in the treasuries of the palace. At that time Hezekiah cut down the door and the door posts of the Temple of the Lord, which King Hezekiah had overlaid [with gold] and gave them to the king of Assryia. (2 Kings 18:14–16)

But this does not begin to measure the success of King Hezekiah. Sennacherib's annals (Oppenheim, 1969a, p. 288) state:

> As to Hezekiah, the Jew, he did not submit to my yoke, I laid siege to 46 of his strong cities, walled forts and the countless small villages in their vicinity, and conquered them . . . I drove out (of them) 200,150 people, young and old, male

and female, horses, mules, donkeys, camels, big and small cattle beyond counting, and considered (them) booty. Himself I made a prisoner in Jerusalem, his royal residence like a bird in a cage. I surrounded him with earthwork in order to molest those who were leaving his city's gate. His towns which I had plundered, I took away from his country and gave them (over) to Mitinti, king of Ashdod, Padi, king of Ekron, and Sillibel, king of Gaza. Thus I reduced his country, but still increased the tribute which I imposed and the *katrū*-presents (due) to me (as his) overlord which I imposed (later) upon him beyond the former tribute, to be delivered annually. Hezekiah himself . . . did send me, later, to Nineveh . . . , together with 30 talents of gold, 800 talents of silver, precious stones, antimony, large cuts of red stone, couches (inlaid) with ivory, *nimedu*-chairs (inlaid) with ivory, elephant hides, ebony-wood. boxwood (and) all kinds of valuable treasures, his (own) daughters, concubines, male and female musicians.

At this point in the history, the editors of Kings stepped in to save face for Isaiah and social reform.[12] There is the suggestion in 2 Kings 18:17ff. that after Hezekiah's payment of tribute, Sennacherib sent out "a large force" from Lachish to Jerusalem, whose spokesman the Rabshakeh called for the surrender of the city. Now, at last, the great Isaiah took action. First he told Hezekiah's ministers that the Lord "will put a spirit in him [Sennacherib]; he will hear a rumor and return to his land, and I will make him fall by the sword in his land" (2 Kings 19:7). Later he sent a message assuring Hezekiah that Sennacherib would not conquer the city (2 Kings 19:32–34): "that night an angel of the Lord went out and struck down one hundred and eighty-five thousand in the Assyrian camp, and the following morning they were all dead corpses. So King Sennacherib of Assyria broke camp and retreated and stayed in Nineveh" (2 Kings 19:35–36). What does all this mean? S. Smith (1975, p. 5) points out that the Chronicle of a later Assyrian king, Esarhaddon (680–669) makes the following reference: "In the 6th year (675 B.C.E.) the troops of Assyria went to Egypt, they fled before a great storm." He adds that the Hebrew words translated as "spirit" and "rumor" mean "wind" and "noise" respectively. These words "may so obviously be interpreted of a storm, as may also 'the angel of the Lord' . . . that it is difficult not to believe that the writer of this part of the verse was referring to the great storm which led to the flight of Esarhaddon's army in 675." I would add only the great storm that allegedly wrecked Esarhaddon's campaign: better to admit retreat before a storm than defeat at the hands of the Egyptian army (see Spalinger 1974, pp. 300–01).

The facts concerning the Assyrian campaign against Judah are, I believe, self-evident and dismal.[13] Sennacherib plundered and partitioned Judah; then in return for a huge tribute, he went home. Nevertheless, the speech delivered by the Assyrian Rabshakeh to Hezekiah's officials[14] before the walls of Jerusalem clearly links the easy victory of the Assyrians with the Hezekiah-Isaiah reforms.

> The Rabshakeh said to them [Hezekiah's officials], "You tell Hezekiah: Thus said the Great King the King of Assyria: What makes you so confident? . . . And if you tell me that you are relying on the Lord your God. He is the very one whose shrines and altars Hezekiah did away with telling Judah and Jerusalem, 'You must worship only at this altar in Jerusalem.' " Come now, make a wager with my master, the King of Assyria: I'll give you two thousand horses if you can produce riders to mount them. (2 Kings 18:19, 22–23)

Perhaps it will be objected that the Rabshakeh's speech is fictional, that diplomacy was not conducted in public before the walls of cities, but it was. This is proven by a letter written in 745 B.C.E. to the Assyrian King Tiglath Pileser III by two of his officials:

> To the king, my lord, your servants Shamash-bunaya and Nabuetir send greeting. . . . On the twenty-eighth day we went to Babylon and stood in front of the Marduk Gate. We argued with the man of Babylon, . . . , [the] servant of Mokin-zu the Chaldean, was beside him. They came out and while they stood with the Babylonians in front of the gate, we spoke to the Babylonians like this . . .

Grayson and Redford (1973, pp. 106–7) report that the rest of the letter is unclear but the basic idea is that the Assyrians were trying to talk the Babylonians into surrender.

Returning to the Rabshakeh's speech, notice how Isaiah's (10:5) prophesy that the Assyrians were the rod of the Lord was thrown back in his face. In fact, Isaiah is never heard from again, and the next prophet of social justice preserved in the Bible is Jeremiah during the affluent reign of Josiah, Hezekiah's grandson. Why did the wealthy Hezekiah lack riders? Because, the Rabshakeh makes clear, he alienated his subjects by defiling Yahweh's shrines and centralizing sacrifice in Jerusalem. This point receives independent confirmation in Sennacherib's annals: the "irregular and elite troops which he [Hezekiah] had brought into Jerusalem . . . in order to strengthen (it), had deserted him . . . " (Pritchard 1969, p. 288). Incredibly, Myers (1965, vol. II, p. 190) concludes: "Not only was Jerusalem spared but Hezekiah's stature rose tremendously . . . " In fact, 2 Chronicles 32:24 tells us that "At that time [after or during the Assyrian invasion] Hezekiah became mortally sick." I would suspect that he suffered a nervous breakdown. It is well to recall that in 2 Kings 20:1–7 Isaiah treated Hezekiah, who was "dangerously ill," by applying a "cake of figs" to his "rash."[15] However, in Greek antiquity one "of the regular duties of the 'seer' [was] the

cure of diseases, especially those of the mind" (Rohde, 1966, p. 590). The
healing process was aided by purifications of a religious nature, including
apparently, cleansing and scouring with figs (Rohde, 1966, p. 590).

There is reason to believe that the Jerusalem troop desertions are no more
than the tip of the iceberg of massive Judean resistance to the Hezekiah-
Isaiah reforms. After surveying the biblical and archaeological evidence, I
am of the opinion that Lachish, Judah's strategic fortress city in the
southwestern foothills, went over to the Assyrians and contributed chariot
forces to the siege of Jerusalem. (1) The Assyrian annals do not list Lachish
among the 46 conquered walled cities (Childs 1967, p. 72). (2) 2 Kings
(18:14, 17; 19:8) and 2 Chronicles (32:9) firmly identify Lachish as
Sennacherib's headquarters. This is reasonable since the city was an ideal
base for operations against the Philistine Plain, the Egyptian border, and
Judah itself. But a ruined city, taken by siege, would hardly offer appropriate
quarters for a great king. (3) Reliefs at Nineveh show a city being stormed
and, according to Ussishkin (1977, p. 30), one of the two accompanying
inscriptions identifies the city as Lachish.[16] However, a letter from Nineveh
to the Assyrian governor in the town ^{al}lu-qa-$še$, which has been identified as
Lachish points in the opposite direction. This letter which concerns the
affairs of the Philistine levees assembled in the town suggests that Lachish
remained under Assyrian control in the first half of the seventh century.
Ussishkin (1977, p. 53) counters that this identification is unacceptable since
"Lachish" is spelled differently in the Amarna letters (fourteenth century
B.C.E.) and the inscription at Nineveh. But not only do spellings change in
600 years (for instance, Šuksu into Šukās, Gubla into Gubāl; see Riis 1970,
p. 128), but the Amarna letters were written in Akkadian by Canaanites.
Even the Assyrian King Assurbanipal (668–627) spoke of "the obscure
Akkadian writing which is hard to master" (C.F. Pfeiffer 1966, p. 27).
Moreover, Ussishkin's argument appears to be circular. How does he know
the spelling of "Lachish" in Nineveh is the correct one? (4) Archaeologists
are divided into two warring camps with respect to the dating of Lachish's
destruction levels. One group dates the destructions of strata III to
Sennacherib and of stratum II to the Babylonians. The second group sees no
destruction level in the late eighth century and dates the destruction of
stratum III to the first Babylonian invasion in 597, and the destruction of
stratum II to the Babylonian invasion of 588.[17] Holladay (1976, pp. 266–67;
see also Stager 1975, pp. 247–50) offers strong evidence in support of two
late sixth-century destructions. There is little difference between the
pottery of Lachish III and that of Lachish II. This is consistent with a brief
period between the destructions. On the other hand, the Lachish III pottery
shows "marked and general differences" from corresponding northern wares

dating from the later-eighth century. To the best of my knowledge the proponents of destruction by Sennacherib have ridiculed Holladay (see Ussishkin 1977, p. 32) but have failed to rebut his analysis. (5) If the debris at a Lachish wall includes the remains of a siege ramp, how can we be sure whether it is of Babylonian or Assyrian construction?

Finally we have the crucial testimony of Micah who prophesied during the reign of Hezekiah (1:1). The Masoretic text of 1:12–16 is as follows:

> For the inhabitant of Maroth waiteth anxiously for good; because evil is come down from the Lord unto the gate of Jerusalem. Bind the chariots to the swift steeds, O inhabitant of Lachish; she was the beginning of sin to the daughter of Zion; for the transgressions of Israel are found in thee. Therefore shalt thou give a parting gift to Moresheth-gath; the houses of Achzib shall be a deceitful thing unto the kings of Israel. I will yet bring unto thee, O inhabitant of Mareshah, him that shall possess thee; the glory of Israel shall come even unto Adullam. Make thee bald, and poll thee for the children of thy delight; enlarge they baldness as the vulture; for they are gone into captivity from thee.

Once again, as in the case of Gilgal, the Septuagint (Thomson) clears away several obscurities and sharpens the focus:

> Who led the way to good for her who was dwelling in sorrows, because evils from the Lord, a sound of chariots and horsemen came down against the gates of Jerusalem? Was it the inhabitant of Lachish? She is a leader to sin for the daughter of Zion. Because in thee have been found the impieties of Israel, therefore even to the inheritance of Gath he will give up idolatrous houses as abandoned. To the kings of Israel they were of no avail. O inhabitant of Lachish! Until the true heirs shall be brought in—O, Odollam! Until an inheritance, the glory of the daughter of Israel shall come,—shave thy locks and make thyself bald for they delicate children; lengthen out they widowhood like an eagle, for they shall be carried from thee into captivity.

Lachish is explicitly linked with chariots, the gates of Jerusalem, the kings of Israel, and idolatrous worship. Moreover, she is accused of behaving like Israel and leading Zion (Judah?) astray. If the "transgressions" and "sins" of Lachish were not those of resisting the Hezekiah-Isaiah reforms, then what were they? Why is Lachish singled out from the other towns in the Shephelah presumably destroyed by Sennacherib's campaign (see Na'aman, 1979, pp. 84–5) and subjected to special condemnation?

According to 2 Kings 22, King Josiah's (640–609) cultural revolution began in the eighteenth year of his reign with the priest Hilkiah's discovery, during Temple repairs, of a "scroll of the Teaching." The latter is usually associated with Deuteronomy. The discovery served as the signal for what may well have been a massive, bloody reign of terror that contributed to the destruction of the state of Judah in 587, and poisoned the atmosphere of

Jewish society for years to come. This is reflected in the Chronicler's (2 Chron. 34–35) account which entirely suppresses Josiah's murders and confines itself to a description of his high-minded vandalism—that is, the smashing of altars, images, and Asherahs, and the defilement of graves (34:3–7). Even more significant, the Chronicler, in a transparent attempt to disassociate Deuteronomy from Josiah's crimes, places the reforms in the twelfth year of his reign, that is, prior to the discovery of the "book of the law of Yahweh given by Moses" (verses, 8–14).

In the Masoretic text, Josiah begins by "suppressing" the idolatrous priests" of all the "high places" in Judah (2 Kings 23:5). In the Septuagint (Thomson) version, he "burned" the idolatrous priests.[18] Then he moved to the north and "abolished all the cult places in the towns of Samaria, which the kings of Israel had built, vexing [the Lord]. He dealt with them just as he had done to Bethel: he slew on the altars all the priests of the shrines who were there, and he burned human bones on them. Then he returned to Jerusalem" (2 Kings 23:19–20). Josiah then "commanded" all the people: "Offer the passover sacrifice to the Lord your God as prescribed in this scroll of the Covenant" (verse 21). Morgenstern (1966, p. 171), however, reasons that the Deuteronomic removal of the Passover celebration from Israelite homes to the central sanctuary "was not popular and probably was never fully accepted, particularly in rural circles, despite the royal enforcement which it received. Probably the old ceremonies continued to be practiced quite extensively in homes throughout the land, although now in unsanctioned and probably therefore in somewhat modified and varied forms."[19] But there is reason to believe that at this time Josiah carried his violent cultural revolution beyond the graveyards and sacrificial altars into the very homes of ordinary Israelites. Verse 24 reports that he "removed" (Thomson) or "did away with" (JPS) the "teraphim" and other "abominations." Since the teraphim or ancestral images were kept in homes it is difficult to see how this removal could have taken place without physical intrusion. Undoubtedly many humble Israelites sought to preserve their heritage by hiding the teraphim while others resisted and perished.[20] Note in this connection, Deuteronomy's legal innovation in which the death penalty was mandated for both the rebellious elder (17:12) and the instigator of idolatry (13:7–12).

Then in 609 Josiah was killed under mysterious circumstances. Verse 29 states that he "went against" Pharaoh Neco, but no battle is reported or even implied. We are told only that Neco "slew him at Megiddo when he had seen him." 2 Chr. 35:22–23 indicates a battle in which "the archers shot king Josiah." Hoschander (1938, p. 11) believes that Josiah was assassinated by Israelites.[21] Certainly he was a hated man and the attribution of his death to the hands of the Egyptians could have been a later invention of Jeremiah's pro-Babylonian party. In this connection an interview between Jeremiah and Judah's last king Zedekiah (598–587) is extremely revealing.

> Then Jeremiah said to Zedekiah, "Thus said the Lord, the Lord of Hosts, the God of Israel: If you surrender to the officers of the king of Babylon, your life will be spared and this city will not be burned down. . . . " King Zedekiah said to Jeremiah, "*I am worried about the Judeans who have defected to the Chaldeans: that they [the Chaldeans] might hand me over to them to abuse me.*" "They will not hand you over," Jeremiah replied. (Jer. 38:17–20; italics mine)

Note the reference to Judean defectors of whom King Zedekiah, a son of Josiah (Myers, 1965, II, p. 222) was in mortal fear.[22] Was it the fact that his father had died at the hands of defectors that aroused his apprehension? Did Zedekiah fear the blood revenge of the kinsmen of those whom Josiah had murdered and defiled? This is very possible.

Finally, the role of Jeremiah deserves comment. How could this man have known the Babylonian surrender terms and how could he have guaranteed Zedekiah's safety unless he were an active Babylonian agent?[23] This is quite consistent with Jeremiah 39:11–14: "King Nebuchadnezzar of Babylon had given orders to Nebuzaradan, the chief of the guards concerning Jeremiah: 'Take him and look after him; do him no harm, but grant whatever he asks of you.' So Nebuzaradan . . . had Jeremiah brought from the [Judean] prison compound. They committed him to the care of Gedaliah son of Ahikam son of Shaphan." The latter was in turn installed as the puppet ruler (Jer. 40:5, 7). Indeed Jeremiah had earlier been charged with defecting to the enemy, and had been incarcerated when he was apprehended trying to leave Jerusalem (Jer. 37:11–15).[24] Note also Jeremiah's 200 mile trips to the Euphrates to first bury and then to recover his linen girdle (Jer. 13:1–11). That Jeremiah was a traitor is clear.[25] His motivation may, at least partially, be clarified by the fact hinted at in 2 Kings 25:12 and Jeremiah 52:16 and stated explicitly in Jeremiah 39:10: that the Babylonians expropriated the vineyards and fields of Judah and redistributed these "among the poor." In this connection it is well to recall that Albrecht Alt (quoted in Zimmerli 1976, p. 74) has argued that the critically emended continuation of Micah 2:1–3 directed against land consolidators threatens a redistribution of the land.[26]

Notes

1. So translated by JPS (1978); JPS (1917), Bewer, and Thomson (see the bibliographic note, Chapter 1, note 2) have: "He shall break down their altars . . . ", that is, the future tense and an ambiguous "He." Some translations attribute the destruction to Yahweh, but as Andersen and Freedman (1980, p. 553) concede "his name does not precede."

2. History periodically repeats itself. Cultic centralization was attempted by the monotheists Akhenaton (ca. 1375–1357 B.C.E.) and Nabonidus (555–537 B.C.E.) in Egypt and Babylon respectively (Oates 1979, pp. 128–34; Budge 1923, pp. 151–52). The former, as Josiah, died under mysterious circumstances while the much reviled Nabonidus was overthrown to the applause of his subjects by Cyrus king of the Persians. Cogan (1974, fn. 67, p. 33) rejects cult centralization by Nabonidus; the evidence, however, points in this direction.

3. For more on Pekah, see H.J. Cook (1964) and Thiele (1966).

4. "There are clear affinities to biblical Hebrew as well as Aramaic. . . . Whether one can call this language Aramaic is really a question of definitions. . . . What is more, Balaam's activities are portrayed in a style and manner reminiscent of biblical poetry and historical narrative." (Levine 1981, pp. 195, 202).

5. An inscription found at Deir 'Alla indicates that a Jewish sanctuary was in use there during the Persian period (De Vaux 1978, p. 583).

6. Does this perhaps explain the strange death of Balaam? After helping the Israelites against Moab, Balaam son of "Beor" is slain by them in connection with an obscure (sexual) trespass in the matter of Peor (Num. 31:7–16). Note the discrepancy between Deuteronomy 2:26–29 in which the Israelites had no difficulties crossing the territory of Moab and the (later?) Balaam pericope (Num. 22:2–24; 25). In Deuteronomy 23:6, "God refused to heed Balaam." Concerning? Balaam's role in the inscription is "to free the goddess from subserviance to the will of the inimical council of the gods . . . It is logical to assume that Balaam succeeded, and that for this reason his exploits were preserved on the wall of a sanctuary. . . . All that the gods could do was to punish Balaam after the fact." (Levine 1981, pp. 196, 204). I find it possible to detect the echo of historical events in this theme.

7. The drying up of the Jordan (Josh. 4), the second circumcision (Josh. 5), Joshua's camp (Josh. 5:10; 10:6, 43; 14:6), Elisha's home (2 Kings 4:38), and more are all associated with Gilgal.

8. Danelius (1967/68, pp. 103–05) notes that: Jeroboam "built" at Shechem (1 Kings 12:25) just as David "built" at Jerusalem (2 Sam. 5:9); David, like Jeroboam "went out" from Jerusalem (2 Sam. 15:16) as a result of Absalom's conspiracy.

9. So translated by JPS (1917) and Bewer; JPS (1978) has "Rebel Israel."

10. So rendered by Thomson; JPS has "made offerings."

11. Tadmor argues that 716/5 is contradicted by a series of synchronisms between Hezekiah and Hoshea in 2 Kings 18:1, 9–10 and he therefore places Hezekiah's accession in 727/6. However, the chronology of 2 Kings 18:13 is supported by an ostracon found in the eighth century destruction layer at Beer-sheba which appears to be dated to Hezekiah's fifteenth year (Aharoni 1973, pp. 71–2). On the question of the age of Egypt's Tarharqa at the time of the Assyrian invasion, see Kitchen (1973).

12. Clements (1980, p. 95) concludes that the narrative of Jerusalem's miraculous deliverance dates from the reign of Josiah, another great reformer.

13. On the contrast between the Bible and Assyrian sources, see Hallo and Simpson (1971, p. 14).

14. These officials included Joah, son of Asaph the recorder (2 Kings 18:18). Again, as in the case of the prophets, the words of the speech were written down for later presentation to the king (2 Kings 18:37; 19:1).

15. On the medicinal qualities of sycamore figs, see Darby, Ghaliouqui, and Grivetti: (1977, vol. 2, pp. 746–48).

16. An inscription of Sennacherib boasts of the capture of Hezekiah's strongholds at Gath (?) and Azekah (Tell Zakariye) by means of siege ramps and battering rams but Lachish is not mentioned (see Na'aman 1974).

17. The Babylonian records do not refer to a destruction of Lachish by Nebuchadnezzar. Na'aman (1979, p. 77) denies that Lachish was attacked in 597: "The time factor (a span of less than three months between his departure from Babylon and the conquest of Jerusalem) precludes the likelihood of a prolonged siege of this city . . . The campaign of 597 was directed at Jerusalem alone."

18. Does Josiah's activity explain the presence at Lachish of a large pit containing the jumbled remains of fifteen hundred bodies covered by a layer of pig and other animal bones? (see Wright 1964, p. 306).

19. Morgenstern (1966, pp. 171, 174) argues that later on the Deuteronomic reformation of the Passover ritual was partially abrogated by the (Priestly) legislation of Exodus 12. He suggests that verses 21–24 and possibly also 42 are from the older (Yahwistic legislation while verses 25–27a are of Deuteronomic origin (pp. 167–68).

20. Rabbinic sources relate how the people sought to conceal their idols from Josiah's religious inspectors (Wieder 1975, p. 66). Does the activity of Josiah (or Hezekiah) explain the finding in a cave on the eastern slope of Jerusalem of numerous female "fertility" figurines as well as horses with discs on their foreheads which are dated by Kenyon (1970, pp. 244–46; see also Holland 1977, pp. 132 ff) to ca. 700 B.C.E. Note in support of this possibility Pritchard's (1943, p. 87) finding that nude female figurines "were apparently, to judge from the frequency of their appearance, the property of private houses rather than merely connected exclusively with the cult." Note also that the "connection of horses with funeral rites is ancient, widespread, and persistent" (Pope 1977a,. p. 167). "On that day, men shall fling away to the flying foxes [?] and the bats, the idols of silver and the idols of gold which they made for worshipping" (Isaiah 2:20).

21. Certain Greek texts (for instance, Symmachus) and the Syrohexaplar have Josiah dying not "in peace" (2 Kings 22:20) but "in Shalem." The latter is a township near Shechem or, perhaps, Shechem itself (Robertson 1950, pp. 170–71).

22. See also Jeremiah 39:9 and 52:15.

23. The use of spies and intelligence agents is well documented in the archives of the Assyrian king Sargon II (721–705 B.C.E.; see R.H. Pfeiffer 1935, pp. 11, 14–15, 57–8). Oppenheim (1968, p. 174) suggests that the use of "to see" and "to hear" in Assyrian court texts of the first third of the first millennium relate to a royal intelligence service.

24. JPS (1978) translates Jeremiah 37:11–12: "When the army of the Chaldeans raised the siege of Jerusalem on account of the army of Pharaoh, Jeremiah was going to leave Jerusalem and go to the territory of Benjamin[a–] to share in some property there[–a] among the people ([a–a] Meaning of Hebrew uncertain)." This is often understood as describing Jeremiah's attempt to take possession of the land he acquired from his cousin in 32:9–15. "However, the context shows that the operative verb *hlq* here means not 'to share, receive a portion' but 'to flee, slip away'. This point was already noted by some medieval Jewish commentators . . . Confirmation of this meaning comes from Akkadian, where the berb *halāqu* means 'to escape, flee'." (Westbrook 1971b, fn. 7, p. 368).

25. The Septuagint version of Jeremiah mentions neither the Judean defectors nor Nebuchadnezzar's order to release the prophet. In fact the Septuagint and Masoretic texts of the book of Jeremiah differ more widely than for any other part of the Bible. According to Driver (1897, p. 269) the number of words in the Hebrew text not found in the Greek amounts to one-eighth of the entire book. The question of the prophets as foreign agents is discussed in Zimmern and Winckler (1903).

Jeremiah's anquish, as reflected in his "Confessions," is understandable, but in no way do his subjective feelings, as one scholar believes, cancel the evidence that he was a quisling. Actually, explicit concern with the psychological state of the prophet is not confined to Jeremiah; it is also found in the Assyrian Vision of the Netherworld which is dated in the earlier 7th century B.C.E.

Buccellanti (1976, p. 70) believes that both texts "give evidence of a general trait which accompanied the prophetic 'profession' in ancient Southwestern Asia. It had become a prophetic 'topos' to express reluctance in front of the divine vocation, a reluctance borne out of a sense of awe for God as the originator of the message, a feeling of inadequacy for one's own potential, and—especially in the case of unpopular messages—the fear of harmful consequences, to the point of persecution and loss of life. . . . But however sincere and understandable the reaction, the fact remains that in the ancient Near East hesitation borne out of fear had become a characteristic reaction of the prophet when he felt himself called, and that this had built up into a real tradition." In short, the anquish of Jeremiah may reflect current prophetic forms, rather than the internal state of the prophet.

26. Note also Isaiah's (23:18) threat against Tyre and Amos's (7:17) threat to the priest Amaziah that his land would be "divided up with a measuring line." Is land redistribution what Jeremiah (32:15) had in mind when he said: "Houses, fields and vineyards shall again be possessed (purchased?) in this land"? Urukagina's reform (see chapter 18 of this book) involved some sort of divinely inspired innovation with respect to the ownership of the city ruler's land (Foster 1981). Is the story of the taking of Naboth's vineyard after a fixed trial by King Ahab (1 Kings 21) intended to justify the expropriation of the royal estates and other landed property? Note Isaiah 3:13: "The Lord will bring this charge against the elders and princes of His people: 'It is you who have ravaged the vineyard; that which was robbed from the poor is in your houses'."

Land redistribution is certainly not a concept that was alien to the ancient mind. Such a policy was proposed in early sixth century B.C.E. Greece but rejected by Solon (see Austin and Vidal-Naquet 1977, pp. 210–12).

18 SOCIOECONOMIC REFORMS AND CONSEQUENCES

The existence of distinct state law codes in ancient Israelite society is only hinted at in biblical passages such as Micah 6:16: "For the statutes of [King] Omri are kept, and all the works of the house of [King] Ahab".[1] However, recent scholarship has not only stressed that several Deuteronomic laws (DLs) as well as laws in Exodus 21–23 (the Covenant Code) are phrased in the manner of Near Eastern case law but has also sought to place these "divine" law codes within the perspective of the great law codes of Near Eastern antiquity.[2] Thus, for example, Kaufman (1979, p. 46) concludes: "DL . . . is unquestionably intended to be a law code in the ancient Near Eastern sense . . . It is constructed according to the principles of such codes. Just as the Law of Hammurapi is a highly stylized, tightly constructed collection of just rulings of Hammurapi (and his courts?), so DL represents God's just rulings and instructions for His people."

It seems not unreasonable to assume that Israel's divine codes bore the same kind of relationship to the legal practices of the Israelite state as did Hammurabi's Code with respect to Babylonian legal practice. Support for this position is provided by Whitelam's (1979, p. 218) observation on the preservation of several royal initiatives, for example, David's decision concerning the distribution of booty (1 Sam. 30:23–25) and Jehoshaphat's judicial reform (2 Chron. 19:4–11), which are reflected in earlier Mosaic stipulations (Num. 31:25ff and Exod. 18): "The reason for this seems to be that later royal promulgations of law have been retrojected to the Mosaic period in order to provide legitimation for such laws and to conform to the general Deuteronomic theological assumption of the divine origin of all Israelite law." A central hypothesis of this book is that Deuteronomy represents an attempt to revise and expand the old divine-law code *and thereby the legal practices of the Israelite state* in the light of the circumstances of a much more affluent society. Certainly, there is concrete evidence linking the content and mode of initiation of the Deuteronomic reforms with Near Eastern social-reform traditions.

In Mesopotamia, as Saggs (1962, p. 171) notes: "The king's status as a guarantor of justice is . . . evidenced by the fact that oaths could be taken either by the gods alone, jointly by the gods and the king, or by the king alone." Thus, during Early Dynastic III Urukagina (2351–2342), the ruler of the prosperous Sumerian city-state Lagash, made a covenant with Ningirsu, the god of Lagash, to remedy certain social problems.

> He [Urukagina] held close to the word which his king [Ningirsu] spoke to him. He banned (literally "threw off") the man in charge of the boatmen from (seizing) the boats. He banned the head shepherds from (seizing) the donkeys and sheep. He banned the man in charge of the fisheries from (seizing) the fisheries. . . . He (Urukagina) amnestied the "citizens" (literally "the sons") of Lagash who (were imprisoned because of) the debts (which they) had incurred, (or because of) the amounts of grain (claimed by the palace for its) stores, or because of) the barley (claimed by the palace for its) stores, or because of theft (or) murder, and set them free. (Finally) Urukagina made a covenant with Ningirsu that a man of power must not commit an (injustice) against an orphan or widow. (Kramer 1963, pp. 318–19, but compare Edzard 1974, p. 149).

Urukagina, the earliest social reformer recorded in history,[3] reigned some eight years before Lagash was destroyed by the neighboring city Umma.

Much later, in 720, probably only a few years before Hezekiah's reforms, Bakenranef (Greek: Bocchoris), a ruler in the Egyptian Delta, initiated a series of reforms. "Bocchoris cancelled all debts not sanctioned by a written contract, freed the debt-burdened properties and the persons enslaved for debt, abolished arrest for debt and instituted *habeas corpus* . . . He published at the same time a law of contract, reduced interest rates to 33 1/3% and limited back interest to 100% of the capital lent." (Pirenne 1962, p. 128)[4] There is reason to believe that the "law of contract" outlawed loans upon the person of the borrower (Westermann 1955, p. 50). Soon afterwards, King Shabaka invaded from Nubia, captured Bocchoris and burned him alive.

Now we know nothing about the initiation of the Deuteronomic reforms of ca. 751 in the northern kingdom, Israel. However, 2 Chron. 29:10 reveals that, prior to initiating his cultural revolution, Hezekiah gathered "the priests and the Levites" and told them: "Now I firmly intend to make a covenant with Yahweh God of Israel that His violent anger may turn away from us." Much more information is available regarding Josiah's procedures.

> And the king went up to the house of the Lord, and all the men of Judah and all the inhabitants of Jerusalem with him, and the priests and the prophets, and all the people, both small and great; and he read in their ears all the words of the book of the covenant which was found in the house of the Lord. And the king stood on the platform [by the pillar] and made a covenant before the Lord, to walk after the Lord, and to keep His commandments, and His testimonies, and His statutes, with all his heart, and all his soul, to confirm the words of this covenant that were written in this book; (2 Kings 23:2–3)

The above passage concludes with the assertion that "all the people stood to the covenant" or "entered into the covenant." But in 2 Chronicles 34:31–32 we read that after Josiah had vowed "to carry out the terms of the covenant as prescribed in this book . . . He caused [made] all that were found in Jerusalem and Benjamin to stand for it. And the inhabitants of Jerusalem did according to the covenant of God, the God of their father." Clearly Josiah's covenant was taken on his own initiative and on his own behalf. Did he possess the resources to force ordinary Israelites to conform to its terms?

Deuteronomy 16:18–20 deals directly with the problem of bureaucratic resources by calling for the appointment of (salaried?) magistrates (judges) and officials (recorders? bailiffs?) in every town.[5] Such officers would then be available to settle controversies "over homicide, civil law, or assault— matters of dispute in your courts" (Deut. 17:8–9) and to determine fitness for military duty (Deut. 20:5, 8–9). That this injunction was fulfilled is suggested by a letter addressed to the governor of the Judean fortress called Mesad Hashavyahu dating from the time of Josiah. The letter, which was found in the guardroom at the gate of the fortress, records the complaints of a reaper in the experienced hand of a scribe. More basically, those Israelite kings who sought by forcible means to implement drastic cultic reforms such as centralization of sacrifice and abolition of ancestral images must have possessed sufficient resources to launch a significant direct attack on socioeconomic problems. Further, we know from Jeremiah 26:18–19 that King Hezekiah was at least influenced by the social reformer Micah, while Jeremiah 22:11–16 tells us explicitly that King Josiah "dispensed justice and equity" and "upheld the rights of the poor and needy."

In Deuteronomy, as in the "Book of the Covenant" (in Exodus (20–23), "law" is used in more than one sense. Some laws are rather obviously exhortations to behave in a socially responsible manner. However, it is not always clear whether we are dealing with civil law or an appeal to conscience. Since the two types of legal change combine and interact in producing social change, it is in order to survey the more important socioeconomic reforms proposed by or reflected in Deuteronomy. We will begin with the new status of women. In the presumably earlier edition of the Decalogue (see Patrick 1977, pp. 156–57), a wife is grouped with her husband's possessions[6]: "You shall not covet your neighbor's house; you shall not covet your neighbor's wife, or his male or female slave, or his ox, or his ass, or anything that is your neighbor's" (Exod. 20:14). But in Deuteronomy 5:18 the wife is singled out and separated from material possessions: "You shall not covet your neighbor's wife. You shall not crave your neighbor's house, or his field, or his male or female slave, or his ox, or his ass, or anything that is your neighbor's."

As in other affluent societies, there is a heightened concern for the welfare of the convicted criminal, for due process of law, and cruel and unusual punishments. Deuteronomy 25:1–3 regulates the flogging of criminals, the victim must be guilty and punishment must be administered in the presence of a judge. "He may be given up to forty lashes, but not more, lest being flogged further, to excess, your brother be degraded in your eyes." Parents are not to be executed for the crimes of their children, nor children for the crimes of their parents (Deut. 24:16).

As for welfare, Deuteronomy 10:17–19 sets the overall tone by maintaining that God "shows no favor and takes no bribe, but upholds the cause of the fatherless and the widow, and befriends the stranger, providing him with food and clothing. You too must befriend the stranger, for you were strangers in the land of Egypt." The seriousness of this provision is underlined by the exclusion of the Ammonites and Moabites from the Israelite congregation "because they did not meet you with food and water on your journey after you left Egypt, and because they hired Balaam son of Beor . . . to curse you" (Deut. 23:4–5). Deuteronomy 24:19–22 gives "the stranger, the fatherless, and the widow" the right to glean in Israelite fields after the crop has been harvested, but Deuteronomy 23:25–26 goes far beyond this by permitting an individual (a migrant?) to satisfy his appetite with the crops grown by another:

> When you enter your neighbor's vineyard, you may eat your fill of grapes, as many as you want; but you must not put any in your vessel. When you find yourself amid the neighbor's standing grain, you may pluck ears with your hand; but you must not put a sickle to your neighbor's grain.

Migratory workers are protected by Deuteronomy 24:14–15, which calls for wages to be paid at the end of each working day. Perhaps most important of all, Deuteronomy 14:28–9 commands that, triennially, a tenth part of agricultural output be set aside for the poor:

> Every third year you shall bring out the full tithe of your field of that year but leave it within your settlement. Then the Levite who has no hereditary portion as you have, and the stranger, and the fatherless, and the widow in your settlement shall come and eat their fill . . .

Surely regulations requiring the prompt payment of wages and taxation for welfare payments could have been enforced by the local magistrates.[7]

During Babylon's great period of affluence, from the early-eighteenth to the mid-seventeenth century B.C.E., it was the custom of Hammurabi (1792–1750) and his successors to issue acts of "justice" or "equity". These *misharum*-acts, Finkelstein (1961, p. 101) tells us, were "mainly characterized by measures designed to remit—at the time of promulgation only— certain types of obligation and indebtedness." Finkelstein elaborates: "The remissive component of the *misharum*-acts had at least some force in the economic life of the period, as evidenced by references to the acts in private documents. The remissive acts, enacted first at the beginning of a reign and possibly afterwards as well if the situation warranted, were acknowledged as among the more important accomplishments of a king, and celebrated in the date-formulae." Apparently, Deuteronomy 15:1–3 went beyond the Mesopotamian practice by incorporating the *misharum*-act in the Israelite constitution![8]

> Every seventh year [at the end of every seven years] you shall practice remission of debts. This shall be the nature of the remission: every creditor shall remit the due that he claims from his neighbor; he shall not dun his neighbor or kinsman, for the remission proclaimed is of the Lord. You may dun the foreigner; but you must remit whatever is due you from your kinsmen [whatsoever of yours is with your brother your hand shall release]. JPS (1974) [JPS (1917)]

Finkelstein (1969a, p. 53) notes that both the *misharum*-edict of Ammiṣaduqa (1646–1626) and Deuteronomy 15 exlude the alien from the benefits of the debt-release and, even more strikingly, that both make technical usage of terms meaning "to oppress, apply pressure (for payment), dun". Deuteronomy enjoins the wealthy not to "harbor iniquitous thoughts when . . . the seventh year is near and look askance at your needy countryman and give him nothing" (15:9). Even an Amos could not have done much to control "iniquitous thoughts," but if Babylonian kings in the second millennium could enforce debt remittances, I see no reason to believe that

Israelite kings were unable to do so also.[9] More will be said concerning the exact nature of the Israelite debt remittance later in this chapter.

Exodus 21:2–3 states that "When you acquire a Hebrew slave, he shall serve six years; in the seventh he shall go free, without payment."[10] But Deuteronomy 15:13 states that when the "Hebrew man or woman" is set free he shall not go "empty-handed" but instead be supplied "out of the flock, threshing floor, and vat". Again minimum standards of compensation could have been set and enforced by the local magistrates and judges. Further, Deuteronomy 23:16–17 seems to forbid the use of the legal machinery for the extradition of a fugitive (both Hebrew and foreign?) slave: "You shall not turn over to his master a slave who seeks refuge with you from his master. He shall live with you in any place he may choose among the settlements in your midst, wherever he pleases; you must not ill-treat him." King Zedekiah's emancipation proclamation raises interesting new questions.

In ca. 588, during Nebuchadnezzar's first invasion of Judah, Zedekiah made a covenant "that everyone should set free his Hebrew slaves, both male and female, and that no one should keep his fellow Judean enslaved" (Jer. 34:8–9). *Misharum*-acts by which all free-born persons were simultaneously emancipated from slavery are not unknown in Mesopotamian history. Lewy (1958, p. 27) cites the prologue of the law code of King Lipit-Eshtar of Isin (1934–1924 B.C.E.), which states that he "effected the release of the sons and daughters of Sumer and Akkad on whose neck slaveship had been imposed." What seems to be unprecedented is that, according to Jeremiah 34:11, the slaveowners repudiated the *misharum*-act. Jeremiah's wording suggests that there is more to this episode than meets the eye: "Thus said the Lord, the God of Israel: I made a covenant with your fathers when I brought them out of Egypt, the house of bondage, saying: 'At the end of seven years each of you must let go any fellow Hebrew who has been sold to you; when he has served you six years, you must set him free' " (Jer. 34:13–14).

M. David (1948, p. 74) points out that Jer. 34:14 is not grammatically homogeneous, since it jumps from the plural to the singular. More importantly, Deuteronomy 15:1–3, which calls for a general release from debt "at the end of every seven years" is confounded with Deuteronomy 15:12: "If a fellow Hebrew, man of woman, is sold to you, he shall serve you six years, and in the seventh year you shall set him free." In my judgment this confounding of laws was deliberate rather than accidental. The key lies in Deuteronomy 15:13–14: "When you set him [the slave] free, do not let him go empty-handed: furnish him out of the flock, threshing floor, and vat . . . " Zedekiah probably mandated emancipation *with compensation* for slaves who had served less than the legally required six years. Evidently this went too far for the Judean public. Indeed, Sarna (1973, p. 144) finds a hint of this reluctance in the language of Jeremiah 34:10.

The formulation of Deuteronomy 19:14 (see also Deuteronomy 27:17) is relatively obscure but I suspect (with L.G. Levy cited in R. North 1954, p. 167) that its aim is to outlaw the sale of land, or at least the alienation of lands in ancient Israelite settlements.[11] (Note that Leviticus 25:29–31 permits the permanent alienation of a house in a walled city after a one-year redemption period while mandating that "houses in villages that have no encircling walls shall be classed as open country; they may be redeemed, and they shall be released through the jubilee.") "You shall not move your neighbor's landmarks, set up by previous generations, in the property that will be alotted to you in the land that the Lord your God is giving you to possess."

The Nuzi material, which consists primarily of the private archives of two prominent families dating from the middle of the second millennium, casts light on this problem. These documents show that at this time real estate could legally be sold or transferred only to the nearest relative of the landowner. In order to circumvent this restriction, the landowner would adopt the buyer or his creditor (or their sons). As D. Cross (1937, p. 5 see also Jankowska 1969, p. 245) points out: "There being no limit on adoption, and adoptive children having first inheritance rights, it was comparatively simple to combine the scale [or mortgage loan] with a deed of adoption to render the transaction perfectly legal." Apparently the authors of Deuteronomy were well aware of the $m\bar{a}r\bar{u}tu$ or (sale-) adoption loophole and sought to close it by means of Deuteronomy 21:15–17:

> If a man has two wives, one loved and the other unloved, and both the loved and the unloved have borne him sons, but the first-born is the son of the unloved one—when he wills his property to his sons, he may not treat as first-born the son of the loved one in disregard of the son of the unloved one who is older. Instead, he must accept the first-born, the son of the unloved one, and allot to him a double portion [literally two thirds] of all he posseses; since he is the first fruit of his vigor, the birthright is his due.

Note that this provision runs counter, not only to the practices of "Nuzi, Alalaḫ, Ugarit and Palestine [where] the father had the right to select a 'first born' as well as making all his heirs share alike, and was not bound by the law of primogeniture," but also to patriarchal practice. In Genesis 48:13–20, "Joseph, the son of the 'loved' woman Rachel is given the double share while Reuben, the son of the 'unloved' Leah (Gen. 29:33), is repudiated as the first born" (Weinfeld 1970, p. 193). (Note also the apparent legal adoption statement in 2 Samuel 7:14: "I will be to him as a father, and he shall be to Me as a son.") Although the framework is humanistic the legal requirement that two-thirds of the father's possessions go to the first-born would have sharply limited the household's ability to sell land or obtain mortgage loans.

Did ancient Near Eastern governments possess the capability to enforce laws regarding land sales or sale adoptions, or were they no more than noble but futile gestures? A text from the time of Hammurabi, or one of his immediate successors, demonstrates that this capability existed and was exercised. The text is an appeal to the king from a petitioner seeking to regain title to real estate he had purchased but was deprived of by a royal *misharum* act. The sale tablets were reviewed by a government official and a decision was rendered. Finkelstein (1965, p. 242) concludes: "Astounding as it must appear to our normally skeptical eyes, there is no way of discounting the factual account of our text that at the promulgation of the *misharum* formal commissions were established to review real estate sales and that they in fact executed their mandate in a presumably conscientous manner." Again there is no reason to believe that Israelite kings were incapable of exercising similar jurisdiction.

Scholars are agreed that Exodus 22:24–25 is the Bible's earliest legal statement regarding the charging of interest on loans. (Gamoran 1971, p. 132). [12] "If you lend silver to My people, to the poor who is in your power, do not act toward him as a creditor: exact no interest from him, If you take your neighbor's garment in pledge, you must return it to him before the sun sets ... " A prohibition on collecting interest from poor countrymen is understandable, perhaps even rational, within the context of early Israelite society. Given that production is largely agricultural and for direct consumption, and taking into account the uncertainties of agricultural output and the relatively high costs of food storage and transport, it becomes apparent that the availability of loans will often make the difference between life and death by starvation. As Posner (1980, pp. 15, 23) has pointed out, societies in this position have sought to provide "hunger insurance" by encouraging generosity toward neighbors and kinsmen. "A 'loan' in primitive society is often just the counterpart to the payment of an insurance claim in modern society— it is the insurer's fulfillment of his contractual undertaking and to allow interest would change the nature of the transaction." But his line of argument, however reasonable, cannot explain why Deuteronomy called for more stringent and comprehensive barriers to the charging of interest, during the affluent, market-oriented eighth–seventh centuries (see Neufeld 1960, pp. 45–6). [13] Note in this connection Kapelrud's (1963, p. 53) perceptive observation that the attack of the classical prophets on the vital sacrificial cult is itself an indication of the growth of urbanization and the spread of markets.

Before turning to Deuteronomy's legal innovation it is well to consider the use of a "garment" as a pledge, since this matter arises in the Mesad Hashavyahu letter. Once again the Nuzi texts provide insight into Israelite practices. They reveal that items of clothing such as *naḫlaptu* and *ḫullānu*, etymologically "cloak" and "jacket" respectively, were relatively expensive items. According to D. Cross (1937, pp. 53, 62) a new cloak or jacket of good quality was worth from 12 to 15 shekels of silver while, on the average, an ox was worth 10 shekels, an ass 6.67 shekels, and a sheep 1.33 shekels of silver. Thus it is at least conceivable that the use of garments as pawns or pledges reflected relatively low storage and transactions costs rather than the abject poverty of the debtor.

As Neufeld (1955, p. 305) has pointed out, Deuteronomy 23:20–21 makes no mention of the economic status of the borrower and, therefore, seems to rule out all interest-bearing loans including consumption loans to the well-off and commercial loans: "Thou shalt not lend upon interest to thy brother: interest on silver, interest on victuals, interest of anything that is lent upon interest. Unto a foreigner thou mayest lend upon interest; but unto thy brother thou shalt not lend upon interest."[14] The blow to the Israelite economy might have been mitigated by access to, say, the Phoenician loan market. Or, perhaps, resident aliens gave loans at interest to Israelites much as in medieval times Jews loaned to Christians and vice versa. But even the most cursory examination of medieval European history starkly reveals the fragile nature of such expedients. In the absence of reasonably inexpensive mechanisms of international enforcement, loan defaults were not infrequent, while Jews and Lombards were hounded, robbed, and ultimately expelled. Any attempt to enforce the Deuteronomic regulations would have raised interest rates or led to credit rationing.

Obviously, a ban on interest would have made it difficult for small farmers to acquire the capital necessary to irrigate their land (see chapter 2). It would appear that Deuteronomy 28:12 (see also Deut. 11:10–14) not only anticipates this objection, but also rebuts it by denying the need for irrigation: "The Lord will open unto thee His good treasure the heaven to give the rain of thy land in its season, and to bless all the work of thy hand; and thou shalt lend unto many nations, but thou shalt not borrow." Possibly Deuteronomy anticipated as well a method of disguising interest payments already visualized in Hammurabi's Code (ca. 1700). This Code lays down legal maximum rates of interest on both silver and grain and then mandates that "If a merchant lent grain or money at interest and when he lent (it) at interest he paid out the money by the small weight and the grain by the small measure, but when he got (it) back he got the money by the (large) weight (and) the grain by the large measure, (that merchant shall forfeit) whatever he lent." As Maloney (1974, pp. 8–9) points out, this provision probably refers to an attempt to raise the interest rate above the legally permitted level by means of dual measures; "a light one when giving out the loan and a heavy one when receiving it back."

While Deuteronomy 25:13–15 makes no specific reference to loans it legislates against dual measures: "Thou shalt not have in thy bag diverse weights, a great and a small. Thou shalt not have in thy house diverse measures, a great and a small. A perfect and just weight shalt thou have; a perfect and just measure shalt thou have. . . . " Moreover, similar concerns may underlie Amos 8:5 on "making the ephah small, and the shekel great" Micah 6:10–11 on "wicked balances" and "deceitful weights," and Leviticus 19:35–36 on "just balances, just weights, a just ephah, and a just hin." (See also Prov. 20:10, 23.)

Some interesting evidence is provided by the Mesad Hashavyahu letter, which dates from the time of King Josiah. The translation provided below is that of Albright (1969, p. 568).

> Let my lord commander hear the case of his servant! As for thy servant, thy servant was harvesting at Hasarsusim (?). And thy servant was (still) harvesting as they finished the storage of grain, as usual before the Sabbath. While thy servant was finishing the storage of grain with his harvesters, Hoshaiah son of Shobai came and took thy servant's mantle. And all my brethren will testify on my behalf—those that were harvesting with me in the heat (?) . . . all my brothers (or brethren[15]) will testify on my behalf! If I am innocent of guilt, let him return my mantle, and if not, it is (still) the commander's right to take (my case under advisement (?) and to send word) to him (asking that he return the) mantle of thy servant. And let not (the plea of his servant) be displeasing to him!

The content indicates that the complainant headed a team of reapers who were probably kinsmen. But as F. M. Cross (1962, p. 46) notes, if we are dealing with a royal corvée or hired labor, then imprisonment, physical punishment, or the nonpayment of wages would be more appropriate modes of retaliation: "The taking of the garment implies the claim of a creditor."

The Nuzi archives dating from the second half of the fifteenth century B.C.E. reveal the existence of *tidennūtu* contracts in which the creditor provided goods while the debtor met the interest payments by allowing the creditor to use his real estate or by "entering the house" of the creditor and performing task work including harvesting, orchard work, meadow work, weaving and carpentry (Eichler 1973, pp. 20, 40–1; Zaccagnini 1979, pp. 7–9).[16] More importantly, Diakonoff (1969, p. 227) and Eichler (1973, p. 7–9) point out that in Middle Assyria (fifteenth–twelfth centuries B.C.E.) loan contracts frequently called for debtors to place reapers at the disposal of the creditor. This practice is also found in our period in eighth–seventh-century Assyria (Postgate 1976, pp. 44–8).[17] A preference for making interest payments in labor power, as opposed to cash or crops, might be understood as an attempt to cope with agricultural wage, price, or yield uncertainty. However, I believe that the explanation may be sought elsewhere. To the extent that "interest on money, interest on victuals, interest on anything that is lent upon interest" is prohibited (Deut. 23:20) or subjected to maximum interest-rate regulations (for instance Article 90 in Hammurabi's Code, see Meek 1969, p. 169), then as E. W. Davies (1981, pp. 68–9) recognizes, economic actors can be expected to seek out second-best alternatives such as the disguise of illegal interest payments as labor services.[18] In fact, the Nuzi *tidennūtu* documents often include a penalty clause which in one case of a loan of "twelve minas of tin" for harvesting services states that "he who violates the agreement shall pay a fine of one ox" (for a seventh-century Assyrian example, see Parker 1954, ND. 2320). Now the Nuzi texts place the value of an ox at 10 shekels and that of a new cloak at between 12 and 15 shekels of silver. Thus the seizure of our reaper's cloak might represent a penalty for defaulting on his interest payment—that is, failing to perform the agreed upon harvesting services. If this explanation of the Mesad Hashavyahu affair is valid, we have indirect evidence that the Judean state sought to enforce the law against interest. An alternative line of explanation entirely in terms of breach-of-contract without reference to a loan transaction is, perhaps, indicated by the Laws of Eshnunna, which date from twentieth-century-B.C.E. Mesopotamia: "Should a man pay [agree to pay?] 1 shekel of silver for a hired man for harvesting—if he does not complete for him the harvest work everywhere he (shall p)ay 10 shekels of silver" (Goetze 1969, p. 162).

The question of enforcement can, however, be approached from another direction. In the standard translation, Deuteronomy 15:1–3. calls for the cancellation of debts every seventh year. But the prohibition on interest in Deuteronomy 23:20 would have eliminated the main motive for lending. If I understand R. North (1954, p. 187) correctly, he is arguing that the seventh-year "release" visualized in Deuteronomy 15:1–3 actually applies to the "pawns" held by the creditor—that is, to the labor or land services pledged to the creditor in lieu of interest.[19] It follows that Deuteronomy may have anticipated and sought to discourage disguised interest payment by means of a seventh-year remittance or, possibly Deuteronomy 15:1–3 is a later innovation triggered by experience with this loophole in the interest prohibition.

Leviticus 17–26, generally referred to by scholars as the "Holiness Code" (H) sets forth several economic reforms. But if this material is to be properly utilized an attempt must be made to date it. The most penetrating and comprehensive analysis of H is that of Driver (1897; for more recent, compact discussions, see Eissfeldt 1965, pp. 233–39 and Noth 1965, pp. 127–28) who makes several key points: (1) "The principle which determines most conspicuously the character of the entire section is that of *holiness—* partly ceremonial, partly moral—as a quality distinguishing Israel . . . , and regulating its life" (p. 48). (2) While H is related to Leviticus 1–16, the Priestly Code, (P), it manifests sharp differences in style, phraseology and motives (p. 47). (3) The above considerations taken together with the miscellaneous nature of H's contents, the recurrence of subjects dealt with in Exodus 20–23 and in P, and the fact that H "opens with instructions repeating the place of sacrifice and closes with a parenetic exhortation, exactly in the manner of the two other Pentateuchal Codes, the 'Book of the Covenant' [Exod. 20:21–23 and 23:20ff] and the code in Deuteronomy (Deut. 12 and 28)" (p. 48) lead to the following conclusion: "The phenomena which the chapters present are explained by the supposition that [H was at] first an independent collection of laws was edited with parentic additions . . . and . . . afterwards the whole thus was formed incorporated in P . . . sometimes with modifications introduced for the purpose of adjusting it more completely to the spirit and system of P, at other times interwoven with elements from P" (Driver 1897, pp. 47–8). Driver (see, more recently Zimmerli 1979, pp. 46–52) then goes on (p. 49) to discuss the "numerous" and "peculiarly striking" affinities between H and the prophet Ezekiel: "the laws comprised in H are frequently quoted by him, and the parenetic passages contain many expressions—sometimes remarkable ones—which otherwise occur in Ezekiel alone." Indeed, the similarities between H and Ezekiel are so pronounced that several scholars have concluded that the prophet himself was the author or compiler of H. Driver himself does not go this far. He raises the possibility that the laws were written at an earlier date, while they were arranged in the closing years of the monarchy. The predominant view among modern scholars is that H probably dates from the period of Ezekiel, which is usually taken to be the early sixth century.[20]

In this event the provision in H regarding interest-bearing loans takes on a new dimension of significance:

> And if thy brother be waxen poor, and his means fail with thee; then thou shalt uphold him; as a stranger and settler shall he live with thee. Take thou no interest [*neshekh*] or increase [*tarbit* and *marbit*]; but fear thy God; that thy brother may

live with thee thou shalt not give him thy money upon interest, nor give him thy victuals for increase. For I the Lord am your God, who brought you forth out of the land of Egypt . . . (Lev. 25:35–38).

Before turning to the substance of this passage it should be noted that it includes two of H's characteristic expressions, that of "fear your God" and "for I the Lord am your God." The latter, in fact, occurs nearly fifty times in H (Driver 1897, p. 49). With respect to content two points stand out. In the first place, H like the corresponding law in the Covenant Code (Exod. 22:24), but unlike that in Deuteronomy (23:20–21), makes explicit reference to the poverty of the borrower. Second, while all three codes use *neshekh*, only H adds the additional terms *tarbit* and *marbit*. These two terms are translated as "increase" and are understood to refer to the collection of accrued interest, while the former, which means "bite," is taken to refer to the deduction of interest in advance (see chapter 6, note 2 of this book on the *ḫubattātu*-loan). But according to Cohn (in the *Encyclopedia Judaica* 1971, vol. 16, pp. 27–8), the most authoritative view is that the various terms are synonyms for interest. This is supported by the fact that the Hebrew *nosheh* or creditor literally means one who lends money upon pledge (Neufeld 1958, p. 375).[22]

What happened, I believe, is that in the years following Josiah's imposition of the Deuteronomic law code, the Judeans learned the hard way that a blanket prohibition of interest is irrational and suicidal, so they retreated to the earlier provision in the Covenant Code.[21] On the other hand, they discovered that their word for interest, *neshekh* (bite), opened an etymological loophole. No doubt those who wished to borrow or lend argued that only advance deduction of interest was prohibited. This argument was settled by adding additional terms such as *tarbit* and *marbit*.

Perhaps the damaging effects of a total ban on the sale of ancestral lands were also perceived for H does not, as does DL(19:14; 27:17), refer to the sin of moving ancient landmarks. Instead, H introduces a Jubilee year when "each of you shall return to his holding" and a "provision for the redemption of the land."[23]

You shall count off seven weeks of years—seven times seven years—so that the period of seven weeks of years gives a total of forty-nine years. Then you shall sound the horn loud; in the seventh month, on the tenth day of the month—the Day of Atonement—you shall have the horn sounded throughout your land you shall hallow the fiftieth year. You shall proclaim release throughout the land for all its inhabitants. It shall be a jubilee for you: each of you shall return to his holding and each of you shall return to his family. That fiftieth year shall be a jubilee for you: you shall not sow, neither shall you reap the aftergrowth or harvest the untrimmed vines, for it is a jubilee. It shall be holy to you: you may only eat the growth direct from the field. . . . When you sell property to your neighbor, or buy any from your neighbor, you shall not wrong one another. In buying from your neighbor, you shall deduct only for the number of years since the jubilee; and in selling to you, he shall charge you only for the remaining crop years: . . . Do not wrong one another, but fear your God; for I the Lord am you God. . . . But the land must not be sold beyond reclaim, for the land is Mine; you are but strangers resident with Me. Throughout the land that you hold, you must provide for the redemption of the land. If your brother is in straits and has to sell part of his holding, his nearest redeemer [closest relative able to redeem the land] shall come and redeem what his brother has sold. If a man has no one to redeem for him, but prospers and acquires enough to redeem with, he shall compute the years since its sale, refund the difference to the man to whom he sold it, and return to his holding. If he lacks sufficient means to recover it, what he sold shall remain with the purchaser until the jubilee; in the jubilee year it shall be released, and he shall return to his holding. (Lev. 25:8–28)

Again note the use of H's characteristic phrases "fear your God" and "for I the Lord am your God." It is not entirely clear whether the redemption provision is available only to those who were poor at the time they sold their land. Such a restriction would probably have been unenforceable. Depending on exactly how the law was interpreted, the land reclamation provision could have operated against long-term capital improvements on the land, but it nevertheless would represent an improvement as compared to total prohibition on land sales (see Soss 1973, pp. 339–41).[24] A final point is that H (Lev. 25:39) appears to have outlawed the transfer of a pledged individual's services to a third party.

The net effect of the economic reforms discussed above is difficult to ascertain. At the very least they would have slowed Israel's rate of economic growth. At the other extreme, the resource misallocations resulting from attempts to eliminate or inhibit land and capital markets and the work-incentive effects of welfare payments had the potential to reduce the living standard in absolute terms. The reactions of the average Israelite to economic regulation were not so dramatic as those he made to the attempt to forcibly convert him to the worship of social justice. Nevertheless, the effects of the economic policies favored by the affluents and their spokesmen added to the disenchantment and alienation of the masses and must have made a contribution to the destruction of the Jewish state and the dispersal of its citizens.

An ironic postscript is provided by the sharp upsurge in genuine moral values and concern for the poor among the brutal but plunder-wealthy Assyrians. Sargon II (721–705) was portrayed as a "helper of the poor who made good their losses" while Sennacherib (704–681) was a "lover of justice . . . who comes to the aid of the needy" (McCown 1943, pp. 222–23). One of Esarhaddon's (680–669) inscriptions attacks the residents of Babylon because they

> answered each other Yes, (in their heart): No; they plotted evil . . . they were oppressing the weak and poor and putting them into the power of the mighty, there was oppression and acceptance of bribe within the city daily without ceasing; they were robbing each other's property; the son was cursing his father in the street . . . then the god (Enlil/Marduk) became angry, he planned to overwhelm the land and to destroy its people. (Weinfeld 1977 (b), p. 194)

Assurbanipal (668–627) attempted to control prices (Dubberstein 1938, p. 42). The monotheist Nabonidus (553–539 B.C.E.) became the last king of Babylon when he tried to centralize worship in the shrine of the god Sin. His subjects eagerly cooperated with the Persian King Cyrus to secure his overthrow.

Notes

1. Translations of JPS unless otherwise specified; see the bibliographic note (chapter 1, note 2).

2. On the Covenant Code, see, for example, Phillips (1970, pp. 12–13).

3. It now appears that Entemena who ruled Lagash about a generation earlier also initiated social reforms (see Edzard 1974, pp. 145–46).

4. This account of Bocchoris's reforms appears to be based on the account provided by the first-century B.C.E. Greek historian, Diodorus of Sicily. The latter, however, does not refer to a 33 ⅓-percent-interest ceiling (see 1933, pp. 271–73, 321–23).

5. No doubt the administration of justice by professional or semi-professional functionaries predates the Deuteronomic reforms. 2 Chronicles 19:5 states that King Jehoshaphat (873–849) appointed judges in the fortified cities of Judah. (Does Isaiah 1:26: "I will restore your magistrates as of old" refer to this reform?) Perhaps the "nobles" who with the "elders" tried Naboth (1 Kings 21:8) represent the existence of professional judges in the northern kingdom, Israel, in the time of Ahab (874–853). More than likely, the earlier judges and legal officials were unsalaried, or nominally salaried, much as the medieval English justices of the peace were appointed by the crown from among the local knights and gentry (see Jewell 1972, especially p. 202). Quite possibly the innovation of Deuteronomy is the introduction of fully salaried law-enforcement officers not dependent on "bribes" (or "gifts") for part of their income. This interpretation is strengthened by Deuteronomy 16:19: "Thou shalt not wrest judgment. Thou shalt not respect persons. Thou shalt not take a bribe." So translated by JPS; Thomson has "gift" not "bribe."

Note also the hostile prophetic references to the judicial role of the "princes" in Hosea 5:10, Micah 3:1, Isaiah 1:23, and Ezekiel 45:9. Note also the hostile references to the judicial role of the "gods" in Psalms 58 and 82. Isaiah 3:14, another attack on the "princes," probably recalls Naboth's trial. See also Whitelam's (1979, chapters 9 and 10) discussion.

6. While the term "ownership" is absent from Hebrew (as well as from Greek and early Latin—see Daube 1979, p. 38), the underlying concept is obvious in the (presumably) earliest Israelite law code.

7. 1 Samuel 8:15 had warned the Israelites that a king would "take a tenth part of your grain and vintage and give it to his eunuchs and courtiers."

8. I say "apparently" because Finkelstein (1965, p. 243; see also 1969, p. 526; Neufeld· 1958, pp. 52–5; Westbrook 1971a, pp. 216–17) maintains that in Mesopotamia the remissive acts were proclaimed at the beginning of reigns and at intervals of seven or more years thereafter.

9. It is interesting to note that eighteenth-century-B.C.E. loan contracts found at an Old Assyrian trading post in Anatolia include a clause calling for repayment even in the event that the king issued a decree "to wash away debt"—that is, to cancel the repayment obligation (Balkan 1974, pp. 31–3). A similar provision is found in a Neo-Assyrian contract dating from our period (see Westbrook 1971a, pp. 218–19). There is no direct evidence that the Israelites utilized similar legal expedients until the time of Hillel's *prozbul*.

The *misharum*-edict of Ammiṣaduqa anticipates attempts to escape its debt-release provision by disguising interest-bearing loans as other types of legally permitted transactions (Finkelstein 1969a, pp. 50, 59–61).

10. "Without payment" (*hinnâm*) might mean "without the slave's giving payment" but in view of Genesis 29:15, in which Laban asks Jacob "are you to serve me without payment?" The use of "without *receiving* payment" seems more appropriate (see R. North 1954, fn, 4, p. 156).

11. Gelb (1979, vol. I, p. 70) refers to a proclamation prohibiting land sales at a certain point within the Ur III period (2112–2004). Note Edzard's (1967, p. 155) remarks:

> As we know, there are, from the [previous] Early Dynastic period, what are quite definitely private land-sale contracts in the area of Akkadian settlement. If land was owned, and therefore bought and sold, by individuals in Sumer in the age of Ur III, we should expect to find records of it, for a society with so elaborate a bureaucracy could surely provide the scribes to make them . . . What we have here is an argument from silence; a second argument is more conclusive. The legal documents of Ur III . . . show us what the objects of litigation were among ordinary men. As we have pointed out, we have no instance of a suit arising from the sale of arable land. . . . There are contracts of lease to private persons, but none of sale, where agricultural land is concerned. After the time of Ur-Ninurta of Isin [1923–1896], private land-sale contracts appear in respectable numbers in the Sumerian south; this can hardly be an accident of archaeology, but points to a change from a previous condition.

The archaeological evidence indicates another policy reversal in southern Babylonia during the reign of Hammurabi's son, Samsuiluna. During the period from 1739 to 1721, contracts for the permanent sale of privately owned fields disappear at Nippur. "A new feature of the sale documents from this period is the high frequency of 'redemption texts'. . . . Theoretically these texts explain that the present buyer is repurchasing property which had previously been sold by his family, but an examination of the personal names shows no obvious genealogical relationship between the seller in the original transaction and the redeemer in the later transaction. . . . It seems possible that the redemption [text] was used in the transfer of property to someone who was outside the circle of legitimate buyers." (Stone 1977, p. 281) Interestingly, loan documents also disappeared for most of this period. For more on Samsuiluna as an economic regulator, see chapter 11 in this book.

12. On the dating of the Elohistic Covenant Code and its narrative framework see, for example, Patrick (1977, pp. 156–57) who suggests that the Code is probably premonarchial while its framework probably dates to the ninth century in the northern kingdom, Israel.

13. The changeover from mutual "hunger insurance" to interest-bearing loans reflects the economic development of Israel, not its "Canaanization."

14. So translated by JPS(1917); JPS(1974) had "deduct" interest instead of "lend upon interest."

15. Cross (1962, p. 45) and Naveh (1960, p. 135) have "brethern" as opposed to Pardee's (1978, p. 37) and Albright's "companions."

16. It is not always clear whether "entering the house" means that the *tidennu* (pledge?) literally resided in the home of the creditor or merely reported there when the time came to perform the contracted for task (see further Eichler 1973, pp. 88–9). (More generally, the distinction, to use the terms of Roman law, between "hypothec" and "mortgage" (*dead* gage) is not always clear, see Hicks 1969, p. 75). A similar kind of ambiguity seems to appear in Roman law: "*Pignus*, pledge was a mode of real security which left the debtor owner of the object pawned: the creditor obtained only possession. In course of time, it became possible to pawn a thing without even handing it over. The creditor, that is, would have a possessory remedy or an action *in rem* only when the debt was due. In most texts, this relaxed variant goes under the old designation *pignus*. A fair number of them, however, call it *hypotheca*—a Greek word." (Daube 1979, p. 43).

17. For additional examples of antichresis, see Eichler (1973, chapter 3). The Assyrian legal tradition is more relevant here than the Nuzi because its "connection with pledge law is far less extensive than in Nuzi. More common is its existence outside the sphere of pledge law, where it is an accessory obligation of the debtor to render antichretic service to the creditor" (Eichler 1973, p. 101). In other words, we are not dealing with self-sale but with an ordinary loan transaction where the interest is paid in labor services.

Eichler (1973, p. 94) provides the following example of a Middle Assyrian antichretic loan contract: "In lieu of the interest on this (borrowed) tin, they shall deliver the yield of a five-*iku* field, the barley and straw, on the threshing floor (at threshing time) to PN (the creditor); should the set term expire (without repaying the loan), they shall, as previously, seed the field." Note the points of resemblance with the Mesad Hashavyahu document.

18. The Roman contract called *nexum* which seems to have involved the payment of interest in labor-services flourished in the fifth and fourth centuries (until abolished in 326 B.C.E.) when interest charges were legally limited or prohibited (see Brunt 1971, pp. 51, 56–7). Finley's (1982, pp. 150–66) discussion is unaware of the economic theory of price controls.

Several loan tablets from a complex of rooms near the palace at Assyrian Calah (Nimrud) dating to the second half of the 7th century appear to call for both interest payments in grain or silver and harvesting services (see Parker 1954, ND. 2092, 2320 and 2334). The specified interest rates of "5 *sutu* for every homer" of barley or "25 percent" for silver, which are found in several other loan tablets, may represent a legal maximum which was evaded by means of supplementary labor services.

See note 9 for attempts in the Mesopotamian area to evade the force of royal debt-release decrees by means of legal expedients. For evidence of interference in the loan market during the reign of Samsuiluna, see note 11.

19. R. North (1954, p. 187) translates Deuteronomy 15:2 as follows: "Every holder of a pawn at his disposition shall release what he *contracted over by pawnbrokerage* with his neighbor" (emphasis in original). In this connection mention should be made of a Neo-Assyrian contract in which Ḫananu transfers the usufruct of a landed estate for a specified period of time to Silim-Aššur in return for 34 shekels of silver. An additional clause reads: "If a release [i.e. of the landed estate] is established, Silim-Aššur will claim his silver" (see Westbrook 1971a, pp. 218–19).

20. Basing his conclusions on the prominence of northern linguistic usages and Aramaisms, the absence of an oracle against Babylon, and several other considerations, J. Smith (1931, pp. 69–71, 79, 98) maintains, however, that: "It is intelligible and chronologically possible that Ezekiel's prophetic activity commenced about 722 either among the Northern exiles or in the

homeland, and that he continued his prophetic labors until c. 669 in Palestine or alternately in Palestine and among the Northern exiles. This scheme . . . accounts for the interpolations and the arrangement of the oracles, and explains why the Redactor wished to convey the impression that Ezekiel was a resident in Babylonia. We look at the Old Testament through Jewish eyes, and the fact that Ezekiel was a prophet of the North is sufficient explanation of the Redactor's method." Smith (pp. 99–100) adds that his hypothesis is consistent with "two sets of oracles delivered by Ezekiel, one set in Palestine and the other in the Diaspora . . . ,it may be that we have a remarkable confirmation of it in the tradition preserved by Josephus that Ezekiel wrote two books, and in the Jewish belief that Ezekiel's prophetic activity commenced in Palestine." A final speculation sharpens our focus on the historical Ezekiel. In 2 Kings 17:27–28 the king of Assyria sends one of the exiled priests to Bethel to teach the new settlers the manner of the God of the land. Is it possible that this priest was Ezekiel? In Ezekiel 3:4 Yahweh orders the prophet: "Go, get thee unto the house of Israel, and speak My words unto them." Smith (p. 96) observes that "the phrase 'lek bo;' (go, get thee) implies a journey of some distance." "So a spirit lifted me up . . . and I went in bitterness, in the heat of my spirit, and the hand of the Lord was strong upon me." (3:14) "There is general agreement," Smith further explains, "that some change is necessary in the text of 3:15 ff. If Ezekiel were 'bethok haggolah' (among the captives) (1:1), he would scarcely be sent to a place so near as another site in exile territory."

21. During the first century C.E., "Hillel the elder is said to have instituted the *prozbul*, by which it became possible for a debt to be repaid after the next sabbatical year [the year of release] by the device of turning the collection over to the court . . . " (Albright 1960, p. 8). This would have facilitated the financing of long-term projects at reasonable interest rates.

The argument in the text accepts the traditional view that Ezekiel belongs to the late-seventh–early-6th centuries. If, however, one accepts J. Smith's (1931, chap. 6) hypothesis that Ezekiel was a northern prophet, the reform of the interest legislation might conceivably date to the aftermath of Jeroboam's imposition of the Deuteronomic law code.

22. Unfortunately, I was unable to obtain a copy of an article by E. Lipiński in *Orientalia Lovaniensia Periodica* (1979).

23. The redemption provision has been compared with the Laws of Eshnunna (twentieth century B.C.E.) which establish a similar right (Zaccagnini 1979, p. 17). See R. North (1954) for a general discussion and references to the literature. Neufeld's (1958, pp. 62–72) article is also informative.

24. Gordon (1965a, p. 239) suggests that a jubilee had been proclaimed in the days of King Hezekiah. He bases this on Isaiah's message to the king: "And this is a sign for you, this year you eat what grows of itself, and the next year what springs from that; and in the third year, sow and reap, and plant vineyards and eat their fruit" (37:30 and 2 Kings 19:29). Gordon adds that the Assyrians timed their invasion to coincide with the forty-ninth and fiftieth years during which the land lay fallow. See also Sarna (1973, p. 149).

19 SUMMARY AND CONCLUSIONS

After the death of King Solomon (c. 922), the United Monarchy of the Israelites split into a northern kingdom, Israel, and a southern kingdom, Judah. During the tumultuous ninth century, while king strove with king for trade routes and priest with priest for a place at the royal table, the Israelite economy grew quietly but strongly. By the beginning of the eighth century, Israel and Judah had been projected into a glittering era of prosperity and power.

During the eighth and seventh centuries, specialized production centers emerged and applied mass-production techniques, most notably in the areas of ceramics and residential housing. Israelite agriculture exported its products and displayed notable technical sophistication, including a rather remarkable adaptation to the desert environment of the Negeb. Testimony to a lively commerce is provided not only by specialized production, but also by the growing use of stone in building, by warehouse facilities, firms with complex managerial structures, brand names, land consolidation, and by the existence of significant population concentrations such as Samaria and Jerusalem. During this period Israel-Judah also expanded territorially gaining control over Bashan's great granary, parts of the fertile Philistine Plain,

247

several ports, and the two major north-south highways, the Via Maris and the King's Highway.

Neither the Bible, archaeology, nor economic theory demonstrates that income differentials widened or became very pronounced. Specifically, there is no reason to believe that the real income or even the relative share of labor had to fall in the eighth and later-seventh centuries.

The new wealth that poured into Israel-Judah was consumed in a variety of forms. There was, first of all, a significant extension in the quantity and quality of housing and other consumer durables. Second, the average Israelite enjoyed a diet that was tastier as well as more varied and nutritious. True bread (raised or leavened bread) was substituted for hard barley-cakes and gruel and finely sifted whiter flour for the coarser varieties. The quantity of meat increased, as did its quality with the substitution of beef for mutton and fattened for unfattened animals. The affluent ancient Israelite being necessarily "poor" in terms of modern amenities chose his luxuries accordingly. He enjoyed his many children and participated in great feasts; he made lavish provision to memorialize his ancestors and gave large public donations; he enjoyed fine art, archaeological objects, gardens, song, and drama; he concerned himself with wisdom and questions of human character and duty; and, of course, he sought to improve the position of those less fortunate then himself.

Since an appreciable number of Israelites became men of means, it is not surprising that the eighth and seventh centuries reverberated with the call for social justice. This theme was most prominent in the prophetic writings but it also penetrated law, history, the literature of prayer (the psalms), and the secular-wisdom literature (the proverbs). The basic thrust of this "prophetic revolution" was the attempt to transform the national God of the Israelites into a God of universalism and social justice. The ordinary Israelite, however, could not be converted to the worship of social justice as long as the ancient religion provided peace of mind and a sense of belonging. Therefore, the prophets bitterly attacked Israel's most sacred religious observances, those honoring God and ancestors by means of sacrifices and *teraphim*.

Amos, Micah, and the other prophets were not poor peasants, hermits, or eccentrics outside the mainstream of Israelite life. Instead, they were educated members of the Establishment who quite possibly, had begun their careers as cultic priests of the second (or prophetic) order. As have all social voluntarists, ancient or modern, they argued that social injustice is neither a private matter nor inevitable. Motivated by idealism or personal ambition they sought with the support of the affluents, to commit the rulers to programs of social amelioration and regeneration. We must not be misled by "the rejection of the 'writing prophets' by their age and [by] the prophetic view of inevitable calamity, these are literary motifs derived from the [traditional Mesopotamian] epic rather than historical facts" (Staples 1966, p. 112). In fact, Isaiah became the "great advisor" or "teacher" of Uzziah and Hezekiah while Amos sought, and may well have secured, a similar position under Jeroboam II. Jeremiah was an associate of the most powerful in the land and probably campaigned for cultic centralization. Micah's social ideas were heeded by Hezekiah while Zephaniah, very likely, was a powerful priest and a relative of King Josiah. Deuteronomy, the basic document of social reform, not only attacks traditional Israelite religion and the market system as the prophets demanded, but also strongly reflects their central ideological tenet, "No social justice, no land of Israel." Indeed Deuteronomy, as the Psalms, is permeated by the very language and images and rhetorical style favored by Amos, Hosea, and Jeremiah. How could this be if the prophets were ineffective in their own time? Traditional historiography influenced, I believe, by Jewish ideas of theodicy in which destruction proves evil doing, Christian ideas of the coming replacement of "ethnic-nationalist religions by the universal faith," and a general intellectual climate of distaste or outright hostility toward markets holds that Israel and Judah fell because the prophetic counsel was ignored. However, as an economist and social scientist, I can testify that whatever its presumed moral virtues, the advice of the classical prophets was destructive from the standpoint of economic affluence and political strength.

Once the prophets and their allies had won the support of the state's armed might, concerted action was taken on two fronts. First, in the interests of an immediate improvement in the *behavior* of the Israelites economic reforms were implemented. Second, in order to teach them to *think* more righteously a program of indoctrination was instituted within the cult. Deuteronomy was designed to fulfill both programmatic objectives. Ancient Israel experienced no less than three such cultural revolutions under Jeroboam II (ca. 751), Hezekiah (ca. 716/5), and Josiah (ca. 621). In each instance the results were disastrous: innocent people were humiliated and murdered, civil war flared, the economy was damaged, and foreign nations took advantage of the opportunity to tear away chunks of Israel-Judah until nothing remained.

In the end the prophets did not succeed in transforming the Israelite. Since they understood neither the man nor Israelite society, they succeeded only in making the former miserable while destroying the latter. Here it is well to avoid misunderstandings. I am not arguing that the economic reforms that must have terminated affluence in eight-century Israel and in seventh–sixth century Judah are enough to also condemn the following periods on economic grounds. As I noted in 1980 (pp. 96–7): *"Reforms that massively undermine incentives cause retro-development, but, in good dialectical*

fashion, the retro-development process includes the destruction of the very
state apparatus that strangled affluence in the name of altruism. Once again
efficient [economic] organization is possible." Thus, for example, the rise of
the Western world took place upon the ruins of the Roman state. On the other
hand, the Chinese state was not smashed but taken over by the Mongols in
the thirteenth century, so the inheritance of affluent Sung China was Oriental
despotism and economic stagnation. What happened in sixth-and fifth-
century Palestine? The Jewish community no longer enjoyed an independent
national life but was a member of a foreign state. This does not, however,
answer the question. The answer depends upon a factual issue: Did the
foreign rulers insist on or permit local Jewish officials to enforce the
economic innovations of Deuteronomy? To the extent that this happened the
road back to affluence would have been blocked. Further exploration is best
left for a second volume.[1]

Of course, traditional scholarship recognizes no causal relationship between the social reforms and the destruction of Israelite society. Thus
Kaufmann (1960, p. 290) remarks: "To what extent a moral-religious book
like Deuteronomy could have become a political constitution is difficult to
say: the experiment was made too near the collapse of Judah to tell." Yerkes
(1959, p. 132) suggests that "Before the drastic reform had been successfully
completed, the temple was destroyed and its ministers deported." Irwin
(1952, p. 132) and Köhler (1956, p. 148) make essentially the same point.
Such comments make as much sense as the story of the peddler who sought to
lower his costs by slightly reducing his horse's feed each day. Unfortunately,
just when the peddler had the creature broken in, it died.

Eliphaz the Temanite, echoing Amos, tells the suffering Job:

> It is because of your piety that He arraigns you, and enters into judgment with
> you? You know that your wickedness is great, and that your iniquities have no
> limit. You exact pledges from your fellows without reason, and leave them naked,
> stripped of their clothes; you do not give the thirsty water to drink; you deny bread
> to the hungry. The land belongs to the strong; the privileged occupy it. You have
> sent away widows empty-handed; the strength of the fatherless is broken.
> Therefore snares are all around you, or darkness, so you cannot see; a flood of
> waters covers you. (Job 22:4–11)

But Job speaking, perhaps, in behalf of a decimated, humiliated Israelite
nation contradicts Amos's (3:7) assertion that "my Lord God does nothing
without having revealed his purpose to his servants the prophets,"[2] suggesting instead that "Even those close to Him cannot forsee His actions" (24:1).
Later Job pleads his case:

> The ear that heard acclaimed me; the eye that saw, commended me. For I saved
> the poor man who cried out, the orphan who had none to help him. I received the

blessing of the wretched; I gladdened the heart of the widow. I clothed myself in righteousness and it robed me; justice was my cloak and turban. I was eyes to the blind and feet to the lame. I was a father to the needy, and I looked into the case of the stranger. I broke the jaws of the wrongdoer, and I wrested prey from his teeth. (29:11–17)

Too little and too late? Of course.

Andersen and Freedman (1980, p. 35) conclude that the "march to ruin was irreversible, as the prophets had insisted almost from the start and as events proved." Mendenhall (1981, p. 190) suggests that the prophets "with a sad success" predicted the destruction of a corrupt and oppressive "petty political power." For Bright (1972, p. 270), "it is evident that the social crimes that Amos had denounced had rent the fabric of society." Coote (1981, p. 61) observes that none of the classical prophets "comes back on stage, victorious or vindicated, to take his final bow as God's effective messenger of justice." His explanation for this is that "The kinds of prophets that were validated by the experience of exile in both north and south were not the kind that were ever well-received by their hearers." In fact, the social fabric was rent and ruin was made inevitable by the predictions, denunciations, good receptions, and reforms themselves.

With respect to the "towering insight" that Israel "would not be able to withstand the dangers that threatened it from outside," are we, as Herrmann (1975, p. 239) believes, dealing with "profound dimensions of prophetic activity"? Or, alternatively, only with more mundane self-fulfilling prophecy? Modern men and women might do well to ponder Hosea's (6:5) parable:

Therefore I have hewn them by the prophets; I have slain them by the words of my mouth.

Notes

1. There are indications that the Assyrian Empire moved from a policy of free trade to one of economic regulation. Very likely the same trend manifested itself in Babylonian (see Oppenheim 1957, p. 34; Saggs 1962, p. 267) and later on, in Persian policy.

2. The participation of prophets in heavenly deliberations is found in Isaiah 6; 44:26 and Jeremiah 23:21–22.

APPENDIX A:
MARKETS AND
ENTREPRENEURS IN THE
ANCIENT NEAR EAST

I have decided not to burden the reader with the details of either the "formalist-substantivist" controversy in economic anthropology (see Lowry 1979, pp. 77–9) or of Polanyi's (for instance, 1977; see also Sabloff and Lamberg-Karlovsky 1975) assertions regarding the absence of true markets in antiquity. Frankly, much of this work is saturated with special pleading and is amateurish with respect to economic analysis. Indeed even the meaning of economics is not grasped. The noted economic historian Douglass C. North (1977, p. 707) who wishes to reinterpret Polanyi's nonmarket-allocation systems in terms of modern transactions costs analysis admits that "It is easy to find fault with Polanyi's analtytical framework. There are numerous parts of his analysis that shou a failure to grasp elementary economic principles. . . . Moreover it is hard to see how one could generate refutable tests of his hypotheses. . . . "

Just as important, while the evidence for Egypt is quite scanty (see Janssen 1975, pp. 158–62, 184–85; 1979, pp. 505–07), modern research has affirmed that ancient Western Asia knew money (in the generic sense of a common medium of exchange[1]), market places,[2] wage labor[3], profit-oriented businessmen and firms, and supply-demand-determined market prices.[4] With respect to the latter two elements, several citations from the relevant scholarly literature should suffice:

> This view of Mesopotamian economy in the third millennium requires a re-appraisal of the role of the merchant in the economy, as well as of the motives underlying his economic activity. The basic premise underlying the conception of the merchant presented here is that the merchant operated *primarily* on the basis of profit and loss and that the state or temple *never* undertook systematically to underwrite his losses. The evidence for this, like the evidence for everything else in the third millennium is disparate, uneven, and indirect, but, on the whole, it is far more compelling than the evidence which can be brought forward to support the view that profit was not an important motive in merchant activity. . . . Moreover, the evidence shows third millennium state executives functioning in much the same regulative activities as their Old Babylonian counterparts. This is not to suggest that market economy dominated third or second millennium Mesopotamian economic processes, but there is sufficient reason to believe that it was a significant factor in the total economic picture. (Powell 1977, pp. 24, 29)

> This preliminary survey of commercial texts from the Sargonic period should conclude by stressing that trade, either institutional or inter-city, may be seen as but one facet of a vital and profitable business activity that flourished throughout the empire of the Sargonic kings and beyond. Individuals, alone or in partnership, the state, on its own behalf or through agents, the king himself, participated in this business activity. . . . From the point of view of the individual businessman, the goal was surely . . . the good life, neatly summed up perhaps in an otherwise cryptic document that lists a donkey, a garden, and a house in Agade. (Foster 1977, p. 42)

> Our texts clearly indicate that the economically decisive element in the Assyrian society [of the second millennium] is not found on the "state level," even though the role played by the temples is still somewhat obscure. Instead, the trade is clearly organized via a great number of large kinship-based groups called "houses," which we may provisionally describe as "firms." The financing of the Old Assyrian trade was organized in long-term partnerships, referred to as *naruqqu*-transactions . . . These partnerships or "societies" appear to have cut across the boundaries of the basic units, the families, and the exact relations are in fact quite unknown. . . . The Old Assyrian commercial colonies in Northern Syria and Anatolia were based on a socioeconomic system of a 'capitalist' type (Larsen 1974, pp. 469–70; 1976, p. 16).

> Both for Anatolia and Assyria occasional changes in the market situation are attested, due to different causes: the season, emergency situations, changes in supply or demand, unfavorable prices, etc. The fluctuations of the prices (for tin once within a fairly short period of time from 13:1 to 16:1, or a difference of more than 20%) do not suggest that prices had been fixed by treaty, as in the system of

'treaty-trade,' advanced by Polanyi. In general the governments on both sides seem to have played a limited role in the actual trading process (Veenhof 1972, p. 400).

[In 7th-6th century B.C.E. Babylonia] barley, like dates, fluctuated in price. . . . That there could be a definite shift in prices even within a single month is illustrated by a contract which provides that: " . . . in Simanu (third month) he shall pay the barley according to the price of Aiaru (second month)." Our information is not sufficient to establish regular seasonal changes, yet it is highly significant that they did exist. (Dubberstein 1938, pp. 26–7; see Leemans 1954, p. 32 for Larsa in the ninteenth century B.C.E.)

Early Mesopotamian societies were demonstrably not organized economically around the temples of the gods. (Yoffee 1979, p. 20)

There is also evidence of sharp fluctuations in grain prices in response to the initiation or lifting of sieges in seventh-century-Babylonia (Ahmed 1968, p. 148), twelfth-century Egypt (Cerny 1933, pp. 176–77), and (probably) ninth-century Israel. A Ugaritic text dating from the second half of the second millennium lists under the heading of cost: "The price; high price; low price; poor price; fixed price; good price; stiff price; fair price; price in town" (Schaeffer 1939, p. 40). Surely, the time has come to put aside once and for all the view that references in the Near Eastern sources to prices, buying, selling, and the like are only the legal fictions of exotic administrative economies monopolized by temple or palace (see, for example, Finley 1957).

Moreover, it is incorrect to characterize ancient Near Eastern societies as economically unprogressive.[5] While a full exploration of this question would be out of place in a work focused on ancient Israel, I offer the hypothesis that Marx's "Asiatic mode of production" (see the discussions of Sawer 1977 and Wittfogel 1957) is a specific phase rather than an eternal feature of ancient or premodern economic life. Both Egypt and Babylonia knew lengthy periods of both economic growth and retrogression; the whole economic system came unglued and was put together several times. The explanation, I suspect, lies in intensified economic intervention and regulation by the state (see Pirenne 1962, pp. 90, 94–5, 107; Leemans 1950, pp. 113–22. I have studied this process for classical Greece, Rome, and Sung China; see Silver 1980.) In a sense one might say that the present work explores the path that carried ancient Israel toward Oriental despotism and destruction.

The antimarket mentality, however, seems to be impervious to evidence, and I have therefore resigned myself to being accused of an anachronistic approach as well as an uncritical acceptance of the entrepreneurial role in economic growth as stated in terms of contemporary economic theory.

Notes

1. On coinage see chapter 5, but here note the frequent references to "sealed lead" in the eighteenth-century-B.C.E. Cappadocian documents (S. Smith 1922, p. 180).

2. Sources on market places: Elat (1979, pp. 184–85, 313); Heichelheim (1960, p. 109); Oppenheim (1977, pp. 128–29); Saggs (1962, pp. 286–87); Schaeffer (1939, p. 19); Veenhof (1972, pp. 350–56). The Bible notes market places in 1 Kings 20:34; 2 Kings 7:1; Jeremiah 37:21; Nehemiah 13:15–16: Jerusalem gates, which appear to have specialized in certain types of merchandise, are the "Fish Gate" (Zeph. 1:10; 2 Chr. 33:14; Neh. 3:3), the "Sheep Gate" (Neh. 3:1, 32; 12:39), and the "Pottery Gate" (Jer. 19:2). The term "streets" (ḥūṣ ōt) has an economic connotation as in Jeremiah 37:21 (the "bakers' street") and, probably, in Ezekiel 26:11–12, which warns that Tyre's streets will be trampled and her riches spoiled. Elat (1979a, fn. 66, p. 543) makes a very interesting observation in this connection: "This extension of the meaning of ḥūṣ ōt may explain why the Targum sometimes translates the ḥūṣ ōt of the Masoretic text as māḥōzīn (Num. 22:39; Lam, 2:19; 4:14), which also means 'market'." Elat provides references on the meaning of mhz in ancient Semitic languages. See chapter 4, note 15 for another economic aspect of "streets." Sargonic texts (2334–2154) refers to goods being "on the street," which means the marketplace or, perhaps, "on the market" in the sense of invested for a profit (Foster 1977, p. 40).

Note also the waterside shops depicted on a Theban tomb (see de Davies and Faulkner 1947) and the market scene described in chapter 3. Note finally the shops excavated at Hazor and the wide distribution of weights at Israelite sites. For ancient Near Eastern evidence on food peddlers, see Oppenheim (1977, fn. 13, p. 356).

Note, however, that while *markets* require mechanisms enabling traders to communicate, they do not require face-to-face gatherings of traders.

3. Sources on wage labor: Diakonoff (1974, p. 50); Gelb (1965, pp. 242–43). According to Mireaux (1960, p. 132), eighth-seventh–century Greece knew wage laborers under the generic title of *thetes*. The available evidence does not suggest that wage labor in antiquity was invariably "causal, spasmodic, marginal." The Bible notes wage labor in Isaiah 16:14; Deuteronomy 15:18, 24:14–15; Leviticus 19:13, 25:39–40; Genesis 29:15 and, perhaps, Genesis 49:14–15.

Even strikes were not unknown. During the reign of Ramses III in ca. 1170 B.C.E. the workers attached to the royal tombs in the Valley of Kings struck on account of overdue pay and other grievances. On one occasion, when the bosses came to get them back to work, an individual named Mose son of Amennakht (possibly a necropolis scribe) said: "By Amon, and by the Ruler, the one whose power is greater than death, if they take me up from here today, he [I?] shall lie down, after having cursed *is*. And I won't." Mose received a beating because of his swearing (literally "the binding himself") by the name of the Pharaoh (see Edgerton 1951, pp. 137–40). The necropolis workers lived in a village that is today called Deir el-Medina and, to judge by their names, were a mixed group consisting not only of Egyptians but also of Asiatics and Nubians (Riefstahl 1964, p. 69). Fifth-century Athens knew a well-established wage-labor exchange (Fuks 1951).

4. Janssen (1975, p. 131; see also pp. 138–39, 183–84) recommends that Egyptologists familiarize themselves with modern peasant societies and warns that knowledge of market economies "proves to be of little value" and, perhaps, even "obnoxious." Note, however, that Janssen (p. 162) refers to the frequent mention of merchants and cites a document "recording the sale of meat, wine and cakes to what seem to be wholesale dealers." Further, while ancient Egypt did not possess coins, it made use, according to Janssen (p. 177), of an obscure system called "money-barter." With respect to the assertion that trading was a state monopoly, Janssen

(p. 163) points out that: "At present there is no material to prove that this is what happened, although there is no document proving the contrary." In the end, Janssen (p. 185) admits that so little data are available that "For the present, a study of the redistribution system in all its aspects seems the only possibility."

5. Muhly (1980, p. 26), for example, uses terms such as "extraordinary" and "astounding" to describe progress in metallurgical technology in the third-millennium in the Near East. In the middle of the third-millennium during the reigns of Lugalanda and Urukagina the agriculturalists of Lagash made use of a plow to which a drill for sowing was attached thereby achieving significant savings both in labor and seed grain. The calculations of Maekawa (1974, especially pp. 41–2) reveal ratios of barley yield to seed volume sharply in excess of medieval Europe. On the "extraordinary" technological progress between 800 and 500 B.C.E. in the Aegean world and the extent of its dependence on Near Eastern sources, see Starr (1977, pp. 82–4). See, further, Gunderson (1982) and Silver (1980, especially 95–6).

APPENDIX B:
HISTORICAL EVIDENCE
ON THE RELATIONSHIP
BETWEEN ECONOMIC
GROWTH AND
LAND CONSOLIDATION

During the period after the political unification of Babylonia under Sargon (ca. 2334 B.C.E.) trade relations were established with distant countries including Cappadocia (in Anatolia), the Mediterranean Sea, Assyria, and the Persian Gulf (Mallowan 1965, pp. 2–3). According to Struve (1969, p. 41) this opening of new markets was accompanied by the consolidation of small land parcels and the appearance for the first time in Babylonia of hired workers in significant numbers.

According to Woodhouse (1938), the emerging international pattern of comparative advantage in the seventh century B.C.E. favored the production in Attica of olives and wine for export, as opposed to cereal for domestic consumption. The result was an agricultural revolution in which land ownership (or control) passed from small independent farmers into the hands of aristocrats who were ready to undertake the required investments in tree and vine stock. The previously independent farmers provided labor services in the legal role of sharecroppers (Lewis 1941, pp. 144–50, 154–55; Mireaux 1960, pp. 134–36; Woodhouse, 1938, pp. 164–65). In view of the relative labor intensity of viticulture, foreign slaves were also imported to augment the labor supply. During the later seventh and sixth centuries many "tenants," having become familiar with the markets for grapes and olives, took loans from landowners and exporters and became independent cultivators (see von Fritz 1943, pp. 30–1).

Similarly, in the later Roman Republic the pattern of comparative advantage became such that domestic cereal production dropped sharply in favor of imported grains from Egypt, North Africa, and Sicily. The Roman countryside switched over to pasturage and the production of wool and meat for the newly affluent urban centers of which Rome itself was the supreme example. This transition was accompanied by the formation of large ranches that spread over Latium, Etruria, and the southern parts of Italy. Livestock raising, of course, is much less labor intensive than is cereals, and it is generally believed that the rural population decreased significantly at this time (Yeo 1948). In Campania, however small grain production was replaced by wine and oil plantations which supplied the new markets in the urban centers, Gaul and Germany, while meeting the need for skilled labor by importing Syrian slaves (Yeo 1952).

Before the thirteenth century, the black monks of the autonomous houses in northern England played only a negligible role in the exploitation of their estates. Dom David Knowles (1948, p. 33) points to the "similarity . . . of the methods and conditions of cultivation in all districts, and to the absence of any considerable production for distant markets." However, beginning in the thirteenth century with the significant growth of urban and international markets for grain and wool "clear sighted abbots and obedientiaries began to gather into hand demesne land as leases fell in, and cultivate grain and raise sheep and cattle with a view to market possibilities" (Knowles 1948, p. 361). Knowles cites several examples including the overseas grain and wool shipments of Christ Church and the Canterbury manors. He adds that the "greater monastic houses played a considerable . . . part . . . and the technique of farming, and questions of distribution of produce for market and the financial administration of a great estate, became of absorbing interest to a large number of abler monks" (p. 36).

The resurgence of cities in earlier medieval Italy (ninth to eleventh centuries) was associated with the emergence of large estates relying on labor services. During the eleventh–fourteenth centuries, however, there was "no considerable progress in the way the soil was cultivated and certainly no progress in agricultural techniques" (Ganshof 1941, p. 282). Beginning in the thirteenth century, the *villa* decomposed and its place was taken by small independent farmers (Mickwith 1941, pp. 323–29, 333, 338). Once the necessary adustments in outlook and knowledge and outlook had taken place, as Pullan (1972, pp. 92–4) notes:

within the towns' range of influence, landlords had many incentives to do away with the cumbersome system of labor services, and to exchange these for cash payments. . . . By the later twelfth century, for example, the feudal tenure [i.e. labor services] had completely disappeared from the area of La Bassa to the south of Milan. . . . In the more advanced regions of Tuscany, manors and serfs had virtually been eliminated by 1300. It would, however, be a mistake to attribute this state of affairs to the pressure applied by the cities—for even in Tuscany the lords had chosen quite freely to emancipate many peasants . . .

Similar trends became apparent especially during and after the fifteenth century in England (Ernle 1936, pp. 46–8) and France (T. Kemp 1971 pp. 14, 21).

In T'ang China, unity and peace encouraged a great increase in trade between the north and the south during the late-seventh–early-eighth centuries C.E. This was accompanied by estate building and the transformation of independent peasants into providers of labor services (Pulleyblank 1955, pp. 27–9). In Sung times a similar trend was triggered in the twelfth and thirteenth centuries by the emergence of a national market in grain, rice and cloth (Elvin 1973, p. 170). As in medieval Italy, these changes gradually penetrated to the grass roots. Then during the sixteenth– seventeenth centuries, local countryside markets increased in importance relative to city markets in a process Elvin (1978, pp. 81–2; see also Elvin 1973, pp. 233, 245) calls "urban devolution." After 1600, more and more landowners moved permanently into the cities, and their holdings became more fragmented" (pp. 82–3). This was accompanied by the rise of independent small farmers and the virtual end of labor services.

The first colonists in northeast Germany did not perform labor services for the lord as had "peasants" in old Germany. This was true even in Prussia as late as the fifteenth century. The colonists were independent farmers who paid for the lord's protection in rent-taxes. In this connection it is worth quoting Aubin's (1941, p. 384) observation that "One difficulty that the German migrants eastward had to face was a lack of those facilities for the division of labor and access to various markets to which they had been accustomed. Early settlements were often isolated from any market at all." Starting, however, in the mid-sixteenth century, the cultivation of grain for export spread throughout northeast Germany. During this period there also occurred the so-called *Bauernlegen*, that is, the elimination of small independent farmers in favor of large wage-paying estates. Mayhew (1973, p. 140) tells us that the managers of these large estates introduced new techniques such as a four-field system that increased grain yields by an eighth, and, in general, "were the main initiators of reform and progress in agriculture." The estates exported through the ports of Danzig and Konigsberg. It is worth noting that the decline in the number of independent farmers was sharpest in the Polish areas that had been the least market oriented. The great magnates in the hinterland of Gdansk were in a better position to store grain and cope with the ups and downs of the Vistula trade than were their smaller, less world-wise neighbors (see Klima 1979, p. 60; Maczak 1968, pp. 79, 88; Tipton 1976, pp. 23–5). Interestingly, by the end of the eighteenth century, as Kula (1976, p. 116, 150) observes, Polish grain exports had declined precipitously from their levels of the beginning of the century and now the great estates shrank and money rents replaced labor rents.

Meanwhile, in western Germany in the eighteenth century rapid change in agricultural practices took place. These included cultivation of the fallow by means of clover, peas, beans, lentils, turnips, hemp, and potatoes. This change was apparently triggered by the greater demand for animal fodder for stall feeding which, in turn, was partially a response to the increased demand for manure. Mayhew's (1973, p. 142) comment that "not surprisingly new ideas took long to reach the grass roots" can be linked to his observation (p. 143) of "a new *Bauernlegen* . . . on a more restricted scale." In several areas noble land owners and bourgeois lessees founded estate villages that utilized wage labor and completely replaced the villages of the independent farmers.

Turning to Muscovy during the second half of the sixteenth century, especially in the Moscow area, we find that growth in the market was accompanied by the cultivation of grain crops on consolidated and enlarged manors in which labor rents overshadowed the money rents of the earlier period (R.E.F. Smith 1977, pp. 126, 142). Later, during the nineteenth century, in the northern half of Russia, the isolated natural economy began to crack under the impact of land and water steam transportation. The ensuing dramatic changes in the "agricultural geography of the country" had been preceded, as Pavlovsky (1968, p. 70) notes, in the course of the first half of the century by farming becoming "very fashionable among the Russian gentry. Agricultural associations were established and foreign improvements studied and imitated." The various innovations rested entirely on the use of labor services.

Our survey of the historical evidence concludes with Japan's great economic take-off in the mid-nineteenth century. In this process agricultural innovation played a major role. And the so-called cultivating landlords who typically played the main role relied on hired labor. As Waswo (1977, p. 33) explains: "Most landlords of the Meiji era were well educated . . . They were better able than other farmers to understand the world outside the village and to negotiate with outsiders" and to take advantage of "new railroads and other improvements in transportation which facilitated the commercial sale of crops." The importance of the innovating landlords declined "in the 1890s and thereafter" (p. 67).

REFERENCES

Abrams, Philip and E. A. Wrigley (eds.), *Essays in Economic History and Sociology* (London: Cambridge University Press, 1978).

Adams, Robert, Mc.C., "Anthropological Perspectives on Ancient Trade," *Current Anthropology* (Sept. 1974): 239–49.

Aharoni, Yohanan, "The Citadel of Ramat Rahel," *Archaeology* (Spring 1965): 15–25.

_____, "Hebrew Ostraca from Tell Arad," *Israel Exploration Journal (vol. 16, (1966): 1–7.*

_____, *The Land of the Bible: A Historical Approach* (Philadelphia, Pa.: Westminster Press, 1967).

_____, "The Israelite Sanctuary at Arad," in Freedman and Greenfield (eds.), *New Directions in Biblical Archaeology* (New York: Doubleday, 1969): 25–39.

_____, "The Hebrew Inscriptions," in Aharoni (ed.), *Beer-Sheba I Excavations at Tel Beer-Sheba, 1969–1971* (Tel Aviv: Tel Aviv University Institute of Technology): 71–7.

_____, *Beer-Sheba I, Excavations at Tel Beer-Sheba, 1969–1971* (Tel Aviv: Tel Aviv University Institute of Archaeology, 1973).

_____, "The Horned Altar of Beer-Sheba," *Biblical Archeologist* (March 1974): 2–6.

_____, *Investigations at Lachish: The Sanctuary and the Presidency (Lachish V)* (Tel Aviv: Gateway, 1975).

_____, "The Negeb and the Southern Border," in Malamat (ed.), *The Age of Monarchies*, (Jerusalem: Massada Press, 1979): 290–307.

_____ and Ruth Amiran, "Arad: A Biblical City in Southern Palestine," *Archaeology* (Spring 1964): 43–53.

_____ and Michael Avi-Yonah, *The Macmillan Bible Atlas*, (rev. ed.), (New York: Macmillan, 1977).

Ahlström, G. W., *Aspects of Syncretism in Israelite Religion* (Lund: Gleerup, 1963).

Ahmed, Sami Said, *Southern Mesopotamia in the Time of Ashurbanipal* (The Hague: Mouton, 1968).

Akurgal, Ekrem, "The Early Period and the Golden Age of Ionia," *American Journal of Archaeology* (October 1962): 369–79.

Albrekston, Bertil, *History and the Gods* (Lund: Gleerup, 1967).

Albright, William Foxwell, *The Archaeology of the Bible* (New York: Revell, 1932).

_____, *The Biblical Period from Abraham to Ezra* (New York: Harper & Row, 1960).

_____, "Some Remarks on the Meaning of the Verb *Shr* in Genesis," *Bulletin of the American Schools of Oriental Research* No. 164 (1961): 28.

_____, (a) *Yahweh and the Gods of Canaan: A Historical Analysis* (New York: Doubleday, 1968).

_____, (b) *Archaeology and the Religion of Israel*, 5th ed. (Baltimore, Md.: The John Hopkins University Press, 1968).

_____, "A Letter from the Time of Josiah," in Pritchard (ed.), *Ancient Near Eastern Texts Relating to the Old Testament* (Princeton, N.J.: Princeton University Press): 568.

Alt, Albrecht, "The Settlement of the Israelites in Palestine," in Alt, *Essays on Old Testament Religion* (New York: Doubleday, 1967), 173–221.

Andersen, Francis I., and David Noel Freedman, *Hosea: A New Translation and Commentary* (New York: Doubleday, 1980).

Anderson, Bernhard W., *The Living World of the Old Testament*, 2d. ed. (London: Longmans, 1967).

_____, *Understanding the Old Testament*, 3d. ed. (Englewood Cliffs, N.J.: Prentice-Hall, 1975).

Anderson, Robert T., "Was Isaiah a Scribe?," *Journal of Biblical Literature* (March 1960): 57–8.

Andrewes, Antony, *The Greeks* (New York: Knopf, 1971).

Ap-Thomas, D. R., "The Phoenicians," in Wiseman (ed.), *Peoples of Old Testament Times* (London: Oxford University Press): 259–86.

Arrow, Kenneth, *The Limits of Organization* (New York: Norton, 1974).

Ashtour, Eliyahu, "An Essay on the Diet of the Various Classes in the Medieval Levant," in Robert Forster and Orest Ranum (eds.), *Biology of Man in History* (Baltimore, Md.: John Hopkins University Press, 1975): 123–62.

Astour, Michael C., "841 B.C.: The First Assyrian Invasion of Israel," *Journal of the American Oriental Society* 91, (1971): 383–89.

Astour, Michael C., "The Merchant Class of Ugarit," in Edzard (ed.), *Gesellschaftsklassen im Aiten Zweistromland und inden Angren Zanden Gebieten*

(Munich: Verlag Der Boyerischer, 1972): 11–26.

Aubin, Herman, "Medieval Colonization Eastwards," in Clapham and Power (eds.), *The Cambridge Economic History of Europe from the Decline of the Roman Empire* (London: Cambridge University Press): 11–26.

Auster, Richard D., and Morris Silver, *The State as a Firm: Economic Forces in Political Development* (Boston: Martinus Nijhoff, 1979).

Austin, M. M., *Greece and Egypt in the Archaic Age*, Proceedings of the Cambridge Philological Society, Supplement No. 2 (Cambridge: 1970).

Austin, M. M., and P. Vidal Naquet, *Economic and Social History of Ancient Greece* (Berkeley, Calif.: University of California Press, 1977).

Avigad, Nachman, "Ammonite and Moabite Seals," in Sanders (ed.), *Near Eastern Archaeology in the Twentieth Century* (New York: Doubleday): 284–95.

———, "Two Hebrew Inscriptions on Wine-Jars," *Israel Exploration Journal* (25, 1975): 101–05.

———, "New Light on the Na'ar Seals," in Cross, Lemke, and Miller (eds.), *Magnalia Dei the Mighty Acts of God* (New York: Doubleday, 1976): 294–300.

———, "Baruch the Scribe and Jerahmeel the King's Son," *Israel Exploration Journal* (28 (1978): 52–6.

———, "Hebrew Epigraphic Sources," in Malamat (ed.), The Age . . . : 20–43.

———. (a) "Jerahmeel and Baruch," *Biblical Archeologist* (Spring 1979): 114–18.

Avi-Yonah, Michael, *The Holy Land from the Persian to the Arab Conquests (536 B.C. to A.D. 640): A Historical Geography* (Grand Rapids, Mich.: Baker Book House, 1966).

———, Abraham Malamat, and Shemayahu Talmon (eds.), *Views of the Biblical World*, 3 vol. (Jerusalem: International Publishing Co., 1960).

———, and Abraham Malamat (eds.), *The World of the Bible, I, The Law* (Yonkers, N.Y.: Education Heritage, 1964).

Aymard, Maurice, "Toward the History of Nutritition: Some Methodological Remarks," in Forster and Ranum (eds.), *Food and Drink in History* (Baltimore, Md.: The John Hopkins University Press): 1–16.

Baer, Klaus, "An Eleventh Dynasty Farmer's Letter to his Family," *Journal of the American Oriental Society* 83, (1963): 1–19.

Bailey, Albert Edward, *Daily Life in Bible Times* (New York: Scribner's Sons, 1943).

Bailey, Cyril, *Phases in the Religion of Ancient Rome* (Berkeley: University of California Press, 1932).

Bakhuizen, S. C., "Greek Steel," *World Archaeology* (October 1977): 220–34.

Bakir, Abd El-Mohsen, *Slavery in Pharonic Egypt* (Le Caire: Imprimerie de L'instiut Francais D'Archeologie Orientale, 1952).

Balkan, Kemal, "Cancellation of Debts in Cappodocian Tablets from Külptepe," in K. Bittel, Ph. H. J. Houwink Ten Cate, and E. Reiner (eds.), *Anatolian Studies Presented to Hans Gustav Güterbock on the Occasion of his 65th Birthday* (Istanbul: Nederlands Historisch-Archaeological Institut, 1974): 29–41.

Baly, Denis, *Geographical Companion to the Bible* (New York: McGraw-Hill, 1963).

Baly, Denis, *The Geography of the Bible* (New York: Harper & Row, 1974).

Baqir, Taha, *Tell Harmal* (Baghdad: Republic of Iraq, Directorate of Antiquities, 1959).

Barag, D., "A Survey of Pottery Recovered from the Sea Off the Coast of Israel," *Israel Exploration Journal,* 13 (1963): 13–19.

Barnett, Richard D., "Phoenicia and the Ivory Trade," *Archaeology* (Summer 1956): 87–97.

Baron, Salo Wittmayer, *A Social and Religious History of the Jews,* vol. I, (2d ed. rev.) (New York: Columbia University Press, 1952). Selections reproduced with permission of Columbia University Press.

Baron, Salo Wittmayer, "The Israelite Population Under the Kings," in Leon A. Feldman (ed.), *Ancient and Medieval Jewish History: Essays by Salo Baron* (New Brunswick, N.J.: Rutgers University Press, 1972): 23–73.

Barrow, R. H., *Slavery in the Roman Empire* (London: Methuen, 1928).

Bartlett, J. R., "The Moabites and Edomites," in Wiseman (ed.), *Peoples*: 229–58.

Barton, George Aaron, *Semitic and Hamitic Origins: Social and Religious* (Philadelphia, Pa.: University of Pennsylvania Press, 1934).

Barzel, Yoram., "An Economic Analysis of Slavery," *Journal of Law and Economics* (April 1977): 87–110.

Bass, George F., (ed.), *A History of Seafaring Based on Underwater Archaeology* (London: Thames & Hudson, 1972).

Beebe, H. Keith, *The Old Testament* (Belmont, Calif.: Dickenson, 1970).

Ben-Tor, Amnon, "Yoqne'am Regional Project Looks Beyond the Tell," *Biblical Archaeology Review* (March/April 1980):30–44.

Bentzen, A., "The Ritual Background of Amos i2–ii16," *Oudtestamentishe Studien* 8 (1950): 81–99.

Bertholet, Alfred, *A History of Hebrew Civilization* (London: Harrows, 1926).

Bewer, Julius A., *The Prophets in the King James Version with Introduction and Critical Notes* (New York: Harper, 1949).

Bic, Milos, "Der Prophet Amos-Ein Haepatoskopos," *Vetus Testamentum* 1 (1951): 293–96.

Bikai, Patricia M., "The Late Phoenician Pottery Complex and Chronology," *Bulletin of the American Schools of Oriental Research* (February 1978): 47–56.

Birmingham, J. M., "The Overland Route Across Anatolia in the Eighth and Seventh Centuries B.C.," *Anatolian Studies* 11 (1961): 185–95.

Bittel, Kurt, *Hattusha: The Capital of the Hittites* (New York: Oxford University Press, 1970).

Bleeker, C. J., "Guilt and Purification in Ancient Egypt," *Numen* (January 1966): 6–87.

Bleeker, C. J., *Egyptian Festivals: Enactments of Religious Renewal* (Leiden: Brill, 1967).

Blenkinsopp, Joseph, *Gibeon and Israel* (London: Cambridge University Press for JSOT, 1972).

Blenkinsopp, Joseph, *Prophecy and Canon* (Notre Dame, Ind.: Notre Dame University Press, 1977).

Bloch, H., "The Roman Brick Industry and its Relationship to Roman Architecture,"

Journal of the Society of Architectural Historians 1 (1941): 3–8.

Blomquist, Thomas W., "The Dawn of Banking in an Italian Commune: Thirteenth Century Lucca," in Center for Medieval and Renaissance Studies, University of California, Los Angeles, *The Dawn of Modern Banking* (New Haven, Conn.: Yale University Press, 1979): 53–75.

De Boer, P. A. H., "The Counsellor," in M. Noth and D. Winton Thomas (eds.), *Wisdom in Israel and in the Ancient Near East* (Leiden: Brill, 1960): 42–71.

Bottéro, Jean, Elena Cassin and Jean Vercoutter, (eds.), *The Near East: The Early Civilizations* trans. from German (New York: Delacorte Press, 1967).

Bottéro, Jean, "The First Semitic Empire," in Bottéro, Cassin, and Vercoutter, (eds.), *The Near East . . .* , 91–132.

Bowker, John, *The Targums and Rabbinic Literature* (London: Cambridge University Press, 1969).

Bowman, Raymond A., "Arameans, Aramaic, and the Bible," *Journal of Near Eastern Studies* (April 1948): 65–90.

Boyer, Majorie Nicé. "Roads and Rivers: Their Use and Disuse in Medieval France," *Medievalia et Humanistica* (June 1966): 68–80.

Bream, Howard N., Ralph D. Heim and Carey A. Moore (eds.), *A Light Unto My Path: Old Testament Studies in Honor of Jacob M. Myers* (Philadelphia, Pa.: Temple University Press, 1974).

Breasted, James Henry, *Development of Religion and Thought in Ancient Egypt* (New York: Harper & Row, 1912).

Bright, John, *A History of Israel*, 2d. ed. (Philadelphia, Pa.: Westminster Press, 1972).

Brinker, R., *The Influence of Sanctuaries in Early Israel* (Manchester: Manchester University Press, 1946).

Broshi, Magen, "The Expansion of Jerusalem in the Reigns of Hezekiah and Manasseh," *Israel Exploration Journal* 24 (1974): 21–6.

Broshi, Magen, "Estimating the Population of Ancient Jerusalem," *Biblical Archaeology Review* (June 1978): 10–15.

Brumbaugh, Robert S., *Ancient Greek Gadgets and Machines* (New York: Crowell, 1966).

Brunt, P. A., *Social Conflicts in the Roman Republic* (New York: Norton, 1971).

Buccellati, Giorgio, "Towards a Formal Typology of Akkadian Similies," in Eichler (ed.), *Kramer Anniversary Volume . . .* , (Verlag Butzon & Verlag Kevelaer, 1976): 59–70.

Budge, E. A. Wallis, *Tutankhamen: Amenism, Atenism, and Egyptian Monotheism* (New York: Bell, 1923).

Budge, E. A. Wallis, *The Book of the Dead: The Papyrus of Ani in the British Museum*, 1895, (New York: Dover, 1967).

Buhl, Marie-Louise, "The Goddesses of the Egyptian Tree Cult," *Journal of Near Eastern Studies* (April 1947): 80–97.

Bulliet, Richard W., *The Camel and the Wheel* (Cambridge, Mass.: Harvard University Press, 1975).

Burford, Alison, "Heavy Transport in Classical Antiquity," *Economic History Review* (August 1960): 1–18.

Burford, Alison, *Craftsmen in Greek and Roman Society* (Ithaca, N.Y.: Cornell University Press, 1972).

Burn, A. R., *The Warring States of Greece: From Their Rise to the Roman Conquest* (New York: McGraw-Hill, 1968).

Burney, Charles, *The Ancient Near East* (Ithaca, N.Y.: Cornell University Press, 1977).

Burrows, Millar, *What Mean These Stones? The Significance of Archaeology for Biblical Studies* (New Haven, Conn.: American Schools of Oriental Research, 1941).

Burstein, Stanley Mayer, *The Babyloniaca of Berossus* (Malibu, Calif.: Undema, 1978).

Carmichael, Colin M., *The Laws of Deuteronomy* (Ithaca, N.Y.: Cornell University Press, 1974).

Cary, M. J. and T. J. Haarhoff, *Life and Thought in the Greek and Roman World* (London: Methuen, 1940).

Casson, Lionel, *Ships and Seamanship in the Ancient World* (Princeton, N.J.: Princeton University Press, 1971).

Cassuto, U., *The Goddess Anath: Canaanite Epics of the Patriarchal Age*, translated from Hebrew, (Jerusalem: Magnes Press, 1971).

Cerny, Jareslav, "Fluctuations in Grain Prices During the Twentieth Egyptian Dynasty," *Archiv Orientalni* 6 (1933): 173–78.

Chadwick, John, *The Mycenaean World* (London: Cambridge University Press, 1976).

Champdor, Albert, *The Book of the Dead: Based on the Ani, Hunefer, and Anhai Papyri in the British Museum* translated from French (New York: Garrett, 1966).

Chevallier, Raymond, *Roman Roads* (Berkeley, Calif.: University of California Press, 1976).

Childs, Brevard S., *Isaiah and the Assyrian Crisis* (Napierville, Ill.: Allenson, 1967).

Chouraqui, André, *The People and the Faith of the Bible* (Amherst, Mass.: University of Massachusetts Press, 1975).

Cipolla, Carlo M., *Before the Industrial Revolution: European Society and Economy, 100–1700* (New York: Norton, 1976).

Clapham, J. H. and Eileen Power (eds.), *The Cambridge Economic History of Europe from the Decline of the Roman Empire, Vol. 1: The Agrarian Life of the Middle Ages* (London: Cambridge University Press, 1941).

Clark, R. T. Rundle, *Myth and Symbol in Ancient Egypt* (New York: Grove Press, 1959).

Clay, Albert T., *The Origin of Biblical Traditions: Hebrew Legends in Babylonia and Israel* 1923 (New Haven, Conn.: Yale University Press, 1980).

Clay, Rachel, *The Tenure of Land in Babylonia and Assyria* (London: University of London Institute of Archaeology, 1938).

Clements, R. E., *Isaiah and the Deliverance of Jerusalem: A Study of the Interpretation of Prophecy in the Old Testament* (Sheffield, JSOT, 1980).

Cogan, Morton, *Imperialism and Religion: Assyria, Judah, and Israel in the Eighth and Seventh Centuries B.C.E.* (Missoula, Mont.: Society of Biblical Literature, 1974).

Cohen, Boaz, "Peculium in Jewish and Roman Law," *Proceedings of the American Academy of Jewish Research* 20 (1951): 135–234.

Cohen, H. Hirsch, *The Drunkenness of Noah* (University, Ala.: University of Alabama Press, 1974).

Cohen, Martin A., "In all Fairness to Ahab: A Socio-Political Consideration of the Ahab-Elijah Controversy," *Eretz-Israel* 12 (1975): 87–94.

Cohen, Martin A., "The Prophets as Revolutionaries: A Sociopolitical Analysis," *Biblical Archaeology Review* (June 1979): 12–19.

Cohn, Haim Hermann, "Usury," in *Encyclopedia Judaica* (vol. 16, 1971): 27–33.

Cole, Dan, "How Water Tunnels Worked," *Biblical Archaeology Review* (March/April 1980): 8–29.

Consitt, Frances, *The London Weaver's Company*, vol. I (London: Oxford University Press, 1933).

Contenau, Georges, *Everyday Life in Babylon and Assyria* (New York: Norton, 1966).

Cook, H. J., "Pekah," *Vetus Testamentum*, vol. 14, (1964): 121–35.

Cook, Stanley A., *The Religion of Ancient Palestine* (London: Constable, 1908).

Cooke, G. A., *A Text-Book of North-Semitic Inscriptions* (Oxford: Oxford University Press, 1903).

Coote, Robert B., *Amos Among the Prophets: Composition and Theology* (Philadelphia, Pa.: Fortress Press, 1981).

Cornfeld, Gaalyah, *Archaeology of the Bible: Book by Book* (New York: Harper & Row, 1976).

Craghan, John F., "The Prophet Amos in Recent Literature," *Biblical Theology Bulletin* 2 (1972): 242–61.

Crenshaw, James L., *Prophetic Conflict: Its Effect Upon Israelite Religion* (Berlin: de Gruyter, 1971).

Crook, John, *Law and Life of Rome* (Ithaca, N.Y.: Cornell University Press, 1967).

Cross, Dorothy, *Movable Property in the Nuzi Documents* (New Haven, Conn.: American Oriental Society, 1937).

Cross, Frank Moore, "Epigraphic Notes on Hebrew Documents of the Eighth–Sixth Centuries B.C. II. The Murabba'ât Papyrus and the Letter Found Near Yahneh-Yam," *Bulletin of the American Schools of Oriental Research* (February 1962): 34–46.

———, "The Old Phoenician Inscription from Spain Dedicated to Hurrian Astarte," *Harvard Theological Review* (April 1971): 189–98.

———, "Leaves From an Epigraphist's Notebook," *Catholic Biblical Quarterly* 36 (1974): 486–94.

———, "Newly Found Inscriptions in Old Canaanite and Early Phoenician Scripts," *Bulletin of the American Schools of Oriental Research* (Spring 1980): 1–20.

——— and Werner E. Lemke, Patrick Miller Jr. (eds.), *Magnalia Dei: The Mighty Acts of God* (New York: Doubleday, 1976).

Crown, Alan D., "Some Factors Relating to Settlement and Urbanization in Ancient Canaan in the Second and First Millennia B.C.," *Abr-Nahrain* 20 (1971): 22–41.

Culican, William, *The First Merchant Venturers: The Ancient Levant in History and Commerce* (New York: McGraw-Hill, 1966).

Cutler, B., and J. Macdonald, "Identification of Na'ar in the Ugaritic Texts," *Ugarit Forschungen* 8 (1976): 27–35.

Curtis, John B., and William W. Hallo, "Money and Merchants in Ur III," *Hebrew Union College Annual* 30 (1959): 103–39.

Daiches, Samuel, *Studies in the Psalms* (London: Oxford University Press, 1930).

Daiches, Samuel, *Moses: The Man and His Vision* (New York: Praeger, 1975).

Dandamayev, M., "The Economic and Legal Character of the Slaves' Peculium in the Neo-Babylonian and Achaemenid Periods," in Edzard (ed.), XVIII-*Rencontre*, 35–9.

Danelius, Eva, "The Sins of Jeroboam ben-Nebat," *Jewish Quarterly Review* 8 (1967/68): 95–114, 204–23.

Darby, William J., and Paul Ghaliougui, Louis Grivetti, *Food: The Gift of Osiris*, 2 vols. (London: Academic Press, 1977).

Daube, David, *The Exodus Pattern in the Bible* (London: Faber & Faber, 1963).

Daube, David, "Fashions and Idiosyncracies in the Exposition of the Roman Law of Property," in Anthony Parel and Thomas Flanagan (eds.), *Theories of Property* (Waterloo, Ont.: Calgary Institute for the Humanities, 1979): 35–50.

David, A. Rosalie, *Religious Ritual at Abydos (ca. 1300 B.C.)* (Warminster: Aris & Philips, 1973).

David, M., "The Manumission of Slaves Under Zedekiah," *Oudtestamentishe Studien* 5 (1948): 63–79.

Davies, Eryl W., *Prophecy and Ethics: Isaiah and the Ethical Traditions of Israel* (Sheffield: JSOT, 1981).

Dayton, J. E., "The Problem of Tin in the Ancient World," *World Archaeology* (June 1973): 123–25.

de Davies, Norman G., and R. O. Faulkner, "A Syrian Trading Venture to Egypt," *Journal of Egyptian Archaeology* 33 (1947): 40–6.

de Geus, C. H. J., "The Importance of Archaeological Research into the Palestinian Agricultural Terraces with an Excursus on the Hebrew Word *gbi*," *Palestine Exploration Quarterly* 107 (1975): 65–74.

de Geus, C. H. J., *The Tribes of Israel* (Assen: Van Gorcum, 1976).

De Graeve, Marie-Christine, *The Ships of the Ancient Near East (c. 2000–500 B.C.)* (Leuven: Department Oriëntalistiek, 1981).

De Vaux, Roland, "The Excavations at Tell El-Far'ah and the Site of Ancient Tirzah," *Palestine Exploration Quarterly* No. 88 (1956): 125–40.

———, *Ancient Israel: Its Life and Institutions* (New York: McGraw-Hill, 1961).

———, "Tirzah," in Thomas (ed.), *Archaeology*, 371–83.

———, "The Revelation of the Divine Name YHWH," in Durham and Porter (eds.), *Proclamation*, 48–75.

———, *The Bible and the Ancient Near East* (Garden City, N.Y.: Doubleday, 1971).

———, *The Early History of Israel* translated from French (Philadelphia, Pa.: Westminster Press, 1978).

Demsky, Aaron, and Moshe Kochavi, "An Alphabet from the Days of the Judges," *Biblical Archaeology Review* (September/October, 1978): 27–8.

Diakonoff, I. M., "A Babylonian Political Pamphlet from about 700 B.C.," in Güterbock and Jacobsen (eds.), *Studies in Honor of Benno Landsberger* (Chicago, Ill.: University of Chicago Press, 1965): 343–49.

———, "Agrarian Conditions in Middle Assyria," in Diakonoff (ed.), *Ancient Mesopotamian Socioeconomic History* (Moscow: Central Department of Oriental Literature, 1969): 204–34.

———, "Slaves, Helots, and Serfs in Early Antiquity," *Acta Antiqua* 22 (1974): 45–78.

Dietrich, B. C., *The Origins of Greek Religion* (Berlin: de Gruyter, 1974).

Van Dijk, J., "Die Inschriftenfunde," *Deutsche Orientgesellschaft* 7 (1962): 39–62.

Diodorus of Sicily, translated C. H. Oldfather, vol. 1 (Cambridge, Mass.: Harvard University Press, 1933).

Diringer, D., "Mizpah," in Thomas (ed.), *Archaeology and Old Testament Study* (London: Oxford University Press, 1967): 329–42.

Dixon, D. M., "A Note on Cereals in Ancient Egypt," in Peter J. Ucko and G. W. Dimbleby (eds.),*The Domestication and Exploitation of Plants and Animals* (Chicago: Aldine, 1969): 131–42.

Dorneman, Rudolph Henry, *The Cultural and Archaeological History of the Transjordan in the Bronze and Iron Ages*, Ph.D. dissertation, University of Chicago, 1970.

Dothan, Moshe, "Ashdod of the Philistines," in Freedman and Greenfield (eds.), *New Directions*, 15–24.

Dougherty, Raymond Philip, *Nabonidus and Belshazzar* 1929 (New Haven, Conn.: Yale University Press, 1980).

Draffkorn, Anne E., "Ilāni/Elohim," *Journal of Biblical Literature* (September 1957): 216–24.

Driver, G. R., and John C. Miles, *The Assyrian Laws* (Oxford: Clarendon Press, 1935).

Driver, S. R., *An Introduction to the Literature of the Old Testament*, 1897, (Gloucester, Mass.: Smith, 1972).

Dubberstein, Waldo H., "Comparative Prices in Later Babylonia (625–400 B.C.)," *American Journal of Semitic Studies* 56 (1938): 20–43.

Duff, A. M., *Freedmen in the Early Roman Empire* (London: Oxford University Press, 1928).

Duncan-Jones, Richard, *The Economy of the Roman Empire: Quantitative Studies* (London: Cambridge University Press, 1974).

Durham, John I., and J. R. Porter (eds.), *Proclamation and Presence* (Richmond, Va.: Knox Press, 1970).

East, W. G., *An Historical Geography of Europe* (London: Methuen, 1967).

Edelstein, Gershon and Mordechai Kislev, "Mevasseret, Yerushalayim: The Ancient Settlement and Its Agricultural Terraces," *Biblical Archaeologist* (Winter 1981): 53–6.

Edgerton, William F., "The Strikes in Ramses III's Twenty-Ninth Year," *Journal of Near Eastern Studies* (July 1951): 137–45.

Edzard, Dietz Otto, "The Third Dynasty of Ur—Its Empire and Successor States," in Bottéro et al. (eds.), *The Near East*, 133–76.

———, " 'Soziale Reformen' Im Zweistromland Bis Ca. 1600 V. Chr.: Realitat Oder Literarischer Topos?," *Acta Antiqua Academiae Scientiarum Hungaricae* 22 (1974): 145–56.

———(ed.), *Gesellschaftsklassen im Alten Zweistromland und in den angrenzenden Gebieten- XVIII. Recontre assyriologique internationale, München, 29. Juni bis 3. Juli 1970* (Munich: Verlag Der Bayerischen Akademie Der Wissenschaften, 1972).

Eichler, Barry L., *Indenture at Nuzi: The Personal Tidennūtu Contract and Its Mesopotamiam Analogues* (New Haven, Conn.: Yale University Press, 1973).

Eichler, Barry L., (ed.), *Kramer Anniversary Volume* (Verlag Butzon and Verlag Kevelaer, 1976).

Eissfeldt, Otto, *The Old Testament: An Introduction* (New York: Harper & Row, 1965).

Eitam, David, "Olive Presses of the Israelite Period," *Tel Aviv* 6 (1979): 146–55.

Elat, M., "Trade and Commerce," in Malamat (ed.), *The Age . . .* , Vol. Five, 173–86.

Elat, M., (a) "The Monarchy and the Development of Trade in Ancient Israel," in Lipinski (ed.), *State and Temple Economy in the Ancient Near East* (Leaven: Dept. of Oriëntalieskek, 1979) vol. II, 528–46.

Elvin, Mark, *The Pattern of the Chinese Past* (Stanford: Stanford University Press, 1973).

Elvin, Mark, "Chinese Cities Since the Sung Dynasty," in Abrams and Wrigley (eds.) *Towns* 79–89.

Encyclopedia Judaica (Jerusalem: Keter, 1971).

Engnell, Ivan, *Studies in Divine Kingship in the Near East*, 1943, (Oxford: Blackwell, 1967).

Eph'al, I., "Israel: Fall and Exile," in Malamat (ed.), *The Age* vol. 4–1, 180–91.

Erman, Adolf, *Life in Ancient Egypt* (New York: Blom, 1894).

Erman, Adolf, *The Literature of the Ancient Egyptians*, translated from German, (New York: Blom, 1927).

Ernle, Lord Rowland E. F., *English Farming Past and Present*, rev. ed. (London: Longmans and Green, 1936).

Evans, Sir Arthur J., "Mycenaean Tree and Pillar Cults and Its Mediterranean Relations," *Journal of Hellenic Studies*, 21 (1901): 99–204.

Evans, Carl D., "Judah's Foreign Policy from Hezekiah to Josiah," in Evans, William W. Hallo and John B. White (eds.), *Scripture in Context* (Pittsburg, Pa.: Pickwick Press for PTMS, 1980): 157–78.

Evenari, Michael, and Leslie Shanah, Naphtali Tadmor, *The Negev* (Cambridge, Mass.: Harvard University Press, 1971).

Face, R. D., "The *Vectuarii* in the Overland Commerce Between Champagne and Southern Europe," *Economic History Review* (December, 1959): 239–46.

Fairman, H. W., (trans. and ed.), *The Triumph of Horus: An Ancient Egyptian Sacred Drama* (Berkeley, Calif.: University of California Press, 1974).

Falkenstein, Adam, *The Sumerian Temple City*, translated from French (Los

Angeles, Calif.: Undema, 1974).

Farbridge, Maurice H., *Studies in Biblical and Semitic Symbolism* (London: Kegan, Paul, Trench, Trubner, 1923).

Fei, John C. H., and Gustav Ranis, "Economic Development in Historical Perspective," *American Economic Review* (May 1969): 386–400.

Feuer, Lewis S., "Some Irrational Sources of Opposition to the Market System," in Ernest van den Haag (ed.), *Capitalism: Sources of Hostility* (New Rochelle, N.Y.: Epoch Books for the Heritage Foundation, 1979): 103–52.

Finklestein, J. J., "The Middle Assyrian *Šulmānu*-Texts," *Journal of the American Oriental Society*, 72 (1952): 77–80.

_____, "Ammisaduqa's Edict and the Babylonian 'Law Codes'," *Journal of Cuneiform Studies* 15 (1961): 91–104.

_____, "Some New Misharum Material and Its Implications," *Assyriological Studies* 16 (1965): 233–46.

_____, "The Edict of Ammisaduqa" and "Additional Mesopotamian Legal Documents," in Pritchard (ed.), *Ancient*, 526–28, 542–47.

_____, (a) "The Edict of Ammisaduqa: A New Text," *Revue d'Assyriologie* 63 (1969): 45–64.

Finley, Moses I., "The Mycenaean Tablets and Economic History," *Economic History Review* (August 1957): 128–41.

_____, *Ancient Slavery and Modern Ideology* (New York: Viking, 1980).

_____: Economy and Society in Ancient Greece (New York: Viking, 1982).

Fohrer, Georg, *History of Israelite Religion*, translated from German (Nashville, Tenn.: Abingdon Press, 1972).

Forbes, Clarence A., "The Education and Training of Slaves in Antiquity," *American Philological Society Transactions* (1955): 321–60.

Forbes, R. J., *Studies in Ancient Technology*, 2d. ed. (Leiden: Brill, 1964–1966).

Forster, Robert and Orest Ranum (eds.), *Food and Drink in History* (Baltimore, Md.: Johns Hopkins University Press, 1979).

Foster, Benjamin R., "Commercial Activity in Sargonic Mesopotamia," *Iraq* 39 (1977): 31–44. Selection reproduced with permission of British School of Archaeology in Iraq.

Foster, Benjamin R., "A New Look at the Sumerian Temple State," *Journal of the Economic and Social History of the Orient* (October 1981): 225–41.

Franken, H. J., "Iron Age Jordan Village," *Illustrated London News* (May 7, 1965): 27.

Franken, H. J., *Excavations at Tell Deir Allā*, vol. I (Leiden: Brill, 1969).

Frankena, R., "The Vassal Treaties of Esarhaddon and the Dating of Deuteronomy," *Oudtestamentlische Studien* 14 (1965): 122–54.

Frederiksen, M. W., "Theory, Evidence and the Ancient Economy," *Journal of Roman Studies* 65 (1975): 164–71.

Free, Joseph E., "The Seventh Season at Dothan," *Bulletin of the American Schools of Oriental Research* (December 1960): 6–15.

Freedman, David Noel, and Edward F. Campbell, Jr., *The Biblical Archaeologist Reader, 2* (New York: Doubleday, 1964).

Freedman, David Noel, and Jonas C. Greenfield (eds.), *New Directions in Biblical*

Archaeology (New York: Doubleday, 1969).

French, A., *The Growth of the Athenian Economy* (New York: Barnes & Noble, 1964).

Friedlander, Stanley, and Morris Silver, "A Quantitative Study of the Determinants of Fertility Behavior," *Demography* 4 (1967): 30–70.

Von Fritz, Kurt, "Once More the 'Ektemoroi," *American Journal of Philology* (January 1943): 24–43.

Fuks, Alexander, "*Kolonos Misthios*: Labor Exchanges in Classical Athens," *Eranos* 44 (1951): 171–73.

Fustel de Coulanges, Numa Denis, *The Ancient City* (Boston: Lee and Shepard, 1896).

Galenson, David W., "The Market Evaluation of Human Capital: The Case of Indentured Servitude," *Journal of Political Economy* (June 1981): 446–67.

Gallery, Leslie Mesnick, "The Garden of Ancient Egypt," in Denise Schmandt-Besserat (ed.), *Immortal Egypt* (Malibu, Calif.: Undema, 1978): 43–9.

Gamoran, Hillel, "The Biblical Law Against Loans on Interest," *Journal of Near Eastern Studies* (April 1971): 127–34.

Ganshof, Francois Louis, "Medieval Agrarian Society in its Prime: France, the Low Countries, and Western Germany," in Clapham and Power (eds.), *Cambridge . . .* , vol, 1, 278–322.

Garnsey, P. D.A., "Economy and Society of Mediolanum Under the Principate," *Papers of the British School of Rome* 44 (1976): 13–27.

Garnsey, P. D. A., "Non-Slave Labour in the Roman World," in Garnsey (ed.), *Non-Slave Labour in the Greco-Roman World*, Supplementary Volume No. 6 (Cambridge: Cambridge Philological Society, 1980): 34–47.

Gelb, I. J., "The Ancient Mesopotamian Ration System," *Journal of Near Eastern Studies* (July 1965): 230–43.

Gelb, I. J., "Household and Family in Early Mesopotamia," in Lipiński (ed.), *State and Temple*, vol. I, 1–97.

Ginsberg, H. L., "Hosea's Ephraim, More Fool Than Knave: A New Interpretation of Hosea 12:1–14," *Journal of Biblical Literature* (December 1961): 339–47.

_____, "The Words of Ahiqar," in Pritchard (ed.), *Ancient* 427–30.

_____, "Isaiah," in *Encyclopedia Judaica* Vol. 9 (1971), 49–60.

_____, "Hosea," in *Encyclopedia Judaica* Vol. 8 (1971),1010–25.

_____, *The Supernatural in the Prophets with Special Reference to Isaiah* Cincinnati, Ohio: Hebrew Union College Press, 1979).

Ginzberg, Eli, "*Studies in the Economics of the Bible,*" *Jewish Quarterly Review* 22 (1931–1932): 343–408.

Gitay, Yehoshua, "A Study of Amos's Art of Speech: A Rhetorical Analysis of Amos 3:1–15," *Catholic Biblical Quarterly* 42 (1980): 293–309.

Glotz, Gustave, *Ancient Greece at Work: An Economic History of Greece from the Homeric Period to the Roman Conquest* (New York: Norton, 1967).

Glueck, Nelson, *The Other Side of the Jordan* (New Haven: American Schools of Oriental Research, 1940).

_____, "Ezion-geber," *Biblical Archelogist* 28 (1965): 70–87.

_____, *The River Jordan* (New York: McGraw-Hill, 1968).

————, "Tell el-Kheleifeh Inscriptions," in Hans Goedicke (ed.), *Near Eastern Studies in Honor of William Foxwell Albright* (Baltimore, Md.: The Johns Hopkins University Press, 1971): 225–42.

Goetze, A., "The Roads of Northern Cappadocia," *Révue Hittite et Asianique* 61 (1957): 91–103.

————, "The Laws of Eshnunna," in Pritchard (ed.), *Ancient*, 161–63.

————. (a) "Instructions for Temple Officials," in Pritchard (ed.), *Ancient*, 207–10.

Göff, Beátrice L., "The 'Significance' of Symbols: A Hypothesis Tested with Relation to Egyptian Symbols," in Jacob Neusner (ed.), *Religions in Antiquity* (Leiden: Brill, 1968): 476–505.

Goodrich, L. Carrington, *A Short History of the Chinese People* (New York: Harper & Row, 1969).

Gordis, Robert, "Studies in the Book of Amos," in Salo W. Baron and Isaac E. Barzilav (eds.), *American Academy for Jewish Research: Jubilee Volume* (Jerusalem: American Academy for Jewish Research, 1980): 201–64.

Gordon, Cyrus H., "Abraham and the Merchants of Ura," *Journal of Near Eastern Studies* (January 1958): 28–31.

————. (a) *The Ancient Near East* 3d. ed. rev. (New York: Norton, 1965).

————. (b) *The Common Background of Greek and Hebrew Civilizations* (New York: Norton, 1965).

Gottwald, Norman K., *All the Kingdoms of Earth* (New York: Harper & Row, 1964).

Gouldner, Alvin W., *The Two Marxisms: Contradictions and Anomalies in Development of Theory* (New York: Seabury, 1980).

Grace, Virginia, *Amphoras and the Ancient Wine Trade* (Princeton: American School of Classical Studies at Athens, 1961).

Grant, Michael, *The Etruscans* (New York: Scribner's 1980).

Gray, George Buchanan, *Sacrifice in the Old Testament: Its Theory and Practice* (London: Oxford University Press, 1925).

Gray, John, *Archaeology and the Old Testament World* (London: Nelson, 1962).

————, *The Legacy of Canaan*, 2d.rev. ed. (Leiden: Brill, 1965).

————, *I & II Kings: A Commentary*, 2d. rev. ed. (Philadelphia, Pa.: Westminster Press, 1970).

Grayson, Albert Kirk, *Assyrian Royal Inscriptions*, Vol. I (Wiesbaden: Harrassowitz, 1972).

Grayson, Albert Kirk, and Donald B. Redford, *Papyrus and Tablet* (Englewood Cliffs, N.J.: Prentice Hall, 1973).

Green, Alberto Ravinell Whitney, *The Role of Human Sacrifices in the Ancient Near East* (Missoula, Mont.: Scholars Press for the American Schools of Oriental Research, 1975).

Greenberg, Moshe, "Hebrew sᵉgullā: Akkadian sikiltu," *Journal of the American Oriental Society* 71 (1951): 172–74.

————, "Another Look at Rachel's Theft of the Teraphim," *Journal of Biblical Literature* (September 1962): 239–48.

————, "Religion: Stability and Ferment," in Malamat (ed.), *The Age,* Vol. 5, 79–123.

Greenfield, Jonas C., "Review of *Magnalia Dei*, ed. F. M. Cross et al," *Bulletin of the American Schools of Oriental Research* (Spring 1980): 83–4.

Gregg, Pauline, *Black Death to Industrial Revolution: A Social and Economic History of England* (New York: Harper & Row, 1974).

Grintz, Jehoshua M., "Do Not Eat On the Blood: Reconsiderations in Setting and Dating the Priestly Code," *Annual of the Swedish Theological Institute* 8 (1972): 78–105.

Gunderson, Gerald A., "Economic Change and the Demise of the Roman Empire," *Explorations in Economic History* 13 (1976): 43–68.

Gunderson, Gerald A., "Economic Behavior in the Ancient World," in Roger L. Ransom, Richard Sutch, and Gary M. Walton (eds.), *Explorations in the New Economic History: Essays in Honor of Douglass C. North* (New York: Academic Press, 1982): 235–56.

Güterbock, Hans G., and Thorkild Jacobsen, (eds.), *Studies in Honor of Benno Landsberger* (Chicago, Ill.: University of Chicago Press, 1965).

Von Hagen, Victor W., *The Roads that Led to Rome* (Cleveland, Ohio: World, 1967).

Haldar, Alfred, *Associations of Cult Prophets Among the Ancient Semites* (Uppsala: Amlqvist & Wiksells, 1945).

Hallo, William W., "Isaiah 28:9–13 and the Ugaritic Abecedaries," *Journal of Biblical Literature* (December 1958): 324–38.

_____, "On the Antiquity of Sumerian Literature," *Journal of the American Oriental Society* 83 (1963): 167–76.

_____, "Antedilvuian Cities," *Journal of Cuneiform Studies* 23 (1970): 57–67.

_____, "The Royal Correspondence of Larsa: I. A. Sumerian Prototype for the Prayer of Hezekiah?" in Eichler (ed.), *Kramer*, 209–24.

_____, "Biblical History in its Near Eastern Setting: The Contextual Approach," in Evans, Hallo and White (eds.), *Scripture*, 1–26.

_____, "Genesis and the Ancient Near Eastern Literature," in Plaut *The Torah: A Modern Commentary* (New York: Union of Hebrew Congregations, 1981): 7–13.

_____ and William Kelly Simpson, *The Ancient Near East: A History* (New York: Harcourt, Brace, Jovanovich, 1971).

Hammershaimb, Erling, *The Book of Amos: A Commentary* (Oxford: Blackwell, 1970).

Hammond, N. G. L., "Land Tenure in Attica and Solon's Seisachtheia," *Journal of Hellenic Studies* 81 (1961): 76–98.

Haran, Menahem, "Amos," in *Encyclopedia Judaica*, vol. 2, (1971): 879–90.

Haran, Menahem, *Temples and Temple-Service in Ancient Israel* (Oxford: Oxford University Press, 1978).

Harden, Donald, *The Phoenicians* (New York: Praeger, 1962).

Har-El, Menashe, "Jerusalem and Judea: Roads and Fortifications," *Biblical Archeologist* (Winter 1981): 8–19.

Harris, Rivkah, "Old Babylonian Temple Loans," *Journal of Cuneiform Studies* 14 (1960): 126–37.

Harris, Rivkah, *Ancient Sippar: A Demographic Study of an Old-Babylonian City* (Nederlands Historisch-Archaelogish Instituut te Istanbul, 1975).

Harris, William V., "Towards a Study of the Roman Slave Trade," in J. H. D'Arms and E. C. Kopff (eds.), *The Seaborne Commerce of Ancient Rome* (Rome: American Academy in Rome, 1980): 117–40.

Harris, William V., (a) "Roman Terracotta Lamps: The Organization of an Industry," *Journal of Roman Studies* 70 (1980): 126–45.

Hawkes, Jacquetta, *The First Great Civilizations* (New York: Knopf, 1977).

Hayes, John H., and J. Maxwell Miller (eds.), *Israelite and Judean History* (Philadelphia, Pa.: Westminster Press, 1977).

Hayes, William C., *The Scepter of Egypt, Part II: The Hyksos Period and the New Kingdom* (New York: Metropolitan Museum of Art, 1959).

Heaton, E. W., *Everyday Life in Old Testament Times* (New York: Scribner's 1956).

———, *The Hebrew Kingdoms* (London: Oxford University Press, 1968).

———, *Solomon's New Men: The Emergence of Ancient Israel as a National State* (London: Thames and Hudson, 1974).

Heichelheim, Fritz M., *An Ancient Economic History*, Vol. I (Leiden: Sijthoff's, 1958).

Heichelheim, Fritz M., "Review of Polanyi et al., *Trade and Market in Early Empires*," *Journal of the Economic and Social History of the Orient* (April 1960): 108–10.

Heltzer, M., "Royal Economy in Ancient Ugarit," in Lipiński (ed.), *State and Temple* vol. II, 459–96.

Herrmann, Siegfried, *A History of Israel in Old Testament Times* (Philadelphia, Pa.: Fortress Press, 1975).

Herzog, Zeev, "The Storehouses," in Aharoni (ed.), *Beer-Sheba I.* 23–30.

Heurgon, Jacques, *The Rise of Rome to 264 B.C.* (Berkeley, Calif.: University of California Press, 1973).

Hicks, Sir John, *A Theory of Economic History* (London: Oxford University Press, 1969).

Hoffner, Harry A., Jr. (ed.), *Orient and Occident* (Germany: Verlag Butzon and Bercker Kevelaer, 1973).

Hoffner, Harry A., Jr., *Alimenta Hethaeorum: Food Production in Hittite Asia Minor* (New Haven, Conn.: American Oriental Society, 1974).

Hoftijzer, Jacob, "The Prophet Balaam in a 6th Century Aramaic Inscription," *Biblical Archeologist* (March 1976): 11–17.

Hoftijzer, Jacob, and G. Van Der Kooij (eds.), *Aramaic Texts from Deir 'Alla* (Leiden: Brill, 1976).

Hogue, Arthur R., *Origins of the Common Law* (Bloomington, Ind.: Indiana University Press, 1966).

Holladay, John S., Jr., "Assyrian Statecraft and the Prophets of Israel," *Harvard Theological Review* 63 (1970): 29–51.

Holladay, John S., Jr., "Of Sherds and Strata: Contributions Toward and Understanding of the Archaeology of the Divided Monarchy," in Cross, et al., *Magnalia* 260–68.

Holland, T. A., "A Study of Palestinian Iron Age Baked Clay Figurines With Special Reference to Jerusalem: Cave 1," *Levant* 9 (1977): 121–55.

Homer, Sidney, *A History of Interest Rates* (New Brunswick, N.J.: Rutgers University Press, 1963).

Hopkins, Ian W. J., "The 'Daughters of Judah' are Really Rural Satellites of an Urban Center," *Biblical Archaeology Review* (September/October 1980): 44–5.

Hopkins, Keith, "Economic Growth and Towns in Classical Antiquity," in Abrams and Wrigley (eds.), *Essays* 35–77.

Hopkins, Keith, (a) *Conquerors and Slaves: Sociological Studies in Roman History* Vol. I (Cambridge: Cambridge University Press, 1978).

Hopper, R. J., *Trade and Industry in Classical Greece* (London: Thames and Hudson, 1979).

Horn, Siegfried H., "Scarabs from Shechem," *Journal of Near Eastern Studies* (January 1962): 1–14.

Hoschander, Jacob, *The Priests and the Prophets* (New York: Jewish Theological Seminary of America, 1938).

Hurvitz, Avi, "The Date of the Prose-Tale of Job Linguistically Reconsidered," *Harvard Theological Review* (January 1974): 17–34.

Interpreter's Bible, Vol. IV, The Book of Psalms, The Book of Proverbs (New York: Abingdon Press, 1955).

Irwin, William A., "The Hebrews: Nation, Society, and Politics," in Henri Frankfort et al., *The Intellectual Adventure of Ancient Man* (Chicago, Ill.: University of Chicago Press, 1946): 326–60.

Irwin, William A., *The Old Testament: Keystone of Human Culture* (London: Abelard-Schuman, 1959).

Ishida, Tomoo, *The Royal Dynasties in Ancient Israel: A Study of the Formation and Development of Royal Dynastic Ideology* (Berlin: de Gruyter, 1977).

Iwry, Samuel, "*Maṣṣēbah* and *Bāmāh* in 1Q Isaiah[a] 6:13," *Journal of Biblical Literature* (September 1957): 225–32.

Jackson, Bernard S., *Theft in Early Jewish Law* (London: Oxford Universtiy Press, 1972).

Jacob, H. E., *Six Thousand Years of Bread: Its Holy and Unholy History* (New York: Doubleday, 1944).

Jacobsen, Thorkild, *The Treasures of Darkness: A History of Mesopotamian Religion* (New Haven, Conn.: Yale University Press, 1976).

Jacobson, V. A. "The Social Structure of the Neo-Assyrian Empire," in Diakonoff (ed.), *Ancient* 277–310.

James, E. O., *The Tree of Life: An Archaeological Study* (Leiden: Brill, 1966).

Jankowska, N. B., "Extended Family, Commune, and Civil Self-Government in Arrapha in the Fifteenth-Fourteenth Century B.C.," in Diakonoff (ed.), *Ancient*, 235–52.

Janssen, Jac J., "Progegomena To The Study of Egypt's Economic History During the New Kingdom," *Studien Zur Altaegyptischen Kultur* 3, (1975): 127–85.

Janssen, Jac J., "The Role of the Temple in the Egyptian Economy During the New Kingdom," in Lipiński (ed.), *State and Temple* vol. II, 505–15.

Jarvis, C. S., *Three Deserts* (London: Murray, 1936).

Jasny, N., "Competition Among Grains in Classical Antiquity," *American Historical Review* (July 1942): 747–64.

Jastrow, Morris, Jr., *The Civilization of Babylonia and Assyria* (Philadelphia, Pa.: Lippincott, 1915).

Jenks, Alan W., *The Elohist and North Israelite Traditions* (Missoula, Mont.: Scholars Press, 1977).

Jensen, Lloyd B., *Man's Foods* (Champaign, Ill.: Garrard Press, 1953).

Jewell, Helen M., *English Local Administration in the Middle Ages* (Newton Abbot: David & Charles, 1972).

Jewish Publication Society. *The Holy Scriptures According to the Masoretic Text* (Philadelphia, Pa.: JPS, 1917).

_____, *The Torah: The Five Books of Moses According to the Masoretic Text* (Philadelphia, Pa.: JPS, 1962, 2d. ed., 1974).

_____, *The Prophets: A New Translation of the Holy Scriptures According to the Masoretic Text* (Philadelphia, Pa.: JPS, 1978).

_____, *The Book of Job: A New Translation According to the Traditional Hebrew Text* (Philadelphia, Pa.: JPS, 1980).

Johnson, Aubrey R., *Sacral Kingship in Ancient Israel* (Cardiff: University of Wales Press, 1967).

Johnston, A. W., "Trademarks on Greek Vases," *Greece and Rome* (October 1974): 138–52.

Johnston, A. W., *Trademarks on Greek Vases* (Warminster: Aris & Philips, 1979).

Johnstone, William, "The Setting of Jeremiah's Prophetic Activity," *Glasgow U. Oriental Society Transactions* 21, (1965/66): 47–55.

Jones, A. H. M., "The Clothing Industry in the Roman Empire," *Economic History Review* (August 1960): 183–92.

Kanawati, Naguib, *The Egyptian Administration in the Old Kingdom: Evidence on its Economic Decline* (Warminster: Aris & Phillips, 1977).

Kang, Shin T., *Sumerian Economic Texts From the Drehem Archive* (Urbana, Ill.: University of Illinois Press, 1972).

Kapelrud, Arvid S., *Central Ideas in Amos* (Oslo: Aschehought, 1956).

_____, *The Ras Shamra Discoveries and the Old Testament* (Norman, Okla.: University of Oklahoma Press, 1963).

_____, *Israel: From the Earliest Times to the Birth of Christ* (Oxford: Blackwell, 1966).

Katzenstein, H. Jacob, *The History of Tyre* (Jerusalem: Schocken Institute for Jewish Research of the Jewish Theological Seminary, 1973).

Kaufman, Stephen A., "The Structure of Deuteronomic Law," *Maarav* (April 1979): 105–58.

Kaufmann, Yehezkel, *The Religion of Israel* (Chicago, Ill.: University of Chicago Press, 1960).

Kees, Hermann, *Ancient Egypt: A Cultural Topography* (Chicago, Ill.: University of Chicago Press, 1961).

Kelso, James L., "A Reply to Yadin's Article on the Finding of the Bethel Seal,"

Bulletin of the American Schools of Oriental Research (October 1970): 65.

Kenik, Helen Ann, "Code of Conduct for a King: Psalm 101," *Journal of Biblical Literature* (September 1976): 391–403.

Kemp, Barry J., "The City of el-Amarna as a Source for the Study of Urban Society in Ancient Egypt," *World Archaeology* (October 1977): 123–39.

Kemp, Tom, *Economic Forces in French History* (London: Dobson, 1971).

Kempinski, Aharon, "Israelite Conquest or Settlement? New Light from Tell Masos," *Biblical Archaeology Review* (September 1976): 25–30.

Kennett, R. H., *Ancient Hebrew Social Life as Indicated in Law, Narrative, and Metaphor* (London: Oxford University Press, 1931).

Kenyon, Kathleen M., *Archaeology in the Holy Land* (New York: Praeger, 1960).

———, "Israelite Jerusalem," in Sanders (ed.), *Near Eastern Archaelogy in the Twentieth Century* (New York: Doubleday): 232–53.

———, *The Bible and Recent Archaeology* (Atlanta, Ga.: Knox Press, 1978).

Kimbrough, S. T., *The Place, Thought, and Importance of Antonin Causse in Old Testament Studies* Princeton, N.J.: Princeton Theological disssertation for Th.D., 1966.

Kitchen, K. A., "Late-Egyptian Chronology and the Hebrew Monarcy: Critical Studies in Old Testament Mythology,I.," *Journal of the Columbia University Ancient Near Eastern Society* 9 (1973): 225–33.

Klima, Arnost, "Agrarian Class Structure and Economic Development in Pre-Industrial Bohemia," *Past and Present* (November 1979): 42–67.

Knowles, Dom David, *The Religious Orders of England*, vol. I (London: Cambridge University Press, 1948).

Kochavi, Moshe, and Aaron Demsky, "An Israelite Village from the Days of the Judges," *Biblical Archaeology Review* (September/October 1978): 18–21.

Köhler, Ludwig, *Hebrew Man*, translated from German, (New York: Abingdon Press, 1956).

Kramer, Samuel Noah, *The Sumerians: Their History, Culture, and Character* (Chicago: University of Chicago Press, 1963).

Kula, Witold, *An Economic Theory of the Feudal System: Toward a Model of the Polish Economy*, translated from Polish (London: New Left Books, 1976).

Lacheman, Ernest R., "Epigraphic Evidences of the Material Culture of the Nuzians," in Richard F. S. Starr (ed.), *Nuzi*, Vol. I (Cambridge, Mass.: Harvard University Press, 1939): 528–44.

Laing, Gordon J., *Survivals of Roman Religion* (New York: Cooper Square, 1963).

Lambdin, Thomas O., "Egyptian Loan Words in the Old Testament," *Journal of the American Oriental Society*, 73 (1953): 145–55.

Lambert, W. G., *Babylonian Wisdom Literature* (London: Oxford University Press, 1960).

Landsberger, Benno L., "Tin and Lead: The Adventures of Two Vocables," *Journal of Near Eastern Studies* (July 1968): 285–96.

Lang, Bernhard, "The Social Organization of Peasant Poverty in Biblical Israel," *Journal for the Study of the Old Testament* (in press).

Langdon, Stephen, "An Early Babylonian Tablet of Warnings for the King," *Journal of the American Oriental Society* 28 (1907): 145–54.

_____, *Tammuz and Ishtar* (Oxford: Clarendon Press, 1914).

_____, *Semitic Mythology* (Baltimore, Md.: Archaeological Institute of America, 1931).

Larsen, Mogens Trolle, "The Old Assyrian Colonies in Anatolia," *Journal of the American Oriental Society* 94 (1974): 468–75. Selection reproduced with permission of the American Oriental Society.

_____ (a), "The City and Its King: On the Old Assyrian Notion of Kingship," in Paul Garelli (ed.), *XIXe Recontre Assyriologique Internationale: Le Palais et la Royauté* (Paris: Geuthner, 1974): 285–300.

_____, *The Old Assyrian City-State and its Colonies* (Copenhagen: Akademisk Forlag, 1976).

Layard, P. R. G., and A. A. Walters, *Microeconomic Theory* (New York: McGraw-Hill, 1978).

Leemans, W. F., *The Old Babylonian Merchant* (Leiden: Brill, 1950).

_____ (a), "The Rate of Interest in Old-Babylonian Times," *Revue International des Droits de l'Antiquite* 5 (1950): 7–34.

_____, *Legal and Economic Records from the Kingdom of Larsa* (Leiden: Brill, 1954).

_____, "The Role of Land Lease in Mesopotamia in the Early Second Millennium," *Journal of the Economic and Social History of the Orient* (June 1975): 134–48.

Leibenstein, Harvey, "Entrepreneurship and Development," *American Economic Review* (May 1968): 72–83.

Leibovitch, Joseph, "Gods of Agricultural Welfare in Ancient Egypt," *Journal of Near Eastern Studies* (April 1953): 73–113.

Leighton, Albert C., *Transport and Communication in Early Medieval Europe, A.D. 500–1100* (New York: Barnes & Noble, 1972).

Lemche, N. P., "The 'Hebrew Slave': Comments on the Slave Law Ex. 21: 2–11," *Vetus Testamentum* 25 (1975): 129–44.

Lemke, Werner E., "The Ways of Obedience: 1 Kings 13 and the Structure of Deuteronomic History," in Cross et al. (eds.), *Magnalia*, 301–26.

Levine, Baruch A., *In the Presence of the Lord: A Study of Cult and Some Cultic Terms in Ancient Israel* (Leiden: Brill, 1974).

_____, "Review of *Temples and Temple Service in Ancient Israel* by M. Haran," *Journal of Biblical Literature* (September 1980): 448–51.

_____, "The Deir 'Alla Plaster Inscriptions," *Journal of the American Oriental Society* 101 (1981): 195–205.

Lewis, Naptali, "Solon's Agrarian Legislation," *American Journal of Philology* (April 1941): 144–56.

Lewy, Julius, (a) "Some Aspects of Commercial Life in Assyria and Asia Minor in the Nineteenth Pre-Christian Century," *Journal of the American Oriental Society* 78 (1958): 89–101.

_____, (b) "The Biblical Institution of $D^e r\hat{o}r$ in the Light of Akkadian Documents," *Eretz Israel* 5 (1958): 21–31.

Lipiński, Edward (ed.), *State and Temple Economy in the Ancient Near East*, 2 Vols. (Leuven: Department Oriëntalistiek, 1979).

Littauer, M. A., and J. H. Crouwel, *Wheeled Vehicles and Ridden Animals in the Ancient Near East* (Leiden: Brill, 1979).

Liver, J., "The Chronology of Tyre at the Beginning of the First Millennium B.C.," *Israel Exploration Journal* 3 (1953): 113–20.

Lowry, S. Todd, "Recent Literature on Ancient Greek Economic Thought," *Journal of Economic Literature* (March 1979): 65–86.

Luckenbill, Daniel David, *Ancient Records of Assyria and Babylonia*, 2 vols. (Chicago: University of Chicago Press, 1926 and 1927).

Lutz, H. F., *Viticulture and Brewing in the Ancient Orient* (Leipzig: Hinrichs, 1922).

Macalister, R. A. Stewart, *The Excavations at Gezer: 1902–1905 and 1907–1909*, 3 Vol. (London: Murray, 1912).

Macalister, R. A. Stewart, *The Philistines: Their History and Civilization* (London: Oxford University Press, 1914).

McCarthy, Dennis J., *Treaty and Covenant: A Study in the Ancient Oriental Documents and in the Old Testament*, new ed. (Rome: Biblical Institute Press, 1978).

McCloskey, Donald N., "English Open Fields as Behavior Towards Risk," in Paul Uselding (ed.), *Research in Economic History: An Annual Compilation of Research*, Vol. 1 (Greenwich, Conn.: JAI Press, 1976).

McCown, Chester Charlton, *The Ladder of Progress in Palestine* (New York: Harper & Bros, 1943).

McCurley, Foster R., Jr., "The Home of Deuteronomy Revisited: A Methodological Analysis of the Northern Theory," in Bream et al. (eds.), *Old Testament*, 295–317.

Macdonald, John, "The Identification of *Bazahātu* in the Mari Letters," *Revue d'Assyriologie* 69 (1975): 137–45.

Macdonald, John, "The Role and Status of the *Suhārū* in the Mari Correspondence," *Journal of the American Oriental Society* 96 (1976): 57–68.

McDonald, William A., "Overland Communications in Greece During LH III," in Emmett L. Bennett, Jr. (ed.), *Mycenaean Studies* (Madison, Wisc.: University of Wisconsin Press, 1964), 217–40.

McKay, J. W., *Religion in Judah Under the Assyrians, 732–609* (Napierville, Ill.: Allenson, 1973).

MacLaurin, E. C. B., "Date of the Foundation of the Jewish Colony at Elephantine," *Journal of Near Eastern Studies* (April 1968): 89–96.

Macnamara, Ellen, *Everyday Life of the Etruscans* (New York: Putnam's, 1973).

Maczak, Anton, "Export of Grain and the Problem of Distribution of National Income in the Years 1550–1650," *Acta Poloniae Historica* 18 (1968): 75–98.

Maekawa, Kazuya, "Agricultural Production in Ancient Sumer," *Zinbun* 13 (1974): 1–60.

Malamat, Abraham (ed.), *The Age of the Monarchies: Culture and Society Vol. Five, The World History of the Jewish People* (Jerusalem: Massada Press, 1977).

Malamat, Abraham, (ed.), *The Age of the Monarchies: Political History, Vol. Four-1, The World History of the Jewish People* (Jerusalem: Massada Press, 1979).

Mallowan, M. E. L., "The Mechanics of Ancient Trade in Western Asia," *Iran (Journal of Persian Studies)* 3 (1965): 1–7.

Maloney, Robert, P., "Usury and Restrictions on Interest-Taking in the Ancient Near East," *Catholic Biblical Quarterly* 36 (1974): 1–20.

Marcus, Ralph, and I. J. Gelb, "The Phoenician Stele Inscriptions from Cilicia," *Journal of Near Eastern Studies* (April 1949): 116–20.

Matthiae, Paolo, *Ebla in the Period of the Amorite Dynasties and the Dynasties of Akkad: Recent Archaeological Discoveries at Tell Mardikh* (Malibu, Calif.: Undema, 1979).

Mayerson, Philip, "Ancient Agricultural Remains in the Central Negeb: The Teleilat El- Anab," *Bulletin of the American Schools of Oriental Research* (February 1959): 19–31.

Mayes, A. D. H., *Deuteronomy* (London: Oliphants, 1979).

Mayhew, Alan, *Rural Settlement and Farming in Germany* (New York: Barnes and Noble, 1973).

Mazar, Benjamin, *The Mountain of the Lord* (New York: Doubleday, 1978).

Mazar, Benjamin, A. Biran, M. Dothan, I. Dunayevsky, " 'Ein Gev: Excavations in 1961," *Israel Exploration Journal* 14 (1964): 1–49.

Meek, Theophile J., "Mesopotamian Legal Documents," in Pritchard (ed.), *Ancient* 163–88, 217–22.

Mendenhall, George E., "Ancient Oriental and Biblical Law," in Edward F. Campbell, Jr. and David Noel Freedman (eds.), *Biblical Archaeology Reader*, vol. III (New York: Doubleday, 1970): 3–24.

_____, "Social Organization in Early Israel," in Cross et al. (eds.), *Magnalia*, 132–51.

_____, *The Tenth Generation: The Origins of the Biblical Tradition* (Baltimore, Md.: Johns Hopkins University Press, 1973).

_____, "Review of *Prophecy and Society in Ancient Israel* by Robert R. Wilson," *Biblical Archeologist* (Summer 1981): 189–90.

Mendelsohn, Issac, "Guilds in the Ancient Near East," *Bulletin of the American Schools of Oriental Research* (December 1940): 17–21.

Mendelsohn, Isaac, *Slavery in the Ancient Near East* (New York: Oxford University Press, 1949).

Meshel, Ze'ev, "Did Yahweh Have a Consort?," *Biblical Archaeology Review* (March/April 1979): 24–35.

Meyers, Carol L., *The Tabernacle Menorah: A Synthetic Study of a Symbol from the Biblical Cult* (Missoula, Mont.: Scholars Press for the American Schools of Oriental Research, 1976).

Michell, H., *The Economics of Ancient Greece* 2d. ed. (New York: Barnes and Noble, 1957).

Mickwith, Gunnar, "Medieval Agrarian Society in Its Prime: Italy," in Clapham and Power (eds.), *Cambridge*, Vol. I, 323–43.

Millard, Alan, "Ezekiel 27:19: The Wine Trade of Damascus," *Journal of Semitic Studies* 7 (1962): 201–03.

Milgrom, Jacob, "The Shared Custody of the Tabernacle and a Hittite Analogy," *Journal of the American Oriental Society* 90 (1970): 204–09.

———, "A Prolegomenon to Leviticus 17:11, *Journal of Biblical Literature* (June 1971): 149–56.

———, "The Alleged 'Demythologization and Secularization' in Deuteronomy," *Israel Exploration Journal* 23 (1973): 156–61.

———, *Cult and Conscience* (Leiden: Brill, 1976).

——— (a), "Profane Slaughter and a Formulaic Key to the Composition of Deuteronomy," *Hebrew Union College Annual* 47 (1976): 1–17.

Mireaux, Emile, *Daily Life in the Time of Homer* (New York: Macmillan, 1960).

Mokyr, Joel, *Industrialization in the Low Countries* (New Haven, Conn.: Yale University Press, 1976).

Moorey, P. R. S., *Biblical Lands* (New York: Dutton, 1975).

Moorey, P. R. S., "Review of M. A. Littauer and J. H. Crouwel, *Wheeled Vehicles and Ridden Animals in the Ancient Near East,*" *Antiquity* (November 1980): 247–48.

Morenz, Siegfried, *Egyptian Religion* (Ithaca, N.Y: Cornell University Press, 1973).

Morgenstern, Julian, *Rites of Birth, Marriage, Death, and Kindred Occasions Among the Semites* (Cincinnati, Ohio: Hebrew Union C. P., 1966).

Moritz, L. A., *Grain-Mills and Flour in Classical Antiquity* (Oxford: Oxford University Press, 1958).

Moscati, Sabatino, *The World of the Phoenicians* translated from Italian, (New York: Praeger, 1968).

Mowinckel, Sigmund, "The 'Spirit' and the 'Word' in the Pre-Exilic Reforming Prophets," *Journal of Biblical Literature* 53 (1934): 199–227.

———, "General Oriental and Specific Israelite Elements in the Israelite Conception of the Sacred Kingdom," in *The Sacral Kingship* (Leiden: Brill, 1959): 283–93.

———, *The Psalms in Israel's Worship*, 2 vols. (Oxford: Blackwell, 1962).

Muffs, Yochanan, *Studies in the Aramaic Legal Papyri from Elephantine* (Leiden: Brill, 1969).

Muhley, James D., "The Bronze Age Setting," in Wertime and Muhly (eds.), *The Coming of the Age of Iron* (New Haven, Conn.: Yale University Press, 1980): 25–67.

Muhley, James D., and T. A. Wertime, "Evidence for the Sources and Use of Tin During the Bronze Age," *World Archaeology* (June 1973): 111–22.

Muilenberg, James, *The Way of Israel* (New York: Harper & Row, 1961).

Mulder, Jan, *Studies on Psalm 45* (Offsetdrukkerij Witsiers-OSS, 1972).

Muller, W. Max, *Egyptian Mythology* (Boston: Jones, 1923).

Murtonen, A., "The Prophet Amos—A Hepatoscoper?," *Vetus Testamentum* 2 (1952): 170–71. 1952 E. J. Brill. Selection reproduced with permission.

Myers, Jacob M., (trans. and notes), *The Anchor Bible: I & II Chronicles* (New York: Doubleday, 1965).

Na'aman, Nadav, "Sennacherib's Letter to God' on His Campaign to Judah," *Bulletin of the American Schools of Oriental Research* (April 1974): 25–39.

Na'amen, Nadav, "Sennacherib's Campaign to Judah and the Date of the *lmlk* Stamps," *Vetus Testamentum* 29 (1979): 61–86.

Naveh, Joseph, "A Hebrew Letter from the Seventh Century B.C.," *Israel Exploration Journal* 10 (1960): 129–59.

Naveh, Joseph, "The Scripts of Palestine and Transjordan in the Iron Age," in Sanders (ed.), *Near Eastern*, 277–83.

Neufeld, Edward, *The Hittite Laws* (London: Luzac, 1951).

———, "The Prohibition Against Loans at Interest in Ancient Hebrew Laws," *Hebrew Union College Annual* 26 (1955): 355–412.

———, "Socio-economic Background of *Yōbēl* and *Šemittā*," *Rivista Degli Studi Orientali* 33 (1958): 53–124.

———, "The Emergence of a Royal-Urban Society in Ancient Israel," *Hebrew Union College Annual* 31 (1960): 31–53.

———, "Inalienability of Mobile and Immobile Pledges in the Laws of the Bible," *Revue Internationale des Droits de l'antiquité* 9 (1962): 33–44.

———, "Fabrication of Objects from Fish and Sea Animals in Ancient Israel," *Journal of the Columbia University Ancient Near Eastern Society* 5 (1973): 310–24.

Niditch, Susan, and Robert Doran, "The Success Story of the Wise Courtier: A Formal Approach," *Journal of Biblical Literature* (June 1977): 179–93.

North, Douglass C., "Markets and Other Allocation Systems in History: The Challenge of Karl Polanyi," *Journal of European Economic History* (Winter 1977): 703–16.

North, Robert, *Sociology of the Biblical Jubilee* (Rome: Pontifical Biblical Institute, 1954).

Noth, Martin, *Leviticus: A Commentary* translated from German (Philadelphia, Pa.: Westminster Press, 1965).

Nylander, C., "A Note on the Stonecutting and Masonry of Tel Arad," *Israel Exploration Journal* 17 (1967): 56–9.

Oates, Joan, *Babylon* (London: Thames and Hudson, 1979).

Obermann, Julian, "Discoveries at Karatepe: A Phoenician Inscription," *Journal of the American Oriental Society, Supplement* (July/September 1948).

O'Connor, David, "Political Systems and Archaeological Data in Egypt: 2600–1700 B.C." *World Archaeology* (June 1974): 15–38.

Oded, B., (a) "Neighbors in the West," in Malamat (ed.), *The Age*, Vol. 4-1, 222–46.

Oded, B., (b) "Neighbors in the East," in Malamat (ed.), *The Age*, Vol. 4-1, 247–75.

Oesterly, W. O. E., *Sacrifices in Ancient Israel: Their Origin, Purposes, and Development* (New York: Macmillan, n.d.).

Ogilvie, R. M., *The Romans and their Gods in the Age of Augustus* (New York: Norton, 1969).

Olmstead, A. T., *The History of Assyria* (Chicago: University of Chicago Press, 1923).

Olmstead, A. T., *History of the Persian Empire* (Chicago: University of Chicago Press, 1948).

Oppenheim, A. Leo, "A Bird's Eye View of Mesopotamian Economic History," in

K. Polanyi et al. (eds.), *Trade and Markets in the Early Empires* (Glencoe, N.Y.: Free Press, 1957): 27–37.

————, "On Royal Gardens in Mesopotamia," *Journal of Near Eastern Studies* (October 1965): 328–33.

————, "Analysis of an Assyrian Ritual (KAR 139)," *History of Religions* (Winter 1966): 250–65.

————, *Letters from Mesopotamia* (Chicago: University of Chicago Press, 1967).

————, "The Eyes of the Lord," *Journal of the American Oriental Society* 88 (1968): 173–80.

————, "Essay on Overland Trade in the First Millennium B.C.," *Journal of Cuneiform Studies* 21 (1967-published 1969): 236–54.

————, (a) "Sennacherib (704–681)," in Pritchard (ed.), *Ancient*, 287–88.

———— and Erica Reiner (rev. ed.), *Ancient Mesopotamia: Portrait of a Dead Civilization* (Chicago: University of Chicago Press, 1977).

Orlinsky, Harry M., "The Seer-Priest and the Prophet in Ancient Israel," in *Essays in Biblical Culture and Bible Translations* (New York: KTAV, 1974): 39–65.

Östborn, Gunnar, *Tōrā in the Old Testament: A Semantic Study* (Lund: Häken, Ohlssons, 1945).

Otwell, John H., *And Sarah Laughed: The Status of Women in the Old Testament* (Philadelphia, Pa.: Westminster Press, 1974).

Page, S. "Joash and Samaria in a New Stela Excavated at Tell al Rimah," *Vetus Testamentum* 19 (1969): 483–84.

Page, S. "Ice, Offerings, and Deities in the Old Babylonian Texts from Tell el-Rimah," in André Finet (ed.), *Actes de la XVIIᵉ Recontre Assyriologique Internationale* (Ham-sur-Heure: Comité belge de recherches en Mésopotamie, 1970): 181–83.

Pardee, Dennis, "The Judicial Plea from Mesad Hahavyahu (Yavneh-Yam): A New Philological Study," *Maarav* (October 1978): 33–66.

Parke, H. W., *The Oracles of Zeus* (Oxford: Blackwell, 1967).

Parke, H. W., and D. E. W. Wormell, *The Delphic Oracle* (Oxford: Oxford University Press, 1956).

Parker, B., "The Nimrud Tablets, 1952-Business Documents," *Iraq* 16 (1954): 29–58.

Parrot, André, *Nineveh and the Old Testament* (New York: Philosophical Library, 1935).

Parrot, André, *Samaria: The Capital of the Kingdom of Israel* (London: SCM Press, 1958).

Patrick, Dale, "The Covenant Code Source," *Vetus Testamentum* (April 1977): 145–57.

Paul, Shalom M., "Prophets and Prophecy in the Bible," in *Encyclopedia Judaica*, Vol. 13 (1971): 1151–1176.

Pavlovsky, George, *Agricultural Russia on the Eve of the Revolution* (New York: Fertig, 1968).

Pečírka, Jan, "Homestead Farms in Classical and Hellenistic Hellas," in M. I. Finley (ed.), *Problèmes de la Terre en Grèce Ancienne* (Paris: Mouton, 1973): 113–47.

Perres, John Weir, *Lord of the Four Quarters: Myths of the Royal Father* (New York: Braziller, 1966).

Peters, John P., *The Psalms as Liturgies* (New York: Macmillan, 1922).

Petrie, W. M. Flinders, *Social Life in Ancient Egypt* (New York: Cooper Square , 1923).

Petrie, W. M. Flinders, *Religious Life in Ancient Egypt* (Boston: Houghton Mifflin, 1924).

Pfeiffer, Charles F. (ed.), *The Biblical World: A Dictionary of Biblical Archaeology* (New York: Bonanza Books, 1966).

Pfeiffer, Robert H., *State Letters of Assyria: A Transliteration and Translation of 355 Official Assyrian Letters Dating from the Sargonid Period (722–625 B.C.)* (New Haven: American Oriental Society, 1935).

Pfeiffer, Robert H., *Religion in the Old Testament: The History of a Spiritual Triumph* (New York: Harper, 1961).

Phillips, Anthony, *Ancient Israel's Criminal Law: A New Approach to the Decalogue* (Oxford: Blackwell, 1970).

Pirenne, Jacques, *The Tides of History*, Vol. 1 (New York: Dutton, 1962).

Plaut, W. Gunther, "Commentary," in *The Torah: A Modern Commentary* (New York: Union of American Hebrew Congregations, 1981).

van der Ploeg, J. P. M., "Slavery in the Old Testament," International Organization of Old Testament Scholars, *Vetus Testamentum Supplements* 22 (1972): 72–87.

Polanyi, Karl, *The Livelihood of Man* (ed. Harry W. Pearson) (New York: Academic Press, 1977).

Polzin, Robert, *Moses and the Deuteronomist: A Literary Study of the Deuteronomic History, Part One* (New York: Seabury, 1980).

Pope, Marvin H., "The Saltier of Atargatis Reconsidered," in Sanders (ed.), *Near Eastern*, 178–96.

———, *Song of Songs: A New Translation with Introduction and Commentary* (New York: Doubleday, 1977).

———, (a) "Notes on the Rephaim Texts from Ugarit," *Memoirs of the Connecticut Academy of Arts and Sciences* (December 1977): 163–82.

———, "Response to Sasson on the Sublime Song," *Maarav* (April 1980): 207–14.

Porten, Bezalel, *Archives from Elephantine: The Life of an Ancient Jewish Military Colony* (Berkeley, Calif.: University of California Press, 1968).

Posner, Richard A., "A Theory of Primitive Society with Special Reference to Law," *Journal of Law and Economics* (April 1980): 1–53.

Postgate, J. N., *Taxation and Conscription in the Assyrian Empire* (Rome: Biblical Institute Press, 1974).

Postgate, J. N., *Fifty Neo-Assyrian Legal Documents* (Warminster, England: Aris & Philips, 1976).

Potter, T. W., *The Changing Landscape of South Etruria* (London: Elek, 1979).

Powell, Marvin A., "Sumerian Merchants and the Problem of Profit," *Iraq* 39 (1977): 23–9. Selection reproduced with permission of the British School of Archaeology of Iraq.

Pratico, Gary, "A Reappraisal of Nelson Glueck's Excavations at Tell el-Kheleifeh," *Newsletter of the American Schools of Oriental Research* 6 (March 1982): 6–11.

Price, Ira Maurice, Ovid R. Sellers and E. Leslie Carlson, *The Monuments of the Old Testament* (Philadelphia, Pa.: Judson Press, 1958).

Pritchard, James B., *Palestinian Figurines in Relation to Certain Goddesses Known through Literature* (New Haven, Conn.: American Oriental Society, 1943).

———— (ed)., *The Ancient Near East: An Anthology of Texts and Pictures* (Princeton, N.J.: Princeton University Press, 1958).

————, "The Inscribed Jar Handles from Gibeon," in Herbert Franke (ed.), *Akten Des Vierundzwanzigsten Internationalen Orientalishten-Kongres* (Wiesbaden, 1959): 213.

————, *Gibeon Where the Sun Stood Still* (Princeton, N.J.: Princeton University Press, 1962).

————, "The First Excavations at Tell es-Sa'idyeh," *Biblical Archeologist* 28 (1965): 10–17.

————, *Ancient Near Eastern Texts Relating to the Old Testament*, 3d. ed., (Princeton, N.J.: Princeton University Press, 1969). Selections reprinted by permission of Princeton University Press.

————, "The Megiddo Stables: A Reassessment," in Sanders (ed.), *Near Eastern*, 268–76.

————, "The Age of Solomon," in Pritchard (ed.), *Solomon and Sheba* (London: Phaidon, 1974): 17–39.

Pullan, Brian, *A History of Early Renaissance Italy: From the Mid-Thirteenth to the Mid-Fifteenth Century* (New York: St. Martin's, 1972).

Pulleyblank, Edwin G., *The Background of the Rebellion of An Lu-Shan* (London: Oxford University Press, 1955).

Purvis, James D., *The Samaritan Pentateuch and the Origin of the Samaritan Sect* (Cambridge, Mass.: Harvard University Press, 1968).

Rahmani, L. Y., "Ancient Jerusalem's Funerary Customs and Tombs: Part II," *Biblical Archeologist* (Fall 1981): 229–35.

Rainey, A. F., "Business Contracts at Ugarit," *Israel Exploration Journal* 13 (1964): 313–21.

Randsborg, Klavs, "Social Stratification in Early Bronze Age Denmark: A Study in the Regulation of Cultural Systems," *Praehistorische Zeitschrift* 49 (1974): 38–61.

Rathje, Annette, "Oriental Imports in Etruria in the Eighth and Seventh Centuries B.C.," in David Ridgway and R. Francesca (eds.), *Italy Before the Romans* (New York: Academic Press, 1979): 145–83.

Rawlinson, George, *History of Ancient Egypt*, Vol. 1 (New York: Dodd Mead, 1880).

Redford, Donald B., *A Study of the Biblical Story of Joseph (Genesis 37–50)* (Leiden: Brill, 1970).

Reed, W. L., "Gibeon," in Thomas (ed.), *Archaeology*, 231–43.

Reiner, Erica, "The Etiological Myth of the 'Seven Sages'," *Orientalia* 30 (1961): 1–11.

Reiner, Erica, "Akkadian Treaties from Syria and Assyria," in Pritchard (ed.), *Ancient*, 531–41.

Reinhold, Meyer, *History of Purple as a Status Symbol in Antiquity* (Brussels: Latomus Revue D'études Laines, 1970).

Revel, Jacques, "A Capital City's Privileges: Food Supplies in Early Modern Rome," in Forster and Ranum (eds.), *Food.* 37–49.

Reynolds, Robert L., *Europe Emerges: Transition Toward an Industrial World-Wide Society, 600–1750* (Madison, Wisc.: University of Wisconsin Press, 1961).

Richter, Gisela M., "The Furnishings of Ancient Greek Homes," *Archaeology* (Spring 1965): 26–33.

Rickman, Geoffrey, *The Corn Supply of Ancient Rome* (Oxford: Clarendon Press, 1980).

Riefstahl, Elizabeth, *Thebes in the Time of Amunhotep III* (Norman, Okla.: University of Oklahoma Press, 1964).

Riis, P. J., *Sūkās I* (Copenhagen: Munksgaard, 1970).

Ringgren, Helmer, *The Faith of the Psalmists* (Philadelphia, Pa.: Fortress Press, 1963).

Ringgren, Helmer, *Religions of the Near East* translated from Swedish (Philadelphia, Pa.: Westminster Press, 1973).

Roberts, J. J. M., "The Davidic Origin of the Zion Tradition," *Journal of Biblical Literature* (September 1973): 329–44.

Robertson, Edward, *The Old Testament Problem* (Manchester: Manchester University Press, 1950).

Roebuck, Carl, *Ionian Trade and Colonization* (New York: Archaeological Institute of America, 1959).

———, "Comment," in *Second International Conference of Economic History,* Vol. I (Paris: Mouton, 1962): 97–106.

———, "Some Aspects of Urbanization in Corinth," *Hesperia* (January/March 1972): 96–127.

Rohde, Erwin, *Psyche: The Cult of Souls and Belief in Immortality Among the Greeks,* Vol. 2 (New York: Harper & Row, 1966).

Rosenbaum, Jonathan, "Hezekiah's Reform and the Deuteronomic Tradition," *Harvard Theological Review* (January/April 1979): 25–43.

Rosenthal, Franz, "Canaanite and Aramaic Inscriptions," in Pritchard (ed.), *Ancient,* 653–62.

Rostovtzeff, M., *Caravan Cities* (London: Oxford University Press, 1932).

Rowley, H. H., *Worship in Ancient Israel: Its Forms and Meaning* (Philadelphia, Pa.: Fortress Press, 1967).

Rowton, M. B., "The Date of the Founding of Solomon's Temple," *Bulletin of the American Schools of Oriental Research* 119 (1950): 20–2.

Saarisalo, Aapeli, "New Kirkuk Documents Relating to Slaves," *Studia Orientalia* 5 (1934): v–100.

Sabloff, Jeremy A., and C. C. Lamberg-Karlovsky (eds.), *Ancient Civilization and Trade* (Albuquerque, N. Mex.: University of New Mexico Press, 1975).

Sabourin, Leopold, *Priesthood: A Comparative Study* (Leiden: Brill, 1973).

Saffirio, L., "Food and Dietary Habits in Ancient Egypt," in D. R. Brothwell and B. A. Chiarelli (eds.), *Population Biology* (London: Academic Press, 1973): 297–305.

Saggs, H. W. F., *The Greatness that was Babylon* (New York: Hawthorn, 1962).

Samhaber, Ernest, *Merchants Make History: How Trade Has Influenced the Course of History Throughout the World* (New York: Day, 1964).

Sanders, James A. (ed.), *Near Eastern Archaeology in the Twentieth Century* (New York: Doubleday, 1970).

Sarna, Nahum M., *Understanding Genesis* (New York: Schocken, 1966).

_____, "Zedekiah's Emancipation of Slaves and the Sabbatical Year," in Hoffner (ed.), *Orient*, 143–49.

_____, "The Chirotonic Motif on the Lachish Altar," in Aharoni (ed.), *Investigations*, 44–6.

Sasson, Jack M., "Canaanite Maritime Involvement in the Second Millennium B.C.," *Journal of the American Oriental Society* 68 (1966): 122–38.

Sasson, Jack M., "The Worship of the Golden Calf," in Hoffner (ed.), *Orient*, 151–59.

Sasson, Victor, "An Unrecognized Juridicial Term in the Yabneh-Yam Lawsuit and in an Unnoticed Biblical Parallel," *Bulletin of the American Schools of Oriental Research* (Fall 1978): 57–63.

Sauneron, Serge, *The Priests of Ancient Egypt* (New York: Grove Press, 1960).

Sawer, Marian, *Marxism and the Question of the Asiatic Mode of Production* (The Hague: Martinus Nijhoff, 1977).

Schaeffer, Claude F. A., *The Cuneiform Texts of Ras Shamra-Ugarit* (London: Oxford University Press, 1939).

Schiffer, Robert L., "The Farms of King Uzziah," *The Reporter* (September 1, 1960): 34–8.

Schlaifer, Robert, "Greek Theories of Slavery from Homer to Aristotle," *Harvard Studies in Classical Philology* 47 (1936): 165–204.

Scott, R. B. Y., "Weights and Measures of the Bible," in Edward F. Campbell Jr. (eds.), *The Biblical Archaelogist Reader 3* (New York: Doubleday, 1970): 345–58.

Segal, J. B., *The Hebrew Passover: From the Earliest Times to A.D. 70* (London: Oxford University Press, 1963).

Seger, Joe D., "The Lahav Research Project in Israel," *Archaeology* (May/June 1979): 50–3.

Seilheimer, Frank H., "The Role of the Covenant in the Mission and Message of Amos," in Bream et al. (eds.), *Old Testament*, 435–51.

Sellin, Ernst (initiated) and Georg Fohrer (completed, revised, and rewritten), *Introduction to the Old Testament* (Nashville, Tenn.: Abingdon Press, 1968).

Semple, Ellen Churchill, *The Geography of the Mediterranean Region: Its Relation to Ancient History* (New York: Holt, 1931).

Shiloh, Yigal, "The Four-Room House: Its Situation and Function in the Israelite City," *Israel Exploration Journal* 20 (1970): 180–90.

_____, "City of David: Excavation 1978," *Biblical Archeologist* (Summer 1979): 165–71.

_____, "The City of David Archaeological Project: The Third Season-1980," *Biblical Archeologist* (Summer 1981): 161–70.

Silber, Rabbi Mendel, *The Origins of the Synagogue* (New Orleans, La.: 1915).

Silver, Morris, *Affluence, Altruism, and Atrophy: The Decline of Welfare States* (New York: New York University Press, 1980).

Silver, Morris, "Adaptations to Information Impactedness: A Survey," in Malcolm Galatin and Robert Leiter (eds.), *The Economics of Information* (Boston: Martinus Nijhoff, 1981): 104–18.

Simpson, William Kelly, *The Literature of Ancient Egypt* (New Haven, Conn.: Yale University Press, 1972).

Smith, James, *The Book of the Prophet Ezekiel* (London: Society for Promoting Christian Knowledge, 1931).

Smith, Morton, *Palestinian Parties and Politics that Shaped the Old Testament* (New York: Columbia University Press, 1971).

Smith, Morton, "A Note on Burning Babies," *Journal of the American Oriental Society* 95(1975): 477–79.

Smith, R. E. F., *Peasant Farming in Muscovy* (London: Cambridge University Press, 1977).

Smith, Sidney, "A Pre-Greek Coinage in the Near East," *Numismatic Chronicle* 2 (1922): 176–85.

Smith, R. E. F., *Babylonian Historical Texts* (Germany: Olms, 1975).

Snaith, N. H., "The Altar at Gilgal: Joshua xxii:23–29," *Vetus Testamentum* (July 1978): 330–35.

Snodgrass, Anthony M., "Iron and Early Metallurgy in the Mediterranean," in Wertime and Muhly (eds.), *The Coming*, 335–74.

Sollberger, E., "Ur-III Society: Some Unanswered Questions," in Edzard (ed.), *XVIII-Rencontre*, 185–89.

Soss, Neal M., "Old Testament Law and Economic Society," *Journal of the History of Ideas* (July/September 1973): 323–44.

Spalinger, Anthony J., "Esarhaddon and Egypt: An Analysis of the First Invasion of Egypt," *Orientalia* 43 (1974): 295–326.

_____, "The Date of the Death of Gyges and Its Historical Implications," *Journal of the American Oriental Society* 98 (1978): 400–09.

Speiser, E. A., *Excavations at Tepe Gawra* Vol. I (Philadelphia, Pa.: University of Pennsylvania Press, 1935).

_____, "The Verb *Shr* in Genesis and Early Hebrew Movements," *Bulletin of the American Schools of Oriental Research* 164 (1961): 23–8.

_____, "*Pālil* and Congeners: A Sampling of Apotropaic Symbols," in Güterbock and Jacobsen (eds.), *Studies*, 389–93.

_____, *Oriental and Biblical Studies: Collected Writings* (Philadelphia, Pa.: University of Pennsylvania Press, 1967).

Sperber, Daniel, *Roman Palestine 200–400. The Land: Crisis and Change in Agrarian Society as Reflected in Rabbinic Sources* (Ramat-Gan: Bar-Ilan University, 1978).

Stager, Lawrence E., *Ancient Agriculture in the Judaean Desert: A Case Study of the Buqê'ah Valley in the Iron Age*, Ph.D. dissertation, Harvard University, 1975.

Stager, Lawrence E., "Farming in the Judaean Desert During the Iron Age,"

Bulletin of the American Schools of Oriental Research 221 (1976): 145–58.

Staples, W. E., "Epic Motifs in Amos," *Journal of Near Eastern Studies* (April 1966): 106–12.

Starr, Chester G., *The Economic and Social Growth of Early Greece, 800–500 B.C.* (New York: Oxford University Press, 1977).

Stech-Wheeler, T., J. D. Muhly, K. R. Maxwell-Hyslop, and R. Maddin, "Iron at Taanach and Early Iron Age Metallurgy in the Eastern Mediterranean," *American Journal of Archaeology* (July 1981): 254–68.

Stein, S., "The Laws on Interest in the Old Testament," *Journal of Theological Studies* 4 (1953): 161–70.

Stern, Ephraim, "Israel and the Close of the Period of the Monarchy: An Archaeological Survey," *Biblical Archeologist* (May 1975): 26–54.

_____, "Craft and Industry," in Malamat (ed.), *The Age*, Vol. 5, 265–78.

Stone, Elizabeth C., "Economic Crisis and Social Upheaval in Old Babylonian Nippur," in Louis D. Levine and T. Cuyler Young Jr. (eds.), *Mountains and Lowlands* (Malibu, Calif.: Undema Publ., 1977): 267–89.

Storch, John and Walter Dorwin Teague, *Flour for Man's Bread: A History of Milling* (Minneapolis, Minn.: University of Minnesota Press, 1952).

Struve, V. V., "The Problem of the Genesis, Development, and Disintegration of the Slave Societies of the Ancient Orient," in Diakonoff (ed.), *Ancient*, 17–67.

Sturdy, John V. M., "The Authorship of the Prose Sermons of Jeremiah," in J. A. Emerton (ed.), *Prophecy* (Berlin: de Gruyter, 1980): 142–50.

Tadmor, H., "The Southern Border of Aram," *Israel Exploration Journal* 12 (1962): 114–22.

_____, "The Me'unites in the Book of Chronicles in the Light of an Assyrian Document," in *Bible and Jewish History: Studies Dedicated to the Memory of J. Liver* (Tel Aviv: 1971): 223–24 (in Hebrew).

_____, "The Chronology of the First Temple Period: A Presentation and Evaluation of the Sources," in Malamat (ed.), *The Age*, Vol. 4-1, 44–60.

Talmon, Shemaryahu, "The Judean 'Am Ha'ares in Historical Perspective," in *Fourth World Congress of Jewish Studies*, vol. I (Jerusalem: World Union of Jewish Studies, 1967): 71–6.

Teall, John L., "The Grain Supply of the Byzantine Empire, 330–1025," *Dunbarton Oaks Papers*, No. 13 (Washington, D.C.: Dunbarton Oaks Research Library, 1959).

Terrien, Samuel, "Amos and Wisdom," in *Studies in Ancient Israelite Wisdom* (New York: KTAV, 1976): 448–55.

Thiele, Edwin R., "Pekah to Hezekiah," *Vetus Testamentum* 16 (1966): 83–107.

Thomas, D. Winton, *Documents from Old Testament Times* (London: Nelson, 1958).

Thomas, D. Winton, *Archaeology and Old Testament Study* (London: Oxford University Press, 1967).

Thompson, T. L., *The Historicity of the Patriarchal Narratives: The Quest for the Historical Abraham* (Berlin: de Gruyter, 1974).

Thomson, Charles (trans.) and C. A. Muses (rev. ed.), *The Septuagint Bible: The Oldest Version of the Old Testament* (Indian Hills, Colo.: Wing Press, 1954).

Tipton, Frank B., Jr., *Regional Variations in the Economic Development of Germany During the Nineteenth Century* (Middletown, Conn.: Wesleyan University Press, 1976).

Torczyner, H., "*Semel Ha-qin'ah Ha-maqneh*," *Journal of Biblical Literature* 65 (1946): 293–302.

Torrey, Charles Cutler, *The Lives of the Prophets: Greek Text and Translation* (Philadelphia, Pa.: Society of Biblical Literature, 1946).

Toynbee, J. M. C., *Death and Burial in the Roman World* (Ithaca, N.Y.: Cornell University Press, 1971).

Tsevat, Matitiahu, *The Meaning of the Book of Job and Other Biblical Studies* (New York: Ktav Publishing House, 1980).

Tushingham, A. D., "A Royal Israelite Seal (?) and the Royal Jar Handle Stamps (part two)," *Bulletin of the American Schools of Oriental Research* (February 1971): 23–35.

Tyumenev, A. I., "The State Economy in Ancient Sumer," in Diakonoff (ed.), *Ancient,* 70–87.

Ussishkin, David, "The Destruction of Lachish by Sennacherib and the Dating of the Royal Judean Storage Jars," *Tel Aviv* 4 (1977): 28–60.

Ussishkin, David, *Excavations at Tel Lachish, 1973–1977: Preliminary Report* (Tel Aviv: Tel Aviv University Institute of Archaeology, 1978).

Van Beek, Gus W., "Frankincense and Myrrh," in Freedman and Campbell (eds.), *The Biblical Archaeologist Reader* (New York: Doubleday, 1964): 99–126.

_____, "Progeomenon," in James A. Montgomery, *Arabia and the Bible* (New York: KTAV, 1969): ix–xxxi.

_____ and A. Jamme, "The Authenticity of the Bethel Stamp Seal," *Bulletin of the American Schools of Oriental Research* No. 199 (1970): 59.

Vaughan, Patrick H., *The Meaning of 'Bāmà in the Old Testament: A Study of Etymological, Textual, and Archaeological Evidence* (London: Cambridge University Press for JSOT, 1974).

Veenhof, K. R., *Aspects of Old Assyrian Trade and Its Terminology* (Leiden: Brill, 1972).

Vermeule, Emily, *Greece in the Bronze Age* (Chicago: University of Chicago Press, 1964).

von Rad, Gerhard, *Genesis: A Commentary* (Philadelphia, Pa.: Westminster Press, 1972).

Vos, Clarence J., *Woman in Old Testament Worship* (Delft: Judels & Brinkman, 1968).

Vriezen, Th C., *The Religion of Ancient Israel* translated from Dutch (Philadelphia, Pa.: Westminster Press, 1967).

Wallace, Anthony F. C., *Religion: An Anthropological View* (New York: Random House, 1966).

Walton, John, "The Antediluvian Section of the Sumerian King List and Genesis 5," *Biblical Archeologist* (Fall 1981): 207–08.

Waswo, Ann, *Japanese Landlords: The Decline of a Rural Elite* (Berkeley, Calif.: University of California Press, 1977).

Watts, John D., "An Old Hymn Preserved in the Book of Amos," *Journal of Near Eastern Studies* (January 1956): 33–9.

Weber, Max, *Ancient Judaism* (translated from German, 1949) (Glencoe, Ill.: Free Press, 1952).

Weeks, Noel, "Mari, Nuzi, and the Patriarchs," *Abr-Nahrain* 16 (1975–76): 73–82.

Weinfeld, Moshe, "Traces of Assyrian Treaty Formulae in Deuteronomy," *Biblica* 46 (1965): 417–27.

_____, "The Covenant of the Grant in the Old Testament and in the Ancient Near East," *Journal of the American Oriental Society* 90 (1970): 184–203.

_____, (a) *Deuteronomy and the Deuteronomic School* (London: Oxford University Press, 1972).

_____, (b) "The Worship of Molech and the Queen of Heaven," *Ugarit-Forshungen* 4 (1972): 133–54.

_____, (a) "Literary Creativity," in Malamat (ed.), *The Age*, Vol. 5, 27–70.

_____, (b) "Ancient Near Eastern Patterns in Prophetic Literature," *Vetus Testamentum* (April 1977): 178–95.

_____, "Burning Babies in Ancient Israel: A Rejoinder to Morton Smith's Article in *JAOS* 95 (1975)," *Ugarit Forschungen* 10 (1978): 411–13.

Weisberg, David, B., *Guild Structure and Political Allegience in Early Achaemenid Mesopotamia* (New Haven, Conn.: Yale University Press, 1967).

Weiser, Artur, *The Psalms: A Commentary* (Philadelphia, Pa.: Westminster Press, 1962).

Welch, Adam C., *The Code of Deuteronomy* (London: Clarke, 1924).

_____, *Prophet and Priest in Old Israel* (London: SCM Press, 1936).

Wertime, Theodore A., and James D. Muhly (eds.), *The Coming of the Age of Iron* (New Haven: Yale University Press, 1980).

Westbrook, Raymond, (a) "Jubilee Laws," *Israel Law Review* 6 (1971): 209–226.

Westbrook, Raymond, (b) "Redemption of Land," *Israel Law Review* 6 (1971): 367–375.

Westermann, William L., "Warehouses and Trapezite Banking in Antiquity," *Journal of Economic and Business History* (November 1930): 30–54.

_____, "Enslaved Persons who are Free," *American Journal of Philology* (January 1938): 1–30.

_____, *The Slave Systems of Greek and Roman Antiquity* (Philadelphia, Pa.: American Philosophical Society, 1955).

_____ and Elizabeth Sayre Hasenoehrl (eds.), *Zenon Papyri: Business Documents of the Third Century B.C. Dealing with Palestine and Egypt*, Vol. 1 (New York: Columbia University Press, 1934).

White, K. D., *Roman Farming* (Ithaca, N.Y.: Cornell University Press, 1970).

Whitelam, Keith, W., *The Just King: Monarchial Authority in Ancient Israel* (Sheffield: Journal for the Study of the Old Testament Supplement Series, 1979).

Whybray, R. N., *The Heavenly Counsellor in Isaiah x1 13–14: A Study of the Sources of the Theology of Deutero-Isaiah* (London: Cambridge University Press, 1971).

Whybray, R. N., *The Intellectual Tradition in the Old Testament* (Berlin: de Gruyter, 1974).

Widengren, Geo., *The King and the Tree of Life in Ancient Near Eastern Religion* (Uppsala: Lundequistka, 1951).

Widengren, Geo., "Royal Ideology and the Testaments of the Twelve Patriarchs," in F. F. Bruce (ed.), *Promise and Fulfillment* (Edinburgh: Clark, 1963).

Widlanski, Michael, "Palace of David or Solomon Found," New York *Times* 23 August 1980, 1, 4.

Wieder, Arnold A., "Josiah and Jeremiah: Their Relationship According to Aggadic Sources," in Michael E. Fishbane and Paul R. Flohr (eds.), *Texts and Responses* (Leiden: Brill, 1975): 60–72.

Wiener, Aharon, *The Prophet Elijah in the Development of Judaism: A Depth-Psychological Study* (London: Routledge & Kegan Paul, 1978).

Wiesen, David S., "The 'Great Priestess of the Tree': Juvenal VI, 544–545," *Classical Journal* (October/November 1980): 14–20.

Will, Elizabeth Lyding, "The Ancient Commercial Amphora," *Archaeology* (July 1977): 264–70.

Willetts, R. F., *Everyday Life in Ancient Crete* (New York: Putnam's Sons, 1969).

Williams, Ronald J., "Egypt and Israel," in J. K. Harris (ed.), *The Legacy of Egypt*, 2d. ed. (London: Oxford University Press, 1971): 257–90.

Williamson, Oliver, "Markets and Hierarchies: Some Elementary Considerations," *American Economic Review* (May 1973): 316–25.

Willis, John T., "Cultic Elements in the Story of Samuel's Birth and Dedication," *Studia Theologica* 26 (1972): 33–61.

Wilson, J. V. Kinnier, *The Nimrud Wine Lists: A Study of Men and Administration at the Assyrian Capital in the Eighth Century B.C.* (London: British School of Archaeology in Iraq, 1972).

Wilson, Robert R., *Genealogy and History in the Biblical World* (New Haven, Conn.: Yale University Press, 1977).

Wilson, Robert R., *Prophecy and Society in Ancient Israel* (Philadelphia, Pa.: Fortress Press, 1980).

Wiseman, D. J., *Peoples of Old Testament Times* (London: Oxford University Press, 1973).

Wiseman, D. J., and Edward Yamauchi, *Archaeology and the Bible: An Introductory Study* (Grand Rapids, Mich.: Zondervan, 1979).

Witt, R. E., *Isis in the Graeco-Roman World* (London: Thames & Hudson, 1971).

Wittfogel, Karl A., *Oriental Despotism* (New Haven, Conn: Yale University Press, 1957).

Wolff, Hans Walter, *Amos the Prophet: The Man and His Background* (Philadelphia, Pa.: Fortress Press, 1973 (1964 German)).

Woodhouse, W. J., *Solon the Liberator: A Study of the Agrarian Problem in the Seventh Century* (London: Oxford University Press, 1938).

Wooley, Leonard, "Excavations at Al Mina, Sueidia," *Journal of Hellenic Studies* (Part 1, 1938): 1–30.

Worden, T., "The Literary Influence of the Ugaritic Fertility Myth on the Old Testament," *Vetus Testamentum* 3 (1953): 273–97.

Wright, G. Ernest, *Biblical Archaeology* (Philadelphia, Pa.: Westminster Press, 1962).

———, "The Lawsuit of God: A Form-Critical Study of Deuteronomy 32," in Bernhard W. Anderson and Walter Harrelson (eds.), *Israel's Prophetic Heritage* (New York: Harper, 1962): 26–67.

———, "Judean Lachish," in Freedman and Campbell (eds.), *Biblical*, 301–09.

———, *Shechem: The Biography of a Biblical City* (New York: McGraw-Hill, 1965).

———, "A Characteristic North Israelite House," in Robert Moorey and Peter Parr (eds.), *Archaeology in the Levant* (Warminster: Aris & Phillips, 1978): 149–54.

Würthwein, E., "Amos-Studien," *Zeitschrift für die alttestamentliche Wissenschaft* 62 (1950): 10–52.

Yadin, Yigael, "An Inscribed South-Arabian Clay Stamp from Bethel?" *Bulletin of the American Schools of Oriental Research* (December 1969): 37–46.

———, "Symbols of Deities at Zinjirli, Carthage, and Hazor," in Sanders (ed.), *Near Eastern*, 199–231.

———, *Hazor: The Rediscovery of a Great Citadel of the Bible* (New York: Random House, 1975).

Yaron, R., "A Document of Redemption From Ugarit," *Vetus Testamentum* (Vol. 10, 1960): 83–90.

Yaron, R., "Foreign Merchants at Ugarit," *Israel Law Review* 4 (1969): 70–9.

Yeivin, S., (a) *A Decade of Archaeology in Israel: 1948–1958* (Istanbul: Nederlands Historisch-Archaeologisch Institut in Het Nabije Ossten, 1960).

———, (b) "Did the Kingdoms of Israel Have a Maritime Policy?", *Jewish Quarterly Review* 50 (1960): 193–228.

———, "Tel 'Erani," in Michael Avi-Yonah and Ephraim Stern (eds.), *Encyclopedia of Archaeological Excavations in the Holy Land*, Vol. 1 (London: Oxford University Press, 1975): 89–97.

———, "Administration," in Malamat (ed.), *The Age*, Vol. 5, 147–71.

———, "The Divided Kingdom: Rehoboam-Ahaz/Jeroboam-Pekah," in Malamat (ed.), *The Age*, Vol. 4-1, 126–78.

Yeo, Cedric, "Transportation in Imperial Italy," *Transactions of the American Philological Society* 77 (1946): 221–44.

———, "The Overgrazing of Ranch-Lands in Ancient Italy," *Transactions and Proceedings of the American Philological Society* 79 (1948): 275–307.

———, "The Development of the Roman Plantation and Marketing of Farm Products," *Finanzarchiv* 13 (1952): 321–42.

Yerkes, Royden Keith, *Sacrifice in Greek and Roman Religions and Early Judaism* (New York: Scribner's, 1952).

Yeshiva University Museum. *Daily Life in Ancient Israel* (New York: Yeshiva University, 1980).

Yoffee, Norman, "The Decline and Rise of Mesopotamian Civilization: An Ethno-archaeological Perspective on the Evolution of Social Complexity," *American Antiquity* (January 1979): 5–35.

Young, Dwight Wayne, "A Ghost Word in the Testament of Jacob (Gen. 49:5)," *Journal of Biblical Literature* (September 1981): 335–42.

Zaccagnini, Carlo, "The Price of the Fields at Nuzi," *Journal of the Economic and Social History of the Orient* (January 1979): 1–31.

Zemer, Avshalom, *Storage Jars in Ancient Sea Trade* (Haifa: National Maritime Museum Foundation, 1977).

Zevit, Ziony, "A Misunderstanding at Bethel: Amos VII:12–17," *Vetus Testamentum* (Vol. XXV, 1975): 783–90.

Zimmerli, Walther, *The Old Testament and the World* (Atlanta: Knox Press, 1976 (1971 German)).

_____, *Exekiel 1: A Commentary on the Book of the Prophet Ezekiel, Chapters 1-24* (Philadelphia: Fortress Press, 1979 (1969 German)).

Zimmern, J., and H. Winckler, *Die Keilinschriften und das Alte Testament* (Berlin: von Reuther & Reichard, 1903).

Index